걸프 사태

# 유엔안전보장이사회 동향 7

걸프 사태

# 유엔안전보장이사회 동향 7

한국학술정보

## | 머리말

걸프 전쟁은 미국의 주도하에 34개국 연합군 병력이 수행한 전쟁으로, 1990년 8월 이라크의 쿠웨이트 침공 및 합병에 반대하며 발발했다. 미국은 초기부터 파병 외교에 나섰고, 1990년 9월 서울 등에 고위 관리를 파견하며 한국의 동참을 요청했다. 88올림픽 이후 동구권 국교 수립과 유엔 가입 추진 등 적극적인 외교 활동을 펼치는 당시 한국에 있어 이는 미국과 국제사회의 지지를 얻기 위해서라도 피할 수 없는 일이었다. 결국 정부는 91년 1월부터 약 3개월에 걸쳐 국군의료지원단과 공군수송단을 사우디아라비아 및 아랍 에미리트 연합 등에 파병하였고, 군 · 민간 의료 활동, 병력 수송 임무를 수행했다. 동시에 당시 걸프 지역 8개국에 살던 5천여 명의 교민에게 방독면 등 물자를 제공하고, 특별기 파견 등으로 비상시 대피할 수 있도록 지원했다. 비록 전쟁 부담금과 유가 상승 등 어려움도 있었지만, 걸프전 파병과 군사 외교를 통해 한국은 유엔 가입에 박차를 가할 수 있었고 미국 등 선진 우방국, 아랍권 국가 등과 밀접한 외교 관계를 유지하며 여러 국익을 창출할 수 있었다.

본 총서는 외교부에서 작성하여 30여 년간 유지한 걸프 사태 관련 자료를 담고 있다. 미국을 비롯한 여러 국가와의 군사 외교 과정, 일일 보고 자료와 기타 정부의 대응 및 조치, 재외동포 철수와 보호, 의료지원단과 수송단 파견 및 지원 과정, 유엔을 포함해 세계 각국에서 수집한 관련 동향 자료, 주변국 지원과 전후복구사업 참여 등 총 48권으로 구성되었다. 전체 분량은 약 2만 4천여 쪽에 이른다.

2024년 3월

한국학술정보(주)

## | 일러두기

· 본 총서에 실린 자료는 2022년 4월과 2023년 4월에 각각 공개한 외교문서 4,827권, 76만여 쪽 가운데 일부를 발췌한 것이다.

· 각 권의 제목과 순서는 공개된 원본을 최대한 반영하였으나, 주제에 따라 일부는 적절히 변경하였다.

· 원본 자료는 A4 판형에 맞게 축소하거나 원본 비율을 유지한 채 A4 페이지 안에 삽입하였다. 또한 현재 시점에선 공개되지 않아 '공란'이란 표기만 있는 페이지 역시 그대로 실었다.

· 외교부가 공개한 문서 각 권의 첫 페이지에는 '정리 보존 문서 목록'이란 이름으로 기록물 종류, 일자, 명칭, 간단한 내용 등의 정보가 수록되어 있으며, 이를 기준으로 0001번부터 번호가 매겨져 있다. 이는 삭제하지 않고 총서에 그대로 수록하였다.

· 보고서 내용에 관한 더 자세한 정보가 필요하다면, 외교부가 온라인상에 제공하는 『대한민국 외교사료요약집』 1991년과 1992년 자료를 참조할 수 있다.

# | 차례

| 정 리 보 존 문 서 목 록 | | | | | |
|---|---|---|---|---|---|
| 기록물종류 | 일반공문서철 | 등록번호 | 2021040202 | 등록일자 | 2021-04-22 |
| 분류번호 | 731.33 | 국가코드 | IQ | 보존기간 | 30년 |
| 명 칭 | 유엔이라크대량살상무기폐기특별위원회(UNSCOM), 1992. 전2권 | | | | |
| 생 산 과 | 국제연합1과/중동1과 | 생산년도 | 1992~1992 | 담당그룹 | |
| 권 차 명 | V.1 1-3월 | | | | |
| 내용목차 | * 2.21-24 Ekeus 특별위원회 의장 이라크 방문 | | | | |

0001

원 본

# 외 무 부

종 별 :

번 호 : UNW-0129 일 시 : 92 0115 1930

수 신 : 장 관(연일,중동일,기정)

발 신 : 주 유엔 대사

제 목 : 걸프사태

1.보도에 의하면, 이락은 걸프전발발전 우라늄가스원심분리 농축기기 10,000 기(년간 핵무기 4-5개 제조가능) 건설에 필요한 부품들을 독일회사들로 부터 사들인것으로 유엔이락 특정무기폐기 특위 (UNSCOM)사찰과정에서 최근 밝혀졌다고 함.

2.지난주 비엔나에서 이락원유 판매문제에 관해 이락-유엔측간 접촉이 있었으며, 2.12 OPEC회의에 앞서 재접촉 예정이라고함.

3.상기관련 유엔측발표나 특기동향이 있는경우 추보예정임.

첨부 FAX:UNW(F)-48 끝

(대사 노창희-국장)

국기국 1차보 중아국 외정실 분석관 청와대 안기부

PAGE 1

92.01.16 10:00 WG

외신 1과 통제관

0002

# IRAQ ADMITS BUYING GERMAN MATERIALS TO MAKE A-BOMBS

## U.N. CALLS ORDERS LARGE

### Purchases Before Gulf War Could Have Produced 4 or 5 Weapons a Year

By PAUL LEWIS
Special to The New York Times

UNITED NATIONS, Jan. 14 — In a new disclosure about President Saddam Hussein's nuclear weapons program, Iraq has admitted buying large quantities of German components for a previously unknown uranium enrichment complex that could have produced enough explosive for four or five weapons a year, officials said today.

The admission was made in Baghdad on Monday to a team of United Nations nuclear inspectors assembled by the International Atomic Energy Agency, based in Vienna, the United Nations officials said. The inspectors had flown to Baghdad on Saturday after learning that German companies had sold Mr. Hussein some of the parts needed to build up to 10,000 uranium gas centrifuge enrichment plants and after receiving a tip-off about where those parts might be concealed.

**Special Magnets**

The United Nations team drew a blank when they raided the suspected site just north of the Baghdad area on Sunday, officials say. But Iraqi nuclear officials later admitted under questioning, the team reported, that they had bought enough special magnets and housings from German companies before the Persian Gulf war to build up to 10,000 centrifuges, although they asserted that these were all destroyed immediately after the cease-fire.

Today, Iraqi officials showed the United Nations inspectors piles of metal debris, saying this was all that remained of their ambitious plan to produce nuclear explosives using the centrifuge enrichment process. Previously, Iraq had said it was only experimenting with centrifuge enrichment techniques and asserted it planned to build no more than 500 centrifuges by 1996.

The International Atomic Energy Agency inspectors took samples of the debris but refused to say whether they believed all the components the German companies supplied had really been accounted for.

**Analysis Is Urged**

"We can't take any view on the Iraqi claim until the samples the team collected have been thoroughly analyzed," said John Scott, acting head of the Special Commission appointed by the United Nations Security Council to oversee the destruction of Iraq's nuclear capability as well as its other weapons of mass destruction.

Last month the International Atomic Energy Agency named 13 companies, most of them German, that it said had supplied equipment for Iraq's nuclear weapons program, including sophisticated machinery needed for the manufacture and assembly of centrifuge enrichment machines.

Agency inspectors have also recently found a centrifuge production plant in Iraq capable of turning out more than 1,000 machines a year. This plant escaped damage by allied bombing during the gulf war.

In Bonn a Foreign Ministry official said five German companies appeared to have sold Iraq centrifuge magnets and housings but added that it was unclear whether they had knowingly violated German export controls. He said the authorities are considering whether to prosecute the companies. Germany has asked the United Nations not to release the names of the companies involved.

Iraq's admission that it was acquiring parts for a huge centrifuge enrichment program is significant for several reasons, United Nations and other officials say.

It confirms once again Iraq's determination to conceal as much as possible of its nuclear program since Baghdad should have reported the purchase and destruction of these centrifuge components to the United Nations under the Security Council resolutions ending the gulf war.

It also illustrates the extent of Baghdad's attempt to acquire nuclear explosives and suggests it was following a multifaceted approach somewhat similar to that taken by the United States at the end of the World War II.

Iraq has already acknowledged trying to produce highly enriched uranium at plants in Tarmiya and Ash Sharqat by the electromagnetic separation technique, which the United States used for its first atomic bomb.

> U.N. officials see another attempt to conceal a nuclear program.

Both plants were destroyed by bombing during the gulf war. But the special commission estimates that each could have produced about 30 pounds of highly enriched uranium explosive annually, or a little less than Iraq probably would need for a bomb.

But Iraq also now appears to have been planning another huge enrichment program, based on the more efficient centrifigue technique, that would have eventually replaced the magnetic separation plants.

**Experiments Admitted**

In addition, it has admitted experimenting with chemical separation techniques and with the gaseous diffusion method, which is generally regarded as the most efficient of all, but which had the disadvantage from Baghdad's view of being difficult to conceal.

The United Nations inspectors have also found evidence that Iraq was trying to design a nuclear weapon and working on such challenging technical problems as building a trigger mechanism or implosion device.

In Washington, the State Department spokeswoman, Margaret D. Tutwiler, called the centrifuge revelation "another exposure of Iraq's duplicity about the extent of its nuclear ambitions" and said it justified maintaining economic sanctions and further United Nations inspections.

It remains unclear, however, wheth-

UNW(F)-48 20115 1930
총504

#UNW-0129
첨부

5-1

0003

er Iraq has obtained all the other components needed to build a 10,000 centrifuge enrichment complex, just as it is also unclear whether Iraq had started building any of the machines before the war and if so what it has done with them now.

**'Immense Production Complex'**

But the fact the German Government told the United Nations it believes Iraq bought enough centrifuge magnets and housings for this number of centrifuge machines, suggests to many experts Iraq was committed to a major enrichment program based on this technology.

"Iraq was buying the parts for an immense production complex that we haven't found any trace of yet," said Gary Milhollin, who directs the Wisconsin Project on Nuclear Arms Control in Washington.

About 2,000 such centrifuge plants would be able to produce about 40 to 50 pounds of highly enriched uranium a year or enough explosive for one bomb. David W. Dorn, an American nuclear weapons expert detatched to the Special Commission from the Lawrence Livermore National Laboratory in California, said that with 10,000 machines in operation, "we are probably talking about a capacity for around three to five bombs a year."

By spinning uranium gas at very high speeds, centrifuges separate out the fissionable uranium 235 isotope from the more common uranium 238.

The machines would be arranged in a "cascade" system, so that each one incrementally "enriches" the gas before passing it on to the next until the percentage of uranium 235 reaches "weapons grade" levels of around 93 percent. Experts say Iraq probably would have started by building a small experimental "cascade" of 100 or so machines before proceeding to full scale production. No trace of any such pilot plant has yet been found.

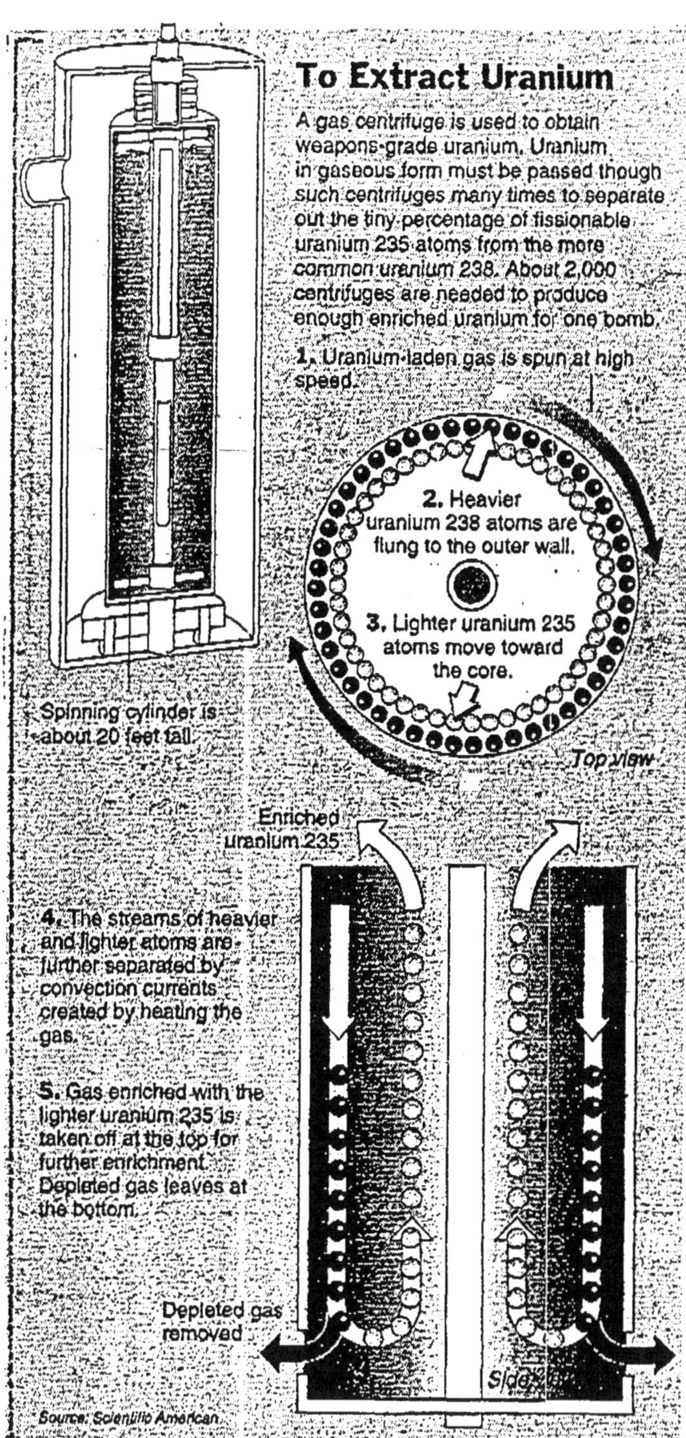


5-2

0004

# Iraq Hiding Missiles, Bush Tells Hill

By R. Jeffrey Smith
Washington Post Staff Writer

President Bush said yesterday that Iraq is continuing to hide large numbers of ballistic missiles and hinder international inspections aimed at eliminating these and other potential weapons of mass destruction.

Bush, who was summarizing his view of Iraq's behavior in a quarterly report requested by Congress, said the government of Iraqi President Saddam Hussein was only cooperating with those inspections involving weapons facilities it wanted to declare. The declarations are required by a cease-fire resolution agreed to by Iraq at the close of the Persian Gulf War last spring.

"In the main, however, Iraq continues to be uncooperative and obstructive with respect to inspection of sites identified . . . as potentially involving clandestine, proscribed activities," Bush said.

He cited, in particular, Baghdad's concealment of ballistic missiles—estimated by intelligence agencies as numbering in the hundreds—and its denial of having financed an ambitious program to develop nuclear weapons.

U.S. concerns about the Iraqi nuclear program were heightened this week by Baghdad's admission that it had purchased thousands of components for centrifuge devices capable of making highly enriched uranium for nuclear weapons.

"It is clear that the large number of centrifuge parts involved and their unambiguous use in uranium enrichment makes clear that Iraq was pursuing production-scale enrichment," said State Department spokesman Margaret Tutwiler. "This is yet another example of Iraqi duplicity about the scope and intent of its nuclear weapon program."

An official of the German Foreign Ministry said in Bonn yesterday that centrifuge magnets and casing materials were supplied to Iraq by five German firms, some of which are under criminal investigation, according to the Associated Press.

Bush's report said Iraq had collaborated with U.N. efforts to inspect and clean up storage sites for poison gas weapons, a monumental task for which Iraq is believed to need outside assistance. The report said Iraq may begin this year under U.N. supervision to destroy the chemical agents.

A total of 62 ballistic missiles, 18 launch pads, 33 missile warheads, 127 missile storage racks and substantial amounts of rocket fuel have been destroyed by the U.N. Special Commission on Iraq, the report said. But it added that "questions remain" about a secret Iraqi capability to make Scud short-range missiles or develop a new long-range missile.

> *"Iraq continues to be uncooperative and obstructive with respect to inspection of sites . . . "*
>
> —President Bush

The report said that a commission established to process Iraqi payments to victims of Iraq's 1990 invasion of Kuwait has completed its preliminary administrative work and set a July 1992 deadline for all claims. But Iraq has not agreed to finance the claims—or the continuing work of the special commission—by selling its oil under international supervision. As a result, the "shortage of funds readily available to the . . . commission has become acute," Bush said.

5-3

0005

# Diplomats Optimistic On Iraqi Oil Sale

## *Talks Likely on Plan to Ease Food Shortage*

By Trevor Rowe
Special to The Washington Post

UNITED NATIONS, Jan. 14—Iraqi and U.N. officials are expected to meet again in Vienna next month to continue negotiations aimed at resolving the impasse that developed after Baghdad refused to sell $1.6 billion in oil under terms set last year by the Security Council, diplomats said today.

The talks are seen as crucial to improving the conditions of Iraq's population, which has suffered from a shortage of food supplies and other basic civilian necessities. Iraq says it lacks foreign currency to pay for them, but it has refused to accept U.N. conditions for a limited sale of its oil.

Last week, the two sides ended three days of negotiations in Vienna on a generally optimistic note with U.N. officials predicting that an arrangement will eventually be worked out. Diplomats said the two sides will probably meet next month, before the session of the Organization of Petroleum Exporting Countries scheduled for Feb. 12.

"OPEC wants to set quotas based on knowledge of the likelihood of Iraq coming back to the oil markets," a diplomat said explaining the choice of dates.

The Security Council considers the proposed $1.6 billion oil sale an exception based on humanitarian concerns and the United States and some of the Western allies have made no secret that they intend the sanctions to remain in force as long as Iraqi President Saddam Hussein is in power.

Last Sept. 19, the Security Council authorized Iraq to sell up to $1.6 billion in oil to pay for food and medical supplies. About 30 percent of that amount was to be used to pay for a fund to compensate those who suffered as a result of Iraq's invasion of Kuwait as well as to cover administrative expenses and the costs of related U.N. operations.

However, Iraq refused to sell the oil, arguing that not only was the amount too little, but the mechanisms set up to monitor oil sales and food distribution violated its sovereignty.

Western officials now say Iraq's participation in the talks and its willingness to continue them may signal a change of heart.

"The fact they showed up for the talks means they've gone from a categorical 'no' to an attitude that 'a few of these things can be taken care of, we can talk,'" a Western official said.

Diplomats noted that the U.N. resolution covers only a period of six months ending in March, thereby giving both sides the opportunity to fashion a new agreement that would be acceptable to each without either being perceived as having given in.

"They might be able to come up with wording that Iraq abides by the resolution and the U.N. agrees to review the situation over the $1.6 billion level set," a Western official said. The Security Council could do this either by adopting a new resolution or extending the existing one.

Diplomats nevertheless are cautious. "In a normal country, you would say that this strikes us as encouraging, but with this country you can't do it," a Western official said.

"There are positive signs but there's also an enormous caveat because [Saddam] is capable of countermanding the decisions taken by his serious technical people," the official added.

Iraq, which was the world's second-largest oil exporter after Saudi Arabia until U.N. sanctions were imposed following its invasion of Kuwait is not expected to regain that position in the foreseeable future.

5-4

0006

# U.N. Guards Can Help Contain Civil Conflict

To the Editor:

Brian Urquhart, one of the fathers of United Nations peacekeeping, has trenchantly addressed the U.N.'s continuing inability to help end the bloodshed and devastation engendered in current civil conflicts ("Who Can Stop Civil Wars?", Op-Ed, Dec. 29).

To the three options he lists — traditional peacekeeping, collective enforcement under the United Nations Charter's Chapter VII, and "armed police actions" under Article 43 — I would add a fourth: the deployment of United Nations Guards, an alternative by now well tried and tested in the crucible of postwar Iraq. The Guards are supplied by countries from diverse regions — from Denmark to Fiji, Czechoslovakia to Ghana, Nepal, Thailand and the Philippines — and are paid for by voluntary contributions to the U.N., under whose command they serve.

The Guards Contingent formula was designed to meet a complex tissue of humanitarian, security and political challenges: the same daunting mix of circumstances we see reflected in other crisis areas today. Massive relief was needed urgently, but its provision was both ineffective and insecure in conditions of civil war. The departure of the coalition forces from northern Iraq was viewed with great trepidation by the Kurds. And yet recourse to peacekeeping under the United Nations Security Council was not considered politically viable.

We had to improvise. The aim was a degree of security without the Security Council, of peace without peacekeeping, of international action without intervention. The Guards' mandate bridges the chasm between relief and security: assigned to protect U.N. personnel and resources, they observe, monitor and report throughout their areas of deployment. They have come to constitute a crucial stabilizing influence. The eyes and ears of the United Nations, they assure a highly visible international presence and attention.

What began with a mere 10 Guards and a solitary U.N. flag at a camp in Zakho, close to the Turkish border eight months ago has evolved into a well-established, 500-strong contingent of 35 nationalities. The experiment has proved its worth. North and south Iraq remain volatile in the extreme; but 1.8 million refugees have returned across the borders and vast quantities of relief supplies have been provided, in both cases safely escorted by the Guards. Their assignment is accepted by all sides and considered indispensable both by U.N. agencies and nongovernmental organizations as well as by the Kurds and others assisted.

Conditions in Iraq in the aftermath of the Persian Gulf war are sui generis; but the innovation of U.N. Guards merits scrutiny for emulation elsewhere. Indeed, the concept was recently considered by some for Dubrovnik, but set aside in favor of the larger peacekeeping option. Possible permutations on the formula could include its adoption by the Security Council, entailing the imposition of Guards with an added political impact. In Iraq, however, the contingent is fully integrated in the Humanitarian Program and deployed with the concurrence of the Government.

The mere deployment of Guards will produce no panacea for strife born of ancient resentments, of rights long denied or ethnic rivalries rekindled by economic deprivation. Whether in Iraq, Yugoslavia or Somalia, Guards or peacekeepers can only be an element in a broader political package; they are no substitute for a solution. Yet they can help contain conflict, create confidence and set a climate within which aid can be delivered; indeed, Guards could become a standard component of humanitarian assistance.

SADRUDDIN AGA KHAN
Geneva, Jan. 2, 1992

*The writer was, until recently, executive delegate of the United Nations Secretary General for a U.N. Inter-Agency Humanitarian Program for Iraq, Kuwait and the Iraq-Turkey and Iraq-Iran border areas.*

5-5

0007

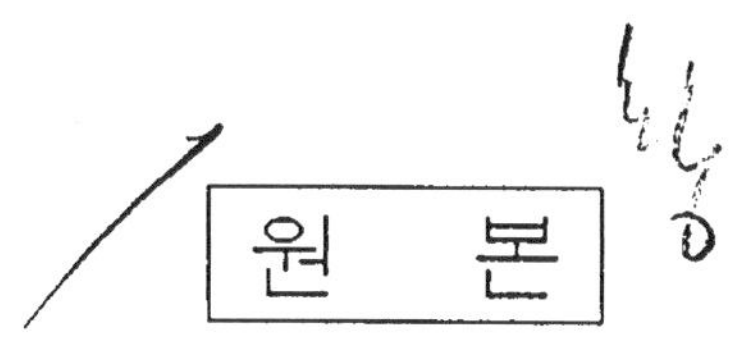


# 외 무 부

종 별 :

번 호 : UNW-0189 일 시 : 92 0121 1930

수 신 : 장 관(연일,중동일,기정)

발 신 : 주 유엔 대사

제 목 : 걸프사태

연: UNW-0129

연호, 유엔의 이락핵관련 9차 사찰 (92.1.12-15)결과에 관한 IAEA 측 발표문 (IAEA/1202-IK/81), 이락원유 판매문제 관련 이락-유엔측 접촉예정에 대한 사무총장 대변인 언급내용을 별첨송부함.

첨부:1. IAEA 이락핵사찰 결과발표문

2.이락원유 판매문제관련 사무총장대변인 언급내용

3. CSM 기사(1.21): UNW(F)-69끝

(대사 노창희-국장)

국기국 1차보 중아국 외정실 분석관 청와대 안기부

PAGE 1 92.01.22 10:17 WG

외신 1과 통제관

0008

(Press Release IAEA/1202-IK/8H UNW(FI)-69 20121 1930 Z204

"The ninth inspection team of the International Atomic Energy Agency (IAEA), with the cooperation and assistance of the United Nations Special Commission on Iraq, visited Iraq from 12 to 15 January. The main objective was to verify recent information received from Governments of Member States, and particularly Germany, concerning Iraqi procurement of large quantities of raw materials and components required for the manufacture of centrifuges to produce enriched uranium.

"The main items discussed with the Iraqi authorities were: special aluminium alloy extrusions specifically for the manufacture of centrifuge vacuum housings; ferrite magnets and other components used in the stator of centrifuge motors; and special equipment needed to fix the stator components in place.

"The Iraqi authorities acknowledged the procurement of these materials and, in addition, stated that they had obtained 100 tons of special high-strength steel (maraging steel) for centrifuge rotors and rotor fittings, and several thousand aluminium forgings for vacuum housing flanges.

"They also stated that these raw materials and components had been destroyed or 'rendered harmless' by melting or crushing before the Agency's inspections began last year. The quantities involved would have sufficed for the manufacture of several thousand centrifuges.

"The team was shown the melted maraging steel stockpile and the powder resulting from the crushing of the ferrite magnets at a site south of Baghdad. Samples were taken for verification purposes. A rough estimate made on-site was consistent with the quantities procured. Full verification must await the results of sample analyses. Verification of the remaining material will be carried out on a future inspection visit.

"The results of this inspection have removed a number of inconsistencies remaining from previous inspections. In the opinion of the experts who took part in the inspection, the Iraqis' centrifuge enrichment programme had not progressed to a point where they could have started a sizeable production of centrifuges, although, given time, they would have been successful.

"The programme had developed to a point, however, where the material necessary for certain key components had been identified. This enabled the procurement of materials as opportunities became available even though the centrifuge design had not been completely finalized or the manufacturing process fully implemented. The operation of a production scale uranium-enrichment centrifuge cascade, given the state of Iraqi centrifuge technology when work stopped, would have required the foreign procurement of large numbers of finished components. Inspections have found no evidence of this.

"The initiative of the German Government has greatly assisted the ongoing inspection effort with regard to the Iraqi centrifuge enrichment programme."

---

NW-0189

He was asked if there was any information on the next round of talks concerning a possible Iraqi oil sale, and whether those talks would be in Vienna. Mr. Ciuliani responded that the date, and place for that matter, were not absolutely clear yet. However, it was anticipated that the talks would take place during the second week of February, possibly in Geneva, where the meeting of the Organization of Petroleum Exporting Countries (OPEC) was to be held on 12 February. 69-2-1

0009

# United Nations Keeps Saddam In Global Spotlight

*Unfinished business includes aid and weapons program*

By Lucia Mouat
Staff writer of The Christian Science Monitor

UNITED NATIONS, N.Y.

TO the consternation of George Bush, Saudi Arabia, and much of the West, Saddam Hussein still rules Iraq.

But a strong and varied United Nations presence there ensures that he rules with much less freedom than he had before the Gulf war.

"The UN mission in effect shines the light of international attention on his every move and it makes it far more difficult for him to rebuild his military potential," says Edward Luck, president of the United Nations Association of the USA. "I think as long as he's in power there's going to be a need for a UN presence there."

The UN played an important role before the war in building a consensus for action. But only at the end of hostilities did the UN's operational role really begin. And a year after the war, the UN still has a laundry list of unfinished business in Iraq:

■ A demarcation commission has yet to determine the precise 200-kilometer (125-mile) border between Iraq and Kuwait.

■ Lightly armed troops from the Iraq-Kuwait Observation Mission monitor the demilitarized zone between the two nations.

■ The UN's August 1990 economic sanctions are still very much in place.

One exception to the sanctions is the Security Council's willingness to allow Iraq to sell up to $1.6 billion in oil. Two-thirds of the money would be used to buy food and medicine. The rest would compensate those who suffered in the Iraqi invasion and underwrite escalating UN expenses. Iraq balks at the UN terms as an invasion of its sovereignty, but will discuss the issue again in February.

■ UN-coordinated humanitarian aid continues. Just two weeks ago the UN released a new six-month, $145 million extension and hopes to move from relief to reconstruction.

■ The Special Commission on Iraqi Disarmament and the International Atomic Energy Agency continue to search for and eliminate Iraq's chemical, biological, and nuclear weapons and the facilities used to produce them.

### Low marks on cooperation

Just last week Iraqi officials admitted – when faced with a stockpile of incriminating evidence – that they had bought thousands of parts for centrifuge devices, which are capable of making enriched uranium for nuclear weapons.

The UN has long given Iraqis low marks on cooperation. Few TV-watchers will soon forget the parking lot standoff last September between Iraqi troops and UN inspectors. Though they have had to fight hard for almost everything they have found, UN officials have uncovered a much larger and more developed nuclear program in Iraq than most experts suspected.

"I find it extraordinary that the [UN] efforts have uncovered so much that the CIA and other intelligence agencies in the world hadn't known," says Mr. Luck. "The fact that we know now is an important step forward."

President Bush noted last week in his quarterly report to Congress that 62 ballistic missiles and numerous other weapons supports and missile warheads have been destroyed. Central Intelligence Agency chief Robert Gates told Congress that Iraq still had several hundred Scud missiles. UN inspectors will be hard pressed to know when to stop their weapons search.

"The problem is that you never know when you've got it all – that's why you want a long-term [UN] presence," says Thomas McNaugher, a defense expert with the Brookings Institution and an Army reservist who helped coordinate emergency relief in Kuwait City last February.

### New line of work for UN?

The UN's unusual role in Iraq could mark the beginning of a major new line of work for the UN. The organization helped to demobilize troops in Nicaragua at the close of that conflict and soon will play a similar role in El Salvador and Cambodia.

"Traditionally, this has not been a role for the UN ... but the whole world is beginning to move from arms control to disarmament," says Luck. One day the UN may even oversee the dismantling of the Soviet nuclear arsenal, he says.

While sanctions now appear firm, there is growing pressure in some quarters to lift them on humanitarian grounds. Any UN-Iraqi deal struck on oil sales would be likely to ease such pressure. But Bush insists the sanctions should remain as long as Saddam is in power. And some experts say the sanctions do not pinch as hard as Saddam would have the world believe.

"My own view is that there is sufficient leakage in the sanctions," says Marvin Zonas, a Middle East expert with the University of Chicago. "So that while the hardship inflicted on the Iraqi people is substantial, it's not so great that sanctions should be discontinued.... We ought to maintain them."

Mr. McNaugher agrees that most Iraqis are probably not as badly off as many suspect. "My understanding is there's a lot of food coming across the borders from Turkey and Jordan," he says.

However, he is concerned that as news about weapons discoveries in Iraq moves off the front pages, pressure may increase to lift sanctions: "I think we're in sort of a slow-motion race between whether Saddam falls first or the international support for sanctions slowly erodes. There's a potential for serious embarrassment there for the president."

69-2-2

0010

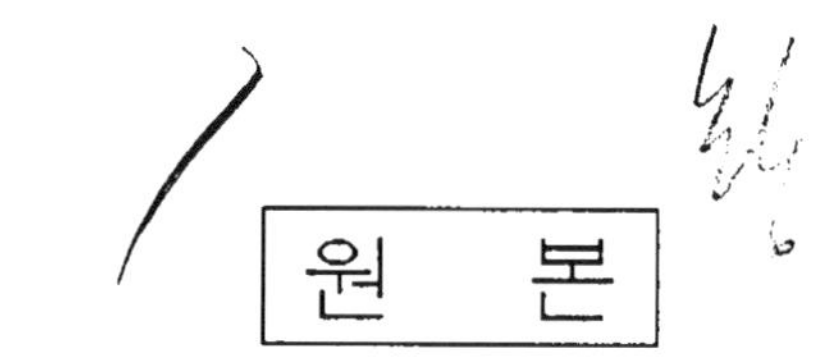


# 외 무 부

종 별 :

번 호 : UNW-0241 일 시 : 92 0124 1830

수 신 : 장 관(연일,중동일,기정)

발 신 : 주 유엔 대사

제 목 : 걸프사태

일부 독일회사들의 대이락 핵시설 부품공급 사례적발과 관련 독일정부는 유엔이락 특정무기 폐기특위 (UNSCOM) 에 대한 협조입장을 강조하는 요지의 안보리문서를 배포하였음.

첨부:1독일 안보리문서

2. NYT 기사(1.24):UNW(F)-84 끝

(대사 노창희-국장)

국기국 1차보 중아국 외정실 분석관 청와대 안기부

PAGE 1

92.01.25 09:08 WG

외신 1과 통제관

0011

UNW(FI)-84 20124 1830
홍 204

UNITED NATIONS

S

# Security Council

Distr.
GENERAL

S/23449
21 January 1992

ORIGINAL: ENGLISH

## LETTER DATED 21 JANUARY 1992 FROM THE PERMANENT REPRESENTATIVE OF GERMANY TO THE UNITED NATIONS ADDRESSED TO THE SECRETARY-GENERAL

Upon instructions from my Government I have the honour to inform you of the visit to Bonn, at the request of the Special Commission established pursuant to Security Council resolution 687 (1991), by its Deputy Executive Chairman, Dr. Robert Gallucci, on 9 January 1992. On the occasion of this visit, my Government made available to him comprehensive information on supplies to Iraq by German companies which it had gathered in the course of investigations. This information has apparently contributed to a more responsive attitude by the Government of Iraq.

My Government continues to be willing to contribute substantially to the work of the Special Commission. In the view of my Government the effective discharge of the tasks set out in resolution 687 and subsequent resolutions enjoys high priority. It is also for this reason that my Government is making every effort to prosecute illegal exports to Iraq and to share the information it has gained with the Special Commission. I am convinced that the Special Commission can fulfil its mandate completely only if all Governments concerned cooperate fully by providing the Special Commission with relevant information on supplies to Iraq. It is in this spirit that my Government wishes to continue its active support of the activities of the Special Commission.

I should be grateful if you would have this letter circulated as a document of the Security Council.

(Signed) Detlev GRAF ZU RANTZAU
Ambassador

-----

#UNW-0241 첨부 84-2-1

92-02538 2861i (E)

# Germany Acts to Curb Arms Exports

## New disclosures put pressure on Parliament

By STEPHEN KINZER
Special to The New York Times

BONN, Jan. 23 — The German Parliament, embarrassed by new disclosures that German companies supplied Iraq with equipment that could be used to build nuclear weapons, approved long-stalled legislation today tightening controls on arms exports.

The bill creates a new Government agency to monitor exports in cooperation with customs officials. Investigators will have the power to open mail and tap telephones in pursuit of evidence against weapons suppliers.

Companies found guilty of violating export laws will be subject to heavy fines, and their executives will be subject to imprisonment. Judges will be empowered to confiscate profits earned from illicit arms sales.

"We want to give officials better tools for preventing the crime of illegal weapons exports," Economics Minister Jürgen Möllemann said in Parliament. "We must make our country as hostile to such activities as other Western countries are."

### Accused of Protecting Company

Mr. Möllemann also defended himself against charges from opposition deputies that he had protected H & H Metalform, a company that has been accused of supplying centrifuge components to Iraq. The company has its headquarters in Mr. Möllemann's parliamentary district.

After one deputy asked if Mr. Möllemann had lent "a protective hand" to the concern, he said such assertions were part of a "smear campaign."

"At no time have I authorized weapons exports to Iraq or Libya," Mr. Möllemann asserted.

The charges against Mr. Möllemann reflected the uncertainty with which Germany has confronted repeated accusations that it is too lax in monitoring arms exports.

Germany is the world's fifth largest arms exporter, and income from foreign weapons sales accounts for about 5 percent of total export earnings. Some industrialists had quietly lobbied against the bill passed today.

The bill was first presented to Parliament nearly a year ago, after disclosures that German concerns had helped Iraq and Libya build plants where poison gas was manufactured. Until this week, however, it had been blocked by objections. Lately it seemed to have faded from Parliament's agenda.

Supporters of the bill found their case suddenly strengthened when the Iraqi Government admitted to United Nations inspectors last week that it had bought specialized nuclear equipment from German companies. The equipment included fortified magnets and housings that would have been sufficient to build 10,000 centrifuges, enough to produce four or five nuclear weapons a year.

Iraqi officials told inspectors that all the equipment was destroyed after the cease-fire that ended the Persian Gulf war last year.

A report issued last month by the International Atomic Energy Agency named 13 companies that it said had contributed to the Iraqi nuclear program. More than half were German.

Adding to the impact of last week's disclosures in Iraq was the Bonn Government's statement on Wednesday that a planeload of German nuclear equipment being sent to Libya in December had been stopped by customs officers only minutes before the plane was to have left Frankfurt. A Government spokesman said the officers acted on a tip provided by an intelligence agency from a foreign country. He declined to identify the country, but press reports said it was the United States.

In today's parliamentary debate, one deputy from the opposition Social Democratic Party, Ernst Schwanhold, criticized the Government for what he said was its failure to supply United Nations inspectors with evidence it had gathered implicating German concerns in weapons transfers to Iraq. He said the evidence was in a report compiled in March 1991 but not made public.

In a briefing for reporters this week, a Government official acknowledged that international publicity about the involvement of German companies in supplying Iraq and Libya had pushed Parliament to act.

84-2-2

0013

'92-01-25 08:46

686 P04 WDI

2/12 신

# 주 국 련 대 표 부

주국련20313- 131 1992. 2. 6.

수신 장관

참조 국제기구국장, 중동아프리카 국장

제목 유엔 이락핵사찰 (안보리)

934

표제관련 안보리문서를 별첨과 같이 송부합니다.

첨 부 : 상기 문서. 끝.

주 국 련 대 사

| 선 결 | | | 결재(공람) | | |
|---|---|---|---|---|---|
| 접수일시 | 1992. 2.10 | 번호 | | | |
| 처리과 | 08382 | | | | |

0014

UNITED
NATIONS

S

# Security Council

Distr.
GENERAL

S/23505
30 January 1992

ORIGINAL: ENGLISH

NOTE BY THE SECRETARY-GENERAL

The Secretary-General has the honour to transmit to the members of the Security Council the attached communication which he has received from the Director General of the International Atomic Energy Agency (IAEA).

92-04341 3181b (E)

/...

0015

Annex

Letter dated 28 January 1992 from the Director General of the International Atomic Energy Agency addressed to the Secretary-General

Please find attached the report of the ninth IAEA Inspection in Iraq under Security Council resolution 687 (1991). You may deem it appropriate to transmit the report to the members of the Security Council. I remain, of course, available with the Chief Inspector, Professor Maurizio Zifferero for any consultations you or the Council may wish to have.

(*Signed*) Hans BLIX

/...

Enclosure

REPORT ON THE NINTH IAEA ON-SITE INSPECTION IN IRAQ

UNDER SECURITY COUNCIL RESOLUTION 687 (1991)

11 - 14 January 1992

**SALIENT POINTS**

- The main objective of the ninth IAEA on-site inspection was to verify recent information obtained from Governments of Member States, and in particular from the Government of Germany, about the procurement of large quantities of stock materials and components needed in the manufacturing of gas centrifuge machines for the production of enriched uranium.

  The materials and components in question included purpose-designed aluminium alloy extrusions used in the production of centrifuge vacuum housings and molecular pumps, and ferrite magnets used in the stators of the centrifuge motors. The quantities involved, which would have been sufficient for the manufacture of the basic static parts of several thousand centrifuges, had not been included in any previous Iraqi declaration.

- This information was discussed with the Iraqi Minister of State for Foreign Affairs in the presence of technical experts from both sides. Subsequent to the discussion, the Iraqi authorities acknowledged the procurement of these materials and components, but stated that all had been destroyed or "rendered harmless" by melting and crushing before the beginning of nuclear inspections in Iraq under resolution 687.

- Further, they acknowledged the procurement of 100 tons of the special high-tensile-strength steel (maraging steel) needed for producing several thousand centrifuge rotors and rotor internal fittings and the procurement of a few thousand aluminium forgings for the vacuum housing top and bottom flanges.

  The Iraqi authorities explained that in this case also the stockpile of maraging steel and aluminium forgings had been "rendered harmless" by melting before the start of the nuclear inspections and offered to present to the team all the materials which they had procured at the location where they were currently stored after being rendered harmless.

/...

0017

- The inspection team verified and sampled the melted maraging steel stockpile and the powder resulting from the crushing of the ferrite magnets, leaving for the next inspection the remaining verifications. A rough estimate of the quantities made on-site appears consistent with the quantities procured. Full verification must await the results of sample analyses and a more accurate assessment of mass.

- The results of this inspection have resolved a number of inconsistencies regarding the Iraqi centrifuge programme remaining from previous inspections. In the opinion of the experts who took part in the nuclear inspection, Iraq had not reached the point where it could start centrifuge production on a sizeable scale, but given time, it would have been successful.

- However, the centrifuge enrichment programme had reached the point where the materials necessary for certain key centrifuge components had been identified, and these materials were being procured as opportunities presented themselves even though the final design had not been completely fixed nor the manufacturing process fully implemented. The operation of any production-oriented centrifuge cascade would have required the procurement of large numbers of finished components, but the nuclear inspection teams have found no evidence of this.

- Initiatives taken by the German Government have greatly assisted the ongoing inspection effort as it relates to the Iraqi centrifuge enrichment programme.

0018 /...

## INTRODUCTION

1. This report summarizes the findings of the ninth inspection carried out by the IAEA in Iraq under Security Council resolution 687 (1991) with the assistance and co-operation of the Special Commission of the United Nations. The inspection took place from 11 to 14 January 1992 and was headed by Mr. Maurizio Zifferero of the IAEA as Chief Inspector. The team consisted of 6 inspectors and 8 supporting staff; it comprised 8 nationalities.

The objectives of the inspection were mainly to:

- verify information, recently received from the German Government, concerning the procurement by Iraq of stock materials and components needed in the manufacturing of gas centrifuges for the production of enriched uranium.

- visit a few previously inspected sites for follow-up actions in order to verify the existence of some machine-tools which might have been associated with the centrifuge enrichment programme.

2. A meeting was held at the Ministry of Foreign Affairs on Sunday, 12 January. The Iraqi delegation was headed by Mr. Muhammad Said al-Sahhaf, Minister of State for Foreign Affairs, and included Mr. Human al-Ghaffar, the Chairman of the Iraqi Atomic Energy Commission (IAEC), Mr. Ibrahim al-Hajjaj, the leader of the Iraqi team for nuclear inspections under resolution 687, and Mr. Abd al-Qadir Ahmad, former Director of the Tuwaitha Nuclear Research Centre and now advisor to the IAEC. The Agency's Chief Inspector gave the Minister a copy of the information recently received from the German Government (see Annex 1) concerning the procurement by Iraq of large quantities of stock materials and components, the nature of which left no doubt about their future utilization in the manufacturing of a large number of centrifuges for producing enriched uranium. In the light of this evidence, the Iraqi authorities were invited to come forward with a comprehensive statement about their procurement of stock materials, components and equipment related to their centrifuge programme.

/...

On the following day a technical meeting was held at the Tuwaitha Nuclear Research Centre. The Iraqi team acknowledged the procurement of the materials and components indicated by the German Government. They further acknowledged the import of additional stock materials including maraging steel and items described later in this report. The Iraqi authorities explained that the entire stockpile of materials and components had been destroyed or "rendered harmless" by melting and crushing before the beginning of nuclear inspections in Iraq under resolution 687. The inspection team was given the possibility to verify the materials and components at the site to which they had been moved for destruction.

3. A site already inspected during the fourth IAEA mission, in the proximity of the Baghdad North Bridge, was thoroughly re-inspected at the request of the Special Commission. The results of the fourth inspection were confirmed in the sense that no immediate evidence of a connection with nuclear activities was found.

4. At the end of the inspection, the team was given a set of documents including written replies to questions asked during the ninth and previous inspections and a set of tables containing a list of items to be reported by Iraq to the Agency under resolution 715. The list of documents received or transmitted in the course of the inspection is contained in Annex 2.

**THE GAS CENTRIFUGE URANIUM ENRICHMENT PROGRAMME**

5. The detailed analysis of centrifuge components removed from Iraq during the seventh and eighth inspections and new data on foreign procurements by Iraq (acknowledged and added to by Iraqi authorities during the ninth inspection) have resulted in a more consistent picture of the Iraqi centrifuge programme. The new data on foreign procurements were provided by IAEA Member States working with the Action Team and, in two significant instances, by Iraq.

6. The Iraqi centrifuge design conforms substantially to early west European designs. However, no component is identical in design; all showed evidence of intelligent adaptation and development based on sound principles. A number of capable scientists and engineers were involved in the Iraqi centrifuge development effort, but it is unlikely that they were able to make the observed design modifications without

/...

outside help. The Iraqi authorities acknowledged "advice from abroad", but they were clearly trying to minimize the extent of foreign involvement. A centrifuge constructed from components found in Iraq, but manufactured to a higher quality standard, would have a separative power greater than that declared by Iraq.

7. Investigations of Iraqi procurements, with the close co-operation of Member State Governments, have become an integral part of the overall inspection effort. Among the data obtained is information from the German Government indicating that large quantities of stock materials intended for the Iraqi centrifuge manufacturing programme had been delivered to Iraq during the period January - May 1990. These stock materials included:

- 300 tonnes of aluminium alloy (AlMgSi 1 F31) tube extrusions for the manufacture of vacuum housings (enough for approximately 2,500 housings). An order for an additional 310 tonnes was stopped by the embargo.

- 84 tonnes of aluminium alloy (AlMgSiPb F28) tube extrusions for the manufacture of molecular pumps (enough for 6,000 pumps);

- 240,000 ferrite magnet spacers (24 per centrifuge stator) and 10,000 soft iron ring band cores (providing material for the manufacture of 10,000 stators for centrifuge motors).

During the ninth inspection, the Iraqi authorities confirmed the receipt of these materials and, in addition, declared the procurement of:

- 100 tonnes of 350-grade maraging steel (material sufficient for approximately 5,000 centrifuges employing maraging steel rotors, end caps and baffles);

- Aluminium forgings sufficient for the manufacture of several thousand top and bottom flanges for the centrifuge vacuum housings.

A schematic showing the various centrifuge components referred to above is presented as Figure 1. The estimate of the numbers of centrifuge components that could have been manufactured from the stated amounts of material implies no

0022.

Figure 1

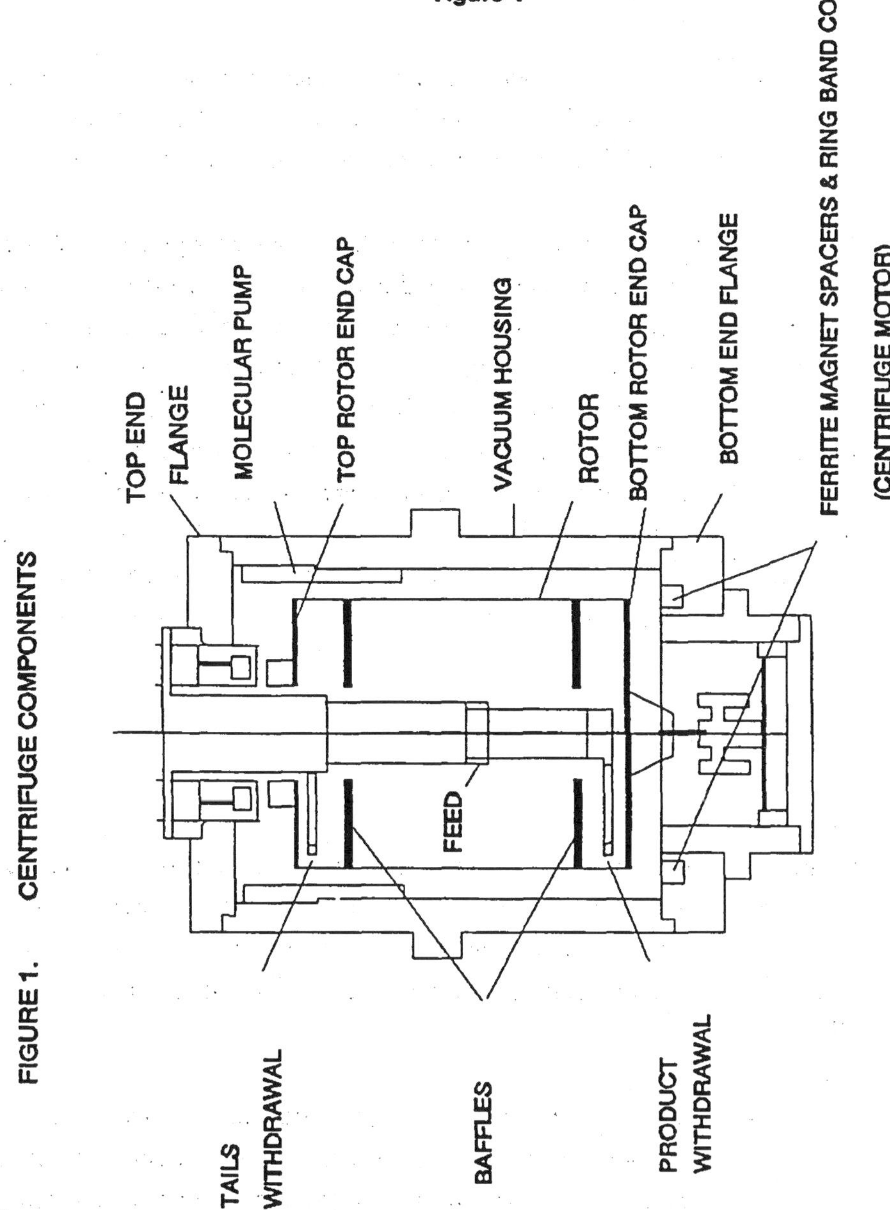


/...

difficulty in meeting the required specifications. A reject rate in the range of 50% for some components was estimated by the Iraqi experts. This reasonably can be expected while the manufacturing process is being implemented.

8. The acquisition of such large quantities of stock materials indicates that Iraq was planning for a much larger and more rapid centrifuge deployment than previously declared. The Iraqi authorities acknowledged this, but argued that there was no contradiction between the very large procurements and the centrifuge development and deployment schedule given to the third and fourth inspection teams; this schedule shows a 500- machine cascade beginning to operate early in 1996. They indicated that the material specifications for important components had been set by mid-1989, but that the final design of the centrifuge was not fixed at the time work stopped because of the Gulf War. Faced with tighter and tighter export controls, they proceeded with the large procurements as opportunities presented themselves, even though they had no immediate plans for the materials in the quantities ordered. Their strategy was to buy whenever there was an opportunity and simply run the risk that some material might not be used.

9. The Iraqi authorities, explaining this material had not been declared, stated that immediately after the Gulf War a political decision had been taken to dismantle and destroy the nuclear programme. In line with this decision, all centrifuge-related materials, equipment and documents were turned over to the Iraqi military for destruction. The actions taken to destroy the materials in question were described as follows:

- The 100 tonnes of 350-grade maraging steel rods and tubes were taken (except for the 3.25 tonnes previously declared to the inspection teams) to the State Establishment for Mechanical Works (a foundry near Iskandariya), melted and poured into "ingots".

- The ferrite magnets and ring band cores were taken to the same establishment. The ferrite magnets were crushed into powder and the ring band cores were melted.

/...

0023

- Aluminium alloys (more than 450 tonnes) in the form of tube extrusions for the manufacture of vacuum housings and molecular pumps and in the form of forgings for the manufacture of end flanges were taken to the Ur Establishment (an aluminium smelter at Al Nassiriya) and melted together.

The Iraqi authorities explained that these materials had been destroyed before the beginning of IAEA inspections, and destroyed in a manner that rendered them useless for centrifuges (e.g. the maraging steel was no longer maraging). Their position was that technically they no longer had maraging steel, special aluminium alloys etc. and, under their interpretation of resolution 687 and later Security Council resolutions, they were not obliged to declare them.

10. Obviously this position can be debated, particularly in view of past Iraqi attempts to hide the true nature and extent of Iraq's nuclear programme. However, justifiable or not, this position suggests that the inspection teams will continue to have difficulty in uncovering and verifying the complete Iraqi programme. The destruction process which began in the immediate aftermath of the Gulf War was, according to the Iraqi authorities, stopped only at the time of the high-level visit by Messrs. Ekéus, Blix and Akashi on 29 June 1991 during the second inspection. The Iraqi statement was that the only centrifuge-related equipment and materials declared by Iraq and verified by inspection teams prior to the ninth inspection were materials and equipment that had not been destroyed as of the end of June 1991. As more procurement data become available, there will probably continue to be mismatches between quantities of materials and equipment delivered to Iraq and quantities declared to and verified by inspection teams. Furthermore, even if the Iraqi position could be accepted, it has not been applied in a consistent manner.

11. The quantities of stock materials were declared by Iraq to be available for inspection at the sites to which they had been taken for destruction. On the last day of the ninth inspection the team went to the State Establishment for Mechanical Works at Iskandariya in order to inspect the melt of the maraging steel and ferrite magnet powder. The team was shown a large pile of flat, irregularly shaped "ingots" in an outside storage area. Samples were taken for the purpose of confirming that the chemical composition is that of maraging steel and that the melting has indeed rendered the material useless for centrifuges. One ingot was selected at random and

/... 0024

weighed (740 kg). This together with a rough count of the number of ingots led to an estimate of the total mass that is reasonably consistent with the Iraqi declaration. Pending confirmation of the chemical composition of the material at Iskandariya, it now appears that the 100 tonnes of maraging steel is generally accounted for - i.e. i) the 1.5 tonnes of maraging steel centrifuge components (end caps and baffles) stopped en route from Switzerland to Iraq at Frankfurt Airport, ii) the maraging steel components declared and inspected at the Ash Shakyli warehouse near Al Tuwaitha and iii) the material seen by the ninth inspection team at Iskandariya. The team was also shown a steel box containing approximately 100 litres of a ceramic powder which, according to the Iraqi authorities, was all that remained of the ferrite magnets; samples were taken to confirm this. More precise assessment of the material stored at Iskandariya and examination of the aluminium melted at Al Nassiriya will be on the agenda of the next inspection.

12. The official Iraqi declaration regarding the number of carbon fibre rotors had been revised upwards from 10 to 20. Twelve of the rotors were seen by inspectors - five were removed from Iraq for analysis and 7 were destroyed during the seventh inspection. Iraq claims that 8 carbon rotors were broken during attempts to install end caps. This is plausible, as an independent assessment of centrifuge components removed from Iraq came to the conclusion that the maraging steel end caps were over-sized vis-a-vis the carbon rotors. The source of the carbon rotors remains unknown. Analysis of them has identified the company which produced the carbon filaments. However, it has been determined that this company has only had one customer for the particular grades of carbon fibre in question and that the customer was not Iraq. Further, the construction of the helix layer is different between at least two of the rotors removed from Iraq and different still from the construction used in Europe. The Iraqi authorities stated that they had procured 20 rotors from a "dealer" and that they had had nothing to do with material and construction specifications. They had chosen to purchase the carbon rotors to support the mechanical endurance and separation testing of single machines as they worked to install the maraging steel rotor line. Immediately before the ninth inspection, the Action Team received a report that three filament winding machines had been delivered to Iraq. The Special Commission indicated that a missile inspection team had seen filament winding machines at the Dhu Al Fiqar factory near Falluja. These machines were inspected. There are three filament winding machines at this location, but expert opinion is that they do not possess sufficient capability for the manufacture of carbon fibre rotors.

0025

/...

As usual, manufacture-related information had been removed from the machines. Action to ascertain whether the machines seen at Dhu Al Fiqar correspond to those reported to have been delivered to Iraq will be taken.

13. The Iraqi plans for the installation of centrifuge manufacturing equipment at Al Furat apparently included five CNC machines in addition to the equipment identified in the seventh and eighth inspection reports. Evidence available to the IAEA inspection team indicates that these five machines were being procured for the manufacture of maraging steel end caps and baffles. The procurement included the demonstration by the manufacturer that the machines were capable of producing the maraging steel pieces to the required specifications. Iraq supplied the manufacturer with maraging steel (presumably from the stock of 100 tonnes described earlier). The return shipment to Iraq of the finished demonstration pieces was intercepted and stopped by German authorities at Frankfurt airport. The full Iraqi order to the European manufacturer was for 15 CNC machines. The five machines referred to above were never delivered. The ten machines that were delivered are, according to Iraqi statements, the machines currently under IAEA seal at the Badr State Establishment. These machines show little signs of use and the analysis of metal turnings taken from some of these machines does not provide evidence that they were used for the manufacture of centrifuge components. It has not been confirmed that the ten machines at Badr are the ten machines originally ordered for the centrifuge programme.

14. Further analysis of the maraging steel rotors, mandrel collar and flow-forming rollers supports Iraqi declarations regarding the extent of use of the flow-forming machine. One of the flow-forming rollers rendered harmless during the eighth mission was removed from Iraq by the ninth team in order to confirm a correspondence between the rollers and the maraging steel rotors. The ninth team also inspected nine flow-forming machines declared by Iraq to have been used in the production of 122-mm and 262-mm rocket bodies. Seven of these machines are installed at the Nasr Establishment at Taji and two are being stored at a subsidiary establishment at Scháula. Eight of the machines are identical, and capable of flow-forming diameters in the range 60-400 mm. The ninth machine (at Scháula) is much larger, and is capable of flow-forming diameters in the range 80-600 mm. All mandrels and other fixtures observed are consistent with Iraqi statements. If the machines were fitted with the appropriate mandrels, rollers, etc., then all machines inspected could have been

0026

/...

used to produce steel centrifuge rotors. The Iraqi authorities reiterated that they had only one mandrel for centrifuge rotors. Most of the machines suffered substantial damage during the Gulf War.

15. The additional five CNC machines referred to in para. 13 above, which are now stated to have been intended for installation at Al Furat, provides a larger potential production capacity than originally estimated by experts. The layout of the Al Furat complex with the planned utilization (as identified by Iraq) is described in Figure 2. The buildings designated as B01, B02 and B03 were far from completion when work stopped.

**OTHER ACTIVITIES**

16. The ninth inspection team conducted a short-notice inspection of the Rashdiya complex, located in the proximity of Baghdad North Bridge. The complex had been designated and inspected by the fourth inspection team. It was constructed in the early 1980s as a project of the Ministry of Agriculture for research and development in water irrigation technology. According to supplied information, the research for which the facility was designed was terminated for lack of success and the entire complex was taken over in 1988 by the Ministry of Industry and Minerals. They partitioned the facility and established an "Engineering Design Centre" (occupying what had been the administration and R & D buildings) in the northern part of the site and were attempting to establish a paper mill/vocational training centre (under the auspices of the Department of Forestry) in the southern portion. The site was physically divided by a wall, the only connection between the two parts being through the main entrances set at two points along the west side of the complex.

17. The Engineering Design Centre was stated to have a staff of 250 technical and administrative personnel. Their work was described as having generally to do with water treatment and water quality, but since the end of the Gulf War most of the staff have been assigned to projects associated with the reconstruction effort. Most offices and laboratories were empty and showed no signs of recent occupancy. The few laboratories where there was activity seemed to be involved in work consistent with Iraqi statements. One typical feature was the complete absence of paper records or reports. The Director of the Centre was unable to produce a single piece of paper related to its projects. His explanation was that all records and reports were

0027

/...

0028

**Figure 2**

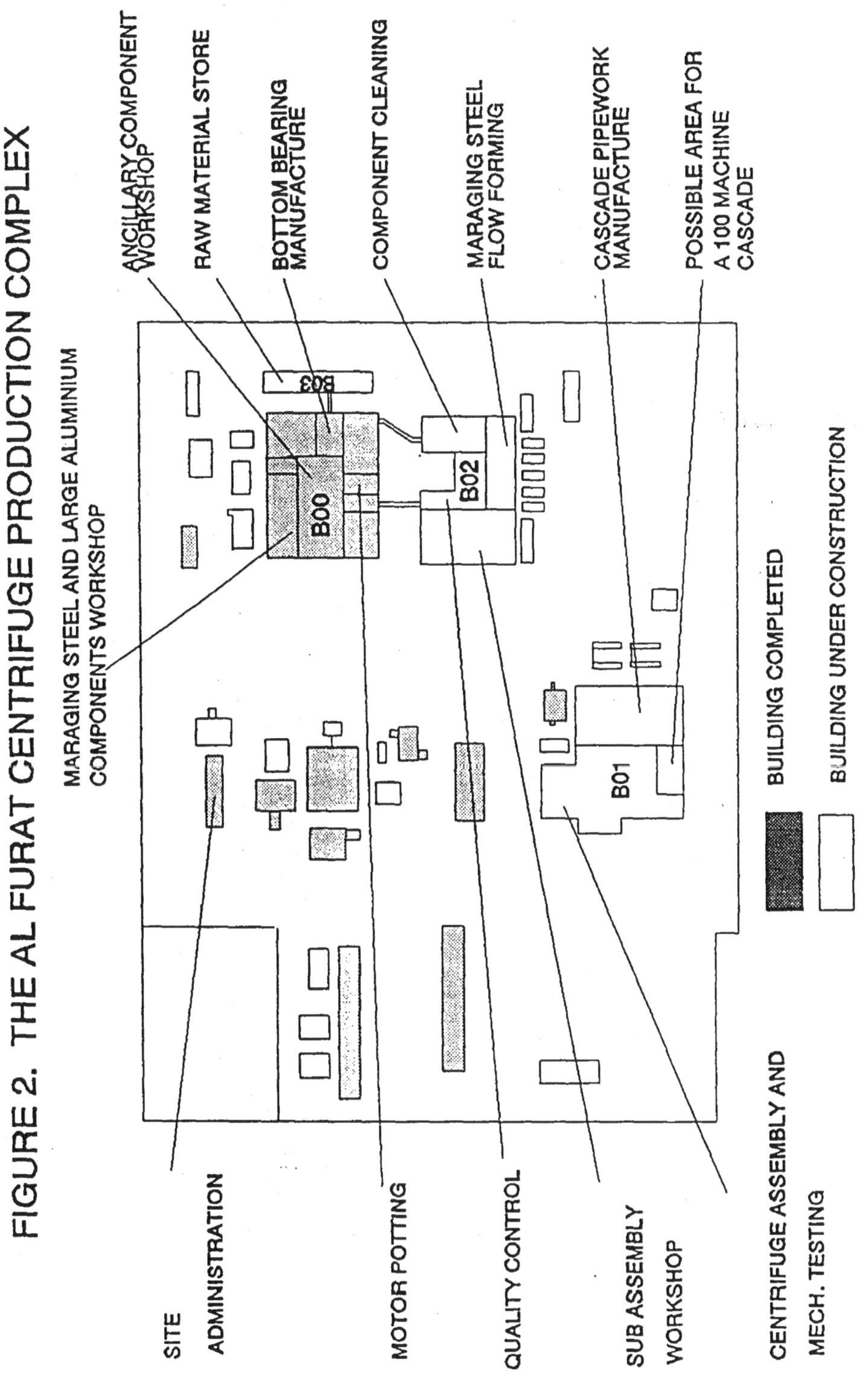

FIGURE 2. THE AL FURAT CENTRIFUGE PRODUCTION COMPLEX

MARAGING STEEL AND LARGE ALUMINIUM COMPONENTS WORKSHOP

ANCILLARY COMPONENT WORKSHOP

RAW MATERIAL STORE

BOTTOM BEARING MANUFACTURE

COMPONENT CLEANING

MARAGING STEEL FLOW FORMING

CASCADE PIPEWORK MANUFACTURE

POSSIBLE AREA FOR A 100 MACHINE CASCADE

B03

B00

B02

B01

SITE ADMINISTRATION

MOTOR POTTING

QUALITY CONTROL

SUB ASSEMBLY WORKSHOP

CENTRIFUGE ASSEMBLY AND MECH. TESTING

BUILDING COMPLETED

BUILDING UNDER CONSTRUCTION

/...

maintained at the field locations where the staff were working or at the Ministry. The Director repeatedly stated that the Centre had never performed any nuclear-related work and that he and his staff had no knowledge of the Petrochemical-3 (PC-3) project.

18. In the southern part of the complex, there are a large main building, settling tanks, a water pump house and three buildings in the early stages of construction. The southernmost area is occupied by a deserted construction camp. The main building has a huge, high-bay hall (approximately 6,000 $m^2$) and a suite of offices along the eastern side. The building is being used to store fertilizers, pesticides and seeds. At the time of the inspection, about 10% of the floor area was being used for this purpose. The rest was empty. The facility has a staff of 3-4 people, who essentially serve as caretakers. It was explained that the main building and the three under construction were intended to be used for wood/paper products R & D and a vocational training centre. Blueprints for the buildings under construction found in a deserted office have titles that appear to confirm this. Construction work stopped at the onset of the Gulf War. At one time, the main building was connected to the R & D building by a first-floor walkway, which has since been walled off. The building has a huge water supply, which Iraqi statements linked to the defunct hydrology project. The north-west corner of the building contains a small room (100 $m^2$) which had been freshly painted and which had a new concrete floor. The manager's explanation was that this room was being prepared for the storage of herbicides that needed to be kept separate from the materials stored in the main hall. There was no physical evidence or other signs of recent modifications which might suggest that this facility served some other purpose than what was declared. A large number of samples were taken.

/...

0029

Appendix I

Letter dated 17 January 1992 from the Alternate to the Resident Representative of Germany to the Office of the United Nations and to the other International Organizations, Vienna, addressed to the Leader of the IAEA Action Team Iraq, established pursuant to Security Council resolution 687 (1991)

With reference to the Action Team's findings on the Iraq centrifuge programme as contained in the reports on the 6th and 7th IAEA on-site inspection, my Government has authorized me to make the following additional information on supplies from Germany to Iraq for the centrifuge programme available to you:

> 240.000 ferrite shaped parts for centrifuge stators and 10.000 pieces of ring sheet material were supplied, in several shipments, to the State Electrical Industries Establishment, Baghdad between January and May 1990, by a German company. A die-casting machine for the manufacture of coil rings for stators was also supplied.

The volume of these supplies may allow some conclusion on the scope and size of the Iraqi centrifuge programme.

Supplementary documentation and drawings are available for examination by experts of the special commission and the IAEA Action Team at the Federal Foreign Office in Bonn, Germany.

(Signed) Klaus UNGER
Alternate to the Resident Representative

/...

0030

Appendix II

## List of documents received or transmitted during the Ninth Inspection

| | |
|---|---|
| 920113 | Letter from Maurizio Zifferero to Al Hajjaj requesting information on German exports in the centrifuge project. |
| 920114 | Letter from Al Hajjaj to Maurizio Zifferero giving information on German procurement on centrifuges. |
| 920114 | Letter from Al Hajjaj to Maurizio Zifferero giving details on the request of radiopharmaceuticals. |
| 920114 | Letter from Al Hajjaj to Dimitri Perricos giving information on the movements of IAEC personnel to the "new site" of Al Atheer. |
| 920114 | Letter from Al Hajjaj to Dimitri Perricos addressing questions raised in writing on 911116 and 911118 on i) staff and equipment transfer to Al-Atheer from Tuwaitha and ii) clarifications regarding activities of Group 4 of PC-3. |
| 920114 | Long table of items as requested in Annex 3 of the long term monitoring plan to complete earlier submission and revised list of radioactive sources. They will provide also an English version and transmit it officially to the UNSG and Dr. Blix. |

-----

0031

International Atomic Energy Agency

# BOARD OF GOVERNORS

GOV/INF/647
31 January 1992

RESTRICTED Distr.
Original: ENGLISH

For official use only

93/

# REPORT ON THE NINTH IAEA ON-SITE INSPECTION IN IRAQ UNDER SECURITY COUNCIL RESOLUTION 687 (1991)

11-14 January 1992

INTERNATIONAL ATOMIC ENERGY AGENCY

92-00372

0032

REPORT ON THE NINTH IAEA ON-SITE INSPECTION IN IRAQ

UNDER SECURITY COUNCIL RESOLUTION 687 (1991)

11 - 14 January 1992

**SALIENT POINTS**

- The main objective of the ninth IAEA on-site inspection was to verify recent information obtained from Governments of Member States, and in particular from the Government of Germany, about the procurement of large quantities of stock materials and components needed in the manufacturing of gas centrifuge machines for the production of enriched uranium.

  The materials and components in question included purpose-designed aluminium alloy extrusions used in the production of centrifuge vacuum housings and molecular pumps, and ferrite magnets used in the stators of the centrifuge motors. The quantities involved, which would have been sufficient for the manufacture of the basic static parts of several thousand centrifuges, had not been included in any previous Iraqi declaration.

- This information was discussed with the Iraqi Minister of State for Foreign Affairs in the presence of technical experts from both sides. Subsequent to the discussion, the Iraqi authorities acknowledged the procurement of these materials and components, but stated that all had been destroyed or "rendered harmless" by melting and crushing before the beginning of nuclear inspections in Iraq under resolution 687.

- Further, they acknowledged the procurement of 100 tons of the special high-tensile-strength steel (maraging steel) needed for producing several thousand centrifuge rotors and rotor internal fittings and the procurement of a few thousand aluminium forgings for the vacuum housing top and bottom flanges.

  The Iraqi authorities explained that in this case also the stockpile of maraging steel and aluminium forgings had been "rendered harmless" by melting before the start of the nuclear inspections and offered to present to the team all the materials which they had procured at the location where they were currently stored after being rendered harmless.

0033

- The inspection team verified and sampled the melted maraging steel stockpile and the powder resulting from the crushing of the ferrite magnets, leaving for the next inspection the remaining verifications. A rough estimate of the quantities made on-site appears consistent with the quantities procured. Full verification must await the results of sample analyses and a more accurate assessment of mass.

- The results of this inspection have resolved a number of inconsistencies regarding the Iraqi centrifuge programme remaining from previous inspections. In the opinion of the experts who took part in the nuclear inspection, Iraq had not reached the point where it could start centrifuge production on a sizeable scale, but given time, it would have been successful.

- However, the centrifuge enrichment programme had reached the point where the materials necessary for certain key centrifuge components had been identified, and these materials were being procured as opportunities presented themselves even though the final design had not been completely fixed nor the manufacturing process fully implemented. The operation of any production-oriented centrifuge cascade would have required the procurement of large numbers of finished components, but the nuclear inspection teams have found no evidence of this.

- Initiatives taken by the German Government have greatly assisted the ongoing inspection effort as it relates to the Iraqi centrifuge enrichment programme.

0034

**INTRODUCTION**

1. This report summarizes the findings of the ninth inspection carried out by the IAEA in Iraq under Security Council resolution 687 (1991) with the assistance and co-operation of the Special Commission of the United Nations. The inspection took place from 11 to 14 January 1992 and was headed by Mr. Maurizio Zifferero of the IAEA as Chief Inspector. The team consisted of 6 inspectors and 8 supporting staff; it comprised 8 nationalities.

The objectives of the inspection were mainly to:

- verify information, recently received from the German Government, concerning the procurement by Iraq of stock materials and components needed in the manufacturing of gas centrifuges for the production of enriched uranium.

- visit a few previously inspected sites for follow-up actions in order to verify the existence of some machine-tools which might have been associated with the centrifuge enrichment programme.

2. A meeting was held at the Ministry of Foreign Affairs on Sunday, 12 January. The Iraqi delegation was headed by Mr. Muhammad Said al-Sahhaf, Minister of State for Foreign Affairs, and included Mr. Human al-Ghaffar, the Chairman of the Iraqi Atomic Energy Commission (IAEC), Mr. Ibrahim al-Hajjaj, the leader of the Iraqi team for nuclear inspections under resolution 687, and Mr. Abd al-Qadir Ahmad, former Director of the Tuwaitha Nuclear Research Centre and now advisor to the IAEC. The Agency's Chief Inspector gave the Minister a copy of the information recently received from the German Government (see Annex 1) concerning the procurement by Iraq of large quantities of stock materials and components, the nature of which left no doubt about their future utilization in the manufacturing of a large number of centrifuges for producing enriched uranium. In the light of this evidence, the Iraqi authorities were invited to come forward with a comprehensive statement about their procurement of stock materials, components and equipment related to their centrifuge programme.

0035

On the following day a technical meeting was held at the Tuwaitha Nuclear Research Centre. The Iraqi team acknowledged the procurement of the materials and components indicated by the German Government. They further acknowledged the import of additional stock materials including maraging steel and items described later in this report. The Iraqi authorities explained that the entire stockpile of materials and components had been destroyed or "rendered harmless" by melting and crushing before the beginning of nuclear inspections in Iraq under resolution 687. The inspection team was given the possibility to verify the materials and components at the site to which they had been moved for destruction.

3. A site already inspected during the fourth IAEA mission, in the proximity of the Baghdad North Bridge, was thoroughly re-inspected at the request of the Special Commission. The results of the fourth inspection were confirmed in the sense that no immediate evidence of a connection with nuclear activities was found.

4. At the end of the inspection, the team was given a set of documents including written replies to questions asked during the ninth and previous inspections and a set of tables containing a list of items to be reported by Iraq to the Agency under resolution 715. The list of documents received or transmitted in the course of the inspection is contained in Annex 2.

## THE GAS CENTRIFUGE URANIUM ENRICHMENT PROGRAMME

5. The detailed analysis of centrifuge components removed from Iraq during the seventh and eighth inspections and new data on foreign procurements by Iraq (acknowledged and added to by Iraqi authorities during the ninth inspection) have resulted in a more consistent picture of the Iraqi centrifuge programme. The new data on foreign procurements were provided by IAEA Member States working with the Action Team and, in two significant instances, by Iraq.

6. The Iraqi centrifuge design conforms substantially to early west European designs. However, no component is identical in design; all showed evidence of intelligent adaptation and development based on sound principles. A number of capable scientists and engineers were involved in the Iraqi centrifuge development effort, but it is unlikely that they were able to make the observed design modifications without

0036

outside help. The Iraqi authorities acknowledged "advice from abroad", but they were clearly trying to minimize the extent of foreign involvement. A centrifuge constructed from components found in Iraq, but manufactured to a higher quality standard, would have a separative power greater than that declared by Iraq.

7. Investigations of Iraqi procurements, with the close co-operation of Member State Governments, have become an integral part of the overall inspection effort. Among the data obtained is information from the German Government indicating that large quantities of stock materials intended for the Iraqi centrifuge manufacturing programme had been delivered to Iraq during the period January - May 1990. These stock materials included:

- 300 tonnes of aluminium alloy (AlMgSi 1 F31) tube extrusions for the manufacture of vacuum housings (enough for approximately 2,500 housings). An order for an additional 310 tonnes was stopped by the embargo.

- 84 tonnes of aluminium alloy (AlMgSiPb F28) tube extrusions for the manufacture of molecular pumps (enough for 6,000 pumps);

- 240,000 ferrite magnet spacers (24 per centrifuge stator) and 10,000 soft iron ring band cores (providing material for the manufacture of 10,000 stators for centrifuge motors).

During the ninth inspection, the Iraqi authorities confirmed the receipt of these materials and, in addition, declared the procurement of:

- 100 tonnes of 350-grade maraging steel (material sufficient for approximately 5,000 centrifuges employing maraging steel rotors, end caps and baffles);

- Aluminium forgings sufficient for the manufacture of several thousand top and bottom flanges for the centrifuge vacuum housings.

A schematic showing the various centrifuge components referred to above is presented as Figure 1. The estimate of the numbers of centrifuge components that could have been manufactured from the stated amounts of material implies no

0037

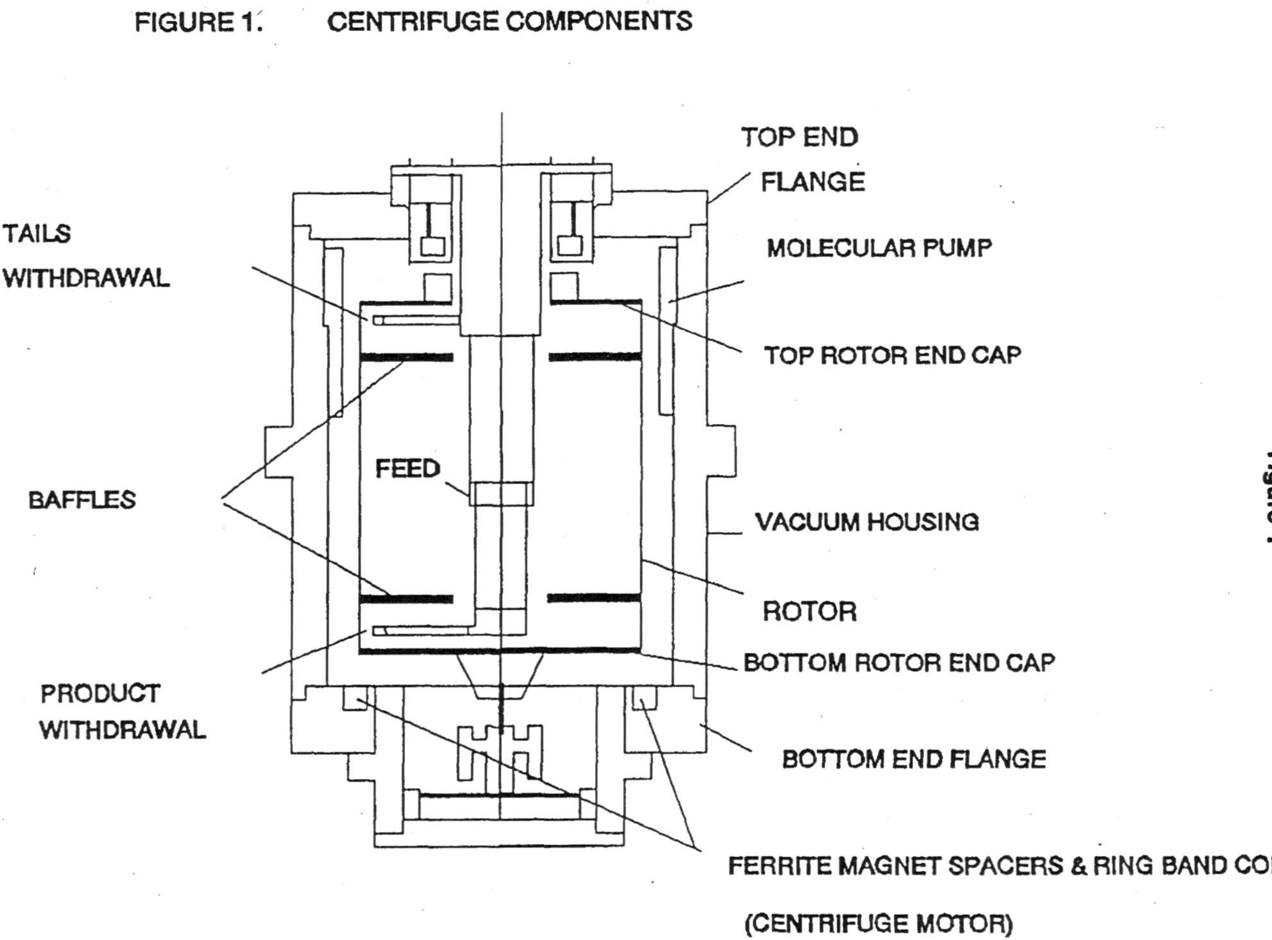


Figure 1

- 6 -

0038

difficulty in meeting the required specifications. A reject rate in the range of 50% for some components was estimated by the Iraqi experts. This reasonably can be expected while the manufacturing process is being implemented.

8. The acquisition of such large quantities of stock materials indicates that Iraq was planning for a much larger and more rapid centrifuge deployment than previously declared. The Iraqi authorities acknowledged this, but argued that there was no contradiction between the very large procurements and the centrifuge development and deployment schedule given to the third and fourth inspection teams; this schedule shows a 500- machine cascade beginning to operate early in 1996. They indicated that the material specifications for important components had been set by mid-1989, but that the final design of the centrifuge was not fixed at the time work stopped because of the Gulf War. Faced with tighter and tighter export controls, they proceeded with the large procurements as opportunities presented themselves, even though they had no immediate plans for the materials in the quantities ordered. Their strategy was to buy whenever there was an opportunity and simply run the risk that some material might not be used.

9. The Iraqi authorities, explaining this material had not been declared, stated that immediately after the Gulf War a political decision had been taken to dismantle and destroy the nuclear programme. In line with this decision, all centrifuge-related materials, equipment and documents were turned over to the Iraqi military for destruction. The actions taken to destroy the materials in question were described as follows:

- The 100 tonnes of 350-grade maraging steel rods and tubes were taken (except for the 3.25 tonnes previously declared to the inspection teams) to the State Establishment for Mechanical Works (a foundry near Iskandariya), melted and poured into "ingots".

- The ferrite magnets and ring band cores were taken to the same establishment. The ferrite magnets were crushed into powder and the ring band cores were melted.

0039

- Aluminium alloys (more than 450 tonnes) in the form of tube extrusions for the manufacture of vacuum housings and molecular pumps and in the form of forgings for the manufacture of end flanges were taken to the Ur Establishment (an aluminium smelter at Al Nassiriya) and melted together.

The Iraqi authorities explained that these materials had been destroyed before the beginning of IAEA inspections, and destroyed in a manner that rendered them useless for centrifuges (e.g. the maraging steel was no longer maraging). Their position was that technically they no longer had maraging steel, special aluminium alloys etc. and, under their interpretation of resolution 687 and later Security Council resolutions, they were not obliged to declare them.

10. Obviously this position can be debated, particularly in view of past Iraqi attempts to hide the true nature and extent of Iraq's nuclear programme. However, justifiable or not, this position suggests that the inspection teams will continue to have difficulty in uncovering and verifying the complete Iraqi programme. The destruction process which began in the immediate aftermath of the Gulf War was, according to the Iraqi authorities, stopped only at the time of the high-level visit by Messrs. Ekéus, Blix and Akashi on 29 June 1991 during the second inspection. The Iraqi statement was that the only centrifuge-related equipment and materials declared by Iraq and verified by inspection teams prior to the ninth inspection were materials and equipment that had not been destroyed as of the end of June 1991. As more procurement data become available, there will probably continue to be mismatches between quantities of materials and equipment delivered to Iraq and quantities declared to and verified by inspection teams. Furthermore, even if the Iraqi position could be accepted, it has not been applied in a consistent manner.

11. The quantities of stock materials were declared by Iraq to be available for inspection at the sites to which they had been taken for destruction. On the last day of the ninth inspection the team went to the State Establishment for Mechanical Works at Iskandariya in order to inspect the melt of the maraging steel and ferrite magnet powder. The team was shown a large pile of flat, irregularly shaped "ingots" in an outside storage area. Samples were taken for the purpose of confirming that the chemical composition is that of maraging steel and that the melting has indeed rendered the material useless for centrifuges. One ingot was selected at random and

0040

weighed (740 kg). This together with a rough count of the number of ingots led to an estimate of the total mass that is reasonably consistent with the Iraqi declaration. Pending confirmation of the chemical composition of the material at Iskandariya, it now appears that the 100 tonnes of maraging steel is generally accounted for - i.e. i) the 1.5 tonnes of maraging steel centrifuge components (end caps and baffles) stopped en route from Switzerland to Iraq at Frankfurt Airport, ii) the maraging steel components declared and inspected at the Ash Shakyli warehouse near Al Tuwaitha and iii) the material seen by the ninth inspection team at Iskandariya. The team was also shown a steel box containing approximately 100 litres of a ceramic powder which, according to the Iraqi authorities, was all that remained of the ferrite magnets; samples were taken to confirm this. More precise assessment of the material stored at Iskandariya and examination of the aluminium melted at Al Nassiriya will be on the agenda of the next inspection.

12. The official Iraqi declaration regarding the number of carbon fibre rotors had been revised upwards from 10 to 20. Twelve of the rotors were seen by inspectors - five were removed from Iraq for analysis and 7 were destroyed during the seventh inspection. Iraq claims that 8 carbon rotors were broken during attempts to install end caps. This is plausible, as an independent assessment of centrifuge components removed from Iraq came to the conclusion that the maraging steel end caps were over-sized vis-a-vis the carbon rotors. The source of the carbon rotors remains unknown. Analysis of them has identified the company which produced the carbon filaments. However, it has been determined that this company has only had one customer for the particular grades of carbon fibre in question and that the customer was not Iraq. Further, the construction of the helix layer is different between at least two of the rotors removed from Iraq and different still from the construction used in Europe. The Iraqi authorities stated that they had procured 20 rotors from a "dealer" and that they had had nothing to do with material and construction specifications. They had chosen to purchase the carbon rotors to support the mechanical endurance and separation testing of single machines as they worked to install the maraging steel rotor line. Immediately before the ninth inspection, the Action Team received a report that three filament winding machines had been delivered to Iraq. The Special Commission indicated that a missile inspection team had seen filament winding machines at the Dhu Al Fiqar factory near Falluja. These machines were inspected. There are three filament winding machines at this location, but expert opinion is that they do not possess sufficient capability for the manufacture of carbon fibre rotors.

0041

As usual, manufacture-related information had been removed from the machines. Action to ascertain whether the machines seen at Dhu Al Fiqar correspond to those reported to have been delivered to Iraq will be taken.

13. The Iraqi plans for the installation of centrifuge manufacturing equipment at Al Furat apparently included five CNC machines in addition to the equipment identified in the seventh and eighth inspection reports. Evidence available to the IAEA inspection team indicates that these five machines were being procured for the manufacture of maraging steel end caps and baffles. The procurement included the demonstration by the manufacturer that the machines were capable of producing the maraging steel pieces to the required specifications. Iraq supplied the manufacturer with maraging steel (presumably from the stock of 100 tonnes described earlier). The return shipment to Iraq of the finished demonstration pieces was intercepted and stopped by German authorities at Frankfurt airport. The full Iraqi order to the European manufacturer was for 15 CNC machines. The five machines referred to above were never delivered. The ten machines that were delivered are, according to Iraqi statements, the machines currently under IAEA seal at the Badr State Establishment. These machines show little signs of use and the analysis of metal turnings taken from some of these machines does not provide evidence that they were used for the manufacture of centrifuge components. It has not been confirmed that the ten machines at Badr are the ten machines originally ordered for the centrifuge programme.

14. Further analysis of the maraging steel rotors, mandrel collar and flow-forming rollers supports Iraqi declarations regarding the extent of use of the flow-forming machine. One of the flow-forming rollers rendered harmless during the eighth mission was removed from Iraq by the ninth team in order to confirm a correspondence between the rollers and the maraging steel rotors. The ninth team also inspected nine flow-forming machines declared by Iraq to have been used in the production of 122-mm and 262-mm rocket bodies. Seven of these machines are installed at the Nasr Establishment at Taji and two are being stored at a subsidiary establishment at Schâula. Eight of the machines are identical, and capable of flow-forming diameters in the range 60-400 mm. The ninth machine (at Schâula) is much larger, and is capable of flow-forming diameters in the range 80-600 mm. All mandrels and other fixtures observed are consistent with Iraqi statements. If the machines were fitted with the appropriate mandrels, rollers, etc., then all machines inspected could have been

0042

used to produce steel centrifuge rotors. The Iraqi authorities reiterated that they had only one mandrel for centrifuge rotors. Most of the machines suffered substantial damage during the Gulf War.

15. The additional five CNC machines referred to in para. 13 above, which are now stated to have been intended for installation at Al Furat, provides a larger potential production capacity than originally estimated by experts. The layout of the Al Furat complex with the planned utilization (as identified by Iraq) is described in Figure 2. The buildings designated as B01, B02 and B03 were far from completion when work stopped.

**OTHER ACTIVITIES**

16. The ninth inspection team conducted a short-notice inspection of the Rashdiya complex, located in the proximity of Baghdad North Bridge. The complex had been designated and inspected by the fourth inspection team. It was constructed in the early 1980s as a project of the Ministry of Agriculture for research and development in water irrigation technology. According to supplied information, the research for which the facility was designed was terminated for lack of success and the entire complex was taken over in 1988 by the Ministry of Industry and Minerals. They partitioned the facility and established an "Engineering Design Centre" (occupying what had been the administration and R & D buildings) in the northern part of the site and were attempting to establish a paper mill/vocational training centre (under the auspices of the Department of Forestry) in the southern portion. The site was physically divided by a wall, the only connection between the two parts being through the main entrances set at two points along the west side of the complex.

17. The Engineering Design Centre was stated to have a staff of 250 technical and administrative personnel. Their work was described as having generally to do with water treatment and water quality, but since the end of the Gulf War most of the staff have been assigned to projects associated with the reconstruction effort. Most offices and laboratories were empty and showed no signs of recent occupancy. The few laboratories where there was activity seemed to be involved in work consistent with Iraqi statements. One typical feature was the complete absence of paper records or reports. The Director of the Centre was unable to produce a single piece of paper related to its projects. His explanation was that all records and reports were

- 12 -

Figure 2

0044

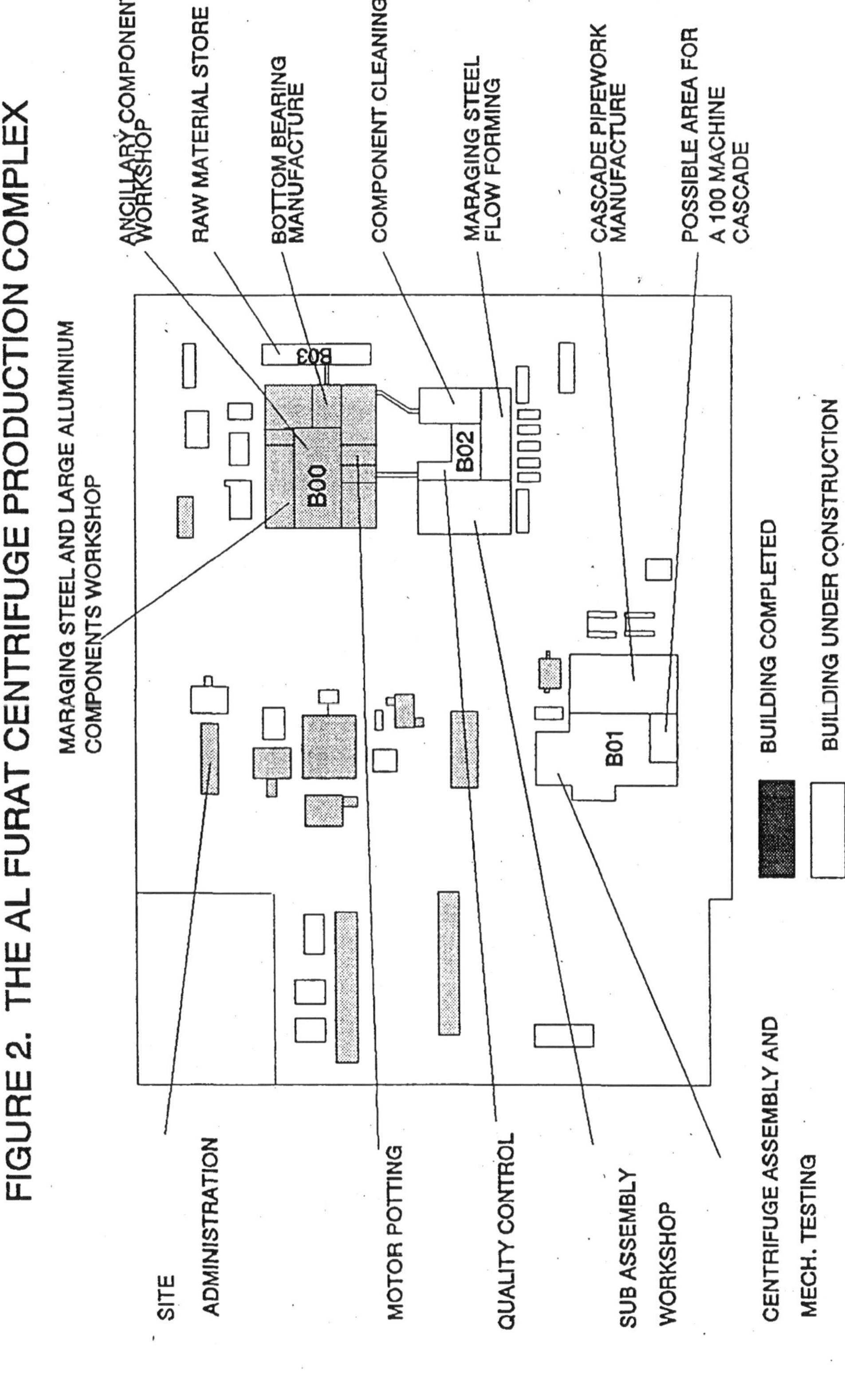

maintained at the field locations where the staff were working or at the Ministry. The Director repeatedly stated that the Centre had never performed any nuclear-related work and that he and his staff had no knowledge of the Petrochemical-3 (PC-3) project.

18. In the southern part of the complex, there are a large main building, settling tanks, a water pump house and three buildings in the early stages of construction. The southernmost area is occupied by a deserted construction camp. The main building has a huge, high-bay hall (approximately 6,000 $m^2$) and a suite of offices along the eastern side. The building is being used to store fertilizers, pesticides and seeds. At the time of the inspection, about 10% of the floor area was being used for this purpose. The rest was empty. The facility has a staff of 3-4 people, who essentially serve as caretakers. It was explained that the main building and the three under construction were intended to be used for wood/paper products R & D and a vocational training centre. Blueprints for the buildings under construction found in a deserted office have titles that appear to confirm this. Construction work stopped at the onset of the Gulf War. At one time, the main building was connected to the R & D building by a first-floor walkway, which has since been walled off. The building has a huge water supply, which Iraqi statements linked to the defunct hydrology project. The north-west corner of the building contains a small room (100 $m^2$) which had been freshly painted and which had a new concrete floor. The manager's explanation was that this room was being prepared for the storage of herbicides that needed to be kept separate from the materials stored in the main hall. There was no physical evidence or other signs of recent modifications which might suggest that this facility served some other purpose than what was declared. A large number of samples were taken.

0045

ACTION TEAM CONFIDENTIAL

Ständige Vertretung der Bundesrepublik Deutschland
bei dem Büro der Vereinten Nationen und bei den anderen
Internationalen Organisationen, Wien

Permanent Mission of the Federal Republic of Germany
to the Office of the United Nations and to the other International Organisations, Vienna

Mission Permanente de la République Fédérale d'Allemagne
auprès du Bureau des Nations Unies et des autres Organisations Internationales, Vienne

A-1220 Wien, 17-12-1991
Wagramer Straße 14

Tel.: 23 15 71-0
Telex: 132755
Fax: 231571-6
Postanschrift: Postfach 160
A-1037 Wien

Az.: 370.25
(Bei Antwort bitte angeben)

Un/Zw

**ANNEX 1**

Professor
Maurizio ZIFFERERO
Leader, IAEA Action Team Iraq
International Atomic Energy Agency
VIC A-2878

<u>Vienna</u>

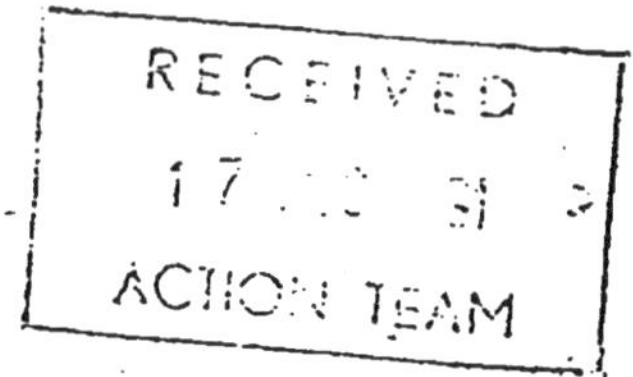


Dear Dr. Zifferero,

with reference to the Action Team's findings on the Iraq centrifuge programme as contained in the reports on the 6th and 7th IAEA on-site inspection, my Government has authorized me to make the following additional information on supplies from Germany to Iraq for the centrifuge programme available to you:

> 240.000 ferrite shaped parts for centrifuge stators and 10.000 pieces of ring sheet material were supplied, in several shipments, to the State Electrical Industries Establishment, Bagdad between January and May 1990, by a German company. A die-casting machine for the manufacture of coil rings for stators was also supplied.

The volume of these supplies may allow some conclusion on the scope and size of the Iraqi centrifuge programme.

Supplementary documentation and drawings are available for examination by experts of the special commmission and the IAEA Action Team at the Federal Foreign Office in Bonn, Germany.

Yours sincerely

(Klaus UNGER)
Alternate to the Resident Representative

0046

## ANNEX 2

## List of documents received or transmitted during the Ninth Inspection

| | |
|---|---|
| 920113 | Letter from Maurizio Zifferero to Al Hajjaj requesting information on German exports in the centrifuge project. |
| 920114 | Letter from Al Hajjaj to Maurizio Zifferero giving information on German procurement on centrifuges. |
| 920114 | Letter from Al Hajjaj to Maurizio Zifferero giving details on the request of radiopharmaceuticals. |
| 920114 | Letter from Al Hajjaj to Dimitri Perricos giving information on the movements of IAEC personnel to the "new site" of Al Atheer. |
| 920114 | Letter from Al Hajjaj to Dimitri Perricos addressing questions raised in writing on 911116 and 911118 on i) staff and equipment transfer to Al-Atheer from Tuwaitha and ii) clarifications regarding activities of Group 4 of PC-3. |
| 920114 | Long table of items as requested in Annex 3 of the long term monitoring plan to complete earlier submission and revised list of radioactive sources. They will provide also an English version and transmit it officially to the UNSG and Dr. Blix. |

0047

원 본

암호수신

# 외 무 부

종 별 :

번 호 : UNW-0427　　　　일 시 : 92 0212 2000

수 신 : 장관(연일,중동일,기정)

발 신 : 주 유엔 대사

제 목 : 걸프사태(이락 대량파괴 무기 관련 협조요청)

1. 유엔 이락 대량파괴 무기폐기 특위(UNSCOM) 는 화생무기 및 탄도미사일 분야관련 이락의 해외장비 및 보급품 수입정보를 수집중인바, 동 특위의 아국앞 협조요청 서한을 별첨송부함.

2. 동 특위는 아국이 여사한 장비및 보급품의 원산지가 된경우 또는 아국에서 수출이 된경우 이를 제보해줄것을 요청하고있음.

3. 한편 핵분야는 IAEA 가 관련국들에게 유사한 제보협조요청을 하였다함.

첨부:USCOM 측서한(2.10):UNW(F)-167 끝

(대사 노창희-국장)

국기국　차관　중아국　안기부

PAGE 1　　　　92.02.13 10:53

외신 2과 통제관 BN

0048

', FEB 12 '92 19:53 KOREA MISSION

P.1

UNITED NATIONS NATIONS UNIES

POSTAL ADDRESS—ADRESSE POSTALE: UNITED NATIONS, N.Y. 10017
CABLE ADDRESS—ADRESSE TELEGRAPHIQUE: UNATIONS NEWYORK

REFERENCE

UNW(F)-167 20212 2000

10 February 1992

304

Excellency,

I have the honour to refer to Security Council resolutions 687 (1991) (section C), 707 (1991) and 715 (1991) relating to the elimination of Iraq's capabilities in regard to weapons of mass destruction and also to ensuring that the acquisition of such weapons is not resumed in the future.

As you are aware, section C of resolution 687 (1991) vests in the Special Commission, established under paragraph 9(b)(i) of that resolution, the responsibilities for discharging the Council's mandate in relation to Iraq's programmes in the fields of chemical and biological weapons and ballistic missiles with a range greater than 150 kilometres while similar responsibilities in the nuclear area are vested in the Director-General of the International Atomic Energy Agency with the cooperation and assistance of the Special Commission.

In order to discharge their responsibilities to the Security Council, the Special Commission and the IAEA are required to develop as detailed and complete a picture as possible of Iraq's activities in the proscribed areas. While the Security Council has called upon Iraq to make a full, final and complete disclosure of its programmes, holdings of weapons, components, production facilities and locations (resolution 707 (1991)), the declarations so far received from Iraq have fallen far short of the disclosure required. When pressed to do so, Iraq has recently indicated that it will only respond to specific information directed to it.

/...

His Excellency
Mr. Chang Hee Roe
Ambassador Extraordinary and Plenipotentiary
Permanent Representative of the Republic
of Korea to the United Nations
New York, New York

#UNW-0427
첨부

167-3-1

0049

UNITED NATIONS  NATIONS UNIES



The Special Commission and the IAEA have therefore had to rely to a considerable extent on the various inspections they have conducted at locations declared by Iraq and, more particularly, at sites designated by the Special Commission, to build up a picture of the Iraqi programmes concerned. Gaps still remain which must be filled, and one of the most important avenues for so doing is to compile as much information as possible on supplies and equipment which Iraq imported and which may have been devoted to activities in the proscribed areas. This will be of particular significance in implementing the Special Commission's and the IAEA's plans (S/22871/Rev.1 and S/22872/Rev.1 and Corr.1) for ongoing monitoring and verification of Iraq's compliance with its obligations, which will involve monitoring future sales of supplies by other countries to Iraq of items relevant to the implementation of the Security Council resolutions (see resolution 715 (1991), paragraph 7).

I am writing to your Excellency in order to seek the assistance of your Government in providing to the Special Commission any information it may have at its disposal, or is able to compile, on equipment and supplies which may have originated in or been exported from the Republic of Korea to Iraq and used in what are now proscribed activities. Any such information would be of great assistance to the Special Commission. It will be treated as confidential and, to the extent it may be used, it will be with a disclaimer to the effect that it carries no implications whatsoever as to whether any infraction of export regulations by the manufacturers is involved.

The Special Commission has so far benefited greatly from information on suppliers it has received from a number of Governments on their own initiative (see, for example, S/23449). This approach to your Government is made in the confidence that the Government will lend its active support to the Special Commission in its efforts to obtain a clear picture of Iraq's foreign procurement programmes in the areas of chemical and biological weapons and ballistic missiles. The request is

/...

167-3-2

0050

FEB 12 '92 19:54 KOREAN MISSION

P.3

UNITED NATIONS  NATIONS UNIES

-3-

limited to these three areas which come within the immediate and direct responsibility of the Special Commission, as the Special Commission understands that a similar approach in the nuclear area has already been made by IAEA to Governments it believed to be in a position to provide it with information.

Accept, Excellency, the assurances of my highest consideration.

Rolf Ekéus
Executive Chairman
Office of the Special Commission

167-3-3

0051

1

| 관리번호 | 92-135 |
|---|---|

원 본

# 외 무 부

종 별 :

번 호 : UNW-0435 일 시 : 92 0213 1720

수 신 : 장관(연일,중동일,미일,기정)

발 신 : 주 유엔 대사

제 목 : 안보리(걸프사태)

1. 언론보도에 의하면 금주초 이락은 이달 의장국인 미국을 통해, 이락의 안보리 결의이행 문제 협의를 위한 92.3 월 자국 외무장관의 안보리 참석을 비공식 제의하여 왔다고함.(2.13 WP 기사)

2. 한편 유엔 핵사찰반은 이락이 플루토니움 생산이 가능한 원자로 1 기 (연간 플루토니움 20 파운드 생산가능)를 은익하고 있다는 정보를 입수하여 조사중이라고 하며 미, 영, 불은 이락이 대량 파괴무기 폐기를 비롯한 안보리 결의상의 제반의무 불이행과 관련 최후통첩 성격의 결의안 또는 의장성명 추진문제를 검토중이라고함.(2.13 NYT 기사)

3. 관련 대표부들에 의하면, 상기 최후통첩 문제에 관한 본격적인 논의는 아직 없으며, 앞으로 당분간 유고, 리비아, 캄보디아 문제로 안보리가 분주해 질것인바 이락문제가 우선적으로 제기될 가능성은 현재로서는 크지 않다고함.

첨부:상기기사:UNW(F)-170 끝

(대사 노창희-국장)

예고:92.12.31. 까지 의거 일반문서로 재분류

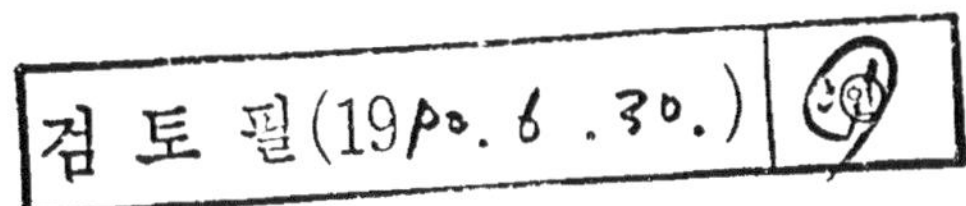


국기국 차관 1차보 2차보 미주국 중아국 외정실 분석관 청와대
안기부

PAGE 1 92.02.14 08:03

외신 2과 통제관 BN

0052

UNW(F)-170 20213 1720 첨부물 · 총 3매
(연알. 중동일. 미일. 기정)

# How to Squeeze Saddam Hussein

A year after the Persian Gulf war, Saddam Hussein still struts. Millions of Iraqi Kurds, Shiites and Sunnis grow restless in the grip of hunger and high prices. The beaten Iraqi Army ponders its loyalties and its own best interests. Can't something *decisive* be done?

President Bush, like many Americans, longs impatiently for such a resolution. Late last year he authorized the C.I.A. to foment internal military action against Saddam Hussein and asked the Pentagon to plan military moves in support of any revolt.

But a forced resolution, however consummately wished, bears greater dangers than benefits. Given the present constellation of political forces in Iraq, U.S. military intervention makes no sense. The most reliable and effective lever for prying the dictator off his perch remains the international economic embargo.

•

One obvious way to try fomenting upheaval involves cliques, sects and rebels, notably the Kurds and Shiites who took up arms against Baghdad last year. Mr. Bush encouraged them — only to stand by and permit their defeat at a time that U.S. forces could have kept Iraqi aircraft out of the skies.

But even if the U.S. could now help such rebels succeed, it would only trade one difficulty for another, more dangerous. Kurdish guerrillas and Shiite devotees of Iran-like theocracy are impressive fighters — but not for democracy.

And even if opposition movements could agree long enough to start a coalition, they would have a hard time holding Iraq together. Today's standoff, admittedly frustrating, might well degenerate into regional war as Turkey, Syria and Iran moved to protect their interests.

If there are dangers to fomenting unrest this way, why not turn instead to secular democratic opponents of the regime? Because there aren't very many of them. They deserve maximum encouragement and diplomatic support. They may have a significant role to play in a future Iraq. But there's no practical way to install them except at gunpoint — and to do that would risk turning true democrats into powerless puppets.

The third way to intervene would be to try inciting rebellion within the Iraqi Army. Other Iraqi commanders, even if they turned out to be just as dictatorial as Saddam Hussein, might nonetheless prove more amenable to the expectations and norms of the outside world. Then again, they might not. The history of C.I.A.-sponsored military coups around the world is not encouraging.

That leaves one other approach — international embargo. It's a slow, unglamorous method. But for certain ends, sanctions work well. Under the present embargo, Iraq can no longer shop the world for arms. It no longer poses immediate danger to its neighbors. Baghdad callously spurns all U.N. offers of humanitarian relief; even so, it pays the price in growing popular discontent.

The U.S. has honorable reason to encourage Iraqis, from the sidelines, to rid themselves of Saddam Hussein. And America has a special interest in encouraging Iraqi democrats to prepare for a larger political role. But there is no reason to risk turning frustration into disaster. Push Saddam Hussein — with sanctions.

170-3-1

0053

# Iraq Bids to Defuse U.N. Tensions

## *Foreign Minister Visit Offered as Resolutions Go Unfulfilled*

By Trevor Rowe
Special to The Washington Post

UNITED NATIONS, Feb. 12—In an effort to defuse mounting international anger over its failure to implement U.N. resolutions, Iraq has proposed sending its foreign minister to discuss the issue with the Security Council, Western diplomats say.

Tension has been building as Iraq continues a blockade of food to its Kurdish population and refuses to abide by a Security Council resolution that calls for Iraq to accept long-term U.N. monitoring of future arms building and purchasing. Baghdad also is criticized for its failure to fully comply with U.N. demands that it return Kuwaiti citizens and goods missing after Iraq's invasion of Kuwait.

Council members are further irritated by Iraq's decision not to use the $1.6 billion in oil it has been authorized by the United Nations to sell to pay for food and medicine badly needed by its population. Baghdad has denounced the council's provision, saying that the amount is too small and that the mechanism to oversee the oil sale and food distribution violates Iraq's sovereignty.

It is unclear what Iraq hopes Foreign Minister Mohammed Saeed Sahaf's visit will achieve, but Western diplomats say it would be difficult to turn the meeting down.

"The idea is that if you deny the fellow the right to attend you look silly. On the other hand, he has a lot of embarrassing questions to answer," said a Western source, adding that the initial reaction to the plan was "why not?"

The Iraqi offer also comes amid increasing pressure from the United States for the overthrow of Iraqi President Saddam Hussein. Diplomats say Baghdad's suggestion could represent an attempt to placate the council.

"The idea is that they [the Iraqis] come to the Security Council to make their case," the source said. As far as most of the council is concerned, the source added, "They don't have one to make."

The source said that the informal offer for Sahaf's visit was conveyed by Iraqi Ambassador Abdul Amir Anbari earlier this week during a meeting with U.S. Ambassador Thomas Pickering, who holds the council's rotating presidency this month. Anbari proposed that the visit take place in March, when the United States no longer has the chair.

The offer also comes as the U.N. Special Commission in charge of scrapping Iraq's weapons of mass destruction is set to begin a new phase of its work—destroying Iraq's arms manufacturing capacity. It is anticipated that the work will be politically sensitive because Iraq is not expected to agree to the destruction of plants that may be capable of producing civilian goods as well.

170-3-2

0054

# Iraq Trying to Make Plutonium, Too, U.N. Aide Says

By PAUL LEWIS
Special to The New York Times

UNITED NATIONS, N.Y., Feb. 12 — United Nations nuclear inspectors now in Iraq are hunting for a secret nuclear reactor capable of producing enough plutonium to make two or more bombs a year, United Nations officials and European diplomats say.

For the first time, the United Nations inspectors searching for President Saddam Hussein's weapons of mass destruction have described intelligence suggesting that Iraq has a previously unknown reactor capable of turning out plutonium.

So far the main thrust of their search has been toward discovering evidence of Iraq's attempt to make highly enriched uranium explosive and to design a weapon capable of using it.

The significance of the new intelligence, experts say, is that President Hussein was trying to build an atomic bomb using plutonium explosive as well.

## 'Reason to Believe'

While the atomic bomb dropped on Hiroshima used uranium as its explosive, the one that destroyed Nagasaki used plutonium, which is also used in most nuclear weapons now.

"We have reason to believe Iraq may have an undeclared plutonium reactor but our inspectors have found nothing significant yet," Rolf Ekeus, the Swedish head of the special United Nations commission, said today.

"All the specialists believe there is a reactor somewhere there," a European diplomat said.

The current search, the tenth the United Nations has conducted, has yielded nothing so far and the team is to leave Iraq on Thursday. On Tuesday the team searched the prison in the northern city of Mosul but again drew a blank.

However the intelligence, much of it from France, suggesting that Iraq has such a reactor has encouraged the United States, France and Britain to consider asking the Security Council to issue a new ultimatum to President Hussein ordering him to cooperate with their efforts to remove his weapons of mass destruction, diplomats say.

## The Unresolved Issues

These three countries, together with the other two permanent Council members, Russia and China, are discussing a possible new Security Council resolution or statement that would address several of their current disputes with Baghdad, according to diplomats.

These include President Hussein's economic blockade against dissident Kurds in the north, trade-sanction violations, the failure of Iraq to account for hundreds of missing Kuwaitis, Iraq's refusal to sell oil under United Nations guidelines to pay for food imports and the President's refusal to cooperate with the Security Council on the weapons issue. Most of these steps were part of the cease-fire agreement ending the Persian Gulf war.

**Nothing is found in the tenth hunt for A-plants.**

Some diplomats said that if Baghdad rejected a new ultimatum, it could help pave the way for a new allied intervention in Iraq, aimed in part at encouraging a coup.

The nuclear inspections mounted by the special commission and by the International Atomic Energy Agency have established that President Hussein had a large nuclear-weapons program that included plans for producing highly enriched uranium explosive using both the centrifuge technique and electromagnetic separation.

Like all other aspects of Iraq's covert nuclear program, possession of a secret nuclear reactor would violate the country's obligation as a signer of the Nuclear Non-Proliferation Treaty to place all its nuclear installations under international safeguards.

Possession of a reactor also violates a similar obligation that Iraq accepted when it agreed to the Security Council resolutions ending the Gulf war.

## Help From China

Last July, a declassified United States Army intelligence document said the United States believed that in 1986, China completed a feasibility study on building a nuclear power plant in Iraq.

The heavily censored document, which was obtained by the Nuclear Control Institute, a Washington research group, revealed that the specifications for the project included "ability to camouflage from satellites," suggesting that the plant was being built for clandestine operation.

However Paul L. Leventhal, president of the Nuclear Control Institute, said he has no evidence the reactor was ever built.

Officials at the United Nations say the intelligence presented so far suggests that Iraq might have concealed a reactor with a power of between 20 and 30 megawatts, which could produce about 20 pounds of plutonium each year. Assuming 10 to 12 pounds of plutonium for each bomb, this amount would allow Iraw to build two nuclear weapons annually.

## How to Use Plutonium

The bomb dropped on Nagasaki has been widely reported as containing about 12 pounds of plutonium. But the United Nations inspectors have already found evidence that Iraqi scientists were experimenting with more modern techniques to increase a bomb's explosive yield, permitting use of less plutonium.

The plutonium that Iraq acquired from a reactor would need to be separated from the residue of its burnt uranium fuel rods. And experts point out that Iraq's Atomic Energy Commission made no secret of its interest in doing this, reporting several separation experiments in recent annual reports.

The United Nations inspectors also discovered that Iraq illicitly produced about 3 grams of plutonium by secretly irradiating uranium in a Soviet reactor that was under international safeguards. The test was carried out between visits by inspectors sent by the international agency to make sure the reactor was not used for military ends.

170-3-3 0055

통 UNSCOM

# UN武器査察團의 이라크 査察 動向

1. UN의 對이라크 大量破壞武器 特別委員會의 「트레반」代辯人은 2.16 UN武器査察團이 미사일을 隱匿한 것으로 推定되는 바그다드의 2개 秘密場所에 대해 空中査察을 할 計劃임을 이라크側에 通告했다고 言及했음.

2. UN의 對이라크 武器査察·經濟制裁 등과 關聯한 最近動向을 보면

가. 이라크은

○ 南北部 飛行禁止區域에서 對空미사일을 철수하고 北部地域 配置 2개 師團 및 레이더基地를 철수(2.13 터키 「세틴」外務長官 言及)하는 등 宥和態度를 지속하면서

○ 美國에 대해 클린턴行政府가 過去를 잊고 相互 關心事와 合法的 權利에 立脚해 새로운 兩國關係 構築의 길을 열 것을 促求(2.13 「후세인」大統領, 「클라크」前 美法務長官 面談시)하는 한편

○ 英國에 대해 이라크資産 凍結解除를 條件으로 이라크이 不法入國 嫌疑로 拘禁한 英國人 事業家 2명의 釋放을 提議(1.31 「아지즈」副總理 및 2.8 「홈마디」公報長官)함과 아울러

○ UN에 대해서는

- 이라크은 30個月된 對이라크 通商禁止를 終結시키기 위해 UN安保理와 協商을 원하며 UN으로부터의 公正한 反應을 呼訴(2.12 「아지즈」副總理)하고

33-29

0056

－「갈리」UN 事務總長에 보내는 書翰을 통해 UN은 이락 國民의 日用品 購入마저 不可能하게 한다면서 制裁措置의 緩和를 要請(2.15 「사하프」外務長官)한데 대해

나. 美國은

○「후세인」大統領의 平和提議를 일축하면서 이락이 UN決議案을 完全遵守할 때까지 美國의 政策에는 변함이 없을 것이라고 言及(2.15 「스테파노풀로스」白堊館 代辯人)하고

○ 이락이 UN 終戰決議를 繼續 違反하고 있기 때문에 美國은 이락에 대한 經濟制裁를 늦추지 않을 것이라고 闡明(2.16 클린턴大統領)하였으며

다. 러시아는 이락이 러시아와의 關係 正常化를 이루기 위해 UN의 諸般 終戰決議案을 履行해야 한다는 점을 表明(2.11「멜레호프」外務部 中東局 副局長)했음.

3. 이번 UN의 바그다드上空 航空査察 推進은

가. UN미사일 査察團(團長 :「파트리세 팔랑크」외 12명)이 미사일基地 査察 및 미사일關聯 技術提供 國家들의 名單 把握을 위해 2.12 - 21간 日程으로 이락에서 査察活動을 전개하고 있는 가운데 提起된 것으로

나. 이락側이 UN査察團의 바그다드上空 飛行을 거부(92.12.17)함에 따라 UN과 이락間에 바그다드上空 飛行制限에 관해 양해된 것(2.16「팔랑크」미사일 査察團長)으로 알려지고 있다는 점에서

33-30

0057

다. 이락側이 UN査察團에 대한 협조 및 對美關係改善 노력을 계속하고 있음에도 불구하고 成果를 보지 못하고 있는 것과 關聯하여 UN側 要求에 不應할 可能性이 있어 UN·이락間 새로운 摩擦要因으로 대두될 것으로 豫想됨.

33-31

0058

원 본

# 외 무 부

종 별 :

번 호 : UNW-0493 일 시 : 92 0219 1820

수 신 : 장 관 (중동일,연일,기정)

발 신 : 주 유엔 대사

제 목 : 안보리 (걸프사태)

1.안보리는 2.19. 비공식 회의를 개최, 유엔 이락대량 파괴무기 폐기 특위(UNSCOM)가 제출한 보고서 ( S/23606) 및 사무총장의 관련보고를 청취하였는바 동 보고 요지는 이락측의 비협조적인 자세로 특위의 임무완료가 불가하였으며 이락측이 안보리 결의를 이행할 의도가 전연 없음에 비추어 안보리의 단호한 대응조치가 필요하다는 내용임.

2.사무총장은 이락측의 결의 이행을 재차 촉구하기 위해 금일오후 EKEUS 특위의장을 이락으로 긴급파견키로 하였으며 안보리는 동의장 방문결과를 내주 재심의 하기로 함. 끝

(대사 노창희-국장)

첨부: FAX (UNW(F)-183)

중아국 1차보 국기국 외정실 분석관 청와대 안기부

PAGE 1 92.02.20 09:58 WG

외신 1과 통제관

0059

UNITED NATIONS UNW(F)-183 20219 1820 첨부물 UNW-0493 **S**

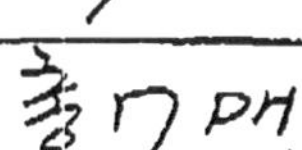

**Security Council**

Distr.
GENERAL

S/23606
18 February 1992

ORIGINAL: ENGLISH

NOTE BY THE SECRETARY-GENERAL

The Secretary-General has the honour to transmit to the Security Council a report submitted by the Executive Chairman of the Special Commission established by the Secretary-General pursuant to paragraph 9 (b) (i) of Security Council resolution 687 (1991).

| 배부처 | 장관실 | 차관실 | 一차보 | 二차보 | 기획실 | 외정실 | 분석관 | 의전장 | 아주국 | 미주국 | 구주국 | 중아국 | 국기국 | 경제국 | 통상국 | 문협국 | 영교국 | 총무과 | 감사관 | 공보관 | 외연원 | 청와대 | 총리실 | 안기부 | 공보처 | 경기원 | 상공부 |
|---|---|---|---|---|---|---|---|---|---|---|---|---|---|---|---|---|---|---|---|---|---|---|---|---|---|---|---|
| | | | | | | | | | | | | 0 | / | | | | | | | | | | | / | | | |

92-07394 3107e (E) 180292 180292 /...

183-7-1

0060

Annex

Special report by the Executive Chairman of the Special Commission established by the Secretary-General pursuant to paragraph 9 (b) (i) of Security Council resolution 687 (1991)

A. Introduction

1. In the Secretary-General's report circulated to the Security Council on 25 January 1992, the Special Commission expressed its most serious concern 1/ at the failure of Iraq to provide full, final and complete disclosure of all aspects of its programmes to develop weapons of mass destruction and to accept its obligations in respect of ongoing monitoring and verification of its compliance with its obligations under section C of Security Council resolution 687 (1991). In the light of the report which the Executive Chairman has received from a special mission which he sent to Baghdad on 27 January 1991, 2/ this failure of Iraq is now clearly tantamount to a rejection by the Government of Iraq of any obligations imposed on it by Security Council resolutions 707 (1991) and 715 (1991), both of which were adopted under Chapter VII of the Charter (see para. 14 below). Instead, Iraq recognizes only its own understanding of obligations imposed on it by paragraphs 10 and 12 of Security Council resolution 687 (1991) which falls far short of what is necessary for the implementation of the plans for ongoing monitoring and verification approved by resolution 715 (1991).

2. For the Special Commission this is a matter of very great importance as the Commission, in the discharge of its responsibilities under the resolutions of the Council, now has to commence in Iraq ongoing monitoring and verification activities. However, monitoring and verification of Iraq's unconditional obligation not to use, develop, construct or acquire any weapons of mass destruction can only be done effectively if Iraq acknowledges and abides by its obligations under resolution 707 (1991) and the plans for ongoing monitoring and verification approved by Council resolution 715 (1991).

B. The basic requirements for ongoing monitoring and verification: Security Council resolutions 707 (1991) and 715 (1991)

(i) Resolution 707 (1991)

3. Ongoing monitoring and verification can only be carried out effectively if the monitoring authorities have the clearest possible picture of what Iraq's capabilities have been in the development and production of weapons of mass destruction and what industrial facilities and materials remain at its disposal or are from time to time acquired which, while devoted to civilian activities, could be converted with relative ease to proscribed military uses. On 15 August 1991, in its resolution 707 (1991), the Security Council demanded that Iraq provide the full, final and complete disclosure of its weapons capabilities required for the clearest possible picture of what those capabilities have been. Iraq has so far failed to provide that disclosure,

/...

183-7-2

0061

although some progress has been made through a procedure of interrogation where specific questions are addressed to Iraq to which it replies.

4. This is not the procedure called for by the resolution, but it is the only way in which it has proved possible to make any progress. This procedure will not achieve the desired result. Experience to date has borne this out. For example, in response to questions put by the special mission dispatched recently to Iraq by the Special Commission, Iraq has admitted that originally it had declared under resolution 687 (1991) only a part of the ancillary equipment for its ballistic missile force. It explained that the undeclared equipment had been destroyed without notification to the Commission in the summer of 1991. The Commission had previously requested Iraq to provide the list of all items that fell under resolution 687 (1991), but which had been destroyed by Iraq without the supervision of the Commission. Up to now no such list has been provided so it is not possible to assess the full implications of these actions by Iraq. However, it is clear that concealment of the destruction of items covered by resolution 687 (1991) has considerably complicated the inspection process and distorted the picture of Iraq's programme of relevant ballistic missiles which has not been completely disclosed under resolution 707 (1991). Furthermore, the unilateral destruction of these items carried out by Iraq without the supervision and consent of the Commission and without prior or subsequent notice is not in accordance with resolution 687 (1991).

5. Iraq is also required to provide a proper accounting for all items that fall under resolution 687 (1991), both under that resolution and under resolution 707 (1991). An example of Iraq's failure in this regard is to be found in Iraq's insistence that its chemical weapons production did not start until 1984, when the United Nations itself concluded that Iraq had used chemical weapons against Iran in 1983. Given that Iraq also inconsistently claims that all its chemical weapons were produced indigenously, this completely undermines the credibility of the figures that Iraq has given for chemical weapons production and use and the material balance that it has provided to the Special Commission. Furthermore, neither documentary nor complete physical supporting evidence has been provided for Iraqi responses to questions concerning the import or production of chemical weapons, chemical warfare agents, related subsystems and production facilities, equipment, etc. In relation to biological weapons, Iraq clearly violated its obligations to hand over to the Commission all its biological weapons-related items when it destroyed buildings at Salman Pak immediately prior to the first Commission inspection there. Explanations provided to date, including those given most recently to the special mission, have not been convincing.

6. Much of the information obtained recently should have been provided by Iraq on its own initiative as part of its compliance with resolutions 687 (1991) and 707 (1991). The examples of Iraq withholding information from the Special Commission until specifically asked show that full, final and complete disclosure of all aspects of its programmes has not been provided as required by resolution 707 (1991). These examples also show that the interrogative approach will not lead to disclosure of all information.

/...

183-7-3

0062

7. A further matter regarding Iraq's compliance with certain provisions of Security Council resolution 707 (1991), other than those relating to reporting, and which impinge upon the privileges and immunities of the Special Commission, has recently become a matter of growing concern. Under that resolution Iraq is required to allow the Commission "to make full use of ... such airfields in Iraq as (it) may determine are most appropriate for the work of the Commission". To date inspection teams entering and leaving Iraq have been required to use the Habbaniyah airfield 100 kilometres from Baghdad, ostensibly because it was the only undamaged operational field available. However, there are now two airfields (Muthanna and Rasheed) within Baghdad city limits which are operational. Iraqi Airways is operating scheduled internal flights out of Muthanna and United Nations helicopters are based at Rasheed. At Habbaniyah Iraq is imposing increasingly onerous requirements on incoming and outgoing United Nations flights to and from Kuwait or Bahrain which considerably delay loading and off-loading and which have come close to harassment. Aircraft are also required to use a runway several kilometres away from the airport ground facilities.

8. Given the distance of Habbaniyah from the Special Commission's centre of operations in Baghdad and the onerous conditions now there imposed, the Commission, on 23 January 1992, made an official approach to the Government recalling the relevant provisions of resolution 707 (1991) and proposing that the Commission's incoming and outgoing flights use Rasheed or Muthanna airports. So far no response has been received and persistent follow-up attempts by the Commission's staff in Baghdad have met with evasive and temporizing replies.

9. The Secretary-General's report of 25 January 1992 refers not only to the difficulties at Habbaniyah airport, but also to Iraq's constant objections to the Special Commission's aerial surveillance flights and to the failure of Iraq to deliver to IAEA part of the documents forcibly removed from a nuclear inspection team in Baghdad on 23 September 1991. The protests on aerial surveillance continue; while the documents have been promised they have not yet been delivered. These two further examples demonstrate Iraq's refusal to acknowledge its obligations under resolution 707 (1991).

10. In the light of past experience, a positive outcome to these matters will only be achieved if a very firm stand is taken.

(ii) Resolution 715 (1991)

11. The most serious difficulty, however, which confronts those responsible for implementing section C of resolution 687 (1991), is Iraq's apparent rejection of the plans for ongoing monitoring and verification submitted to the Council by the Secretary-General and by the Director-General of IAEA (S/22871/Rev.1 and S/22872/Rev.1 and Corr.1). These plans were approved by the Council in its resolution 715 (1991). By the same resolution, the Council demanded that Iraq meet unconditionally all its obligations under the two plans and cooperate fully in carrying them out. It is of great importance that Iraq expressly recognize its obligations under the two plans and resolution 715 (1991).

/...

183-7-4

0063

12. Iraq's position on resolution 715 (1991) and the plans approved thereunder was formally stated in a letter of 19 November 1991 which the Foreign Minister of Iraq addressed to the President of the Security Council. In the letter Iraq strongly attacked the plans for ongoing monitoring and verification, claiming that they were "aimed at objectives incompatible with the letter and spirit of the United Nations Charter, the norms of international law and international and humanitarian pacts and covenants". The letter further asserted that the plans "constituted a dangerous precedent, causing the gravest damage to the credibility of the United Nations and its fundamental role in the protection of the independence and territorial sovereignty of Member States".

13. With the letter of 19 November 1991, Iraq transmitted "information required under resolution 687 (1991)". This information, however, did not correspond to the declarations required under the plans approved by resolution 715 (1991). This failure by Iraq to comply with the plans was reported to the Council in the Secretary-General's report of 25 January 1992, where detailed information was provided on the steps being taken by the Special Commission to seek Iraq's compliance with Security Council resolution 715 (1991). As was indicated in that report, the Commission was sending a special mission to Baghdad, at the end of January 1992, to underline the Commission's most serious concern with Iraq's failure to provide the full, final and complete disclosure of its programmes in the field of weapons of mass destruction demanded by resolution 707 (1991) and to comply with resolution 715 (1991).

14. That special mission has now returned and reported to the Executive Chairman. While it obtained some of the information which should previously have been supplied under resolution 707 (1991), this had to be done by the interrogative procedure referred to above. On resolution 715 (1991), the special mission met with absolutely no success. Iraq, at the level of the Minister of State for Foreign Affairs, reiterated that the Government maintained its position expressed in the letter of 19 November 1991.

15. It is now completely clear that Iraq has arrogated to itself the determination of how paragraphs 10 and 12 of section C of Security Council resolution 687 (1991) should be applied. The Special Commission has thus regretfully concluded that, despite the Commission's best endeavours, Iraq has no intention of meeting its obligations under the plans approved under, and the provisions included in, Security Council resolution 715 (1991).

C. <u>Conclusions</u>

16. As such a position is contrary to the Security Council resolutions, the Special Commission and the IAEA would be precluded from carrying out effectively a programme of ongoing monitoring and verification of the nature and scope approved by the Council. Should the Commission now seek to initiate the ongoing monitoring and verification phase of its mandate under these circumstances, it will be sending a message that, in fact if not in law, it is prepared to operate this phase of its responsibilities under Iraq's, not the Council's conditions. Past experience in Iraq has demonstrated the very

/...

183-7-5

0064

serious inadequacies of such an approach. The Commission is therefore not legally able nor is it prepared to adopt it. In such circumstances the Commission has felt that it had no alternative but to report this matter immediately to the Council for its instructions.

17. The statement issued on behalf of the Council on 31 January 1992, at the conclusion of the 3046th meeting of the Council held at the level of Heads of State and Government, stresses that all of the resolutions adopted by the Council on this matter remain essential to the restoration of peace and stability in the region and must be fully implemented. The circumstances above show that the longer firm action is delayed, in the face of Iraq's repeated refusal to acknowledge any obligations under Security Council resolutions 707 (1991) and 715 (1991), the more intransigent the Government's position is likely to become. If this attitude is not changed the third and final phase of the responsibilities of the Special Commission under paragraph 10 of resolution 687 (1991) cannot be implemented, nor can resolutions 707 (1991) and 715 (1991).

Notes

1/ S/23514, paras. 15 to 26.

2/ See para. 14 below.

-----

183-7-6

0065

(Second revised text)

PRESIDENTIAL STATEMENT

19 February 1992

The members of the Security Council express their gratitude to the Secretary-General for the report submitted to the Security Council on 18 February 1992 (S/23606).

The members of the Security Council note that while progress has been made, much still remains to be done to implement the relevant resolutions of the Council. The members of the Council are gravely concerned by Iraq's continued failure to acknowledge all its obligations under Council resolutions 707 (1991) and 715 (1991), and its continued rejection of the plans of the Secretary-General and of the Director-General of the International Atomic Energy Agency (S/22871/Rev.1 and S/22872/Rev.1 and Corr.1 as approved by resolution 715 (1991)) for ongoing monitoring and verification of Iraq's compliance with its obligations under paragraphs 10, 12 and 13 of resolution 687 (1991).

Ongoing monitoring and verification of Iraq's obligations is an integral part of Security Council resolution 687 (1991) which established a cease-fire and provided the conditions essential to the restoration of peace and security in the region. Such ongoing monitoring and verification is a step of the utmost importance towards the goal set out in paragraph 14 of that resolution.

Iraq's failure to acknowledge its obligations under resolutions 707 (1991) and 715 (1991), its rejection up until now of the two plans for ongoing monitoring and verification, and its failure to provide the full, final and complete disclosure of its weapons capabilities constitute a continuing material breach of the relevant provisions of resolution 687 (1991). Unconditional agreement by Iraq to implement these obligations is one of the essential preconditions to any reconsideration by the Council under paragraphs 21 and 22 of resolution 687 (1991) of the prohibitions referred to in those paragraphs.

The members of the Council support the decision of the Secretary-General to dispatch a special mission headed by the Executive Chairman of the Special Commission to visit Iraq immediately to meet and discuss with the highest levels of the Iraqi Government for the purpose of securing the unconditional agreement by Iraq to implement all its relevant obligations under resolutions 687 (1991), 707 (1991) and 715 (1991). The mission should stress the serious consequences if such agreement to implement is not forthcoming. The Secretary-General is requested to report on the results of the special mission to the Security Council upon its return.

-----

4188E

183-7-7

0066

02/28/92 23:43 ☎202 797 0595 EMBASSY OF KOREA ➝ WOI ☑004

# 주 미 대 사 관

USW(F) : 1185 년월일 : 920228 시간 : 2330

수 신 : 장 관 (미일, 중동일)

발 신 : 주 미 대 사

제 목 : 이락, 유엔미사일장비제거협 거부 (출처 : WP )

| 보 안<br>통 제 | |
|---|---|

# Baghdad Defies U.N. Deadline

## Council Orders Iraq To Allow Destruction Of Missile Equipment

By Trevor Rowe
Special to The Washington Post

UNITED NATIONS, Feb. 28—Iraq today refused to allow a U.N. team to begin destruction of equipment used for the construction of ballistic missiles, escalating its confrontation with the Security Council.

In a letter to the Security Council, Baghdad instead proposed holding further discussions on the subject during a visit of a high-level Iraqi delegation here next month.

Iraq's negative response today prompted the Security Council to meet for consultations. The council later issued a statement in which the 15 members said they "deplore and condemn" Iraq's failure to comply with U.N. demands.

"The members of the council require the government of Iraq to communicate directly to the council without further delay an authoritative and unconditional acknowledgement of its agreement to accept and implement the above noted oligations, including specifically the determination ... requiring the destruction of ballistic missile-related equipment," the Security Council statement said.

The council also formally invited the Iraqi delegation, which will be headed by Deputy Prime Minister Tariq Aziz, to hold talks, provided the delegation arrived by the week of March 9. A U.S. official said the council could then move to take punitive action against Iraq.

U.S. Ambassador Thomas Pickering, who holds the rotating presidency of the Security Council this month dismissed the Iraqi letter as

( 1185 - 2 - 1 )

| 외신 1과<br>통 제 | |
|---|---|

| 배부처 | 장관 | 차관 | 1차보 | 2차보 | 기획실 | 의전실 | 분석관 | 의전장 | 아주국 | 미주국 | 구주국 | 중아국 | 국기국 | 경제국 | 통상국 | 문협국 | 영교국 | 총무과 | 감사관 | 공보처 | 안기부 | 청와대 | 총리실 | 안기부 | 공보처 | 경기원 | 상공부 |
|---|---|---|---|---|---|---|---|---|---|---|---|---|---|---|---|---|---|---|---|---|---|---|---|---|---|---|---|
| | / | | | | | | | | | 0 | | / | | | | | | | | | | / | / | | | | |

0067

# 주 미 대 사 관

USW(F) : 년월일 : 시간 :

수 신 : 장 관

발 신 : 주 미 대 사

| 보 안 통 제 | |
|---|---|

제 목 : (출처 : )

---

**IRAQ, From A1**

"totally unacceptable. . . . It's seven pages of 'no.' "

The confrontation comes slightly more than a year after Iraq agreed in writing to abide by U.N. terms for a formal cease-fire in the Persian Gulf War.

Last week, the Security Council warned Iraq that it faced "serious consequences" unless it agreed to implement U.N. resolutions requiring the elimination of Iraq's weapons of mass destruction. U.N. officials said the latest confrontation began Wednesday when Baghdad refused to allow a U.N. weapons-destruction team to carry out its duties.

Iraq then requested two additional delays that ended on an agreed upon deadline of today at 2 p.m. EST, close to the time Iraq submitted a letter outlining its refusal. At the center of the dispute is the destruction of equipment that has a "dual" function also capable of being used for civilian purposes.

"The destruction of a missile with a range of over 150 kilometers [94 miles] is clear under the requirements of Resolution 687," said the letter written by Mohammed Saeed Sahaf, Iraq's minister of state for foreign affairs. He was referring to the resolution that set the terms for a cease-fire in the Persian Gulf War.

"It is neither clear nor justifiable, however, that destruction should indiscriminately include machines and equipment which can be modified and changed in such a way as will turn them totally incapable of being used in the productions of any weapon or prohibited material," he added.

Before beginning this sensitive phase of the U.N. team's mission, Rolf Ekeus, the head of the U.N. commission charged with scrapping Iraq's weapons of mass destruction, traveled to Washington and secured the support of national security adviser Brent Scowcroft.

A U.S. official said Thursday that if the high-level Iraqi mission failed to satisfy the Security Council, Washington would press for the adoption of a resolution putting more pressure on Iraq. While sanctions are still being imposed on Iraq, diplomats said that theoretically, Iraq's communication links could still be cut.

British Ambassador David Hannay told reporters after the Security Council meeting that when the high-level Iraqi delegation comes to New York, it will have to heed the demands of the international community. "If they don't pay attention, I fear they will be making one of those classical miscalculations of which they have made a number in the past, to the great detriment of their people."

Some diplomats said continued Iraqi defiance could lead to pressure for some kind of military action.

For the time being, however, diplomats say they want to convey a message of firmness. "We have to show a calm determination," said a French official. The Security Council "refuses to get hot-tempered even though the matter is taken very seriously."

During the council's deliberations, a Russian diplomat reportedly told his fellow members that "the Iraqis seem to feel they are they are the cat and we're the mouse. It's time they understand the contrary."

( 1185 - 2 - 2 )

| 외신 1과 통 제 | - |
|---|---|

0068

| 관리 번호 | 92/189 |
|---|---|

원 본

# 외 무 부

종 별 : 지 급

번 호 : UNW-0574 일 시 : 92 0229 1000

수 신 : 장 관(중동일,연일,기정)

발 신 : 주 유엔 대사대리

제 목 : 안보리(걸프사태)

연:UNW-0493

1. 안보리는 금.2.28. 저녁 공식회의를 소집, 연호 EKEUS 특위의장의 92.2.21-24 간 이락방문결과 보고서(S/23643)를 심의하고 별첨 안보리 의장 성명을 채택함

2. 동성명은 이락의 안보리 결의불이행을 비난하고 조속한 이행조치를 촉구하는 한편 이락측이 제안한바있는 고위대표단 파견제의를 수락, 이락 대표단을 안보리회의에 초청하여 늦어도 3 월 9 일 주간에 본건을 재심의할수 있도록함

3. EKEUS 특위의장은 동보고서에서 이락방문기간중 TARIQ AZIZ 부수상, HUSSEIN 외무장관등 고위인사를 접촉, 결의이행을 촉구한데 대해 이라측의 성실한 결의이행 약속을 보장받을수 없었다고 결론짓고 있음

4. 금일 공식회의에 앞서 개최된 비공식협의에서 미국등 주요이사국은 이락의 태도를 안보리에 대한 중대한 도전으로 간주하고 이락대사대리를 불러 안보리의 엄중한 항의를 전달하였다고함

5. 안보리내의 분위기는 이락의 태도에도 불구, 군사적인 대응조치는 현재 검토되지 않고 있으며 현재의 경제제재 조치를 계속하는 한편, 구두비난만으로는 불충분할 경우에 대비한 대응책을 강구하고 있다고함

(대사대리 신기복-국장)

예고:92.6.30 까지

예고문에 의거 일반문서로 재분류(1992.6.30)

첨부:UNW(F)-0206

92.6.30. 일반

중아국 1차보 국기국 외정실 분석관 안기부

PAGE 1 92.03.01 01:06

외신 2과 통제관 FM

0069

UNW(G)-0206 20F19 1000
(공동외, 연외, 7/36)
#정보

28 February 1992
6:45 p.m.

Presidential Statement

The members of the Security Council express their gratitude to the Secretary-General for the report submitted to the Council on 27 February 1992 (S/23643), transmitting the results of the special mission dispatched to Iraq by the Secretary-General pursuant to the statement of the President of the Council of 19 February 1992 (S/23609). The members of the Council approve in full the conclusions of the special mission as contained in the report and in particular its finding that Iraq is not prepared to give its unconditional agreement to implement all of its obligations under resolutions 687 (1991), 707 (1991) and 715 (1991).

The members of the Council deplore and condemn the failure of the Government of Iraq to provide the special mission with full, final and complete disclosure, as required by resolution 707 (1991), of all aspects of its programmes to develop weapons of mass destruction and ballistic missiles with a range greater than 150 kilometrés, including launchers, and of all holdings of such weapons, their components and production facilities and locations, as well as all other nuclear programmes; and the failure of Iraq to comply with the plans for ongoing monitoring and verification (S/22871/Rev.1 and S/22872/Rev.1 and Corr.1) approved by resolution 715 (1991). In a statement made on 19 February 1992 prior to the dispatch of the special mission to Iraq the Council noted that Iraq's behaviour constituted a material breach of ~~the~~ resolution 687 (1991). Regrettably this continues to be the case.

Furthermore, the members of the Council equally deplore and condemn Iraq's failure, within the time prescribed by the Special Commission at the request of Iraq, to commence destruction of

2066-27

0070

ballistic missile-related equipment designated for destruction by the Special Commission. The members of the Council reaffirm that it is for the Special Commission alone to determine which items must be destroyed under paragraph 9 of resolution 687 (1991). Therefore, the Government of Iraq's letter of 28 February 1992 to the Executive Chairman of the Special Commission is unacceptable. Iraq's refusal to implement the determinations of the Special Commission constitutes a further material breach of the relevant provisions of resolution 687 (1991).

The members of the Council demand that Iraq immediately implement all its obligations under Council resolution 687 (1991) and subsequent resolutions on Iraq. The members of the Council require the Government of Iraq to communicate directly to the Council without further dalay an authoritative and unconditional acknowledgement of its agreement to accept and implement the above noted obligations, including specifically to comply with the determination of the Special Commission requiring the destruction of ballistic missile-related equipment. The members of the Council emphasize that Iraq must be aware of the serious consequences of continued material breaches of resolution 687 (1991).

The members of the Council note that an Iraqi delegation is prepared to come to New York as soon as it is invited to do so. The members of the Council have asked its President to extend such an invitation to the delegation to come to New York without further delay. The members of the Council intend in any event to continue their consideration of this question no later than the week beginning 9 March 1992.

206-2-2

0071

# 주 국 련 대 표 부

주국련20313- 220 1992. 2. 28.

수신 장관

참조 국제기구국장, 중동아프리카국장

제목 걸프사태(안보리)

연 : UNW - 0493

연호 대량파괴무기 폐기특위(UNSCOM) 보고서 및 특위 의장의 이라크 방문과 관련한 이라크측의 입장을 설명한 자료가 안보리 문서로 배포된바, 별첨 송부합니다.

첨 부 : S/23606, S/23636. 끝.

No. 발송 1992. 2. 28 주유엔대표부

주 국 련 대 사

| 선 결 | | 결재(공람) | | |
|---|---|---|---|---|
| 접수일시 | 1992. 3 2 | | | |
| 처리과 | 12567 | | | |

0072

UNITED
NATIONS

S

# Security Council

Distr.
GENERAL

S/23606
18 February 1992

ORIGINAL: ENGLISH

## NOTE BY THE SECRETARY-GENERAL

The Secretary-General has the honour to transmit to the Security Council a report submitted by the Executive Chairman of the Special Commission established by the Secretary-General pursuant to paragraph 9 (b) (i) of Security Council resolution 687 (1991).

92-07394 3107e (E) 180292



/...

## Annex

## Special report by the Executive Chairman of the Special Commission established by the Secretary-General pursuant to paragraph 9 (b) (i) of Security Council resolution 687 (1991)

### A. Introduction

1. In the Secretary-General's report circulated to the Security Council on 25 January 1992, the Special Commission expressed its most serious concern 1/ at the failure of Iraq to provide full, final and complete disclosure of all aspects of its programmes to develop weapons of mass destruction and to accept its obligations in respect of ongoing monitoring and verification of its compliance with its obligations under section C of Security Council resolution 687 (1991). In the light of the report which the Executive Chairman has received from a special mission which he sent to Baghdad on 27 January 1991, 2/ this failure of Iraq is now clearly tantamount to a rejection by the Government of Iraq of any obligations imposed on it by Security Council resolutions 707 (1991) and 715 (1991), both of which were adopted under Chapter VII of the Charter (see para. 14 below). Instead, Iraq recognizes only its own understanding of obligations imposed on it by paragraphs 10 and 12 of Security Council resolution 687 (1991) which falls far short of what is necessary for the implementation of the plans for ongoing monitoring and verification approved by resolution 715 (1991).

2. For the Special Commission this is a matter of very great importance as the Commission, in the discharge of its responsibilities under the resolutions of the Council, now has to commence in Iraq ongoing monitoring and verification activities. However, monitoring and verification of Iraq's unconditional obligation not to use, develop, construct or acquire any weapons of mass destruction can only be done effectively if Iraq acknowledges and abides by its obligations under resolution 707 (1991) and the plans for ongoing monitoring and verification approved by Council resolution 715 (1991).

### B. The basic requirements for ongoing monitoring and verification: Security Council resolutions 707 (1991) and 715 (1991)

#### (i) Resolution 707 (1991)

3. Ongoing monitoring and verification can only be carried out effectively if the monitoring authorities have the clearest possible picture of what Iraq's capabilities have been in the development and production of weapons of mass destruction and what industrial facilities and materials remain at its disposal or are from time to time acquired which, while devoted to civilian activities, could be converted with relative ease to proscribed military uses. On 15 August 1991, in its resolution 707 (1991), the Security Council demanded that Iraq provide the full, final and complete disclosure of its weapons capabilities required for the clearest possible picture of what those capabilities have been. Iraq has so far failed to provide that disclosure,

/...

0074

although some progress has been made through a procedure of interrogation where specific questions are addressed to Iraq to which it replies.

4. This is not the procedure called for by the resolution, but it is the only way in which it has proved possible to make any progress. This procedure will not achieve the desired result. Experience to date has borne this out. For example, in response to questions put by the special mission dispatched recently to Iraq by the Special Commission, Iraq has admitted that originally it had declared under resolution 687 (1991) only a part of the ancillary equipment for its ballistic missile force. It explained that the undeclared equipment had been destroyed without notification to the Commission in the summer of 1991. The Commission had previously requested Iraq to provide the list of all items that fell under resolution 687 (1991), but which had been destroyed by Iraq without the supervision of the Commission. Up to now no such list has been provided so it is not possible to assess the full implications of these actions by Iraq. However, it is clear that concealment of the destruction of items covered by resolution 687 (1991) has considerably complicated the inspection process and distorted the picture of Iraq's programme of relevant ballistic missiles which has not been completely disclosed under resolution 707 (1991). Furthermore, the unilateral destruction of these items carried out by Iraq without the supervision and consent of the Commission and without prior or subsequent notice is not in accordance with resolution 687 (1991).

5. Iraq is also required to provide a proper accounting for all items that fall under resolution 687 (1991), both under that resolution and under resolution 707 (1991). An example of Iraq's failure in this regard is to be found in Iraq's insistence that its chemical weapons production did not start until 1984, when the United Nations itself concluded that Iraq had used chemical weapons against Iran in 1983. Given that Iraq also inconsistently claims that all its chemical weapons were produced indigenously, this completely undermines the credibility of the figures that Iraq has given for chemical weapons production and use and the material balance that it has provided to the Special Commission. Furthermore, neither documentary nor complete physical supporting evidence has been provided for Iraqi responses to questions concerning the import or production of chemical weapons, chemical warfare agents, related subsystems and production facilities, equipment, etc. In relation to biological weapons, Iraq clearly violated its obligations to hand over to the Commission all its biological weapons-related items when it destroyed buildings at Salman Pak immediately prior to the first Commission inspection there. Explanations provided to date, including those given most recently to the special mission, have not been convincing.

6. Much of the information obtained recently should have been provided by Iraq on its own initiative as part of its compliance with resolutions 687 (1991) and 707 (1991). The examples of Iraq withholding information from the Special Commission until specifically asked show that full, final and complete disclosure of all aspects of its programmes has not been provided as required by resolution 707 (1991). These examples also show that the interrogative approach will not lead to disclosure of all information.

/...

0075

7. A further matter regarding Iraq's compliance with certain provisions of Security Council resolution 707 (1991), other than those relating to reporting, and which impinge upon the privileges and immunities of the Special Commission, has recently become a matter of growing concern. Under that resolution Iraq is required to allow the Commission "to make full use of ... such airfields in Iraq as (it) may determine are most appropriate for the work of the Commission". To date inspection teams entering and leaving Iraq have been required to use the Habbaniyah airfield 100 kilometres from Baghdad, ostensibly because it was the only undamaged operational field available. However, there are now two airfields (Muthanna and Rasheed) within Baghdad city limits which are operational. Iraqi Airways is operating scheduled internal flights out of Muthanna and United Nations helicopters are based at Rasheed. At Habbaniyah Iraq is imposing increasingly onerous requirements on incoming and outgoing United Nations flights to and from Kuwait or Bahrain which considerably delay loading and off-loading and which have come close to harassment. Aircraft are also required to use a runway several kilometres away from the airport ground facilities.

8. Given the distance of Habbaniyah from the Special Commission's centre of operations in Baghdad and the onerous conditions now there imposed, the Commission, on 23 January 1992, made an official approach to the Government recalling the relevant provisions of resolution 707 (1991) and proposing that the Commission's incoming and outgoing flights use Rasheed or Muthanna airports. So far no response has been received and persistent follow-up attempts by the Commission's staff in Baghdad have met with evasive and temporizing replies.

9. The Secretary-General's report of 25 January 1992 refers not only to the difficulties at Habbaniyah airport, but also to Iraq's constant objections to the Special Commission's aerial surveillance flights and to the failure of Iraq to deliver to IAEA part of the documents forcibly removed from a nuclear inspection team in Baghdad on 23 September 1991. The protests on aerial surveillance continue; while the documents have been promised they have not yet been delivered. These two further examples demonstrate Iraq's refusal to acknowledge its obligations under resolution 707 (1991).

10. In the light of past experience, a positive outcome to these matters will only be achieved if a very firm stand is taken.

(ii) Resolution 715 (1991)

11. The most serious difficulty, however, which confronts those responsible for implementing section C of resolution 687 (1991), is Iraq's apparent rejection of the plans for ongoing monitoring and verification submitted to the Council by the Secretary-General and by the Director-General of IAEA (S/22871/Rev.1 and S/22872/Rev.1 and Corr.1). These plans were approved by the Council in its resolution 715 (1991). By the same resolution, the Council demanded that Iraq meet unconditionally all its obligations under the two plans and cooperate fully in carrying them out. It is of great importance that Iraq expressly recognize its obligations under the two plans and resolution 715 (1991).

/...

0076

12. Iraq's position on resolution 715 (1991) and the plans approved thereunder was formally stated in a letter of 19 November 1991 which the Foreign Minister of Iraq addressed to the President of the Security Council. In the letter Iraq strongly attacked the plans for ongoing monitoring and verification, claiming that they were "aimed at objectives incompatible with the letter and spirit of the United Nations Charter, the norms of international law and international and humanitarian pacts and covenants". The letter further asserted that the plans "constituted a dangerous precedent, causing the gravest damage to the credibility of the United Nations and its fundamental role in the protection of the independence and territorial sovereignty of Member States".

13. With the letter of 19 November 1991, Iraq transmitted "information required under resolution 687 (1991)". This information, however, did not correspond to the declarations required under the plans approved by resolution 715 (1991). This failure by Iraq to comply with the plans was reported to the Council in the Secretary-General's report of 25 January 1992, where detailed information was provided on the steps being taken by the Special Commission to seek Iraq's compliance with Security Council resolution 715 (1991). As was indicated in that report, the Commission was sending a special mission to Baghdad, at the end of January 1992, to underline the Commission's most serious concern with Iraq's failure to provide the full, final and complete disclosure of its programmes in the field of weapons of mass destruction demanded by resolution 707 (1991) and to comply with resolution 715 (1991).

14. That special mission has now returned and reported to the Executive Chairman. While it obtained some of the information which should previously have been supplied under resolution 707 (1991), this had to be done by the interrogative procedure referred to above. On resolution 715 (1991), the special mission met with absolutely no success. Iraq, at the level of the Minister of State for Foreign Affairs, reiterated that the Government maintained its position expressed in the letter of 19 November 1991.

15. It is now completely clear that Iraq has arrogated to itself the determination of how paragraphs 10 and 12 of section C of Security Council resolution 687 (1991) should be applied. The Special Commission has thus regretfully concluded that, despite the Commission's best endeavours, Iraq has no intention of meeting its obligations under the plans approved under, and the provisions included in, Security Council resolution 715 (1991).

C. Conclusions

16. As such a position is contrary to the Security Council resolutions, the Special Commission and the IAEA would be precluded from carrying out effectively a programme of ongoing monitoring and verification of the nature and scope approved by the Council. Should the Commission now seek to initiate the ongoing monitoring and verification phase of its mandate under these circumstances, it will be sending a message that, in fact if not in law, it is prepared to operate this phase of its responsibilities under Iraq's, not the Council's conditions. Past experience in Iraq has demonstrated the very

/...

0077

serious inadequacies of such an approach. The Commission is therefore not legally able nor is it prepared to adopt it. In such circumstances the Commission has felt that it had no alternative but to report this matter immediately to the Council for its instructions.

17. The statement issued on behalf of the Council on 31 January 1992, at the conclusion of the 3046th meeting of the Council held at the level of Heads of State and Government, stresses that all of the resolutions adopted by the Council on this matter remain essential to the restoration of peace and stability in the region and must be fully implemented. The circumstances above show that the longer firm action is delayed, in the face of Iraq's repeated refusal to acknowledge any obligations under Security Council resolutions 707 (1991) and 715 (1991), the more intransigent the Government's position is likely to become. If this attitude is not changed the third and final phase of the responsibilities of the Special Commission under paragraph 10 of resolution 687 (1991) cannot be implemented, nor can resolutions 707 (1991) and 715 (1991).

Notes

1/ S/23514, paras. 15 to 26.

2/ See para. 14 below.

-----

**UNITED NATIONS**

**S**

## Security Council

Distr.
GENERAL

S/23636
24 February 1992
ENGLISH
ORIGINAL: ARABIC

LETTER DATED 24 FEBRUARY 1992 FROM THE CHARGE D'AFFAIRES A.I. OF THE PERMANENT MISSION OF IRAQ TO THE UNITED NATIONS ADDRESSED TO THE SECRETARY-GENERAL

On instructions from my Government, I have the honour to transmit to you herewith a letter dated 24 February 1992 from Mr. Ahmed Hussein, Minister for Foreign Affairs of Iraq, concerning the visit made to Baghdad by the special mission headed by Ambassador Rolf Ekeus, Chairman of the Special Commission.

I should be grateful if you would have this letter and its annex distributed as a document of the Security Council.

(Signed) Samir K. K. AL-NIMA
Chargé d'affaires a.i.

92-08252 2857c (E) 240292 240292 240292

/...

Annex

Letter dated 24 February 1992 from the Minister for Foreign Affairs of Iraq addressed to the Secretary-General

[Original: Arabic/English]

Sir,

I have the honour to inform you that the Republic of Iraq has welcomed the mission dispatched by the Security Council and headed by Ambassador Rolf Ekeus, the Executive Chairman of the Special Commission, which visited the country from 21 to 24 February 1992. Ambassador Ekeus has had three meetings with H.E. Mohammed Said Al-Sahaf, the Minister of State for Foreign Affairs, in addition to one extended meeting with H.E. Tariq Aziz, the Deputy Prime Minister, H.E. Minister of State Al-Sahaf and myself.

All matters of interest and concern to both sides were discussed in depth during these meetings at which also prevailed an atmosphere of candour and clarity as to the exchange of views on those matters.

During the meetings, the Iraqi side submitted its views towards reaching a common understanding based on objectivity, fairness and goodwill towards the matters under discussion, which were as follows:

I. Iraq reaffirms its willingness to cooperate and deal constructively with the mission headed by Ambassador Ekeus and with the Special Commission, and wishes to point out the following grounds:

1. Iraq is of the opinion that it has provided all the necessary information required of it. Iraq is ready to cooperate in the provision of any related additional information still deemed necessary and clearly related to the subject. Iraq believes that the best modality for implementing what is mentioned above is to have the opportunity to conduct an expert-level dialogue with the Special Commission to clarify the overall picture of each of the programmes concerned, and reach specific conclusions, especially in respect of the modification of equipment for non-prohibited purposes within a specified period of time.

2. Once this has been accomplished within a specified period of time, the Special Commission and the IAEA should then report to the Security Council that Iraq is in substantial compliance with its

His Excellency Mr. Boutros Boutros-Ghali
Secretary-General of the United Nations
New York

/...

0080

obligations under Security Council resolution 687 (1991), and that Iraq requests the Security Council to draw a fair balance between the level of progress achieved at this stage and the position on the sanctions with a view to lifting them.

3. Iraq insists that the Special Commission take a clear position as to the first stage (the destruction of weapons and the identification of the equipment which produces them), in view of the link between this position and the position on the sanctions. Iraq also insists that the Special Commission present to the Security Council a fair and accurate factual report on this subject.

II. Proposed action

1. Iraq proposes that Iraqi experts be invited to present, in a consolidated form, the information required from Iraq, and to respond to the questions relating thereto.

2. To respond to any questions that may be raised by the Special Commission in this regard.

3. To enable adequate material balances to be established for all weapons and their components.

4. To provide credible detailed information on items destroyed unilaterally by Iraq.

5. To provide, upon specific requests, any available evidence relating to Iraq's declarations.

6. To discuss the scope of destruction proposed by the Special Commission, so as to ensure the specific non-prohibited use of the facilities, equipment, materials and components in an irreversible manner.

III. Plans for ongoing monitoring and verification

Iraq does not reject the plans for ongoing monitoring and verification. By recognizing resolution 687, Iraq has accepted the principle that the Security Council should ascertain and verify that industry in Iraq is not directed in a manner which does not satisfy the Security Council as to the non-production of prohibited weapons. In this regard, Iraq can deal with the Security Council and the Special Commission on the basis of respect for sovereignty and the requirements of national security, and of refraining from methods of provocation and infringement upon Iraq's industrial capabilities which will be devoted to peaceful purposes or to military purposes not prohibited by Security Council resolution 687.

/...

IV. The Iraqi delegation to be dispatched to talk to the Security Council will convey Iraq's position on resolutions 707 and 715.

You are kindly requested to distribute this letter as a document of the Security Council.

Please accept the assurances of my highest consideration.

(Signed) Ahmed HUSSEIN
Minister for Foreign Affairs
The Republic of Iraq
Baghdad
24 February 1992

-----

0082

朝鮮日報
1992. 3. 3. 화, 3면

# 「제2걸프戰」우려 고조

## 美,「시간벌기」이라크에 武力시위

## "최종목표는 北韓 核사찰" 시각도

조선 3.3.3면

1일부터 페르시아灣에 배치된 美항공모함에서는 전투기가 매일 출격하고있다. 对이라크 감시用이자 무력시위用 비행이다. 이 전투기들은 「공격개시」라는 명령이 떨어지면 언제든지 바그다드로 날아갈채비를 하고있다.

이라크가「대량살상무기 및 스커드미사일, 그리고 그 생산시설을 폐기하라」는 유엔안보리 결의를28일 거부하고 나서자, 이 지역엔 또 한차례 긴장이 고조되고있다. 걸프전 終戰 1주년을 맞은 시점에서 「제2의 걸프전」이 발발하는 것이 아니냐는 우려의 목소리가 높아지고 있는것이다.

유엔안보리는 이라크가 폐기거부의사를 밝힌 직후 강력한 对이라크 비난성명을 발표한데 이어, 이라크가 끝내 고집을 부릴 경우 「심각한 결과」를 초래하게 될 것이라고 경고했다.

미국을 비롯한 서방측 반응이 워낙 강경하자, 이라크는 유화적인 제스처를 보이고 나섰다. 타리크 아지즈 이라크부총리는 1일 이라크국영 TV방송을 통해「유엔에 대표단을 파견, 무기폐기와 관련된 이라크의 입장을 설명하겠다」면서『이라크는 유엔 결의를 준수할 것』이라고 거듭 강조했다.

그러나 이라크가 유엔이 요구하는 수준의 군비감축을 성실히 이행할 것인지는 미지수다. 이라크는 지난달말 유엔특별위원회가 입국했을때,당초 약속했던 스커드무기 생산공장폐기를, 이 시설이 평화적목적으로 이용할 수 있다는 이유를 들어 거부했었다.

이라크는 최대한「시간벌기작전」을 펴며 안보리결의 이행을 회피하리라고 보는 것이 합리적이다. 문제는 이때 미국이 군사행동을 강행할 것이냐는 점이다. 여기에는 몇가지 고려사항이 있다.

냉전구도가 무너진후 미국은「対蘇견제」와 같은 뚜렷한전략목표를 상실했다. 그 와중에 잠정적으로 떠오른 목표가 핵무기를 포함한 대량살상무기의 확산방지다. 특히 이같이 위험한 무기가 분쟁가능성이 높은 지역에 유입되는것을 막기 위해 미국을 포함한 서방국가들은 총력을 기울이고 있다. 이라크가 이미 旧소련의 핵과학자 50명을 채용했다는 소식은 미국을 더욱 초조하게 하고 있을지도 모른다.

미국은 이라크가 안보리 결의안을 거부하고 나섰다는 점도 중시하고 있다. 미국은 新국제질서 메커니즘을 작동시키는데 있어 유엔안보리를 그 중심축으로 활용하고 있다. 蘇聯이라는 존재가 사라진 상황하에서 안보리는「미국의 의도를 국제사회의 의지로 둔갑시키는 요술상자」역할을 할 수 있기 때문이다.『유엔안보리는 미국의 국익을 대변하는 기구로 전락했다』는 이라크의 비난은 이런 점에서 일리가 있다. 미국은 안보리의 권위를 유지하기 위해서라도 뭔가 행동을 보이지 않을 수 없는 형편인 것이다.

「미국의 총구는 이라크를 향하고 있지만, 바라보고 있는 곳은 북한」이라는 지적도 나오고 있다. 미국은 북한이 핵무기를 보유하는 사태를 가장 경계하고 있다. 「북한이 최근 핵무기 관련 시설을 제3의 장소로 이동시키고 있다」는 정보기관 분석은 IAEA사찰로는 근본적인 문제해결이 어렵다는 사실을 말해주고 있다. 그러나 미국이 북한을 상대로 군사행동을 벌이는데는 엄청난 정치적 부담이 따른다.

따라서 만만한 패전국 이라크를 상대로 무력시위를 벌인뒤 겁에 질린 북한을 협상테이블로 불러들인다는 구도가 성립될 수 있는 것이다.

美국방관계자들은 지금 「제2의 걸프전」과 관련된 손익계산서를 뽑고 있을지도 모른다. 저울 한쪽엔 군사행동을 주장하는 매派의 논리가, 반대쪽엔 각종 비용명세서가 놓여있다. 여기에다「대통령선거를 앞둔 부시의 국내인기」라는 항목이 저울 어느쪽에 놓여질지에 대한 계산이 끝나면 미국의 선택이 결정될 것이다.

〈金昌均기자〉

0083

| 관리 번호 | 92 -197 |
|---|---|

| 분류번호 | 보존기간 |
|---|---|
| | |

# 발 신 전 보

번 호 : WUN-0491 920303 1836 ED 종별 :

수 신 : 주 유엔 대사. 총영사

발 신 : 장 관 (연일)

제 목 : 안보리 - 이라크 무기폐기관련

대 : UNW-0574

이라크의 안보리 결의 이행문제와 관련한 최근 안보리의 제반 움직임과 관련, 미, 영, 불등 상임이사국 및 여타 주요이사국의 입장과 안보리의 향후 행동계획등에 대하여 파악, 보고하고 금후 본건 진전사항을 예의 관찰, 수시 보고바람. 끝.

(국제기구국장 김재섭)

1992.6.30. 에 예고문에 의거 일반문서로 재분류됨

| 보안 통제 | |
|---|---|

| 앙 고 재 | 92년 3월 3일 | 유엔1과 | 기안자 성명 | | 과 장 | 심의관 | 국 장 | | 차 관 | 장 관 |
|---|---|---|---|---|---|---|---|---|---|---|
| | | | | | | | | | | |

| 외신과통제 |
|---|
| |

0084

| 관리 번호 | 92-196 |
|---|---|

# 외 무 부

종 별 :

번 호 : UNW-0600 일 시 : 92 0303 2200

수 신 : 장 관(연일,중동일,기정)사본:유종하대사

발 신 : 주 유엔 대사대리

제 목 : 안보리-이라크 대량 파괴무기 폐기

대:WUN-0491

연:UNW-0574

1. 당관에서 관련 대표부에 탐문한바에 의하면 TARIQ AZIZ 부수상을 단장으로한 15 명의 이라크 대표단이 3.9. 당지에 도착, 3.11. 안보리 회의에 참석예정으로 있음

2. 연호 2.28. 안보리 의장성명 채택후 안보리의 향후 행동계획은 동 안보리회의에서의 이라크측의 대응태도를 보아가며 결정될것인바, 대부분 이사국들은그간의 이라크 태도에 비추어 지금까지와 동일한 비타협적인 입장을 반복할 것으로 기대한바 이라크가 2.28. 자 성명을 중대하게 받아 들인경우 태도변경도 배제할수 없으므로 일단 상기 회의시까지는 안보리의 대응조치를 보류해둔다는 입장이라고 함

3. 당지 안보리 주요이사국 담당관에 따르면 2.28. 의 의장성명은 최후통첩의 성격은 결코아니며 그간의 이라크의 비협조적이고 회피적인 태도를 만족할만한 성과가 없을경우에는 미, 영, 불의 주도로 새로운 대응조치가 강구될것이며 동대응조치에는 제한적인 군사행동을 포함한 모든종류의 조치가 고려가능하나 안보리 전체이사국과의 충분한 협의를 거쳐 결정될 것이라고 함

4. 안보리내 비동맹 그룹은 현재 이라크측이 명백히 안보리 결의를 위반하고 있으므로 이라크측에 대한 동정은 고려할수 없으며 계속 비타협적인 태도를 고수한다면 주요 이사국들의 강경대응조치에 동의할수 밖에 없는 입장이라고함

5. 본건진전사항 추보예정임

(대사대리 신기복-국장)

예고:92.6.30 일반

| 국기국 | 장관 | 차관 | 1차보 | 2차보 | 중아국 | 국기국 | 외정실 | 분석관 |
|---|---|---|---|---|---|---|---|---|
| 청와대 | 안기부 | | | | | (대사) | | |

PAGE 1

92.03.04 13:19

외신 2과 통제관 BN

0085

| 관리 번호 | 92/206 |
|---|---|

# 외 무 부

종 별 :

번 호 : UNW-0601 일 시 : 92 0303 2200

수 신 : 장 관(연일,연이,중동일,중동이,기정)사본:유종하 대사

발 신 : 주 유엔 대사대리

제 목 : 안보리(92.3월 주요의제)

금월 안보리 의장국 베네주엘라는 금 3.3. 오후 비공식 회의를 개최,3 월중안보리 작업일정을 협의한바 주요내용 아래 보고함

1. 이락의 안보리 결의(대량파괴무기 폐기)이행

-3.11. 이락 대표단을 출석시켜 이락측의 결의 불이행을 추궁하고 EKEUS 특위의장등 관련전문가로 하여금 이라측의 입장설명에 대해 대질신문을 하는 기회를 갖도록 함. 경우에 따라서는 2-3 회정도 회합을 고려하고 있음 (상세별도보고)

2. 펜암기 폭파사건

-사무총장 특사로 리비아에 파견되었던 SAFRONCHUK 의 보고서가 명 3.4. 안보리에 제출되어 동보고서를 심의하고 안보리의 대응방향을 협의함

-명 3.4. 사무총장보고서를 심의함

4. 상기외에 이스라엘 점령지역, 소말리아사태, 유고사태등에 대해서도 심의예정임

(대사대리 신기복-국장)

예고:92.6.30 까지

92. 6. 30. 일반

| 국기국 | 장관 | 차관 | 1차보 | 2차보 | 중아국 | 중아국 | 국기국 | 국기국 |
|---|---|---|---|---|---|---|---|---|
| 외정실 | 분석관 | 청와대 | 안기부 | | | | | |

PAGE 1 92.03.04 13:20

외신 2과 통제관 BN

0086

주 미 대 사 관

USW(F) : 1283 년월일 : 92.3.5 시간 : 15:00

수 신 : 장 관 (미일, 중동일, 중동이, 정안)

발 신 : 주 미 대 사

제 목 : 이라크, 미사일 은닉 사찰

(출처 : WT)

| 보 안 | |
|---|---|
| 통 제 | |

# Hidden Iraqi missiles sought

By Rowan Scarborough and Bill Gertz
THE WASHINGTON TIMES

The United States is conducting an urgent hunt for more than 100 Iraqi Scud missiles that spy agencies believe are hidden underground near Baghdad.

Iraqi leader Saddam Hussein's persistence in protecting his Scuds is spurring interest among five Middle East countries, plus Turkey, in buying U.S.-made Patriot missiles, according to Bush administration sources.

The sources said the State Department has notified Congress it is discussing the possibility of transferring $16 billion in Patriot anti-missile systems to Saudi Arabia, Kuwait, the United Arab Emirates, Bahrain, Qatar and Turkey.

Allied forces used the Patriot to intercept Iraqi-launched Scuds during the Persian Gulf war.

Administration officials said intelligence reports indicate Baghdad constructed underground storage sites to circumvent U.N. cease-fire agreements. U.S. reconnaissance — including satellites and spy planes — has been unable to locate the cache so U.N. inspection teams can move in and supervise the missiles' destruction.

The new hunt in Iraq for the suspected Scuds began three weeks ago, according to an administration intelligence official.

"They have done quite a bit of underground [construction] work," the official said. "They are probably storing the missiles down there."

Iraq's refusal to declare the location of Scud ballistic missiles and other weapons material has irked President Bush, who has weighed the option of ordering renewed military action against Baghdad to force compliance with U.N. resolutions.

The Pentagon is keeping warplanes, including the F-117A stealth fighter, in Saudi Arabia and deploys Navy carriers in the region.

The United States interprets the U.N. resolutions as already authorizing military action. The agreements require Iraq to destroy Scud missiles and related equipment and all weapons of mass destruction.

Mr. Bush and the United Nations consistently have charged Baghdad with violating the accords, which Iraq agreed to March 3, 1991.

The administration has told Congress Iraq is harboring "hundreds" of Scuds, the weapon it launched into Israeli and Saudi cities during the 44-day Gulf war.

U.S. intelligence sources said the exact number of remaining Iraqi Scuds may be as high as 800.

The United Nations recently confronted Iraq on its refusal to destroy Scud-related components. Iraq maintained it should be allowed to keep the equipment and use it for non-military manufacturing.

The U.N. Security Council has given Iraq until next week to comply or face unspecified "serious consequences." Officials said options include tightening economic sanctions that already have hurt Iraq's economy and hindered efforts to rebuild its bombed-out infrastructure.

An Iraqi delegation headed by Deputy Prime Minister Tariq Aziz is scheduled to come to New York on Monday to argue for a relaxation of sanctions.

The Security Council has stated that the embargo will stay in place until Iraq complies.

Mr. Bush has gone further, saying the trade restrictions will stick as long as Saddam is in power.

Senior administration officials have predicted Saddam's downfall. But the Iraqi president has stubbornly clung to power a year after his Gulf war defeat, protected by an ever-tightening ring of security forces.

Iraq has outmaneuvered sanctions to some extent by shipping goods by air into Jordan, then trucking them to Baghdad, according to several knowledgeable intelligence sources.

Although a number of Iraq's neighbors want the United States to sell them Patriots, it is unlikely the administration will approve all the deals and submit them to Congress, according to an administration official.

This official said the administration will ask Congress to approve sales for Saudi Arabia and Kuwait, although the timing of the notifications is still being discussed.

Kuwait, its military crushed by Iraq's swift invasion in August 1990, wants to build an integrated air defense system of U.S.-made Hawk anti-aircraft missiles and longer-range Patriots, which can knock out aircraft and tactical ballistic missiles.

But Turkey, a strong U.S. ally during the war, cannot afford to buy Patriots, the source said. Most of its U.S. military aid is tied up in buying jet fighters and other American-made weapons. Likewise, Bahrain lacks the needed cash and would need the Saudis' financial help.

Officials said these countries not only fear Iraq, but also Iran and Syria, which are bolstering their arsenals of ballistic missiles capable of hitting cities in the region.

| 외신 1과 | |
|---|---|
| 통 제 | |

1283-1-1

92.3.5
WT

0087

# 주 미 대 사 관

USW(F) : 1358 년월일 : 92.3.9 시간 : 11:30

수 신 : 장 관 (중동일, 미이, 미이)

발 신 : 주 미 대 사

제 목 : 이라크 핵문제

| 보 안 통 제 | |
|---|---|

(출처 : WP )

# Iraq, U.N. Prepare for Key Talks

## *Britain Says It Would Back Military Action*

By Trevor Rowe
Special to The Washington Post

UNITED NATIONS, March 8—With the arrival here Monday of an Iraqi delegation headed by Deputy Prime Minister Tariq Aziz, the U.N. Security Council is gearing up for the highest-level face-to-face public confrontation with Iraq since the outbreak of the Persian Gulf War.

The meeting, scheduled for Wednesday, was requested by Iraq and comes amid Western threats of military and other kinds of punitive action to force Baghdad to comply with U.N. cease-fire resolutions.

Today, British Prime Minister John Major said he would back a military strike against Iraq if it refuses to comply with resolutions requiring the elimination of its weapons of mass destruction. Major told the BBC that he would support the military action if it is sanctioned by the United Nations.

British officials said Friday that Major agreed in a telephone conversation with President Bush that they would use any means necessary to force Iraqi President Saddam Hussein to comply with the resolutions, Reuter reported.

So far, Baghdad has refused to agree to fully implement resolutions dealing with the long-term monitoring and elimination of nuclear, chemical, biological and ballistic weapons as well as to the destruction of facilities used in their production. It especially opposes the destruction of equipment that it says has dual military-civilian use and has made clear that it resents the U.N. monitoring as an intrusion on its sovereignty.

U.N. officials said Iraq has cooperated in the destruction of its declared stockpiles of chemical, biological and ballistic missiles. But last month Baghdad refused to allow a U.N. team to begin destruction of facilities used for construction of ballistic missiles, which include Scuds. U.N. officials say Iraq also has not fully cooperated in providing all relevant information about the weapons programs, and they suspect that some programs or manufacturing equipment—including that used for making nuclear weapons—could still be hidden.

In a report in late January, U.N. Secretary General Boutros Boutros-Ghali stated that while there had been "significant progress" made in implementing aspects of the U.N. cease-fire resolutions, "much remains to be done." He also stressed the need for a change of policy on the part of Iraq to one of "candor, transparency and cooperation at all levels."

Many Western diplomats view the mission of the Iraqi delegation as a diplomatic offensive aimed at softening international resolve on economic sanctions. Iraq has complained bitterly about the sanctions, which are to remain in force until Baghdad has fully complied with the cease-fire resolutions.

However, one diplomat said: "The odds are stacked against them [the Iraqis]. While they may argue they've complied with 60 to 70 percent of the demands, this is not sufficient for the council."

There is speculation that one aim of the Iraqi visit is to shift domestic resentment over shortages of food and consumer goods away from Saddam's regime and onto the United Nations.

Iraqi officials said that Mohammed Said Sahaf, minister of state for foreign affairs, will accompany Aziz, as will the deputy minister of industry and a top member of the agency in charge of atomic energy production. Security Council President Diego Arria of Venezuela has said the session could continue into Thursday.

Diplomats predict that if Iraq fails to satisfy the council's demands, some kind of punitive action is likely to be considered. One idea being discussed among the United States and its allies is a military strike at plants engaged in the production of weapons of mass destruction.

92.3.9 WP

| 외신 1과 통 제 | |
|---|---|

1358 2 1

| 배 | 장관 | 차관 | 1차보 | 2차보 | 기획실 | 의전실 | 외정실 | 분석관 | 아주국 | 미주국 | 구주국 | 중아국 | 국기국 | 경제국 | 통상국 | 문협국 | 영교국 | 총무과 | 감사관 | 공보관 | 외연원 | 청와대 | 총리실 | 안기부 | 공보처 | 경기원 | 상공부 |
|---|---|---|---|---|---|---|---|---|---|---|---|---|---|---|---|---|---|---|---|---|---|---|---|---|---|---|---|
| 부처 | / | / | / | | | / | / | | | 2 | 0 | | | | | | | | | | | / | / | / | | | |

92- 3-10 ; 14:38 ; #8

# 주 미 대 사 관

USW(F) : 년월일 : 시간 :

수 신 : 장 관

발 신 : 주 미 대 사

제 목 :

| 보 안 통 제 | |
|---|---|

(출처 : )

Rowland Evans and Robert Novak

## An October Surprise?

In an effort to repeat past glories and exploit his foreign policy strong point, President Bush has amassed a wealth of new intelligence justifying a massive air attack against Saddam Hussein in a pre-election surprise that might revive Bush's forlorn presidency.

Bush has been given data showing that the United States underestimated by 50 percent Iraq's weapons of mass destruction: nuclear, chemical and biological. Two defectors claim Iraq had eight nuclear research facilities, double the four that were known. Even worse, the CIA now believes 800 Scud missiles remain intact, far more than reported at war's end.

The president will trumpet this new intelligence if he decides to strike against the Iraqi president and his war machine, which Bush boasted had been destroyed in Desert Storm. In a fortuitous throw of the political dice, the new intelligence could be used to justify putting Bush back at the helm in a glorious foreign policy crisis. His fallen presidency is in need of revival, as is his chaotic, leaderless reelection campaign.

But presidential aides are aware of the high political risk of a new foreign adventure that might fail. Even if it succeeded in ending Saddam's rule, voter suspicion of Bush's political motivation is so strong today, it might backfire. One administration source privately calls Bush "almost craven" in the abject way he is courting voters with self-criticism and sudden policy shifts that shatter his old principles.

Signals of possibly imminent action against the Iraqi dictator are plentiful in Washington, at the United Nations and in the government of British Prime Minister John Major. Major himself faces an early election. On Thursday, for the second time in five days, British Foreign Secretary Douglas Hurd raised the option of a military strike against Saddam Hussein. If Saddam persists in defying U.N. orders, he said, Major's government will consider a military strike—surprising language for the tired old British lion unless the United States was known to agree.

Commander-in-Chief Bush is well prepared for such a strike. He has stationed a "composite" air wing in Saudi Arabia, with stealthy F-117Cs, F-15Es and other strike aircraft. In the Persian Gulf and the nearby Arabian Sea, Bush now has an awesome capacity of 1,500-kilometer Tomahawk missiles. Backup submarines and aircraft carriers are available from the Mediterranean.

The threat of Iraq's hidden Scud arsenal has already had a frightening impact on Saudi Arabia, Kuwait, Bahrain, the United Arab Emirates and Qatar. These states alone, according to the intelligence estimates, have placed orders for more than $16 billion in U.S.-manufactured Patriot missiles. Although the Patriot's performance was far from perfect in the anti-Scud war before U.S.-led forces threw Iraq's forces out of Kuwait, it is still the best weapon available.

For months, Democratic politicians have been wondering whether Bush would try an "October surprise," a phrase coined in 1980 by Republicans who feared that President Carter would pull a pre-election "surprise" and negotiate the freedom of American hostages in Tehran.

As Bush has sunk deeper into the quicksand of recession and faced humiliation from Patrick J. Buchanan in his campaign for the Republican presidential nomination, a decision by the president to unsheathe his national security sword has looked more likely. Bush's surrogate campaigners have attacked Buchanan for having opposed the war against Iraq before it actually started.

A new war, which the Pentagon has informed the White House could be "packaged" at between four and 10 days of air attacks, might help dramatize Buchanan's 1990 pre-war opposition to freeing Kuwait. In fact, however, Buchanan's current "America first" foreign policy theme may fit the views of average voters today better than a new foreign adventure.

Thus Bush's tub-thumping over his victory in Desert Storm seems to leave many citizens more angry than grateful. They've forgotten, or want to forget, that long-ago war because it cannot solve unemployment, the high cost of homes, poor schools, dangerous streets or drugs—the meat and potatoes of the 1992 election.

In assessing the political effect of a new war against Saddam, the president's men will serve him better if they do not forget these mundane considerations.

| 외신 1과 통 제 | |
|---|---|

92.3.9 WP

1358-2-2

0089

주 영 국 대 사 관

UKW(F) : 041P 년월일 : 720309 시간 : 1830
수 신 : 장 관 (중동이, 연일)
발 신 : 주영대사
제 목 : 이라크 정세

| 보 안 | |
| --- | --- |
| 통 제 | |

(출처 : )

THE TIMES (92.3.9)

# Aziz seeks to head off action by UN on dismantling weapons

**BY CHARLES BREMNER IN NEW YORK AND JILL SHERMAN**

TARIQ Aziz, the Iraqi deputy prime minister, flew to New York from Jordan last night to face a public tongue-lashing by the United Nations Security Council over Baghdad's failure to co-operate in dismantling its nuclear, chemical, biological and ballistic weapons programmes.

When he appears before the council on Wednesday, Mr Aziz, the first senior Iraqi official to visit America since the Gulf war, is likely to try to head off new action to force Baghdad to comply with the UN's resolutions.

In the past week Britain and America have evoked the possibility of using force to remove suspected nuclear facilities and missile caches, but diplomats consider military action unlikely given the political pitfalls and opposition from within the American armed forces to new military entanglements in Iraq.

Several members of the House of Representatives foreign affairs committee, including Dante Fascell, its chairman, urged President Bush yesterday to consider military action. Iraq is obliged to scrap its weapons under Resolution 687, which covered the Gulf ceasefire.

In London, John Major said yesterday he would back military action against Iraq if sanctioned by the United Nations. He said on Radio 4's *Sunday* that he would not rule out a strike if Iraq continued to obstruct destruction of its missiles. "If that proves to be necessary, the answer is yes. I would support it," the prime minister said.

Among options being examined by the security council is a scheme to confiscate part of Iraq's assets, estimated at up to $5 billion (£3 billion), frozen after the invasion of Kuwait in August 1990. Most of the assets are held in America, Britain and Switzerland, but legal and practical difficulties would need to be overcome before they could be confiscated.

Mr Aziz is expected to link further co-operation with calls for a relaxation of the embargo that has crippled the Iraqi economy, an approach the UN will almost certainly reject. Western officials believe President Saddam Hussein is intent on wearing down the UN's resolve over time.

US warships were reported yesterday to be preparing to intercept two North Korean ships approaching the Gulf from the Indian Ocean and said to be carrying sophisticated Scud missiles for Iran and Syria.

Mr Bush said on Saturday that he would not rule out American intervention to prevent the delivery of the weapons. Israel, which was hit by Scuds during the Gulf war, has urged the United States to take action against the vessels.

Page
041P-1-1)

| 외신 1과 | |
| --- | --- |
| 통 제 | |

| 차관보 | 1차보 | 2차보 | 기획실 | 의전실 | 분석관 | 의전장 | 아주국 | 미주국 | 구주국 | 중아국 | 국기국 | 경제국 | 통상국 | 문협국 | 영교국 | 총무과 | 감사관 | 공보관 | 외연원 | 청와대 | 총리실 | 안기부 | 공보처 | 경기원 | 상공부 |
| --- | --- | --- | --- | --- | --- | --- | --- | --- | --- | --- | --- | --- | --- | --- | --- | --- | --- | --- | --- | --- | --- | --- | --- | --- | --- |
| / | | / | / | | | | | | | 0 | / | | | | | | | | / | / | | / | | | |

0090

| 관리 번호 | 92 — 216 |
|---|---|

원 본

# 외 무 부

종 별 :

번 호 : UNW-0668　　　　일 시 : 92 0310 2000

수 신 : 장관(연일,중동일,기정) 사본:유종하대사

발 신 : 주 유엔 대사

제 목 : 안보리-이라크 대량파괴무기 폐기

대: WUN-0491

연: UNW-0600

1.3.9. 당지 도착한 TARIG AZIZ 부수상은 3.10. 오전 안보리의장 (베네주엘라 대사)을 면담하고 이어 안보리 비동맹이사국 (CAUCUS) 과 회담한후 오후에는사무총장을 면담함.

2. 안보리는 3.11. 공식회의에 대비 금일 비공식 협의에서 이사국간 의견조정 및 3.11. 공식회의 진행절차를 협의한바 금일 합의된 내용은 다음과 같음.

- 3.11.10:30 에 회의를 개최, 별첨 안보리의장 성명을 낭독하고 각 이사국의 개별 발언 및 이라크 대표의 발언 청취

- 이어 각 이사국 및 EKEUS 대량파괴무기 폐기 특위의장의 질문에 대해 이라크 측의 답변이 있게됨.

- 쿠웨이트 및 BLIX IAEA 사무총장도 동회의에 참석함.

3. 안보리의장은 금일 오전 AZIZ 부수상과의 면담후 행한 기자회견에서 이라크 측으로 부터 받은 느낌은 이라크 측이 안보리 결의를 무조건적으로 이행하여야 한다는 사실을 잘 이해하고 있었으며 금번 대표단 파견의 목적은 이라크 측이 안보리 결의를 이행하는 경우 안보리가 대 이라크 경제제재 조치를 철회교섭토록 임무를 부여받은것 같다고 논평함.

4. 금일 오전의 안보리 비동맹 이사국과의 면담시에도 이라크 측은 안보리 결의 이행과 경제제재 조치 철회를 연계하는 문제를 제안하였다고 하는바 명일 회의에 따른 안보리의 대응방향등 진전사항 추보 예정임. 끝

(대사대리 신기복-국장)

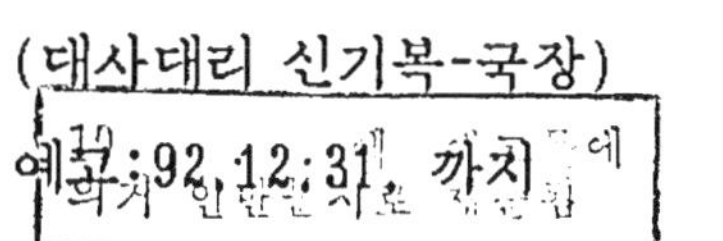


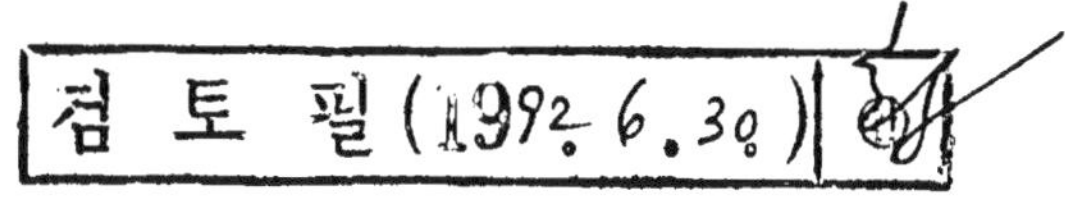


| 국기국 | 장관 | 차관 | 1차보 | 2차보 | 중아국 | 국기국 | 외정실 | 분석관 |
|---|---|---|---|---|---|---|---|---|
| 청와대 | 안기부 | | | | | | | |

PAGE 1　　　　92.03.11 10:29

외신 2과 통제관 BX

0091

첨부: FAX (UNW(F)-238)

PAGE 2

0092

UNW(F)-238 20310 2000 첨부물 총 1304

10 March 1992

(연일. 중동일, 기정)

Revised

# STRUCTURE OF THE DRAFT INTRODUCTORY PRESIDENTIAL STATEMENT

I. GENERAL OBLIGATION

II. SPECIFIC OBLIGATIONS

(a) Respect for the inviolability of the international boundary

(b) Weapons-related obligations

(c) Repatriation of and access to Kuwaiti and third-country nationals in Iraq

(d) Iraq's liability under international law

(e) Repayment and servicing of Iraq's foreign debt

(f) Return of property

(g) Monthly statements of gold and foreign currency reserves

(h) Undertaking not to commit or support acts of international terrorism

III. CONCLUDING OBSERVATION

238-13-1

0093

10 March 1992

Second revision

DRAFT STATEMENT BY THE PRESIDENT OF THE SECURITY COUNCIL

Following consultations among members of the Council, I have been authorized to make the following statement on behalf of the Council.

I. GENERAL OBLIGATION

1. The resolutions concerning the situation between Iraq and Kuwait impose a number of general and specific obligations upon Iraq.

2. As regards the general obligation, Iraq is required, under paragraph 33 of Security Council resolution 687 (1991), to give official notification to the Secretary-General and to the Security Council of its acceptance of the provisions of that entire resolution.

3. Iraq signified its unconditional acceptance in letters dated 6 and 10 April 1991 (S/22456 and S/22480, respectively) and 23 January 1992 (S/23472).

4. When the Security Council met at the level of Heads of State and Government on 31 January 1992 the concluding statement made by the President of the Council, on behalf of its members (S/23500), contained the following passage:

"Last year, under the authority of the United Nations, the international community succeeded in enabling Kuwait to regain its sovereignty and territorial integrity, which it had lost as a result of Iraqi aggression. The resolutions adopted by the Security Council remain essential to the restoration of peace and stability in the region and must be

238-13-2

fully implemented. At the same time the members of the Council are concerned by the humanitarian situation of the innocent civilian population of Iraq."

5. On 5 February 1992, the President of the Security Council issued a statement on behalf of its members (S/23517) in which he stated, among other things:

"In connection with the Secretary-General's factual report [S/23514] on Iraq's compliance with all the obligations placed upon it by resolution 687 (1991) and subsequent relevant resolutions, the members of the Security Council note that while much progress has been made, much remains to be done. ... The members of the Council are disturbed by the lack of Iraqi cooperation. Iraq must implement fully resolution 687 (1991) and subsequent relevant resolutions as was stated in the statement read out by the President of the Council on behalf of its members in the meeting held on 31 January 1992 with the participation of the heads of State and Government (S/23500)."

6. In a statement made on behalf of the Council on 28 February 1992 (S/23663), the President said:

"The members of the Council demand that Iraq immediately implement all its obligations under Council resolution 687 (1991) and subsequent resolutions on Iraq. The members of the Council require the Government of Iraq to communicate directly to the Council without further delay an authoritative and unconditional acknowledgement of its agreement to accept and implement the above noted obligations, including specifically to comply with the determination of the Special Commission requiring the destruction of ballistic missile-related equipment. The members of the Council emphasize that Iraq must be aware of the serious consequences of continued material breaches of resolution 687 (1991)."

7. I must also draw attention to the further report of the Secretary-General on the status of complianca by Iraq with the obligations placed upon it (S/23687).

0095

8. From the aforementioned statements by the President and in view of the reports of the Secretary-General, it will be seen that, despite Iraq's statements of unconditional acceptance of Security Council resolution 687 (1991), the Security Council has determined that Iraq is not in full compliance with all of its obligations.

## II. SPECIFIC OBLIGATIONS

9. In addition to the general obligation to accept the provisions of resolution 687 (1991) in their entirety, several Security Council resolutions impose specific obligations upon Iraq.

### (a) Respect for the inviolability of the international boundary

10. By paragraph 2 of resolution 687 (1991) the Security Council demands that Iraq respect the inviolability of the international boundary and the allocation of islands previously agreed upon between Iraq and Kuwait. Pursuant to paragraph 3 of that resolution, the Secretary-General established a Boundary Demarcation Commission to demarcate the boundary between Iraq and Kuwait. Paragraph 5 of the same resolution requires Iraq and Kuwait to respect a demilitarized zone (DMZ) established by the Security Council. The Council has been informed that Iraq has respected the DMZ and that it has fully participated in the work of the Boundary Demarcation Commission. It has also been informed that Iraq refuses to withdraw a number of police posts that are not in line with UNIKOM's principle that both sides

0096

should stay 1,000 metres from the boundary line shown on UNIKOM's map.

(b) Weapons-related obligations

11. Section C of resolution 687 (1991) imposes certain specific obligations upon Iraq with respect to its chemical and biological weapons programmes, its ballistic missile programmes with a range greater than 150 kilometres and its nuclear programmes. These obligations are elaborated upon in resolutions 707 (1991) and 715 (1991). The obligations are defined in paragraphs 8, 9, 10, 11, 12 and 13 of resolution 687 (1991) and they are elaborated upon in paragraphs 3 and 5 of resolution 707 (1991) and paragraph 5 of resolution 715 (1991).

12. The information relevant to Iraq's compliance with the obligations laid down in the paragraphs of the Security Council resolutions to which I have just referred is reproduced in annex I to the Secretary-General's report (S/23687).

13. By resolution 699 (1991), the Security Council decided that the Government of Iraq shall be liable for the full costs of carrying out the tasks authorized by section C of resolution 687 (1991). No funds have so far been received from Iraq to meet this liability.

14. The Council has noted that since the adoption of resolution 687 (1991) progress has been made in the implementation of section C of that resolution but that much remains to be done. There is serious non-compliance with the obligations concerning the programmes for weapons of mass destruction and ballistic

238-13-5

0097

missiles and the members of the Council have found this to be a continuing material breach of resolution 687 (1991).

15. The Special Commission has informed the Council about the outstanding matters that would at the present time appear to be the most important. The Council's attention is invited again to annex I of the Secretary-General's report, S/23687 of 7 March 1992.

16. The Council has also noted the statement by the International Atomic Energy Agency (IAEA) contained in the Secretary-General's report of 25 January 1992 (S/23514 section C of the annex). The attention of the Council is drawn to information annexed to the further report of the Secretary-General, S/23687 (annex II), of 7 March 1992, relative to the two last inspections by the IAEA, on Iraq's compliance with its obligations under United Nations Security Council resolutions as they relate to nuclear activities.

17. In a statement issued on behalf of the members of the Council (S/23609), the President stated on 19 February 1992 that:

> "Iraq's failure to acknowledge its obligations under resolutions 707 (1991) and 715 (1991), its rejection up until now of the two plans for ongoing monitoring and verification and its failure to provide the full, final and complete disclosure of its weapons capabilities constitute a continuing material breach of the relevant provisions of resolution 687 (1991)."

18. In a further statement made on 28 February 1992 on behalf of the Council (S/23663), the President said:

> "The members of the Council deplore and condemn the failure of the Government of Iraq to provide the Special Commission with full, final and complete disclosure, as

0098

required by resolution 707 (1991), of all aspects of its programmes to develop weapons of mass destruction and ballistic missiles with a range greater than 150 kilometres, including launchers, and of all holdings of such weapons, their components and production facilities and locations, as well as all other nuclear programmes; and the failure of Iraq to comply with the plans for ongoing monitoring and verification approved by resolution 715 (1991). ... Furthermore, the members of the Council equally deplore and condemn Iraq's failure, within the time prescribed by the Special Commission at the request of Iraq, to commence destruction of ballistic missile-related equipment designated for destruction by the Special Commission. The members of the Council reaffirm that it is for the Special Commission alone to determine which items must be destroyed under paragraph 9 of resolution 687 (1991)."

(c) Repatriation of and access to Kuwaiti and third-country nationals in Iraq

19. As regards Kuwaiti and third-country nationals in Iraq, Security Council resolutions 664 (1990), 666 (1990), 667 (1990), 674 (1990), 686 (1991) and 687 (1991) impose an obligation on Iraq to release, facilitate repatriation of, and arrange for immediate access to them, as well as the return of the remains of any deceased personnel of the forces of Kuwait and of the Member States cooperating with Kuwait pursuant to resolution 678 (1990). Furthermore, paragraph 30 of resolution 687 (1991) requires Iraq to extend all necessary cooperation to the International Committee of the Red Cross (ICRC) in connection with the above obligations.

20. The Security Council was informed by the ICRC in January 1992 that almost 7,000 persons have returned from Iraq to their countries since the beginning of March 1991. The ICRC also

238-13-7 0099

- 7 -

stated that despite all its efforts, there are still thousands of persons reported missing by the parties to the conflict.

21. A special commission composed of the representatives of France, Iraq, Kuwait, Saudi Arabia, the United Kingdom and the United States has met under the auspices of the ICRC, to try to reach an agreement on, among other things, the implementation of paragraph 30 of resolution 687 (1991). However, the ICRC has informed the Council that it has not yet received any information as to the whereabouts of the persons reported missing in Iraq. Nor has it received detailed and documented information on the search conducted by the Iraqi authorities. Finally, it is also still awaiting information on persons who have died while in custody.

22. The attention of the Council is drawn to section 4, paragraphs 12 to 14, of the Secretary-General's report contained in document S/23687 of 7 March 1992.

(d) Iraq's liability under international law

23. Another obligation concerns Iraq's liability under international law. In resolution 674 (1990), the Security Council reminds Iraq "that under international law it is liable for any loss, damage or injury arising in regard to Kuwait and third States and their nationals and corporations, as a result of the invasion and illegal occupation of Kuwait by Iraq". Its liability under international law is reaffirmed in paragraph 2 (b) of resolution 686 (1991) and paragraph 16 of resolution 687 (1991). Resolution 687 (1991) further specifies that it "is

0100

liable under international law for any direct loss, damage, including environmental damage and the depletion of natural resources, or injury to foreign Governments, nationals and corporations, as a result of Iraq's unlawful invasion and occupation of Kuwait".

24. By paragraph 18 of the same resolution, the Security Council created a Fund to pay compensation for claims that fall within paragraph 16, to be financed by a percentage of the value of the exports of petroleum and petroleum products from Iraq. In view of the existing economic sanctions against Iraq under resolution 661 (1990), Iraq was permitted by the Security Council under resolutions 706 (1991) and 712 (1991) to sell a limited quantity of oil, as an exception, a portion of the proceeds from which would be used to provide financial resources for the Fund. To date, it has not availed itself of this possibility. The Council notes that this authorization is due to lapse on 18 March 1992. The members of the Council are aware of a request by Iraq for a five-year moratorium on meeting its financial obligations, including payments into the Compensation Fund.

(e) Repayment and servicing of Iraq's foreign debt

25. With regard to another obligation, the Security Council, in paragraph 17 of resolution 687 (1991), demands that Iraq scrupulously adhere to all of its obligations concerning servicing and repayment of its foreign debt.

26. The attention of the Council is drawn to paragraphs 17 and 18 of the Secretary-General's report (S/23637) of 7 March 1992.

238-13-9

0101

(f) Return of property

27. I now turn to the question of return of property. The Security Council, in paragraph 2 (d) of resolution 686 (1991), demands that Iraq immediately begin to return all Kuwaiti property seized by it, to be completed in the shortest possible period. The members of the Council have noted with satisfaction that, as stated in the further report of the Secretary-General, Iraqi officials involved with the return of property have extended maximum cooperation to the United Nations to facilitate the return.

(g) Monthly statements of gold and foreign currency reserves

28. Another obligation is set out by paragraph 7 of resolution 706 (1991), under which the Government of Iraq is required to provide to the Secretary-General and appropriate international organizations monthly statements of its gold and foreign currency reserves. To date, no such statements have been provided to the Secretary-General or to the IMF.

(h) Undertaking not to commit or support acts of international terrorism

29. By paragraph 32 of resolution 687 (1991), Iraq is required not to commit or support acts of international terrorism or allow any organization directed towards commission of such acts to operate within its territory and to condemn unequivocally and renounce all acts, methods, and practices of terrorism.

238-13-10

0102

30. The Council notes Iraq's statements contained in letters dated 11 June 1991 (S/22687 and S/22689) and 23 January 1992 (S/23472) that it is a party to international conventions against terrorism and that it has never pursued a policy favourable to international terrorism as defined by international law.

-32

## III. CONCLUDING OBSERVATION

33. In view of the observations on the record of Iraq's performance, the Security Council has considered itself justified in concluding that Iraq has not fully complied with the obligations placed upon it by the Council. It is the Council's hope and expectation that this meeting will prove an invaluable opportunity to advance in the consideration of this issue as required in the interest of world peace and security, as well as that of the Iraqi people.

238-13-11

(31) ~~30~~. I should now like to refer to the demands by the Security Council with respect to the Iraqi civilian population. In paragraph 2 of resolution 688 (1991), the Security Council demands that Iraq, as a contribution to removing the threat to international peace and security in the region, end the repression of its civilian population. In paragraphs 3 and 7, the Security Council insists that it allow immediate access by international humanitarian organizations to all those in need of assistance in all parts of Iraq, and demands its cooperation with the Secretary-General to these ends.

(32) ~~31~~. The Security Council remains deeply concerned at the grave human rights abuses that, despite the provisions of resolution 688 (1991), the Government of Iraq continues to perpetrate against its population. The Security Council notes that this situation is confirmed by the report of the Special Rapporteur of the Commission on Human Rights (E/CN.4/1992/31, also to be circulated in document S/23685) and by the comments of the Office of the Executive Delegate of the Secretary-General contained in the further report of the Secretary-General.

32. The members of the Council are particularly concerned at the reported restrictions on the supplies of essential commodities, in particular food and fuel, which have been imposed by the

238-13-12 0104

- 5 -

Government of Iraq on the three northern governorates of Dohuk, Erbil and Suleimaniya. In this regard, as the Special Rapporteur has noted in his report, inasmuch as the repression of the population continues, the threat to international peace and security in the region mentioned in resolution 688 (1991) remains.

238-13-13

0105

6/103

원 본

# 외 무 부

암호수신

종 별 :

번 호 : UNW-0687 일 시 : 92 0311 2300

수 신 : 장관(연일,중동일,기정) 사본:유종하대사

발 신 : 주 유엔 대사

제 목 : 안보리-이라크 대량파괴무기 폐기

연: UNW-0668

1. 안보리는 3.11. 오전 공식회의를 개최, 연호 진행절차에 따라 의장의 성명낭독, 각 이사국의 발언, AZIZ 부수상의 발언을 청취하고 오후에는 BLIX IAEA 사무총장, EKEUS 대량파괴무기 폐기특위 의장, 쿠웨이트 대표의 발언과 이사국의질의가 있었는바 명일 오전에 회의를 속개, 이라크 측의 답변을 청취하기로 함.

2. 주요 발언내용

가. 의장성명 (연호 자료 참고)

안보리 결의에 따라 이라크의 분야별 결의 이행상황을 상세히 점검한바 결론적으로 이라크의 결의이행 실적이 아직 완전하지 못하며 금번회의를 통해 진전을 기대함.

나. 미국

- 걸프사태 종결을 위한 안보리 결의 687 은 이라크측이 이를 수락 하였음에도 불구하고 무기개발계획의 허위자료 제출, 핵시설 은폐등으로 의무이행을 회피하고 있음.

- 상기외에 국경선 준수문제, 쿠웨이트 재산반환, 실종자 확인작업등에 있어서도 이라크측은 성실한 의무이행을 하지않고 있으며 특히 쿠르드족 및 남부지역 시아파에 대한 경제봉쇄를 행함으로써 이들 소수민족의 생활실태는 극도로 악화됨.

- 안보리 결의 이행을 재차 촉구하며 이의 완전한 이행이 없이는 경제제재 조치 해제는 불가함. 동 결의가 이행되지 않을경우 중대한 결과를 초래할것임.

다. 영국

- 사무총장의 보고서는 이라크의 결의 불이행 내용을 상세히 기록하고 있는바 이라크측의 협력을 재촉구함.

- 대량파괴무기 폐기 관련, 협상의 여지는 없으며 이락측의 결의 이행만이

국기국 장관 차관 1차보 2차보 중아국 국기국 외정실 분석관
정와대 안기부

PAGE 1 92.03.12 13:25

외신 2과 통제관 BZ

0106

문제인바 이는 다른사항과 연계가 불가함.

- 작년 안보리 결의를 심각하게 받아들이지 않아 기회를 놓쳤는바 금번에는기회를 상실차 않을것을 기대함.

라. 상기외에 15 개 이사국 전원이 발언한바, 주로 이라크의 결의이행을 재차 촉구하고 경제제재 해제는 추후 고려할 문제라는 점을 강조함.

마. 이라크 대표 (별첨 자료 참조)

- 안보리 결의는 충실히 이행하여 왔음. 즉 대량파괴무기도 유엔감시하에 폐기하고 장비 및 생산시설도 일방적으로 파기하였음.

- 687 결의이행에 따라 경제제재 조치를 해제 촉구한바 있으나 안보리 일부이사국은 이라크의 정치지도층 교체시 까지 제재조치 해제를 보류하고 있음.

- 유엔특위 (SCOM) 및 IAEA 와 협조하여 유엔이 요구하는 모든점에 대해 확인해줄 준비가 되어있음.

- 따라서 모든문제에 대한 답변을 일정한 기한내에 제출함으로써 이문제 종결을 희망하며 이라크의 주권 및 안전이 보장되는 방법으로 특위 및 IAEA 측과 향후 이행계획을 작성, 시행할것을 제안함.

- 이라크가 의무이행을 완료한 만큼 안보리의 경제제재 해제조치가 있어야 할것임.

3. 오후 회의에서 IAEA 사무총장 및 EKEUS 특위의장은 오전 이라크측의 발언에 대해 반박하고 이라크 측의 비협조적 자세로 안보리 결의에 따른 완전한 임무수행을 할수 없었다고 밝힘. 또한 앞으로의 미진한 부분에 대해 이라크측 협조가 계속 필요함을 언급함.

4. 쿠웨이트 대표는 이라크의 쿠웨이트인 억류, 재산반환, 국경선 확정문제등에 대해 언급함.

5. 영국, 미, 인도, 불란서 등 4 개국이 질의한바 특히 영국 및 미국은 이락 대표발언이 종래 태도를 반복한것에 불과하며 실망을 금치 못한다고 함. 질의내용은 다음과 같음.

가. 영국

- 대량파괴무기 폐기관련, SCOM 및 IAEA 결정사항을 이라크가 무조건 수락할것인지 여부

- 쿠르드 및 남부 시아파에 대한 경제봉쇄 해제 용의

나. 미국

- 결의이행에는 유엔측과의 협상여지가 없으며 이라크 측의 일방적인 완전한 이행만이 문제이므로 이점을 명확히 이해하기 바람.

-대량 파괴무기 폐기 계획 제출시기등 이락측이 미이행중인 모든사항에 대한이라측의 이행 용의

다. 인도

- 이락내 외국인 송환 가능시기

라. 불란서

- 이락 대표 발언을 수락할수 없으며 안보리에 대한 도전으로 간주함.

- 군사계획에 대한 완전한 자료 (FULL PICTURE) 제출요구

-유엔의 인도적 활동을 위해 이라크내 유엔센타 설치 허용 및 쿠르드 에 대한 경제봉쇄 해제 용의

6. 전망

- 주요 이사국들은 이라크측의 금일 태도로 보아 명일 회의에서도 특별한 태도변화를 기대할수 없으며 안보리의 현지 분위기가 바그다드 정부에 전달된후 그 결과를 보아가며 향후 대응방향을 강구한다는 입장임.

- 금번 회의후 별도 결의안 채택은 없으며 대신 의장성명을 발표할 예정인바, 이라크측이 계속 결의불이행을 고수할 경우에도 안보리는 현재의 경제제재를계속하는 외에 별도의 군사조치는 현재로선 고려하지 않고 있다고 함. 끝

(대사대리 신기복-국장)

첨부: UNW(F)-245

UNW(주)-245 20311 2300 첨부물
총 17매
(연일. 중동일. 기정)

STATEMENT

DELIVERED

BY

HIS EXCELLENCY TARIQ AZIZ

DEPUTY PRIME MINISTER

OF THE REPUBLIC OF IRAQ

BEFORE

THE SECURITY COUNCIL

NEW YORK

11 MARCH 1992

245-17-1

'92-03-12 12:04

*TRANSLATION*

Mr. President,

This is the first time for us to have been given the opportunity to submit our point of view before the Security Council at this level in respect of the Council's dealing with Iraq.

Military force was used against Iraq during the period from 17 January to 28 February 1991 under the umbrella of Resolution 678 adopted by the Council on 28 November 1990. Indeed, even after the cessation of military operations, some formations of our armed forces continued to receive air strikes such as those of 2 March 1991.

The whole world knows the way in which this resolution has been implemented to inflict, in a deliberate manner, a total destruction of the whole civilian infrastructure in Iraq: the roads, bridges, power plants, water treatment plants, civilian factories (including an infant-milk factory), dams, and communication centres. In addition to all of this, there was the damage and destruction inflicted on the civilian population, their properties and their residential centres, on mosques, churches, schools and colleges, hospitals and medicine stores, civilian shelters and food stuff storage buildings.

The facts of the terrible, full-scale and iniquitous destruction are now known to all fair-minded people in the world. Dozens of books and reports have been published on the subject, many documentary films made, and several symposia held in various parts of the world, including this city. I quote here Ambassador Marti Ahtisaari, the Assistant Secretary-General of the United Nations, who visited Baghdad during 10-17 March 1991 and wrote a report on the visit; the report forwarded by the Secretary-General to the President of the Security Council with a letter dated 30 March 1991. Ambassador Ahtisaari wrote: "Most means of modern life support have been destroyed or rendered tenuous. Iraq has, for some time to come, been relegated to a pre-industrial age".

-1-

245-17-2

0110

*Not only we, but also members of the Security Council, including permanent members, have said that the operations of destruction carried out had gone beyond the framework of Resolution 678 which became a political tool used to destroy a free independent country.*

*However, you are aware that Iraq informed the Council on 28 February 1991 of its acceptance to comply fully with Resolution 660 and all the other resolutions of the Security Council.*

*Then came Resolution 686 on 2 March 1991. That resolution contained a fundamental principle confirmed by the Council stating a reaffirmation of the commitment of all member-states to Iraq's independence, sovereignty and territorial integrity.*

*Having adopted this resolution, the Council moved on to formulating the grounds and measures necessary for an official ceasefire to be declared. Resolution 687 was then adopted on 3 April 1991.*

*This resolution came up with such measures and conditions as had never been precedented in the whole history of the United Nations; for these measures and conditions transcended by a large degree the initial limits and declared objectives of the Council's previous resolutions. As an independent sovereign state, Iraq stated its views about this resolution on the basis of UN Charter, international law and the principles of fairness and justice. However, the Iraqi government accepted the resolution in order to ward off the dangers threatening the people of Iraq.*

*More than eleven months have elapsed now since resolution 687 was adopted, during which Iraq has seriously endeavoured to implement its provisions. And I wish to point out in this respect that the Iraqi Minister of Foreign Affairs had sent, on 23 January 1992, a comprehensive letter in which he demonstrated in an objective manner, supported by evidence, how much Iraq had implemented of the provisions contained in the resolution. The contents of that letter, which I hope all members have read in depth, makes clear that the fundamental contents of the resolution had already been implemented.*



245-17-3

0111

Mr. President,

While I request that the contents of the comprehensive letter of the Iraqi Minister of Foreign Affairs to which I have reffered be regarded as a part connected with the contents of the present statement on the Council's assessment of the situation, I ask you to permit me to focus in some detail on certain aspects of the subject; aspects that have, since last summer, often become cause for problems and allegations thrown at Iraq without careful examination.

The weapons which Iraq is prohibited from possessing have been totally destroyed. Whatever remains, especially in the missiles and chemical ammunition fields, is being successively destroyed under the supervision of the inspection teams and according to a plan about which there is no argument between the Iraqi authorities concerned and these teams. As to the equipment used, or allegedly used, in producing those weapons, they have all been identified; for the ispection teams have visited all the factories and sites they wanted to visit, saw the equipment there, examined them and marked them with lables ensuring their non-use henceforth.

During the period from April 1991 to February 1992, 29 inspection teams visited Iraq with an overall membership of nearly 400 inspectors who spent a total of 240 days in the country; i.e. about eight months of continuous work, during which the inspection teams conducted 415 inspection operations including 127 surprise visits made without prior notice to locations spread all over Iraq, and for which they used the most advanced and sophisticated means of detection, communications, reconnaissance and transport, including the helicopters used for conducting large-scale aeria surveys over many plants of Iraq. The number of survey operations conducted with these planes was about 45, while the numer of flights made for this and other purposes was about 120, each flight lasting between 4 and 8 hours.

During this period too, US U2 reconnaissance planes conducted 32 operations over Iraq. The aerial survey and reconnaissance operations conducted by these planes took an

-3-

245-17-4

0112

'92-03-12 12:06

average of 3-4 hours each.

The various inspection teams have supervised 40 oprations of destruction of missile systems, chemical weapons, equipment and their accessories. The items already destroyed under the supervision of the inspection teams have reached a total of around 14000. These have ranged from half-manufactured parts to missiles and rocket launchers, from machines and equipment to empty chemical ammunition shells.

In addition, the Iraqi side has destroyed more than 270,000 items ranging from parts and pieces to machines and equipment, the remains of which have been examined by the inspection teams. More than 1500 tons of raw materials have also been destroyed.

The number of the various machines and equipment, which the inspection teams have put their seals on and prevented from being moved, has reached nearly one thousand, in addition to what was destroyed during the military operations, which left none of the locations of the said activities without inflicting great damage on its buildings and equipment.

The clear conclusion to be left with from all this is that Iraq is no longer in possession of any weapons, munitions or major or minor systems prohibited by Resolution 687. The equipment used, or allegedly used, in producing such items have been identified, and their use has either been frozen or turned to civilian industries or to industries not prohibited by Resolution 687. All this is taking place under the supervision of the inspection teams. This fundamental fact has been deliberately hidden from the Council with a view to keeping it in a climate of suspicion as to the position of Iraq.

Let me now address a second matter which has also been used as a pretext to raise doubts and ill-intended allegations against Iraq. Since 4 March 1991, the Iraqi authorities concerned have repatriated, in cooperation with the International Committee of the Red Cross, 6520 Kuwaiti and third-country nationals. There are now in Iraq 3594 Kuwaitis who are not detainees there, but live in freedom and are registered with the ICRC office



248-17-5

0113

in Baghdad. But the Kuwaiti authorities have agreed to the return of only 468 of them.

It is worth mentioning that while the Kuwaiti authorities which have submitted a list containing 2242 persons claimed to be in Iraq, 233 of these are proven to have been returned to Kuwait through the ICRC and 59 of them remain in Iraq awaiting approval from the Kuwaiti authorities for their return.

We have stated our position on this matter to the Council more than once, as well as to the League of Arab States from which we received an envoy who came to see the facts of the situation. The false allegation, however, that Iraq is holding Kuwaiti individuals as detainees, continues to be thrown about by certain governments, without bothering to ask themselves the obvious question: Why should Iraq do this thing? And I wish to ask: What benefit dose Iraq expect to gain from detaining one or two thousand Kuwaiti citizens when Iraq has already repatriated high-ranking Kuwaiti officers and other high officials including 20 members of the ruling family in Kuwait? In order to remove any vagueness or equivocation and reach the truth, we addressed an official note to the ICRC, on 20 February 1992, in which we requested that this whole matter be entrusted to the ICRC to take whatever measures it deems appropriate in order to determine the facts.

The same thing goes for the subject of properties. We have submitted inventories, expressed willingness to return the items, and have indeed returned great numbers and huge quantities of them. That there are other items to be returned is not an Iraqi responsibility but the responsibility of the Secretary-General's delegate entrusted to take the measures required for the properties to be received from Iraq which has reiterated its readiness to cooperate and facilitate the task.

While I find it sufficient to mention these matters in relation to the provisions of Resolution 687, I wish to reaffirm that Iraq, as it is clearly stated in the letter of the Foreign Minister of Iraq to which I have referred, has indeed fulfilled the greatest and most fundamental part of the



245-17-6

0114

provisions of the resolution in relation to the other matters addressed in sections A, B, D and H of the resolution. The implementation of the remaining provisions, which by their nature require a period of time to be fully implemented, is being carried out in the proper manner, and Iraq is extending serious and professional cooperation in order to achieve such implementation.

Mr. President

Paragraph 21 of resolution 687 stipulates that the Security Council review the provisions of paragraph 20 which provides for the continuation of the embargo in light of the implementation of the relevant resolutions of the Council, in order that the Council should determine whether to ease or lift the sanctions reffered to in the said paragraph.

The Council has continued, since it conducted its first review of Iraq's compliance in June 1991, to declare after each review that Iraq had not yet fully complied with the resolution, which meant that the embargo upon Iraq remained in place and the sufferings of 18 million Iraqis continued unmitigated.

We have sent many notes and letters to the Council, and our Permanent Representative spoke repeatedly before the Council explaining Iraq's position and the extent of its fulfillment of the provisions of Resolution 687. But all these efforts have been ignored under pressure from a small, but influential and perhaps even tyrannical, number of members in the Council. Now and again, storms of false allegations and ill-intended extremist conclusions were raised against Iraq's position on one subject or the other. The Council was repeatedly put in an atmosphere of distortion aimed to suggest non-compliance by Iraq with the provisions of the resolution. Some members of the inspection teams visiting Iraq have been selected from people linked to the intelligence services of certain countries in order to create proplems and hence keep the Council in this atmosphere of distortion.

I wish here to remind the Council that the first steps of implementing Resolution 687 were



245-17-7

0115

'92-03-12 12:08

*taken during the weeks and months immediately following the cesseation of the military operations, when Iraq was suffering bitterly from the impact of the total destruction which had left the country without electricity, communications or transport, and resulted in the destruction of its buildings, documents and other damages caused by tens of thousands of tons of explosives dropped all over Iraq. None of the parties adopting the resolution has attempted to show any understanding of, or sympathy with, the terrible tragic situation forced upon Iraq. A series of demands and decisions on the implementation of this or that paragraph of the resolution was taken in rapid succession and came hammering down regardless of the facts of the situation suffered by Iraq.*

*I am also forced here to remind the Council, and through it the international community, that the countries to which I have made referrence, did not stop at Iraq's compliance with the provisions of Resolution 687 as a condition to lifting the economic sanctions. Weeks after the resoltion had been adopted and Iraq begun implementing its provisions, those countries announced that they would not be prepared to lift the economic embargo until the political leadership of Iraq was replaced. These countries continue reiterating this precondition despite its flagrant contradiction with the principles of the UN Charter and with contents of the resolutions issued by the Council itself.*

*Thus, those states have exploited Resolution 687 to achieve political objectives not accommodated for in the resolution, in the way as they exploited Resolution 678 as I explained earlier.*

*The noisy storms new-fangled by certain elements in the inspection teams who came to serve the objectives of those countries, were exploited to issue new Council resolutions containing provisions even more extremist than those contained in Resolution 687, without regard to Iraq's difficult circumstances. the objective was to blackmail Iraq, keep the finger of accusation pointed at it, use this false and distorted climate to maintain the inquitious economic embargo imposed upon the people of Iraq, and ultimately exploit the situation in a manner that would enable the said*

-7-

245-17-8

0116

countries to issue, whenever they chose to, threats of the use of force against Iraq once again in order to accomplish the objectives envisaged by them for a change of the political system in Iraq, and indeed to complete the fulfillment of the dream to destroy Iraq.

Mr. President,

In our notes and letters to the Council, while talking to Ambassador Ekeus during his three visits to Baghdad, particularly the last visit, we have said: you keep raising doubts about this issue or that. So let us sit together at the level of experts from both the Special Commission and from Iraq, in order to review every aspect and every question. Let us discuss every subject, and we are ready to cooperate, as we have done on many occasions with the inspection teams when the Iraqi experts had the chance to sit together with the members of those teams and conducted with them scientific professional discussions in a constructive atmosphere. The Iraqi experts responded to thousands of questions put to them and provided the teams with thousands of documents of information and data requested by the teams. The most recent of such discussions were those held with the two members of the Special Commission in late January 1992 which were also most fruitful and positive.

Amongst the 29 inspection teams that have so far visited Iraq, 24 heads of such teams have issued fair and objective statements, pointing to the good cooperation extended by the Iraqi authorities and to the positive result achieved. I wish, in this respect, to refer to the positive statement recently made by Mourizio Zifferero of the tenth nuclear inspection team, in which he stressed and praised the cooperation of the Iraqi side with the inspection teams. So why don't we adopt this objective and constructive approach? And why do we keep seeing provocation and accusation restorted to? The reason is clearly political, completely ill-intended and has nothing real to do with the process of fulfilling the provisions of Resolution 687.

Mr.President,



245-17-9

0117

757 P09 WOIMUCOM 1 '92-03-12 12:10

We have come to this meeting in good faith and with a true desire to make the facts clear, reach an understanding with the Council on the matter relevant to implementing Resolution 687, clarify the matters about which doubts and allegations are raised, and to address the issues that need to be solved. Our delegation is hereby ready to clarify to the distinguished Council all relevant points which they wish to know about.

I also wish to make the following observations on a number of issues raised, particularly in the Presidential Statement recently issued by the Council on 28 February 1992:

1. Iraq is ready to continue cooperating with the Special Commission and the IAEA in order to accomplish the tasks stipulated in Resolution 687.
2. Having submitted huge amounts of data, information and documents and answered thousands of questions put by inspection teams, Iraq is ready to continue cooperating in this respect in order to complete the picture in accordance with the goals of Resolution 687.
3. Iraq is ready to reach a practical solution to the question of the Security Council verification of Iraq's capabilities to produce the weapons prohibited by resolution 687.
4. Iraq is ready to reach a practical mechanism regarding the issue of the equipment covered by the provisions of paragraph (8) of Resolution 687, with a view to rendering these equipment harmless.

Iraq is willing to do this on the basis of respect to its sovereignty and dignity and of non-infringement upon its national security, and on this basis not allowing the objectives stipulated in Resolution 687 to be turned into means of preventing our people and country from living its free normal life like all other free people in the world.

Mr. President,

On the question of completing the information and data, about which doubts and allegations continue to be raised, our delegation proposes that a technical meeting be held, at the

-9-

245-17-10

0118

earliest time convenient to the Council, between Iraqi representatives and representatives from the Special Commission, and attended by representatives from all member-states of the Security Council. The Special Commission will submit at this meeting all its demands for data and information and put all questions connected with Resolution 687. During this meeting, a comprehensive review will be made of all data, information and documentation presented by Iraq at the request of the Special Commission. Following this, a comprehensive report on the situation will be presented to the Council, with a specific period of time, in order that we may bring this issue out of the cycle of allegations, frictions, misunderstandings and ill-intended political positions, and place it in its right objective framework, so the Council can see the facts as they actually are.

Through this, the Council's demand for a full, complete and final declaration of the programmes in question will have been accomplished in scientific, objective and reliable manner.

Regarding the operations of verifying Iraq's capabilities to produce prohibited weapons in the future, we have reaffirmed our willingness to cooperate while underlining the necessity of respect to cosiderations of Iraqi sovereignity and national security. Practical arrangements should be reached within the framework of the objective identified by the Security Council. Such arrangements should not go beyond this framework to achieve political and intelligence purposes. The Special Commission has, for instance, chose to use U2 aircraft to conduct flights over Iraqi territory. This aircraft belongs to the United States of America whose adminstration has been announcing on daily basis its intention to strike at and destroy the political leadership of Iraq. Are we to accept that this aircraft is used sololy for the tasks of the Special Commission, or is it being used for intelligence purposes? We have a right here to raise doubts and apprehensions, for how can we interpret the fact that we have seen this aircraft conduct around 15 flights over Baghdad alone, each flight lasting 3-4 hours; and this operation was repeated several times within one month earlier this year? Why is it that we

-10-

0119

fail to choose another aircraft from an impartial state to operate from an Iraqi airfield with an Iraqi pilot accompanying its crew, in order that we may be satisfied that the opration will be to accomplish the objectives of Resolution 687 and not another political or intelligence objectives threatening Iraq's security? How long will these extraordinary measures continue for? Doesn't the basic principle of respect to Iraq's sovereignty and security call for a reasonable period be determined for these suspect reconnaissance operations to be brought to an end? It is imperative, therefore, that this subject be discussed in a serious and fair manner.

In order to determine the issue of ongoing monitoring in final and constructive manner, we propose that a common discussion be conducted of the plans related thereto. The inspection teams have evinced understanding of this view when we proposed it to them during their visits to Iraq.

As regards the equipment which can be modified to non-prohibited use in accordance with Resolution 687, we must ask: What is the real objective sought in Paragraph (8) of Resolution 687? Is it to prevent Iraq from becoming an industrialized country and to destroy all its industries and all the advanced industrial property in its possession. Or is the objective to verify the non-production of weapons prohibited under Resolution 687? If the first is the objective, can any people accept a situation in which it is deprived of its advanced industrial base and pushed back to the pre-industrial age which was the threat I received from the US Secretary of State during our meeting in Geneva on 9 January 1991? The people of Iraq will never accept that. But if the objective of the Council is to verify the non-use of those equipment in producing prohibited weapons on the basis of Resolution 687, then we are ready to cooperate in this regard.

The current resolutions and plans , with their general language, are capable of being used in this or that direction. What we ask is for the language to be carefully selected in the light of the objective set; and for methods of implementation and conduct to be determined for the Special Commission and the IAEA to follow, again in the light of the objective set.

-11-

245-17-12

0120

'92-03-12 12:12

It is possible that we reach a resonable formula by which the objective can be achieved, while preserving, at the same time, Iraq's legitimate rights and its sovereignty and security.

On this question, we wish to make certain points. There is an extremist approach in interpreting item (B) of Paragraph (9) of Resolution 687, which determines the mechanism of implementing Pragraph (8). This approach calls only for destruction, whereas the original paragraph allows such equipment to be rendered harmless.

The overwhelming part of the equipment and machines in question are for general use, and can only be turned to special use by attaching dies, tools and fixtures. This fact is basic knowledge to everyone involved in the field of industry. Why is it not enough to destroy these accessories and thus guarantee that machines and equipment are not turned to prohibited use? Why this insistence on the total destruction of these machines and equipment? How, for instance, can we understand the insistence on total destruction of a computer system, simply because it has been used to calculate the performance of the rocket motor, when it will be sufficient to erase the programme from the computer disc, or even destroy the disk itself? How can we interpret the destruction of ordinary cooling equipment which had been used to cool the chamber housing the rocket motor. How can we interpret the demand that building should be destroyed simply because it housed machines which were to be used in producing the dodies for the rocket motors? How can we understand the demand for the destruction of equipment that can be used in the production of the tooth-fillings and bone replacement and of testing equipment for communication and electricity network systems.

In order to solve all these matters, our delegation proposes that the Special Commission prepare a complete and final list of all the machines and equipment concerned, which the Commission proposes for destruction or for being rendered harmless. The Special Commission can do this without difficulty because it has already inventored all the machines and equipment relating to Resolution 687. The list is to be submitted to *the Security Council with representatives from Iraq attending to convey our view on whether it is or is not possible to use the equipment for prohibited purposes. If it is thought that the Council, in its present form, can not carry out this task then every member state could be represented by specialized experts capable of verifying the data and information submitted by both the Special Commission and the Iraqi representatives. Thus it will be possible to come to a decision based on objective grounds and related to the goal indentified in Resolution 687.*

*In this way, the goal can be achieved away from suspicion, allegation, and the atmosphere of tension, and away from ill-intended political objectives.*

*The Security Council has entrusted to the Special Commission certain tasks. But these tasks should remain technical in nature, and the Council should not relinquish its authority in taking the final decision on matters of a political and legal nature relating to the destiny of a free people and of the fate of such properties as this people cherishes and finds of use to helping it move towards regaining its prosperity.*

*Keeping matters vague and unresolved, preserving to the Special Commission alone the absolute power of issuing decisions means that the fate of properties belonging to the people of Iraq, indeed the very destiny, sovereignty and security of this people shall remain indefintely in the hands of a body which does not exist in the UN Charter, without allowing Iraq to have any say on the matter. Is this the objective which the Security Council set for itself by adopting its resolutions?*

*Finally, what is the position of the Security Council on the subject of the economic embargo?*

*In spite of all that has been fulfilled in the context of implementing the provisions of Resolusion 687, the Council has not budged an inch its position on the question of the embargo. Nor has the Council taken into consideration adherence to the UN Charter and international law in respect of the rights of civilian poulation.*

*Thirteen months have now gone by since we had the ceasefire and Resolution 660 on the basis of which the economic embargo was imposed, and the people of Iraq remain deprived of their right to normal life and importing all their humanitarian needs. In theory, Iraq has been allowed to import medicines and foodstuffs. But Iraqi assets in other countries continue to be frozen. Despite the fact that the Security Council had decided to authorize the countries concerned to take their own decisions to unfreeze the assets in question, most countries have failed to take such decisions, particularly the Council member-states. Iraq is not allowed, on the other hand, to export any commodity or goods whatsoever, in order that it may use the revenues made through such exports to purchase food, medicine and other humanitarian needs.*

*Iraq is a country which has made an outstanding contribution to the establishment of human civilization. The museums of London, Paris, Berlin, and New York are full of treasures highlighting the greatness of Iraqi civilization. It was from amongst the people of Iraq that Abraham, the father of all prophets, emerged to the world; and it was this people that invented writing and established the world's first legal code determining the rights and obligations of man. This people is subjected today to such injustice and such iniquity. How long will this ancient nation endure this situation for? And how long, indeed, will humanity bear to let it go for?*

*This people is prohibited from importing the chlorine it needs to sterilize its drinking water. And now demands are made that the factory producing chlorine be destroyed. Iraq is further prevented from importing or producing the materials it needs to combat such plant diseases as may claim a major share of its agricultural produce, under the pretexts that these are chemical materials which can be used in weapons production. Indeed the Sanctions Committee has gone so far as to prevent Iraq from importing even soap and detergents.*

*This people of Iraq, which has given the world, throught a history of six thousand years, philosophers, poets and men of letters, and which*



2ㅇ5-17-15

0123

established the worlds earliest university, is being prevented today from importing all of its needs of educational materials and of the paper needed to print school text-book and student note-books.

Allow me at this point to reiterate a fact underscored by Prince Sadruddin Aga Khan, the former Excutive Delegate of the Secretary-General, at a press conference held here in the United Nations building, on 22 July 1991. He said in response to a question that it would be difficult to deny the fact that Iraqi people was being punished through the economic sanctions, while this had not been the objective sought by the resolutions of the Security Council.

The question constantly asked by (18) million Iraqis, together with millions more of honest free people in the world is: For how long will this iniquitous seige continue to be imposed upon Iraq? And for how long will the Sanctions Committee continue to hold the absolute and arbitrary powers to determine the needs of Iraqi people? How can the right of veto given to five member-states since the founding of the United Nations Organization be interpreted in such a way as to be used in determining whether a people should be allowed to purchase soap, printing paper or children's toys.

You, Gentlemen, ask Iraq to implement this and comply with that; and Iraq has been fulfilling its obligations month after month. We have submitted to you a comprehensive factual report of what has been fulfilled, and expressed our willingness to cooperate on sound bases emanating from the UN Charter and from the principles of justice and fairness. What obligations has the Council, for its part, fulfilled towards the people of Iraq? The answer is: Nothing whatsoever. Even when the Council adopted a resolution formally and theoretically allowing Iraq to export limited quantities of oil in order to be able to pay for food and medical purchases, the Council included, both in the resolution itself and in its implementation plan, an endless list of preconditions, all of which infringe upon Iraq's sovereignty and security; preconditions which constitute flagrant interference in Iraq's internal affairs and which stem from ill-intended political

-15-

245-17-16

0124

*objectives. The Council imposed further preconditions which practically prevent Iraq from securing its people's needs of food and medicine.*

*We call upon the Security Council to abondon this position for an objective and fair one. We have demonstrated, in good faith, our readiness to cooperate. The Security Council ought, for its part, to show willingness to fulfill its obligations towards the people of Iraq and proceed from good faith in dealing with Iraq.*

*THANK YOU*
*MR. PRESIDENT*



245-17-17

원 본

# 외 무 부

종 별 :

번 호 : UNW-0697 일 시 : 92 0312 2030

수 신 : 장관 (연일,중동일,기정) 사본:유종하대사

발 신 : 주 유엔 대사

제 목 : 안보리-이라크 대량파괴무기 폐기

연: UNW-0687

1. 안보리회의가 3.12. 오전 속개되어 3.11. 안보리 의장 성명 및 각이사국의 질문에 대한 AZIZ 부수상의 답변을 청취하고 이사국간의 협의를 거쳐 작성된 안보리 의장 성명을 발표함.

2. 이라크 측 답변 주요 내용

가.3.11. 자 안보리의장 성명에 관한 부분

0 이라크-쿠웨이트 국경선 존중: 국경선으로 부터 1 KM 이내에 있는 이라크측 경찰초소를 1KM 밖으로 이동하는것은 문제없다고 봄.

0 무기관련 의무 (WEAPON-RELATED OBLIGATIONS)

- 안보리 결의 687 에서 규정한 화학무기등 대량파괴무기는 전부 폐기하였음.

- 무기개발계획 자료제출 요구에는 모든 계획에 대한 완전한 자료를 제출할 준비가 되어있으며 이를 위해 즉각 SCOM 및 IAEA 와 기술적인 문제를 협의 예정임.

- 무기제조 장비 및 시설 폐기관련, 결의 687 은 무기제조 목적으로 사용된 장비폐기를 규정하고 있으므로 민수용으로 개조 가능한 것은 추후 확인을 조건으로 폐기대상에서 제외되어야 함.

- 향후 대량파괴무기의 구입, 개발, 사용등을 방지하기 위한 유엔 감시 및 검증원칙을 수락하며 이를위해 SCOM 및 IAEA 와 협의를 개시하겠음.

0 외국인 억류, 실종

- ICRC 가 이라크내 감옥을 방문토록 허가하고 실종자 확인을 위한 신문광고를 게재하겠음.

0 보상문제

-국제법에 따라 공평히 보상이 청구되어야 하나 보상청구 과정에서 이라크의

국기국 장관 차관 1차보 2차보 미주국 중아국 외정실 분석관
청와대 안기부

PAGE 1

92.03.14 00:29

외신 2과 통제관 FM

0126

입장이 전연 방영되지 않았음.

0 국제 채무 및 이자

- 국제채무를 인정하나 유류 수출이 제한된 상황에서 채무를 변제할 방법이없음.

0 재산반환

- 유엔측에 충분한 협조를 제공하였음.

0 금 및 외환보유 증명

- 이라크는 식량, 의약품등 인도적인 목적의 물품구입을 위해 안보리 이사국에 유류를 수출하고 동 국가로 부터 상기 물품을 구입할것을 제안함.

0 쿠르드족등에 대한 경제봉쇄등

- 안보리 결의 688 은 국내문제 간섭으로 간주하나 그럼에도 불구 유엔의 이라크내 구호활동에 전적으로 협력중임.

- 쿠르드족에 대한 경제봉쇄 및 남부지역 사이파에 대한 억압은 사실과 다름.

나. 이사국 질문에 대한 답변

- 인도대표가 질문한 억류자 송환문제에 대해서는 ICRC 에 모든 자료를 제공하겠다고 하고 미, 영, 불이 질문한 내용에 대해서는 상기 각 부문별 답변으로 대체하거나 이와 동일한 내용의 답변을 행하고 자신의 금번 방문은 친선 (GOODWILL) 목적이며 앞으로도 매 60 일 마다 행해지고있는 안보리의 이라크 결의 이행여부 심의시 이라크 대표단 파견을 제안하였음.

3. 상기 이라크측 답변이 끝난후 미국 (PICKERING 대사)은 이라크측의 답변에서 몇가지 새로운 긍정적인 변화를 감지할수 있으나 무기 폐기관련 아직도 완전한 이행이 이루어지지 않고있으므로 말보다 행동으로 이를 증명하여 줄것을 촉구함. 영국도 이라크 측의 답변이 회피적 (EVASIVE) 이라고 발언함.

4. 안보리는 이어 잠시 정회를 가진후 다음 내용의 안보리 의장성명 (별첨)을 발표함.

- 안보리는 3.11. 자 의장성명을 전폭 지지하며 이라크 측은 안보리 결의를 완전히, 무조건적으로 준수하지 않고있음.

- 이라크 부수상이 보여준 친선이 행동으로 연결되기를 희망함.

5. 전망

- 연호 보고와 같이 안보리는 이라크측의 후속태도를 보아가며 대응방향을 강구할 예정인바 상기 회의후 가진 기자회견에서 AZIZ 부수상은 금번 방문이 만족스럽진

PAGE 2

0127

못하지만 상호 이해를 증진시킨 유용한 기회였다고 하고 앞으로 IAEA 및 SCOM 과 긴밀히 협력하겠다고 언급한 점에 비추어 이라크의 태도변화가 예상됨.

- 영국대사는 비공식적으로 이라크의 결의 불이행이 계속될 경우 다음단계는 제한적 군사조치 밖에는 없다고 언급한바 있으나 안보리는 당분간 IAEA 및 SCOM 과 이라크 측의 협력 과정을 지켜보게 될것으로 전망됨. 끝

(대사대리 신기복-국장)

첨부: UNW(F)-248

UNW(F)-248 20312 2030 첨부물 총 1매
(연안. 중동일. 기정)

The views of the Security Council, having been expressed through its President and by the statements of its members on the extent of compliance by the Government of Iraq with its obligations under the relevant Security Council resolutions, the Security Council has listened with close attention to the statement by the Deputy Prime Minister of Iraq and his responses to the questions posed by Council members.

The members of the Security Council wish to reiterate their full support for the statement made by the President of the Council on their behalf at the opening of the 3059th meeting (S/23699).

In the view of the Security Council, the Government of Iraq has not yet complied fully and unconditionally with those obligations, must do so and must immediately take the appropriate actions in this regard. It hopes that the goodwill expressed by the Deputy Prime Minister of Iraq will be matched by deeds.

0129

UNITED
NATIONS

**S**

# Security Council

PROVISIONAL

S/PV.3059 (Resumption 1)
11 March 1992

ENGLISH

PROVISIONAL VERBATIM RECORD OF THE THREE THOUSAND
AND FIFTY-NINTH MEETING (Resumption 1)

Held at Headquarters, New York,
on Wednesday, 11 March 1992, at 5.05 p.m.

| | | |
|---|---|---|
| President: | Mr. ARRIA | (Venezuela) |
| Members: | Austria | Mr. HOHENFELLNER |
| | Belgium | Mr. NOTERDAEME |
| | Cape Verde | Mr. BARBOSA |
| | China | Mr. LI Daoyu |
| | Ecuador | Mr. AYALA LASSO |
| | France | Mr. MERIMEE |
| | Hungary | Mr. ERDOS |
| | India | Mr. MENON |
| | Japan | Mr. HATANO |
| | Morocco | Mr. SNOUSSI |
| | Russian Federation | Mr. LOZINSKY |
| | United Kingdom of Great Britain and Northern Ireland | Sir David HANNAY |
| | United States of America | Mr. PICKERING |
| | Zimbabwe | Mr. MUMBENGEGWI |

This record contains the original text of speeches delivered in English and interpretations of speeches in the other languages. The final text will be printed in the Official Records of the Security Council.

Corrections should be submitted to original speeches only. They should be sent under the signature of a member of the delegation concerned, within one week, to the Chief, Official Records Editing Section, Department of Conference Services, room DC2-750, 2 United Nations Plaza, and incorporated in a copy of the record.

92-60392 8445V (E)

0130

S/PV.3059 (Resumption 1)
116-120

The meeting was resumed at 5.05 p.m.

The PRESIDENT (interpretation from Spanish): The next speaker is Mr. Hans Blix, Director General of the International Atomic Energy Agency (IAEA), to whom the Council has extended an invitation under rule 39 of its provisional rules of procedure. I invite Director Blix to take a place at the Council table and to make his statement.

Mr. BLIX: Under a series of Security Council resolutions, beginning with resolution 687 (1991), the IAEA has been mandated, working together with the Special Commission, to map nuclear programmes and facilities in Iraq intended for, or susceptible of being used for, nuclear weapons production or the production of weapons-usable material; to remove, destroy or render harmless proscribed items; and to plan and perform future ongoing monitoring and verification of Iraq's compliance with all the Security Council resolutions in the nuclear sphere. I propose to focus on the Agency's work in these three areas.

In the 11 months that have passed since the adoption of resolution 687 (1991), the IAEA has sent 10 inspection missions to Iraq, removed 12 kilograms of highly enriched unirradiated uranium from Iraq, ordered and supervised the destruction or rendering harmless of a considerable amount of proscribed equipment and prepared a plan for the long-term monitoring of permitted nuclear activities.

0131

(Mr. Blix)

This considerable activity would not have been possible without a certain amount of cooperation by Iraq, but the results would have come much faster and with much less pain if Iraq had fully and spontaneously complied with its obligations under the resolutions of the Council and the exchange of letters with the Secretary-General of the United Nations.

As described by the IAEA in the report submitted by the Secretary-General on 25 January 1992, Iraq has often followed a pattern of denial of clandestine activities until the evidence is overwhelming, followed by cooperation until the next case of concealment is revealed. The denial of activities has in many cases been accompanied by active concealment and deception. In a number of cases serious confrontation occurred when Agency inspection teams were denied the right to unrestricted access to sites or the removal of pertinent documents.

It is perfectly clear that in the face of these attitudes the IAEA could not have carried out the inspection programme and the mapping of the Iraqi nuclear programme but for the firm and consistent support of the Security Council. I should like to express the appreciation of the IAEA for this support. The present meeting of the Council is testimony to the continuation of this support in view of concrete difficulties which the Special Commission and the IAEA are currently encountering. Like several speakers this morning, I do hope that this meeting will contribute to a solution of these difficulties. I shall describe these difficulties but also briefly point to the results which have been achieved.

Important results have been obtained in the identification and mapping of Iraq's extensive efforts to acquire nuclear-weapons capability. After 10 months of work, including 10 inspections, after many sessions of intense

0132

(Mr. Blix)

questioning of Iraqi technical teams, after the screening of masses of documents and after assessment of the analytical investigations of many hundreds of samples taken in Iraq, a fairly consistent and coherent picture is emerging of the Iraqi nuclear programme. Information supplied by Iraq, often after prior lack of cooperation, has been of great importance in several ways, but the picture that we draw is by no means a simple reflection of this information; it is based on direct observation and inspection of nuclear facilities, equipment and material, on authentic documents and proven information from other countries and on our own experts' considerable experience of nuclear programmes. There are, however, still some gaps or gray areas. In view of these gaps and Iraq's track record of non-revelation, inspections need to continue. Further information obtained about sites having possible clandestine nuclear facilities must also be followed by inspection. Indeed, we do not exclude that the need for further inspections can arise even as future ongoing monitoring and verification begin.

A general shortcoming in Iraq's attitude has been the lack of full and explicit acceptance of Security Council resolutions 707 (1991) and 715 (1991). I fear that this is an expression not only of reluctance but also of resistance, which is incompatible with the binding nature of these resolutions. In raising this matter during his recent visit to the Government of Baghdad, the Chairman of the Special Commission, Ambassador Ekeus, was speaking not only for the Commission but also at the request of the IAEA. The Security Council's insistence on the matter is important, not only as a question of the authority of the Council but as a matter that underlies the many specific points of non-compliance that we noted. A detailed list of such points was prepared by the IAEA in document S/23514, now supplemented and updated by information in document S/23687.

0133

(Mr. Blix)

While, as the Deputy Prime Minister of Iraq said, the IAEA noted some improvements in the attitudes of the Iraqi authorities in the course of recent IAEA inspections, lack of cooperation and non-compliance still persist in the provision of information concerning sources of procurement of critical material and equipment. This information is of great significance since in many cases it is the only means for independent verification of the correctness of Iraqi statements and is basic to future monitoring. Further, the initial information needed to establish the future ongoing plan for monitoring and verification, required to be supplied by Iraq under resolution 715 (1991), has been provided only in a partial and incomplete way. The Deputy Prime Minister of Iraq referred this morning to the readiness of his Government to cooperate to solve current difficulties. A statement by Iraq of readiness to provide procurement information and to complete the information required under resolution 705 (1991) would eliminate important hurdles.

I now turn to the question of removal, destruction or rendering harmless of proscribed nuclear items. A large part of the Iraqi nuclear facilities, including most of the facilities known to us to have been used in the nuclear-weapons development programme, was either fully destroyed or heavily damaged in the course of the Gulf War. This has been true in the case of Tuwaitha, the main research-and-development centre of the Iraqi nuclear programme; of Tarmiya, the industrial complex for electro-magnetic isotope separation (EMIS) enriched uranium production; of Ash Sharqat, the intended second site for EMIS industrial-scale activities; of Al Jesirah, the large chemical complex, where the natural uranium feed material for enrichment activities was produced, and of Al Quaim, where uranium concentrates from indigenous uranium-bearing phosphate ores were produced.

0134

(Mr. Blix)

In addition, by admission of the Iraqi authorities, a number of items such as components and equipment were subsequently damaged or destroyed by the Iraqi military in an attempt to remove evidence of the clandestine nuclear programme. In spite of this extensive destruction there are still sites, facilities, equipment and material which suffered little or no damage and therefore fall into the category of items requiring destruction, removal or rendering harmless under resolution 687 (1991).

This is the case of the Al Atheer site, specificially designed for weaponization activities, and of some buildings in Tarmiya and Ash Sharqat. In addition, some of the equipment, machine tools and materials, with little or no repair or modification, might be useful to Iraq should it seek to resurrect its nuclear-weapons programme.

The issue of destruction, removal and rendering harmless has been discussed at length between the IAEA and the Special Commission, and we are agreed to implement these activities on the basis of a common approach.

Progress to date in this area of destruction, removal or rendering harmless can be summarized as follows:

First, the removal of highly enriched uranium suitable for direct use in nuclear weapons has been given high priority. This material, in the form of fresh and irradiated fuel elements for the Iraqi research reactors, has been in the custody of the Agency since the first inspection, in May 1991. All the fresh fuel was removed from Iraq last November. Negotiations are being held with French and British companies to remove the remaining irradiated fuel, for which adequate funding is still required.

(Mr. Blix)

Secondly, a large number of components of calutrons and ultracentrifuges relevant to the production of enriched uranium have been assembled and destroyed under the supervision of the Agency.

Thirdly, hot cells, glove boxes, remote-handling manipulators and other equipment used in research activities for laboratory-scale separation of plutonium from irradiated fuel have been destroyed or rendered harmless. Dedicated equipment and machine tools used in the manufacturing of these components have also been destroyed.

Fourthly, dual-use items - that is, equipment and machine tools which, in principle, could be utilized in non-prohibited as well as prohibited activities - are being inventoried and placed under Agency seal. The destruction or release of these items is being dealt with on a case-by-case basis. Obviously, release of any such items will only be made provided that there can be effective future monitoring of their agreed-upon use.

Fifthly, buildings such as laboratories, plants and other facilities where research and development, production or testing directly relevant to activities prohibited under resolution 687 (1991) were conducted are currently being assessed for destruction. This is, for instance, the case of Al Atheer. A complete inventory of such facilities is being prepared. Any request for use in non-proscribed activities would have to be evaluated in the light of the possibility of effective monitoring of agreed-upon use.

Although the Agency has not so far met with resistance on the part of Iraq to its request for destruction, removal or rendering harmless of proscribed material, facilities or equipment, we are keenly aware that the

(Mr. Blix)

Special Commission has encountered such resistance. The Security Council's support for the authority of the Special Commission and of the IAEA to determine what is to be destroyed, removed or rendered harmless and Iraq's corresponding duty to accept and to implement such requests is, therefore, much appreciated. The elimination of facilities and equipment that would be of use in a resurrection of the clandestine nuclear programme is clearly of great importance.

0137

(Mr. Blix)

Large facilities and large amounts of equipment required for the production of nuclear-weapons-usable material and nuclear weapons by Iraq have been destroyed, removed or rendered harmless. New facilities cannot easily be built without detection, and the import or production of new relevant equipment will meet great obstacles. What certainly remains in Iraq, however, is a large number of highly trained scientists and engineers who were engaged in its nuclear programme. Information supplied to our inspection teams suggests that these people are currently engaged in the civilian reconstruction of the country. Needless to say, it is important that these highly qualified cadres remain engaged in non-proscribed activities.

To conclude, it is essential that the measures prescribed by the Council for Iraq succeed, not only to allay fears about Iraq reviving a programme of weapons of mass destruction, notably nuclear weapons, but also to demonstrate that international verification is a viable means to create confidence. That experience is necessary if actions taken in Iraq are to represent steps towards the goal of establishing in the Middle East a zone free of weapons of mass destruction, as envisaged in paragraph 14 of resolution 687 (1991). The IAEA is committed to successful implementation of the Council's resolutions on Iraq and looks to the Security Council for guidance and support in its efforts to contribute to this result.

The PRESIDENT (interpretation from Spanish): The next speaker is Mr. Rolf Ekeus, Executive Chairman of the Special Commission, to whom the Council has extended an invitation under rule 39 of its provisional rules of procedure. I invite him to take a place at the Council table and to make his statement.

0138

Mr. EKEUS: The Special Commission has one fundamental aim. That aim is to be in the position to report to the Security Council as soon as possible that Iraq has met in full all its obligations under section C of resolution 687 (1991) as elaborated upon in resolutions 707 (1991) and 715 (1991). The speed with which the Special Commission can carry out its responsibilities and report to the Council that its task is successfully and fully executed does not lie solely within the Commission's control. It is determined by the degree of cooperation which is received from Iraq and the openness and transparency of that State.

Let me examine the cooperation, openness and transparency which is required in relation to the provision of information to which the Deputy Prime Minister referred this morning. Iraq claims to have provided all the necessary information. But this is not the case. Iraq has indeed given information. However, this information is neither complete nor systematized. The Commission has evidence of the continued existence and concealment of undeclared weapons and the means of their delivery. Iraq has not provided the full, final and complete disclosure of all aspects of its prohibited programmes as required under resolution 707 (1991). The very fact that Iraq has not even acknowledged resolution 707 (1991) undermines the credibility of the information it has provided.

In that context, it must be stated that it is very difficult for the Special Commission to carry out a dialogue with Iraq if such a dialogue must be carried out under the cloud of Iraq's outright refusal to give full, final and complete disclosure in accordance with the language of resolution 707 (1991).

The credibility of Iraq is further reduced by the failure to furnish the documentary and material evidence necessary to verify the information.

0139

(Mr. Ekeus)

Instead of full, final and complete disclosure, Iraq has proposed a dialogue in which the Special Commission would seek to elicit the information from Iraq through an inquisitorial approach. Such an approach shifts the onus of seeking and compiling the information onto the Commission, whereas the Council's decisions properly place that onus on Iraq. It is Iraq which has in its possession the full information, not the Special Commission.

Thus, Iraq must provide, first, all information on the evolution of the programmes and the links between all the elements in each programme; secondly, all information on procurement to support the programmes, including a detailed year-by-year breakdown of production and imports, and their sources; thirdly, full records of the use of all relevant weapons and components thereof; fourthly, credible detailed information on items destroyed unilaterally by Iraq - I shall come back to that point; and, fifthly, sufficient credible supporting documentation and physical evidence for all declarations made by Iraq.

Just this morning in his statement before the Security Council, the Deputy Prime Minister of Iraq declared that Iraq has destroyed more than 270,000 items unilaterally. The Special Commission has requested, but not received from Iraq, the list fully accounting for all these items, which clearly relate to proscribed programmes. In the view of the Special Commission, the unilateral destruction by Iraq of these items is not in conformity with resolution 687 (1991), which provided for disposal of prohibited items only under international supervision. The number of items involved indicates that many gaps remain in the picture of Iraq's prohibited-weapons programmes. It is up to Iraq to fill those gaps by complying with the requirements of resolution 707 (1991) to provide a full, final and complete disclosure of its proscribed programmes.

0140

S/PV.3059 (Resumption 1)
129-130

(Mr. Ekeus)

Concerning the Special Commission's responsibility for the destruction, removal or rendering harmless of Iraq's weapons and capabilities in the proscribed areas, I have to state that the destruction of weapons already declared by Iraq is now under way with the cooperation of the Iraqi authorities - and that cooperation has been good.

0141

(Mr. Ekeus)

With regard to the disposal of the capabilities for the production of such weapons we are, however, in another situation. It will be recalled that under paragraph 9 (b) (ii) of Security Council resolution 687 (1991) Iraq is required to destroy, under the supervision of the Special Commission, all its proscribed missile capabilities, including launchers and repair and production facilities.

As members of the Council know, a ballistic missile team recently had to be withdrawn from Iraq because of the refusal of the authorities in Iraq to proceed with the destruction of certain missile-producing capabilities. These had been identified for destruction by the Special Commission after a long process of exchanges with Iraq and careful and thorough consideration, on a case-by-case basis, of every request made by Iraq. As a result, a final decision was made by the Special Commission and a list of items was communicated to Iraq in a letter dated 14 February 1992 (S/23673).

Iraq is continuing to refuse to comply with this decision and seeks to confuse the issue, despite the statement of the President of the Security Council dated 28 February 1992 on behalf of all the members of the Council, which clearly reaffirmed that it is for the Special Commission alone to determine which items must be destroyed under paragraph 9 of resolution 687 (1991).

For some months now the Special Commission has discussed and has notified Iraq of how it intends to proceed in the matter of the destruction, removal or rendering harmless of Iraq's capabilities for producing weapons of mass destruction. Iraq has sought to argue that nearly every building and every piece of equipment which has been devoted to its proscribed-weapons programmes should be kept and should be converted to what it has said would be

(Mr. Ekeus)

civilian use. Iraq has argued that otherwise the Special Commission would be depriving the country of its civilian industrial base. This argument does not stand up to even the most cursory examination. There is not a single structure or item which is or will be earmarked for destruction that has formed part of Iraq's civilian industrial base. These structures and items have been devoted to the production of weapons of mass destruction and not to the production of articles for civilian use. The Special Commission would be failing in its responsibilities to the Security Council if it did not ensure that items used by Iraq for production of weapons of mass destruction were either destroyed, removed or rendered harmless. In this latter sense, the items must be modified to such a degree that they no longer possess specific features that render them capable of use by Iraq in prohibited activities or amenable to reconversion.

Thus we come to the third stage of the Special Commission's responsibilities, and that is the ongoing monitoring and verification of Iraq's compliance with its obligations under section C of Security Council resolution 687 (1991). In this case, the existence of an impasse is now amply confirmed. By its resolution 715 (1991), adopted in October 1991, the Security Council approved plans for ongoing monitoring and verification submitted by the Secretary-General and by the Director General of the International Atomic Energy Agency (IAEA). Since November, the official position of Iraq has been that stated in a letter to the President of the Council from the Minister for Foreign Affairs of Iraq. This position was reaffirmed to the Special Commission at the end of January 1992. That letter states that the plans are aimed at objectives incompatible with the letter and spirit of the United Nations Charter, the norms of international law, and international and humanitarian pacts and covenants. Most recently -

0143

(Mr. Ekeus)

during my visit to Baghdad - Iraq has said that the statement does not amount to a rejection of the plans. However, the Special Commission cannot understand it otherwise than as rejection, in the light of the language to which I just referred. The rejection by Iraq is confirmed by the fact that Iraq has so far failed to file with the Special Commission two declarations which were required under the Commission' plans in November 1991 and January 1992. Without these declarations, which would provide the basic information required to set up a satisfactory monitoring regime, such monitoring which would comply with the Security Council's requirement, cannot be instituted.

Iraq has argued that the plans infringe upon its independence, sovereignty and national security. However, the plans have been formulated on the basis of existing international norms and those currently under negotiation for the forthcoming international convention on the elimination of chemical weapons, which is intended to have universal application.

To the extent that general provisions in the plans appear intrusive, this is in large measure a result of the conduct of Iraq. The intrusive elements were approved by the Security Council against a background of concealment, movement of proscribed items and violation of the privileges and immunities of inspection teams which are well known to the Council. If Iraq cooperates, the intrusive elements will not need to be invoked; in any event, the Special Commission and the International Atomic Energy Agency have no need to excuse or justify plans which have the unanimous endorsement of the Council in its resolution 715 (1991), adopted under Chapter VII of the United Nations Charter.

Prompt and successful implementation of all the stages of the work of the Special Commission and of the IAEA require that their facilities, privileges

(Mr. Ekeus)

and immunities are fully implemented. These facilities, privileges and immunities flow from the Council resolutions, from relevant international conventions to which Iraq is party, and from the express provisions of the status agreement between the United Nations and Iraq which entered into force on 14 May 1991.

To take one example, from the beginning Iraq has interposed difficulties in regard to the operations and landing rights of United Nations aircraft in Iraq. These difficulties continue, and, where landing rights are concerned, all the Special Commission's approaches to resolve them are met with silence. This should not continue if Iraq has a real interest in the full cooperation necessary to expedite implementation of section C of Security Council resolution 687 (1991)

(Mr. Ekeus)

The Deputy Prime Minister also referred to high-altitude aircraft operations over Iraq. I have to remind him that in resolution 707 (1991) the Council specifically approved such aerial surveillance. The aircraft is provided to the Special Commission by a Member State. A large number of Governments provide us with information and logistical support. The Special Commission makes use of personnel from many countries: so far we have used inspectors and technical experts from 35 countries. We also use helicopters and a heavy transport capability provided by one Government.

The aerial surveillance flights are undertaken with the full control and command of the Special Commission. It is the Special Commission that indicates which areas shall be covered. It is correct that a large number of such flights have taken place over the Baghdad area. There is a very simple explanation. In the vicinity of Baghdad there is a large number of facilities to which resolution 687 (1991) relates. It goes without saying, that the pilot carries a United Nations certificate, that the plane is provided with United Nations insignia and that Iraq is notified in advance of each flight, both of the time-frame within which the flight is to take place and the point of entry and the point of departure from Iraqi territory.

The special mission headed by me which was sent to Iraq recently under the Council's aegis to secure unconditional agreement by Iraq to implement all its relevant obligations under resolutions 687 (1991), 707 (1991) and 715 (1991) failed to obtain that agreement. The failure by Iraq to provide it resulted in the condemnation and warning contained in the statement of 28 February 1992 by the President of the Council on behalf of the Council

0146

(Mr. Ekeus)

members. The Commission must act in accordance with the resolutions of the Council and the statements of its President on behalf of its members. It cannot negotiate away any of the provisions of the resolutions, the statements or the plans approved by resolution 715 (1991), for instance.

In the absence of the undertaking by Iraq to comply fully with the Council's decisions, and until practical experience is gained to confirm that such an undertaking is being honoured, the Special Commission will be seriously hindered in the phases of its operations concerning the identification and destruction of prescribed items and it will be precluded from instituting the ongoing monitoring and verification phase. In such a situation the possibility of the Special Commission's certifying Iraq's compliance with its obligations under section C of resolution 687 (1991) does not even arise.

The PRESIDENT (interpretation from Spanish): The next speaker is the representative of Kuwait. I invite him to take a place at the Council table and to make his statement.

Mr. ABULHASAN (Kuwait) (interpretation from Arabic): I am pleased on behalf of the State of Kuwait to congratulate you, Sir, on presiding over the Security Council's work for this month. We know you as a seasoned diplomat representing a friendly country with which we share many interests, a country which works with Kuwait for peace based on justice throughout the world. We are confident that you will be successful in conducting the Council's business.

I should also like to extend our thanks to our friend, Ambassador Thomas Pickering, Permanent Representative of the United States, for his presidency of the Security Council last month.

0147

(Mr. Abulhasan, Kuwait)

The Council is meeting today to consider Iraq's compliance in implementing the provisions of resolution 687 (1991). At this meeting, which is attended by a high-level delegation from the Iraqi regime, the Council also aims to examine Iraqi's claims to have implemented that resolution and therefore to have the right to the benefits outlined in the resolution to be given when it is fully implemented.

Kuwait is the main party whose rights are enshrined in the operative paragraphs of the resolution, for whose implementation specific responsibilities rest upon the Iraqi regime. Kuwait wishes objectively and impartially, and with a sense of historic responsibility towards the people of Kuwait, its interests, security and stability, and towards the security and stability of the region, wishes to make the following points.

First, resolution 687 (1991) is binding on Iraq for two reasons. The first is that the resolution was adopted under Chapter VII of the Charter and under its umbrella and therefore is binding not only on Iraq, as a main and immediate party, but also on all the other countries of the world. Secondly, the Iraqi legislature, the National Assembly, accepted resolution 687 (1991) unconditionally, thus negating all reservations and remarks made by Iraq in its preliminary letter of acceptance, which the Security Council rejected.

The second point is that, for all the reasons I have given, Iraq has become absolutely bound to implement resolution 687 (1991), without any negotiation concerning its provisions or any interpretation by Iraq of them. Implementation is, however, to be in accordance with the interpretations, mechanisms and reports prepared by the Secretary-General of the United Nations and approved by the Security Council.

0148

(Mr. Abulhasan, Kuwait)

Thirdly, a follow-up of Iraq's conduct and its behaviour in regard to the operative paragraphs of resolution 687 (1991) demonstrates that it has reneged on its absolute acceptance of the resolution and that it is attempting to evade the obligations based upon the interpretation of these operative paragraphs, under the pretext used by the Iraqi regime in its preliminary letter of acceptance of resolution 687 (1991) - which, again, the Security Council rejected at that time.

The following remarks are made because they form the general background governing the implementation by Iraq of the provisions of resolution 687 (1991). I shall give examples of what I have just said, in relation to questions that concern Kuwait exclusively, in particular in resolution 687 (1991), by making these points:

I turn first to the question of prisoners of war and missing persons who are Kuwaiti or third-country nationals.

First, paragraphs 2 (c) and 3 (c) of resolution 686 (1991) and paragraph 30 of resolution 687 (1991) provide for the immediate release of all prisoners of war and detainees who belong to Kuwait or who are third-country nationals and request the assistance of the International Committee of the Red Cross (ICRC) in this regard.

Second, immediately following the cease-fire, and with the assistance of the ICRC, the Iraqi regime set free 6,920 prisoners and detainees who were Kuwaiti or who were third-country nationals.

Third, a large number of prisoners and detainees who are Kuwaiti or are third-country nationals are still in Iraq's prisons and detention camps. Full lists of their names were presented to the ICRC last September. Iraq, however, has never responded to the repeated requests of the ICRC to be

0149

(Mr. Abulhasan, Kuwait)

allowed to visit them and register their names. Many meetings were held. Some of them took place between coalition representatives and three representatives of the Iraqi regime, in the presence of the Red Cross; and others, between the Red Cross and representatives of the Iraqi regime. These meetings resulted in these main requests made to Iraq on 16 October 1991: publication of Kuwaiti and Saudi lists of all missing persons in all Iraqi media and at various times; and visits in all freedom by the International Committee of the Red Cross to detention camps in Iraq, in accordance with standard procedures of the ICRC. The Iraqi response to these requests, on 12 November, was incompatible with the requests. It was therefore officially rejected by the representatives of the coalition forces. Publication in only one Iraqi newspaper is not sufficient. A single visit by the ICRC to each detention camp and prison, with prior notification, is inconsistent with the rules. Moreover, resolution 686 (1991) and 687 (1991) provide no basis or support for the principle of reciprocity regarding the procedures governing this case.

Fourth, throughout this period, the ICRC has received no information as to the whereabouts of the persons reported missing. Nor has it received any detailed and documented information on the search operations launched by the Iraqi authorities. The ICRC is also still awaiting information on persons who died during the detention.

Fifth, the ICRC, in paragraph 15 of its report to the Secretary-General in document S/23514, expressed its regret that it had been unable to reach an agreement.

Sixth, Iraq submitted to the ICRC a list containing the names of 3,700 persons alleged by Iraq to be Kuwaitis wishing to return to Kuwait. On

0150

(Mr. Abulhasan, Kuwait)

the other hand, the Red Cross said it could not confirm their nationalities, and these persons are claiming that they lived in Kuwait and have expressed a desire to go back to their former place of residence. These persons are now living in various places in Iraq and enjoying freedom of movement inside Iraqi territory. Some of them do not fall into the category of detained prisoners envisaged in resolutions 686 (1991) and 687 (1991) but, rather, fall into the category of "family reunion". Kuwait has accepted each and every one of them who fall into that category, but it has rejected the rest of them because they are not Kuwaitis and do not fall into the category of "reunion"; or their names were not listed in the civil record, the Kuwaiti census which was deposited with the United Nations and which includes the names of all Kuwaitis and others who had lived in Kuwait until 1 August 1990 - that is, one day before the Iraqi invasion of Kuwait.

The Iraqi authorities are attempting to give world public opinion the illusion that the Government of Kuwait does not want its sons back. Kuwait, that kind, loving mother, would in no circumstances ever reject any of its sons. But we cannot accept that persons who have nothing to do with Kuwait should be planted in Kuwait. It is well known that when Iraq committed its aggression against Kuwait it confiscated many passports and identity cards of Kuwaitis and forged all of them to bear the names of those whom it wanted to plant in Kuwait so that they could sow the seeds of dissension.

Seventh, on 28 February 1992, four and a half months after the presentation to Iraq, through the ICRC, of the coalition proposals regarding the publication of names in newspapers and the visits to prisons and detention camps in all freedom, the Foreign Minister of the Iraqi regime sent a letter

0151

(Mr. Abulhasan, Kuwait)

in which he accepted these conditions. As a matter of fact, this acceptance was belated and, at the same time, was a conditioned acceptance. The letter from the Foreign Minister of the Iraqi regime was based on the allegation that Iraq had implemented paragraphs 2 (c) and 3 (c) of Security Council resolution 686 (1991) and paragraph 30 of resolution 687 (1991). As is known, those Security Council resolutions demand the return of all prisoners and detainees. They do not talk about an intention to return them, let alone agreement to publish their names or arrange for visits to prisons and detention camps in order to locate them.

(Mr. Abulhasan, Kuwait)

With that rationale the Iraqi régime is attempting to give the Security Council the false impression that it has met its obligations with regard to Kuwaiti detainees and third-country nationals.

Through you, Mr. President, I wish to put two questions to the representative of the Iraqi régime on the matter of these prisoners. First, why will Iraq not accept the standard rules and procedures of the ICRC with respect to visits to prisons and Iraqi detention camps? Secondly, why has Iraq not yet given a serious response to specific cases set out in the comprehensive files on Kuwaiti and Saudi prisoners of war submitted as early as last October?

These innocent Kuwaitis and their families and these third-country nationals are pinning their hopes on this meeting; they expect the Council to shoulder its responsibility to help them overcome the suffering they have experienced since their detention. We ask the Council to make the Iraqi regime accept its responsibilities just as the Iraqi regime asks the international community to understand the suffering of the Iraqi people - suffering ultimately due to the policies of that very regime. We in Kuwait and in other countries whose nationals remain in Iraqi prisons and detention camps call on the international community to understand the suffering of those detainees and to put pressure on the Iraqi regime to facilitate the ICRC mission, in accordance with standard Red Cross procedures, to locate them, to release them, to ensure their repatriation or to determine their fate.

Kuwait wishes to take this opportunity to express its gratitude to the ICRC for the humanitarian role it has played, and to commend its efforts, which have thus far been fruitless owing to the Iraqi regime's obduracy. We call upon the Council to help the ICRC accomplish its lofty mission.

0153

(Mr. Abulhasan, Kuwait)

I turn now to the demarcation of the boundary between Iraq and Kuwait. In his report of 2 May 1991, on the basis of which the Iraq-Kuwait Boundary Demarcation Commission was established, in accordance with paragraph 3 of resolution 687 (1991), the Secretary-General specified the Commission's tasks and course of action, and determined that its decisions would be final. Consequently, the substantive work carried out by the Iraq-Kuwait Boundary Demarcation Commission represents a legal demarcation of the international boundary which is binding on both parties. Moreover, the Security Council in paragraph 4 of its resolution 687 (1991), which is legally binding on Iraq, decided to guarantee the inviolability of the boundary as demarcated.

Kuwait notes that Iraq's delegation in the Commission has participated in the majority of its work, contributed to formulating the Commission's internal rules of procedure and shared in preparing the records and reports of its meetings. That is further evidence of Iraq's acceptance of the binding nature of the Commission's decisions. While Kuwait is of the view that the work of the Boundary Demarcation Commission is progressing in a constructive, if very slow, manner, some statements and comments made by the representative of Iraq during Commission meetings, which appear to have been based on instructions from his Government, make us doubt the seriousness of Iraq's commitment to the binding nature of the work of the Commission, and make us wonder about Iraq's intentions with respect to that work - especially since the main objective of the Commission is to guarantee stability and security along the border. In that connection, I draw the attention of the Council to two paragraphs of an official intervention in which, during a meeting held in Geneva in August 1991, the Iraqi representative rejected, completely and in detail, the establishment by the Secretary-General of the Iraq-Kuwait Boundary Demarcation Commission.

0154

(Mr. Abulhasan, Kuwait)

That and other positions do not further or conform to Iraq's obligations under resolution 687 (1991). Through you, Mr. President, I should like to ask a specific question of the representative of the Iraqi regime: What is the meaning of that statement made by your representative in the Boundary Demarcation Commission, particularly the part at the conclusion referring to Iraq's objection to the whole process from the outset and describing the Commission as a strange creature?

The presence of that Iraqi statement in the meeting records of the Boundary Demarcation Commission is further demonstration of Iraq's lack of commitment to resolution 687 (1991). Therefore, clarifying Iraq's position on this question is of the utmost importance to the security and stability of the entire region. For our part, we reiterate our full respect for and commitment to all decisions of the Boundary Demarcation Commission. We should like also to express our appreciation for the scientific and professional methods used by the Commission and for the neutrality and objectivity with which it is conducting its business.

I turn now to the return of stolen Kuwaiti property. Since 26 March 1991, when the Secretary-General appointed an official responsible for coordinating the return of Kuwaiti property stolen by the Iraqi regime, Kuwait has submitted detailed lists of property stolen from 25 ministries, institutions and government establishments. Some of this property was included in inventory lists prepared by the Iraqi occupying authhorities and found after the expulsion of the Iraqi forces from Kuwait.

The special coordinator appointed by the Secretary-General, and his staff, are to be commended for their notable efforts to return the property which Iraq declared its willingness to return. Property belonging to the

(Mr. Abulhasan, Kuwait)

following institutions has been returned: the Central Bank of Kuwait, the Central Library of Kuwait, the National Museum of Kuwait, the Kuwait News Agency and Kuwait Airways Corporation. Some aircraft and military helicopters have also been returned. Some other property belonging to the Ministries of Defence and Health are being returned; the modalities of the return are being set up. It must be said, however, that most of the property was deliberately destroyed.

Kuwait has several points to make on this subject.

First, to date the Iraqi authorities have not commented on the fate of property belonging to other ministries and government institutions.

Secondly, the Iraqi authorities have officially rejected their liability for the return of property stolen from the private sector. The value of this property is estaimated to exceed hundreds of millions of dollars.

0156

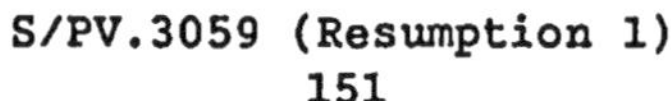

(Mr. Abulhassan, Kuwait)

Some of these were stolen and removed to Iraq under inventory lists prepared by Iraqi ministries, accompanied by the signatures and seals of governmental agencies that had come to Kuwait to supervise the operations of theft and transport. We have some of the photocopies and some of the originals left by the Iraqi regime after it had been expelled.

If Iraq does not complete the return of both public and private property, it will be in violation of the provisions of resolutions 686 (1991) and 687 (1991). It is liable for compensation of properties destroyed during the theft and return operations.

Having reviewed the extent of Iraq's compliance with the provisions relevant to Kuwait of resolutions 686 (1991) and 687 (1991), I should like to add the following points, which demonstrate Iraq's lack of seriousness for the letter and spirit of those resolutions.

First, the Secretary-General said in his report on the United Nations Iraq-Kuwait Observation Mission (UNIKOM)

> "The continued presence of Iraqi police posts on the Kuwaiti side of the line shown on UNIKOM'S map remains a matter of concern. I have instructed the Chief Military Observer of UNIKOM to persevere in his efforts to have these police posts pulled back behind the line."
> (S/23106, para. 35)

Despite the efforts made by UNIKOM, Iraq still insists on keeping these posts, and informed Major-General Greindl that it would not pull back the posts because of the political implications resulting therefrom.

There is no question that the continued presence of the seven Iraqi police posts inside Kuwaiti territory represents a violation by Iraq of Kuwait's sovereignty and territorial integrity. Moreover, Iraq's stubborn refusal to remove the posts contravenes its announced commitment to cooperate

0157

(Mr. Abulhassan, Kuwait)

with UNIKOM. The Iraqi position as such cannot be described as full compliance with resolution 687 (1991).

Secondly, Iraq still rejects resolutions 706 (1991) and 712 (1991), which authorized the export of $1.6 billion of Iraqi oil to finance the purchase of foodstuffs and medicines and to pay its contribution to the compensation fund as laid down in a main paragraph of resolution 687 (1991).

Such intransigence and rejection on the part of Iraq of the two aforementioned resolutions is harmful to the Iraqi people and adds to their pain and suffering. That attitude is a denial of the rights of large numbers of people affected by the Iraqi invasion and aggression against Kuwait, who would benefit from the compensation fund.

The nationals of many countries have been affected by Iraq's refusal to accept resolutions 706 (1991) and 712 (1991). These continued practices by Iraq represent a major violation of resolution 687 (1991), which gave rise to reparations and the establishment of a compensation fund and its financing mechanism.

The most blatant example of Iraq's violation of Security Council resolutions is the fact that it declines to reveal, destroy and accept the monitoring of all stockpiles of weapons of mass destruction.

In the final paragraphs of his report, the Secretary-General made it perfectly clear that Iraq has thus far failed to meet its obligations. This grave situation implies two risks: the continued aggressive intentions of that regime towards its neighbours and towards security and peace in the region; and the intent to make use of such capabilities, if they escaped destruction, the Iraqi regime having decided to reveal its intention of rejecting the remaining provisions of resolutions 687 (1991) and of reneging on everything it had accepted. The Iraqi regime's record is replete

(Mr. Abulhassan, Kuwait)

with broken promises. Its abrogation of the Algiers Agreement with Iran and its eight-year war with that country bear witness to the nature of this regime, its promises and the extent of its respect for its commitments.

In this meeting the Council is called upon in the presence of the Iraqi high-level delegation to guarantee that peace and security in the area are not obstructed by the capricious, aggressive nature of this regime.

Guarantees that deter the regime's capability of aggression are a victory for peace, security and stability in the region and will render a service to the people of Iraq and promote security and prosperity for all the peoples in the area.

The PRESIDENT (interpretation from Spanish): I thank the representative of Kuwait for his kind words addressed to me.

I shall now set aside a period exclusively for directing questions at His Excellency Mr. Tariq Aziz, Deputy Prime Minister of Iraq, who, in accordance with his request of this morning, will deal with these questions at the meeting tomorrow morning.

Sir David HANNAY (United Kingdom): I listened with very great care this morning to the lengthy statement made by the Deputy Prime Minister of Iraq. While I was somewhat disappointed that it did not reflect a more wholehearted response to the unanimous view of this Council, which is seeking to achieve full compliance by Iraq of its obligations, I nevertheless would welcome the opportunity to ask one or two questions about various sections of his statement. I noted that he referred to a quotation from the report by Mr. Ahtisaari about Iraq having been propelled back into the pre-industrial age. I am only bound to say that at the time Mr. Ahtisaari wrote that report,

0159

S/PV.3059 (Resumption 1)
154-155

(Sir David Hannay, United Kingdom)

and entirely unbeknownst to him, Iraq was in fact still pursuing a nuclear weapons programme, which is not normally an appurtenance of a State in the pre-industrial age.

0160

(Sir David Hannay, United Kingdom)

Now, a number of the questions related to the weapons of mass destruction are very important and of great concern to the Council. The first question I would like to ask the Deputy Prime Minister to consider is whether the four points on page 9 of the English text of his statement are completely unconditional and unqualified, or whether the 8 lines of text below the four points are in fact the left hand taking away what the right hand has just given. I think it is extremely important that the Council should know that these four undertakings are entirely unqualified and unconditional.

My second question in this connection would relate to point four of those four points, where it is stated that Iraq is ready to reach a practical mechanism regarding the issue of the equipment covered by the provisions of paragraph 8 of resolution 687 (1991). I would like to ask whether the fact that this reference is only to paragraph 8, which refers to chemical and biological weapons and ballistic missiles but not to nuclear materials and nuclear matters, which are dealt with in paragraph 12, is a deliberate omission or simply an oversight? It is obviously a matter of some considerable significance if this undertaking does not relate to nuclear matters, as it appears not to do on the face of the text.

Then, I would like to address the ideas put forward by the Deputy Prime Minister for involving the Council in discussions about the handling of weapons of mass destruction. I think it must be clear from what was read out by our President at the beginning, and in particular from the statement by the Council on 28 February, that the view of the Council is that it is not the business of the Council to get involved in the detailed decisions that have to be taken by the Special Commission and the International Atomic Energy Agency (IAEA). But I would like to assured - and this is the point of my

0161

(Sir David Hannay, United Kingdom)

question - that if, as a result of further contacts between the Deputy Prime Minister and his delegation and the Special Commission and the IAEA, certain determinations and decisions are taken by the Special Commission and the IAEA, Iraq will accept those decisions and determinations as fully binding and will implement them? That is also very important for the Council to know.

On matters outside the scope of the weapons of mass destruction section of Security Council resolution 687 (1991), the Deputy Prime Minister referred to a number of products which it was impossible to import into Iraq because of lack of funds, and I would like to ask the Deputy Prime Minister whether, if the Council - as my delegation hopes it will - renews resolutions 706 (1991) and 712 (1991), the Government of Iraq will be prepared to resume the contacts with the Secretariat which it was holding in the months of December and January with a view to implementing a scheme which would enable humanitarian supplies to reach the people of Iraq.

And finally, I would like to express the extreme regret of my delegation that the Deputy Prime Minister did not at any moment address Iraq's obligations under Security Council resolution 688 (1991). These are serious matters which have given great concern to the Council, which has noted a risk to international peace and security arising from the way in which the population of the north and the south of Iraq was treated last year, and I would like to ask the question as to when the Government of Iraq intends to lift the economic blockade on a part of its country so that any humanitarian supplies which are sent by the United Nations agencies or others are able to reach all parts of the Iraqi population and are not prevented from reaching those whom the Government of Iraq does not wish them to reach.

Those are the questions I would like to put, and I will look forward with lively interest to hearing the answers tomorrow morning.

Mr. PICKERING (United States of America): I want to assure you at the outset, Mr. President, that I do have some questions, but I would ask your permission also, in the course of presenting my questions, to comment briefly, if I may, on the statement we heard this morning, which does not lend itself very well to questions, because the questions have more to do with what was not in the statement than with what was in it.

In any event, let me begin by saying that we were disappointed in what we heard from the Deputy Prime Minister this morning, and that perhaps might be guilty of being a serious understatement. The approach which he made to the Council did not, in our view, either address the issues nor did it very much advance the process.

The statement itself appeared to be directed towards trying to destroy at least in part the confidence of the Security Council in the Special Commission and in the International Atomic Energy Agency (IAEA) and their work. In several areas it suggested that the Council now had to put itself into the process of actually implementing its own resolutions. Even worse, perhaps, it suggested that the Council enter into a negotiating process with Iraq for the implementation of what we all know to be mandatory resolutions of the Council. This perhaps reflects a continued fundamental misunderstanding on the part of Iraq about mandatory resolutions and a serious miscalculation of the intention and purpose of the Council in dealing with Iraq's programmes of weapons of mass destruction in particular.

Specifically, the Deputy Prime Minister suggests that with respect to the declarations required of Iraq under resolution 687 (1991), Iraq would be ready to sit down with the Council and the Special Commission and apparently negotiate out what it is that Iraq will declare. This is not the approach of the Council nor, obviously, the purpose of its resolutions.

(Mr. Pickering, United States)

Secondly, with respect to the issue of the destruction of its weapons of mass destruction and the programmes in Iraq for the production of those weapons, it seeks a similar negotiating-oriented approach. It suggests that there is confusion about what the Special Commission and the International Atomic Energy Agency have asked to be destroyed. It suggests that the Council put itself into the middle of this process to decide what elements must be destroyed. It ignores the firm position on the part of the Council that the Special Commission and the IAEA will be the technical mechanism for the designation of what should be destroyed or rendered harmless or removed in the Iraqi programme and in the production base which supports that programme. We understand the Special Commission conducted several rounds of conversation with Iraqi technical experts and has come up with final lists on certain ballistic missile and related production items which Iraq now refuses to destroy. We fail to see how further conversations and negotiations are a real answer to the problem. The problem is really full compliance with the resolution as it stands and the designations made carefully by the Special Commission.

Finally, we appear to have roughly the same proposal coming out of the statement this morning with respect to the issue of long-term monitoring. Again, long-term monitoring plans presented by the Council to Iraq and approved in resolutions which are mandatory are clearly not subject to negotiation. Such efforts are not in keeping with mandatory resolutions, and we continue to expect a full and clear Iraqi commitment to comply.

(Mr. Pickering, United States)

A drawn-out discussion and negotiation of compliance with resolutions is certainly not in the interest of regional peace and stability, and it is not - at least in our view - the intention of the members of the Council, nor is it is provided for in the resolutions with which Iraq must comply.

It is disappointing that the Iraqi statement made no serious effort to address the numerous outstanding questions in the minds of the members of the Council, some of which I will turn to in a minute. At the end of his statement the Deputy Prime Minister must clearly have understood this, and we, on our part, welcome his commitment to address these questions - with, one hopes, his answers - tomorrow morning. We look forward in that regard to hearing what he has to say.

Finally, other portions of the statement merely seem to repeat the old and tired arguments of the past. In that respect we saw very little that was new in the statement, and it did not serve to advance the process of Iraqi compliance, which is, again, deeply disappointing.

We are also disappointed, as are others, that nowhere in the Iraqi statement this morning did we see references to resolution 688 (1991), to the United Nations important role in providing humanitarian assistance to the citizens of Iraq, or a discussion of what Iraq will do to alleviate the plight, particularly of the Kurds and the Shi'a.

0165

(Mr. Pickering, United States)

This only serves to lend greater credence to our fears about Iraq's refusal to observe universal standards of human rights and its oppression of the Kurds and Shi'a, its own citizens, unfortunately in their own country.

On the other hand, we react positively to the one small portion of the statement in which the Deputy Prime Minister seemed to break new ground by promising, starting today, to publish the names of missing persons in several Iraqi newspapers once a week for a period of several weeks. We could only hope that Iraq would comply rapidly with the rest of its obligations with the same degree of directness. This especially includes providing unrestricted access to the International Committee of the Red Cross (ICRC) to all Iraqi prisons and places of detention.

Iraq has made frequent references to its sovereignty and to internal affairs. However, Iraq knows as well as all of us that the Council is operating with regard to its resolutions on Iraq under Chapter VII. Such resolutions are mandatory and fall under the last portion of paragraph 7 of Article 2 of the Charter, which makes it clear that the principle of non-intervention "shall not prejudice the application of enforcement measures under Chapter VII". The measures that Iraq complains of are clearly enforcement measures under Chapter VII.

It is clear that the author of all this destruction and difficulty is Iraq itself. Iraq was frequently warned by the Council to cease its aggression and to abandon its illegal occupation of Kuwait. Iraq brought these measures upon itself and Iraq now holds the key to their relaxation. It is clear that Iraq must comply with the Security Council resolutions. Attacks on the views of the members of the Council and attacks on the cohesion of the Security Council and most particularly on the independence of its individual

(Mr. Pickering, United States)

members are not the way to achieve a change in the present situation. Similarly, attacks on the Special Commission and the IAEA do not assist.

As I said this morning, Iraq should begin by committing itself to full compliance and then to immediately taking on the follow-up actions rapidly and expediently to carry out that compliance. Unfortunately, nothing we have heard here today so far suggests that Iraq understands this need. It is clear that Iraq has not yet fully complied with the resolutions. But again, we hope to hear tomorrow as we did not today that Iraq intends to do so.

Now I should like to turn, in the light of our session planned for tomorrow morning, to a few questions which we believe clearly need answers.

First, on weapons of mass destruction, is Iraq ready to make full, final and complete disclosure of its programmes of weapons of mass destruction, and when will it do so?

Secondly, is Iraq prepared to commence destruction of its ballistic missile production and repair facilities, as requested by the Special Commission's letter of 14 February and under United Nations supervision, and will it do so immediately?

Thirdly, will Iraq return to the IAEA the nuclear documents seized from and never returned to the sixteenth Special Commission inspection team in September 1991, and will it do so immediately?

Fourthly, will Iraq today provide unconditional acceptance of the long-term monitoring and verification plans laid out in resolution 715 (1991) and make the required declarations of its equipment and facilities? When will Iraq begin to observe the full range of privileges and immunities to be accorded to the Special Commission and to the IAEA?

With respect to the boundary demarcation and border posts, does Iraq now recognize its obligations to accept the work of the Boundary Commission to

0167

(Mr. Pickering, United States)

demarcate the Iraq-Kuwait border? Will Iraq remove immediately its border police posts from the Kuwaiti side of the border on the map used by the United Nations Iraq-Kuwait Observer Mission?

With respect to detainees, refugees and humanitarian interests, will Iraq resolve as soon as possible the matter of missing Kuwaitis, Saudis, and missing third-country nationals from the Gulf war by conducting detailed documented searches for those missing and sharing the full results of those searches with the ICRC; by providing to the ICRC information on Kuwaitis and third-country nationals who died while in custody; by granting the ICRC unrestricted access to all Iraqi places of detention in its effort to trace the missing? When will Iraq meet the humanitarian needs of the Iraqi people by implementing resolutions 706 (1991) and 712 (1991)? When will Iraq permit the establishment of United Nations humanitarian centres throughout Iraq, including Kirkuk and Mosul? When will Iraq guarantee the United Nations humanitarian programme unrestricted access to vulnerable groups throughout Iraq?

As to Iraqi economic blockades within its own country, when will Iraq dismantle the checkpoints blocking roads into northern Iraq and lift the blockade in northern Iraq? When will Iraq allow Iraqi citizens formerly resident in the Kirkuk area to return to their homes and businesses? Will Iraq cease attacks on civilians, including artillery bombardment of urban areas? And when will Iraq and the Iraqi military end their encirclement of the southern marsh area, a de facto blockade confining up to 500,000 persons, and permit the United Nations to visit?

On the return of property, when will Iraq make a final accounting of and return of all both military and non-military property taken from Kuwait? And, finally, when will Iraq begin providing the Secretary-General and appropriate

0168

(Mr. Pickering, United States)

international organizations a monthly statement of Iraq's gold and foreign currency reserves, as required by resolution 706 (1991)?

Mr. MENON (India): The Deputy Prime Minister of Iraq, Mr. Tariq Aziz, has provided the Council with details of his country's position on various aspects relating to the implementation of Council resolutions. I should like to refer to one issue of humanitarian concern that members of the Council and Mr. Aziz have spoken of - the repatriation of Kuwaiti and other nationals from Iraq. My delegation raises this issue consistent with its stand that the overall humanitarian aspect demands special attention and redress.

It appears to my delegation that, besides the problem of identification, registration and actual repatriation, there is a clear divergence of views on what has been done so far and what further needs to be done. The Deputy Prime Minister has stated his country's willingness to scrutinize this issue in detail with the International Committee of the Red Cross (ICRC) and with other authorities concerned with a view to expediting repatriation. Concentrated and effective action in this regard is of great importance, given the suffering and anxiety of those involved.

Against this backdrop, the question we would like to pose is the following: Could Mr. Aziz throw further light on this with a view to confirming that Iraq will be able in the very near future to expedite full repatriation of Kuwaiti and other nationals in cooperation with the ICRC?

Mr. MERIMEE (France) (interpretation from French): I regret to have to say that my delegation cannot regard as acceptable the comments made by Mr. Tariq Aziz, for they do in fact challenge the resolutions of the Security Council and the mechanisms laid down and endorsed in those resolutions.

0169

(Mr. Mérimée, France)

Having made this general comment, my delegation would confine itself to three questions, which, we think, relate to the most important issues.

My first question is on the obligation that Iraq has to give a full and complete picture of its military programme. From the various reports, *inter alia* that from the Special Commission, we think that this full picture has not been provided. The French delegation's question is as follows: When will Iraq be able to provide this full picture?

My second question is just as straightforward. When will Iraq make known to the Security Council its unconditional acceptance of the monitoring plan approved under resolution 715 (1991)? My delegation would be happy if, at tomorrow's meeting, the Iraqi delegation could solemnly enter into that commitment.

My third and final point is that my delegation noted that Mr. Tariq Aziz, in his statement this morning, refrained from mentioning resolution 688 (1991) or the particular difficulties obtaining in some regions of Iraq. My delegation would like to know the reasons for the impediments which the Iraqi Government continues to put in the way of the opening of United Nations humanitarian centres in Kurdistan and in the south of the country. My delegation asks the Iraqi Government when it will open those centres and when it will lift the blockade it has imposed on part of its population.

The PRESIDENT (interpretation from Spanish): As there are no further speakers on my list, I shall now suspend the meeting until tomorrow, Thursday 12 March, at 10.30 a.m.

*The meeting was suspended at 6.45 p.m.*

03/13/92 18:45 ☎ 071 589 9134 ROK EMBASSY UK P.04

주 영 국 대 사 관

UKW(F) : 440 년월일 : 20313 시간 : 1800

수 신 : 장 관 (중동1, 연일)

발 신 : 주영대사

제 목 : 이라크 관계

| 보 안 | |
|---|---|
| 통 제 | |

(출처 : )

(92.3.13) THE TIMES

# UN heads for showdown with Iraq on nuclear arms

FROM JAMES BONE IN NEW YORK

IRAQ failed yesterday in its bid to convince the United Nations Security Council that it was ready to comply with UN resolutions and should be rewarded with a relaxation of sanctions.

Addressing the 15-nation council for a second day, Tariq Aziz, Iraq's deputy prime minister, maintained a hard line — offering only to start talks on key UN demands. As a result, the UN now seems to be heading for what could be its most serious showdown with Iraq since the end of the Gulf war.

After hearing Mr Aziz, the security council agreed on a statement repeating that Iraq had "not yet complied fully and unconditionally" with the terms of the Gulf war ceasefire and "must immediately take the appropriate actions in this regard".

Thomas Pickering, the American ambassador, said: "We are once again in a cat-and-mouse game... There is every willingness to discuss at great length, but no willingness to accept the need for compliance, much less to begin the actions to comply."

Britain and the United States appear to have decided to make the destruction of Iraq's main nuclear weapons' facility at Al Atheer a test case of Iraqi compliance with UN resolutions.

The International Atomic Energy Agency has told Iraq that UN inspectors will soon try to dismantle Al Atheer. Western diplomats suggest the installation would make an appropriate allied bombing target if Iraq refuses to co-operate.

America is also considering seeking a new UN resolution seizing Iraqi assets already frozen abroad. Britain and France plan to ask the UN to appoint a special representative to focus attention on Baghdad's maltreatment of its Kurdish and Shia Muslim populations.

Mr Aziz answered point-by-point a list of complaints delivered by the council president on Wednesdey. On the key demands of the elimination of Iraq's weapons of mass destruction and the long-term monitoring of its defence industries, he simply offered to enter into technical talks which would lead to a relaxation of sanctions.

He also refused to make a UN-approved oil sale to pay for relief supplies, again objecting to the requirement that part of the money be diverted to pay war compensation and to finance the elimination of Iraq's weapons of mass destruction. He said, however, that Iraq was ready to resume talks on a new oil sale scheme.

He expressed no willingness to lift the present economic blockade of the Kurds in northern Iraq and he called a UN resolution criticising their mistreatment a "blatant interference" in Iraq's internal affairs.

Page

(440 - 1 - 1)

| 외신 1과 | |
|---|---|
| 통 제 | |

| 배부처 | 장관실 | 차관실 | 1차보 | 2차보 | 기획실 | 외정실 | 분석관 | 외연원 | 미주국 | 구주국 | 중아국 | 국기국 | 경제국 | 통상국 | 문협국 | 영교국 | 총무과 | 감사관 | 공보관 | 외연원 | 청와대 | 총리실 | 안기부 | 공보처 |
|---|---|---|---|---|---|---|---|---|---|---|---|---|---|---|---|---|---|---|---|---|---|---|---|---|
| | / | / | | | / | / | | | | 0 | / | | | | | | | | | / | | / | | |

0171

03/18/92 14:50 ☎202 797 0595 EMBASSY OF KOREA --- WOI 002

# 주 미 대 사 관

이1차

USW(F) : 1617 년월일 : 92.3.18 시간 : 14:15

수 신 : 장 관 (미일, 중동일, 중동이, 국연)

발 신 : 주 미 대 사

제 목 : 대이락 제재

| 보 통 | 안 제 |
|---|---|

(출처 : NYT )

# U.N., Hinting at Force, Gives Iraq a Week to Scuttle Arms

By PAUL LEWIS
Special to The New York Times

UNITED NATIONS, March 17 — The United Nations has given Iraq until March 26 to come up with a detailed plan for destroying a long list of equipment and buildings used for constructing and repairing its banned ballistic missiles, United Nations officials and Western diplomats said today.

The deadline, which carried at least an implicit threat of the use of force, was given last week to Deputy Prime Minister Tariq Aziz, Iraq's special envoy here, by Rolf Ekeus, the Swedish chief of the special commission set up to oversee the elimination of Iraqi weapons of mass destruction.

This constitutes a critical first test of the vague agreement by Mr. Aziz to cooperate more closely with the Security Council's gulf war cease-fire terms.

Although Iraq had rejected an earlier destruction order, arguing that the material could be converted to peaceful uses, officials say Mr. Aziz appeared to accept the new deadline. But these officials emphasize that any destruction program that Baghdad follows must be a complete one and acceptable to the special commission.

A 35-member team of United Nations ballistic missile experts is in Baghdad waiting to receive the Iraqi plan next week. If President Saddam Hussein's Government meets the deadline and produces an acceptable schedule of arms destruction, the team will stay on to oversee the work, officials say.

Otherwise it plans to leave, raising the possibility the United States and its allies might opt for a military strike to destroy the nuclear-related sites.

*New Resolution*

It is unclear whether the allies, for political reasons, would seek a new Security Council endorsement of such military action or whether they would operate on the basis that since Iraq refuses to comply with the cease-fire terms, that truce is no longer in effect and they are free to attack again.

The United States already has a bomber foerce in Saudi Arabia, as well as planes aboard a carrier in the Persian Gulf. In addition, B-52 bombers have recently arrived in Britain on what are described as exercises.

In Washington today, Defense Secretary Dick Cheney insisted that the Bush Administration was still committed to using United Nations diplomacy rather than force to eliminate the Iraqi

Continued on Page A11, Column 1

92.3.18 NYT

1617 - 2 - 1

| 외신 통 | 1과 제 |
|---|---|

| 배부처 | 장관실 | 차관실 | 一차보 | 二차보 | 의정실 | 분석관 | 아주국 | 미주국 | 구주국 | 중아국 | 국기국 | 경제국 | 통상국 | 정문국 | 청와대 | 안기부 | 공보처 | 경기원 | 상공부 | 재무부 | 농수부 | 동자부 | 환경처 | 과기처 | | |
|---|---|---|---|---|---|---|---|---|---|---|---|---|---|---|---|---|---|---|---|---|---|---|---|---|---|---|
| | / | / | / | | / | / | | O | | /2 | / | | | / | / | / | | | | | | | | | | |

021 P12 WOI '92-03-19 04:47 0172

# U.N. Gives the Iraqis a Deadline For Destroying Missile Capacity

*Continued From Page A1*

weapons of mass destruction. But Mr. Cheney did not rule out the use of force.

The Security Council has warned Iraq four times since the end of the gulf war a year ago that it is violating the truce terms and that it would face serious consequences unless it complied with them.

Last week President Bush said he would "contemplate all alternatives" if Mr. Hussein did not bow to United Nations pressure. The British Prime Minister, John Major, has said he would back a military strike.

The Council, after its latest warning to Baghdad, summoned Mr. Aziz and his delegation for a series of meetings. There, members called for full and immediate compliance with their orders and said they would not negotiate these.

Iraq has been ordered to turn over full details of its banned weapons-development programs including remaining nuclear installations, to cooperate with plans to monitor its arms industry to insure that no new projects are begun, and to destroy the buildings and equipment designated by the special commission.

### Pressure on Libya, Too

Big-power pressure at the United Nations is not limited to Iraq. The United States, Britain and France have circulated the draft of a resolution to Security Council members that would impose an array of new sanctions on Libya unless it turned over intelligence agents they have accused of blowing up Pan Am Flight 103 ofer Lockerbie, Scotland, and a U.T.A. flight over sub-Saharan Africa, with a combined loss of 440 people.

The resolution, which the Council is expected to approve in the next few days, severs all airline links with Libya, bans the sale of aircraft, spare parts and maintainance services as well as all military deliveries, and requires governments to reduce the size of Libyan diplomatic missions and restrict the movement of Libyan envoys in their countries.

In January, the Council ordered Libya to hand over two men accused in the destruction of Pan Am 103 for trial in Britain or the United States and to allow a French magistrate to question those accused of blowing up the U.T.A. plane.

But so far Libya has refused, but has offered to put them on trial and has asked the accusing Western Governments to provide evidence against them.

In a news conference this afternoon at the United Nations, the Libyan representative condemned the proposed resolution.

The envoy, Ali el-Houderi said: "This draft resolution does not reflect the will of the entire Security Council, but only the wishes of the three co-sponsor countries," referring to the United States, Britain and France. "Any pressure that might be applied against member countries of the Security Council to adopt this draft resolution will be considered as coercion and domination in its worst and most blatant form."

He said the resolution "gets close to declaring war by using the Security Council."

### Destruction of Iraqi Installation

The United Nations plans in the next few days to test Iraq's willingness to accept the destruction of most of its Al Atheer nuclear-weapons plant south of Baghdad. The special commission and the Vienna-based International Atomic Energy Agency, a United Nations specialized agency, will send the Iraqis a list of the installations they want eliminated.

Al Atheer was undamaged in the gulf war because the allies did not realize at the time that it was where Iraq planned to build and test a bomb. At last week's Security Council meeting with Mr. Aziz, the United States called for the plant's destruction.

Mr. Aziz, officials say, took a more flexible approach with Mr. Ekeus on two other issues where it appeared to be heading toward a fresh confrontation with the Security Council.

The Iraqis gave Mr. Ekeus an Arabic document that they say is the list of military industries requested by the special commission to monitor these factories, insuring that they are not used to make weapons of mass destruction. But it will take about two weeks before the document is translated into English and the commission can assess its value.

92.3.18
NYT

1617-2-2

0173

원 본

# 외 무 부

종 별 :

번 호 : UNW-0760 일 시 : 92 0318 1900

수 신 : 장 관(연일,중동이)

발 신 : 주 유엔 대사

제 목 : 이라크 대량 파괴무기 및 팬암기사건

1. 표제관련 3.18.자 NYT 기사 송부함.

2.GIULIANI 사무총장 대변인은 동기사 내용중 3.26. 최후통첩 보도 내용은 사실과 다르며 무기폐기특위 (SCOM)는 3.21. 이라크를 방문할 예정으로 있다고 설명함. 끝

(대사대리 신기복-국장)

첨부: UNW(F)-275

국기국 중아국

PAGE 1 92.03.19 09:24 WG

외신 1과 통제관

0174

UNW(G)-0175 20710 1900 UNW-0760 의 첨부

# U.N. Demands an Iraqi Plan By March 26 to Scrap Arms

By PAUL LEWIS
Special to The New York Times

UNITED NATIONS, March 17 — The United Nations has given Iraq until March 26 to come up with a detailed plan for destroying a long list of equipment and buildings used for constructing and repairing its banned ballistic missiles, United Nations officials and Western diplomats said today.

The deadline, which carried at least an implicit threat of the use of force, was given last week to Deputy Prime Minister Tariq Aziz, Iraq's special envoy here, by Rolf Ekeus, the Swedish chief of the special commission set up to oversee the elimination of Iraqi weapons of mass destruction.

This constitutes a critical first test of the vague agrement by Mr. Aziz to cooperate more closely with the Security Council's gulf war cease-fire terms.

Although Iraq had rejected an earlier destruction order, arguing that the material could be converted to peaceful uses, officials say Mr. Aziz appeared to accept the new deadline. But these officials emphasize that any destruction program that Baghdad follows must be a complete one and acceptable to the special commission.

A 35-member team of United Nations ballistic missile experts is in Baghdad waiting to receive the Iraqi plan next week. If President Saddam Hussein's Government meets the deadline and produces an acceptable schedule of arms destruction, the team will stay on to oversee the work, officials say.

Otherwise it plans to leave, raising the possibility the United States and its allies might opt for a military strike to destroy the nuclear-related sites.

**New Resolution**

It is unclear whether the allies, for political reasons, would seek a new Security Council endorsement of such military action or whether they would operate on the basis that since Iraq refuses to comply with the cease-fire terms, that truce is no longer in effect and they are free to attack again.

The United States already has a bomber force in Saudi Arabia, as well as planes aboard a carrier in the Persian Gulf. In addition, B-52 bombers have recently arrived in Britain on what are described as exercises.

In Washington today, Defense Secretary Dick Cheney insisted that the Bush Administration was still commit-

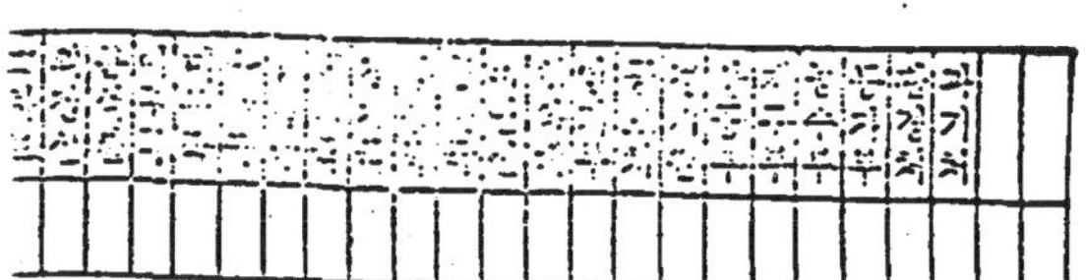

275-2-1

0175

# ...Demands Iraqi Weapons Plan by March 26

Continued From Page A1

ted to using United Nations diplomacy rather than force to eliminate the Iraqi weapons of mass destruction. But Mr. Cheney did not rule out the use of force.

The Security Council has warned Iraq four times since the end of the gulf war a year ago that it is violating the truce terms and that it would face serious consequences unless it complied with them.

Last week President Bush said he would "contemplate all alternatives" if Mr. Hussein did not bow to United Nations pressure. The British Prime Minister, John Major, has said he would back a military strike.

The Council, after its latest warning to Baghdad, summoned Mr. Aziz and his delegation for a series of meetings. There, members called for full and immediate compliance with their orders and said they would not negotiate these.

Iraq has been ordered to turn over full details of its banned weapons-development programs including remaining nuclear installations, to cooperate with plans to monitor its arms industry to insure that no new projects are begun, and to destroy the buildings and equipment designated by the special commission.

### Pressure on Libya, Too

Big-power pressure at the United Nations is not limited to Iraq. The United States, Britain and France have circulated the draft of a resolution to Security Council members that would impose an array of new sanctions on Libya unless it turned over intelligence agents they have accused of blowing up Pan Am Flight 103 over Lockerbie, Scotland, and a U.T.A. flight over sub-Saharan Africa, with a combined loss of 440 people.

The resolution, which the Council is expected to approve in the next few days, severs all airline links with Libya, bans the sale of aircraft, spare parts and maintainance services as well as all military deliveries, and requires governments to reduce the size of Libyan diplomatic missions and restrict the movement of Libyan envoys in their countries.

In January, the Council ordered Libya to hand over two men accused in the destruction of Pan Am 103 for trial in Britain or the United States and to allow a French magistrate to question those accused of blowing up the U.T.A. plane.

> A veiled threat to use force against nuclear building and repair sites.

But so far Libya has refused, but has offered to put them on trial and has asked the accusing Western Governments to provide evidence against them.

### Libyan Expresses Outrage

In a news conference this afternoon at the United Nations, the Libyan representative condemned the proposed resolution.

The envoy, Ali el-Houderi said: "This draft resolution does not reflect the will of the entire Security Council, but only the wishes of the three cosponsor countries," referring to the United States, Britain and France. "Any pressure that might be applied against member countries of the Security Council to adopt this draft resolution will be considered as coercion and domination in its worst and most blatant form."

He said the resolution "gets close to declaring war by using the Security Council."

The United Nations plans in the next few days to test Iraq's willingness to accept the destruction of most of its Al Atheer nuclear-weapons plant south of Baghdad. The special commission and the Vienna-based International Atomic Energy Agency, a United Nations specialized agency, will send the Iraqis a list of the installations they want eliminated.

Al Atheer was undamaged in the gulf war because the allies did not realize at the time that it was where Iraq planned to build and test a bomb. At last week's Security Council meeting with Mr. Aziz, the United States called for the plant's destruction.

Mr. Aziz, officials say, took a more flexible approach with Mr. Ekeus on two other issues where it appeared to be heading toward a fresh confrontation with the Security Council.

The Iraqis gave Mr. Ekeus an Arabic document that they say is the list of military industries requested by the special commission to monitor these factories, insuring that they are not used to make weapons of mass destruction. But it will take about two weeks before the document is translated into English and the commission can assess its value.

### Some Give and Take

The Iraqis also said they were prepared to give the commission a requested list of the materials they have imported in their push to build nuclear, chemical and biological arsenals.

But the Iraqis appeared unwilling to provide names of the companies that supplied these goods, as the commission also wants. And Mr. Aziz repeated that his Government does not accept Security Council Resolution 715, which provides for this long-term monitoring, calling this a breach of its sovereignty.

0176

원 본

# 외 무 부

종 별 :

번 호 : UNW-0826 일 시 : 92 0324 1800

수 신 : 장 관(연일,중동일,기정)

발 신 : 주 유엔 대사

제 목 : 안보리-이라크 대량파괴무기 폐기

연:UNW-0760(1),786(2)

1.3.21. 부터 이라크를 방문중인 유엔특위 (SCOM)팀은 3.23. 이라크측이 SCUD 미사일을 기폐기, 매장하였다고 주장하는 현장을 방문, 검증활동중이며, 이라크측으로부터 미사일 생산장비 폐기를 위한 관련 문건도 인계받아 특위의 검토가 끝나는 대로 폐기작업에 들어갈 예정이라고함

2. 연호(2)에 따라 이라크 및 유엔 대표단은 3.26비엔나에서 식량, 약품등 긴급 물품 수입을 위한 이라크의 석유수출 허용문제를 협의할 예정임

(대사 유종하-국장)

첨부:UNW(F)-0299

국기국 1차보 중아국 외정실 분석관 안기부

PAGE 1

92.03.25 09:39 WG

외신 1과 통제관

0177

MAR 24 '92 17:32 KOREAN MISSION P.1

Press Release

Department of Public Information • News Coverage Service • New York

UNW(F)-0299 20324 1800 UNW-0826 의 첨부

Note No. 4985
23 March 1992

NOTE TO CORRESPONDENTS

UNITED NATIONS AND IRAQ TO BEGIN NEGOTIATIONS CONCERNING OIL EXPORTS AT VIENNA ON 26 MARCH

VIENNA, 20 March (UN Information Service) -- Secretary-General Boutros Boutros-Ghali announced yesterday at a press conference at United Nations Headquarters that negotiations between the representatives of the United Nations and Iraq on possible resumption of petroleum exports by Iraq are scheduled to begin at Vienna on 26 March.

The United Nations team will be led by Assistant Secretary-General for Political Affairs, Giandomenico Picco.

At a brief meeting of the Security Council late yesterday afternoon, the Council President Diego Arria (Venezuela) read out a statement on behalf of Council members in which he said they were prepared to authorize the sale of Iraqi oil as provided for in Council resolutions 706 (1991) and 712 (1991). (For details see Press Release SC/5386 of 19 March.)

By resolution 706, the Council stipulated terms for the limited sale of Iraqi oil and oil-products under strict conditions and close United Nations monitoring. Under the resolution's provisions, Iraq's oil could be sold for a six-month period with full payment by the purchasers to be deposited into an escrow account controlled by the United Nations. Funds would be allocated from that account to purchase essential foodstuffs and supplies and to meet Iraq's financial obligations under previous Council resolutions. The resolution specifies that the sum to be produced by Iraq's limited oil exports cannot exceed $1.6 billion.

Under resolution 712, the Council, confirming its ceiling of $1.6 billion in limited Iraqi oil sales, approved recommendations contained in a report of the Secretary-General (document S/23006) outlining a basic structure and measures for the sale of Iraqi oil, aimed at meeting that country's humanitarian requirements.

* *** *

299-2-1

7288P

For information media--not an official record

0178

Press Release

Department of Public Information • News Coverage Service • New York

IK/93
23 March 1992

**INSPECTION TEAM VISITS SITES WHERE IRAQ SAYS IT DESTROYED SCUD-TYPE MISSILES; IRAQIS HAND OVER PLANS FOR DESTRUCTION OF BALLISTIC MISSILES EQUIPMENT**

The following information was received from the Special Commission set up under Security Council resolution 687 (1991) in connection with the disposal of Iraq's weapons of mass destruction:

On 23 March, the team visited two sites at which the Iraqi side claims that the remains of some of the SCUD-type missiles they destroyed unilaterally last summer are buried. Initial excavation revealed some pieces of such missiles. The Iraqi side has been asked to conduct a full excavation to enable verification to be undertaken. When these preparations are complete, the team will resume verification activities at these sites.

The Iraqi authorities also handed over the plans for the destruction of equipment associated with the ballistic missiles programmes that they had failed to deliver to the previous inspection team. These plans are now being studied. If they meet the requirements of the Special Commission, destruction will commence during this team's inspection.

* *** *

299-2-2

7292P

For information media—not an official record

0179

원 본

# 외 무 부

종 별 :

번 호 : UNW-0877 일 시 : 92 0326 2100

수 신 : 장 관(연일,중동일)

발 신 : 주 유엔 대사

제 목 : 안보리-이라크 대량파괴 무기폐기

연:UNW-0826

이라크 방문중인 유엔특위(SCOM)팀의 미사일 폐기 검증활동에 관한 보도자료 별첨 송부함

(대사 유종하-국장)

첨부:UNW(F)-0318

국기국 중아국

PAGE 1

92.03.27 13:09 WH

외신 1과 통제관

0180

# United Nations

## Press Release

Department of Public Information • News Coverage Service • New York

UNW(F)-0318 2032Z/00 UNW-0877 시 첨부

IK/94
25 March 1992

DESTRUCTION OF IRAQ'S BALLISTIC MISSILES EQUIPMENT BEGINS

The following has been received from the Special Commission set up under Security Council resolution 687 (1991) in connection with the disposal of Iraq's weapons of mass destruction:

The ninth United Nations ballistic missiles inspection team today witnessed the start of the destruction of Iraq's ballistic missiles production and repair facilities. The team was able to verify the complete destruction of some of the nine items that the Iraqi authorities had refused to destroy during the previous inspection. Destruction and verification activities are scheduled to continue.

The team visited three technical establishments to the south and west of Baghdad. The principal machinery destroyed was highly specialized mixer equipment used in the production of solid rocket propellant. Other items included machinery and electronic testing equipment. The items were destroyed by cutting or crushing.

The team remains in Baghdad. It will continue its other inspection activities and its efforts to verify Iraq's statement of 19 March that it had unilaterally destroyed ballistic missiles and associated equipment last summer.

* *** *

318-2-1

# United Nations

## Press Release

Department of Public Information • News Coverage Service • New York

IK/95
26 March 1992

UN INSPECTION TEAM EXAMINES MISSILES DESTROYED BY IRAQ

The following has been received from the Special Commission set up under Security Council resolution 687 (1991) in connection with the disposal of Iraq's weapons of mass destruction:

The ninth ballistic missiles inspection team today examined the remains of a significant number of ballistic missiles that had been destroyed unilaterally by Iraq. Team members identified parts unique to each missile as well as some missile guidance sets.

Those activities took place at various sites to the north and south of Baghdad where, for the past four days, the Iraqi Army has been excavating the buried debris.

* *** *

318-2-2

7345P

For information media—not an official record

0182

원 본

암 호 수 신

# 외 무 부

종 별 :

번 호 : UNW-0895 일 시 : 92 0327 2100

수 신 : 장 관(연일,중동일)

발 신 : 주 유엔 대사

제 목 : 안보리-이라크 제재조치

안보리는 금 3.27 비공식 회의에서 안보리 결의이행을 위한 최근의 이라크측의 조치에 대해 안보리 결의 687 호 제재조치를 해제하기에는 미흡하다는 별첨안보리의장 성명을 발표하기로 하였음.

(대사 유종하-국장)

첨부;UNW(F)-0321

국기국 장관 차관 1차보 2차보 중아국 외정실 분석관 청와대 안기부

PAGE 1

92.03.28 10:57

외신 2과 통제관 BX

0183

UNW(F)-0321 20327 1100 #첨부물

27 March 1992

DRAFT

**NOTE BY THE PRESIDENT OF THE SECURITY COUNCIL**

The members of the Security Council held informal consultations on 27 March 1992 pursuant to paragraphs 21 and 28 of resolution 687 (1991) and paragraph 6 of resolution 700 (1991).

After hearing all the opinions expressed in the course of the consultations, the President of the Council concluded that there still was no agreement that the necessary conditions existed for a modification of the regimes established in paragraph 20 of resolution 687 (1991), as referred to in paragraph 21 of that resolution; in paragraphs 22, 23, 24 and 25 of resolution 687 (1991), as referred to in paragraph 28 of that resolution; and in paragraph 6 of resolution 700 (1991). Recent initial offers of cooperation by the Iraqi authorities ~~have not yet been~~ would be fully matched by actual deeds.

The members of the Security Council expressed the hope that

321-1-1

0184

<table>
<tr><th colspan="6">정 리 보 존 문 서 목 록</th></tr>
<tr><td>기록물종류</td><td>일반공문서철</td><td>등록번호</td><td>2021040203</td><td>등록일자</td><td>2021-04-22</td></tr>
<tr><td>분류번호</td><td>731.33</td><td>국가코드</td><td>IQ</td><td>보존기간</td><td>30년</td></tr>
<tr><td>명 칭</td><td colspan="5">유엔이라크대량살상무기폐기특별위원회(UNSCOM), 1992. 전2권</td></tr>
<tr><td>생 산 과</td><td>국제연합1과/중동1과</td><td>생산년도</td><td>1992~1992</td><td>담당그룹</td><td></td></tr>
<tr><td>권 차 명</td><td colspan="5">V.2 4-12월</td></tr>
<tr><td>내용목차</td><td colspan="5">* 7.6 안보리 비공식 회의(이라크의 농무부 청사에 대한 사찰 거부문제 논의)<br>7.28-29 농무부 청사 사찰 실시</td></tr>
</table>

0001

원 본

| 관리번호 | 92-337 |
|---|---|

# 외 무 부

종 별 :

번 호 : UNW-1030　　　　일 시 : 92 0407 1930

수 신 : 장 관(연일,중동일,기정)

발 신 : 주 유엔 대사

제 목 : 걸프사태(이락 대량무기 폐기 유엔특위)

1. 이락 대량무기 폐기유엔특위(UNSCOM) EKEUS 위원장은 4.3. 본직앞 서한을 통하여 이락의 화학무기 폐기를 위한 UNSCOM 작업단 설치계획을 통보하고 동작업단에 아국의 참여를 요청하여 왔는바 동서한을 별첨 송부하니 검토후 회시바람.

2. 서한내용

가. UNSCOM 은 92.6-12 월간 이락 MUTHANNA STATE ESTABLISHMENT 에 있는 화학무기 폐기를 위한 작업단을 구성키로 하였음

나. 작업단의 규모는 추후결정 예정이나 영어를 구사하는 자로서 화학무기에 관한 지식을 갖춘 민간인이나 군인및 기술자, 화학무기 탐지전문가, 의료인, 건물철거기술자들로 구성됨

다. 필요장비는 방독의복, 화학무기제거및 탐지장비, 폐쇄회로 TV 등임

라. 동화학무기폐기 작업단 설치에 한국정부의 참여를 희망함

3. 동위원회측에 문의한바에 의하면 동작업단은 약 30-35 명으로 구성 예정이며 현재 안보리 상임이사국을 포함 27 개국(아시아에서는 호주, 인도, 일본, 뉴질랜드, 파키스탄, 중국, 태국포함)에 작업단 참여를 요청하였으며 각국이 1-2 명의 화학무기 제거 전문가를 파견하여 줄것을 희망하고 있음

(대사 유종하-국장)

예고:92.12.31 일반문에 의거 인반문서로 재분류

첨부:UNW(F)-0365

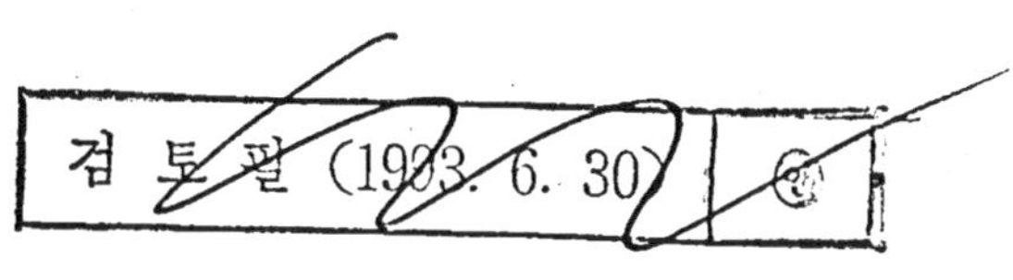


국기국 안기부 | 장관 | 차관 | 1차보 | 2차보 | 중아국 | 외정실 | 분석관 | 청와대

PAGE 1　　　　92.04.08 09:25

외신 2과 통제관 BZ

0002

APR 07 '92 18:21 KOREAN MISSION P.3

UNW(під)-0365 20407 1930 # 외무부

UNITED NATIONS  NATIONS UNIES

Amb. Shin.

POSTAL ADDRESS—ADRESSE POSTALE UNITED NATIONS, N.Y. 10017
CABLE ADDRESS—ADRESSE TELEGRAPHIQUE: UNATIONS NEWYORK

REFERENCE:

3 April 1992

Excellency,

I have the honour to advise you that with the deployment of UNSCOM 29/CD1 on 18 February 1992 the formal programme for the destruction of Iraq's Chemical Warfare capability has commenced. Shortly, following the soon-to-be completed construction of a nerve agent hydrolysis plant and mustard incinerator, we will initiate the destruction of the bulk of Iraq's CW agents which are either stored or have been relocated to the Muthanna State Establishment. This chemical destruction programme will continue concurrently with other Special Commission activities, and will require substantial personnel and other resources. To carry out this task I must yet again turn to your Government for support.

I have decided to establish a team comprising personnel serving on a 3-6 monthly basis, at the Muthanna State Establishment, from June 1992 until the end of 1992 at least. The exact size and detailed composition of the team is yet to be determined; however, it will require English speaking civilians or military officers and technicians with appropriate chemical defence and destruction process knowledge, decontamination and detection experts, medical personnel, technical storemen and occasional short tour calls on structural engineers, demolition engineers, EOD personnel and analytical experts. There will also be requirements for protective clothing, decontamination, detection, agent monitoring, closed circuit television equipment and possibly analytical instruments in support of this operation.

The establishment of this standing team will not preclude occasional requests for personnel and equipment for chemical destruction operational requirements at other locations.

Inevitably, as the programme evolves, there will be modifications. You will be advised promptly of any changes.

/...

H.E. Mr. Chang Hee Roe
Ambassador Extraordinary and Plenipotentiary
Permanent Representative of the Republic
of Korea to the United Nations
New York, New York

Explosive Ordnance Disposal

0003

UNITED NATIONS  NATIONS UNIES

- 2 -

It would be appreciated if your Government could contribute to the establishment of the UNSCOM programme at the Muthanna State Establishment. In the event you are prepared to participate in this important task, kindly inform UNSCOM of the nature of your contribution.

Accept, Excellency, the assurances of my highest consideration.

Rolf Ekéus
Executive Chairman
Office of the Special Commission

0004

원 본

# 외 무 부

종 별 :

번 호 : UNW-1033 일 시 : 92 0407 1930

수 신 : 장 관(연일,중동일,기정)

발 신 : 주 유엔 대사

제 목 : 걸프사태(이락 대량무기 폐기 유엔특위)

1.이락의 대량무기 폐기와 관련, 당관이 입수한유엔특위 (UNSCOM) EKEUS 위원장의 4.3.자 안보리의장앞 서한내용을 하기보고함

2.서한내용

가.이락 외무장관이 UNSCOM 위원장앞 92.3.19자 서한을 통하여 최초로 밝힌바에 의하면

0 이락은 유엔감시하에 91.7월 폐기된 미사일 62기외에 92기를 보유하고 있었으나, 91년 여름일방적으로 폐기하였다함 (UNSCOM 에 폐기잔재확인)

0 또한 이락정부는 유엔에 통보하지 않는 45개의 화학탄두를 포함한 135개의 미사일탄두와 8개의 이동 미사일 발사태를 보유하고 있었으나, 91.7월이를 일방적으로 폐기하였으며 (UNSCOM 에서확인불가) 다량의 화학무기도 일방적으로 폐기하였다함

나.상기와 같은 이락의 일방적 폐기는 국제감시하에 폐기토록 되어있는 안보리결의(687)를 위반하는 것이며 이락이 최근까지도 보유한 무기관련 정보를 UN 에 숨기고 있었음

다.이락은 유엔이 요청한 미사일관련 폐기대상물중 (S/23673 ANNEX A) 최초로 92.3.21-309개 대상물을 폐기하였으며 여타 폐기대상물의 폐기계획안을 UNSCOM 에 제출하였음

라.유엔감시하에 화학무기 2.5톤을 2.21-3.24중 폐기하였음

마.유엔조사단이 4월초순 이락을 방문, AL ATHEER에 있는 핵무기 생산관련 시설및 장비의 파괴를 감독, 확인 예정이며 파괴방법은 IAEA가 현재 검토중임

바.이락의 상기 조치는 유엔결의 이행의 진전이나 이락의 유엔결의를 충실히 이행할지는 좀더두고 보아야함

(대사 유종하-국장)

첨부UNW(F)-360

국기국 1차보 중아국 외정실 분석관 안기부

PAGE 1 92.04.08 09:44 WG

외신 1과 통제관

0005

APR 07 '92 18:34 KOREAN MISSION P.1

FROM UN SECURITY COUNCIL FRI 04.03.'92 11:03 NO.2 PAGE 7

UNW(F)-0360 20407 1930

2/7

UNW-1033의 첨부

UNITED NATIONS  NATIONS UNIES

2 April 1992

Excellency,

I have the honour to refer to our meeting of 1 April at which you indicated that the members of the Security Council would appreciate an update on developments since the visit of the Iraqi Deputy Prime Minister to the Security Council. I hereby attach such an update.

Accept, Excellency, the assurances of my highest consideration.

Rolf Ekéus
Executive Chairman
Office of the Special Commission

0006

3|7

ANNEX

Introduction

1. The following is an update on the developments relating to section C of Security Council resolution 687 (1991) since the visit of the Deputy Prime Minister of Iraq to New York 10-14 March 1992, to attend the Security Council meeting on the implementation of that resolution.

New disclosures

2. On 19 March 1992, the Government of Iraq, in a letter from the Minister of State of the Ministry for Foreign Affairs to the Executive Chairman of the Special Commission, for the first time, disclosed that it had possessed 89 proscribed operational ballistic missiles and 3 training missiles in excess of the 62 missiles which had been formally declared to the United Nations in connection with Security Council resolution 687 (1991) and which had been destroyed under the supervision of the Special Commission in early July 1991. According to the letter, the 92 non-declared missiles had been unilaterally destroyed by Iraq during the summer of 1991. An inspection team of the Special Commission (UNSCOM 31) last week identified the remnants of 86 destroyed missiles.

3. Furthermore, the Government of Iraq disclosed another 135 hitherto undeclared missile warheads, including 45 warheads for chemical warfare. It also disclosed 4 imported mobile missile launchers, 4 locally produced mobile missile launchers, 4 launch and test vehicles and a number of related equipment and spare parts. The Special Commission has so far not been able to verify all of these items which like the missiles are reported by Iraq to have been unilaterally destroyed late in July 1991.

760-6-2

0007

2

4. In addition, Iraq has informed the Commission about a large number of chemical munitions unilaterally destroyed during the summer of 1991.

5. All these destruction activities were conducted in violation of Security Council resolution 687 (1991), which provides for international supervision of the destruction of any proscribed item. Furthermore, the admissions in the letter are proof that Iraq had been concealing important information from the Special Commission until the letter was delivered.

Destruction of ballistic missiles related production equipment

6. Iraq stated in the letter of 19 March that it was now prepared to begin implementing the decision of the Commission on the destruction of equipment and buildings (see document S/23673). During the period 21-30 March, the ballistic missiles team referred to above oversaw the destruction of the nine items of equipment identified for destruction by the eighth ballistic missiles inspection team but which the Iraqi side had refused to destroy at that time. The full list is as follows:

| Site | Item destroyed | Date destroyed/verified |
|---|---|---|
| Dhu al-Fiqar | Computer DEA | 25 March |
| | INSTRON cooling chamber | 25 March |
| | INSTRON measurement | 25 March |
| | Motor case transport dollies | 25 March |
| | Coolers and compressors | 27 March |
| Taj al-Ma'arik | 300-gallon mixer (2) | 27 March |
| | 300-gallon mixer bowls (4)1/ | 25 March |
| Al-Yawm al-Azim | Cradle for BADR-2000 | 25 March |
| | Electronic test equipment | 25 March |

1/ Document S/23673 of 4 March 1992 mentioned only 3 of these mixer bowls. An additional mixer bowl was discovered by the eighth ballistic missiles inspection team.

760-6-3

0008

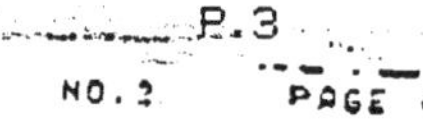



7. These items were destroyed by either cutting with a plasma torch or by crushing. This destruction represents the first step in the destruction of all the items in List A contained in document S/23673. The Iraqi authorities have handed over their proposals on how they intend to destroy the items on List A. These proposals are now being studied by the Special Commission. A further ballistic missiles inspection team will visit Iraq in the near future to continue this destruction process.

## Chemical Weapons Destruction

8. A chemical weapons inspection team was in Iraq during the period 21 February to 24 March to undertake destruction activities at Khamisiyah Storage Site, some 400km south of Baghdad.

9. The munitions destroyed included fully-, partially- and un-filled rockets. The chemical agent was a nerve agent. A full breakdown of rockets destroyed is as follows:

| | |
|---|---|
| 1. Filled rockets | 389 |
| 2. Partially filled rockets | 36 |
| 3. Unfilled rockets | 38 |
| Total | 463 |

(ie approximately 2.5 tonnes of agent)

## Nuclear issues

10. In the nuclear field, an inspection team will arrive in Iraq early next week inter alia to supervise and verify the destruction of plant and equipment at Iraq's nuclear weapons design centre at al Atheer. The methods of destruction to be used are currently under consideration by the IAEA.

360-6-4

0009

4

Declarations due under resolutions 707 and 715 (1991)

11. The Iraqi Government has stated that they wish to make a new start in their dealings with the Special Commission. In their letter of 19 March, the Iraqi Government stated that they will make available a "dossier of comprehensive, final and complete information on relevant programmes." In discussions with the Special Commission, Iraq has also undertaken to make the initial declarations required under the plans for the future ongoing monitoring and verification of its obligations not to reacquire proscribed items. However, the Special Commission have not yet received any indication of Iraq's readiness to acknowledge its obligations under resolutions 707 and 715 (1991). Nor have the promised information or declarations been received from Iraq. Without the clear acknowledgement by the Government of Iraq of its obligations under resolutions 707 and 715 (1991), there would be no firm political basis for the proper implementation of these resolutions. Moreover, any information or declaration received without clear acknowledgement will be of doubtful credibility.

Conclusions

12. In spite of the serious concealment of the items and equipment admitted in the letter of 19 March 1992, the actions above represent a development towards the implementation of resolution 687 (1991) and subsequent relevant resolutions - i.e. the full dismantling of Iraq's weapons of mass destruction capabilities and the establishment of an effective regime for ongoing monitoring and verification to ensure that Iraq does not reacquire such capabilities. However, much remains to be done before this goal is reached in full:

- complete destruction, removal or rendering harmless of Iraq's prohibited weapons capabilities - ie equipment and facilities associated with its weapons of mass

360-6-5

0010

5

destruction and ballistic missiles programmes and the destruction of Iraq's stocks of chemical munitions, agents and precursors;

- acceptance by Iraq of its obligations under Council resolutions 707 and 715 (1991);

- provision by Iraq of the required full, final and complete disclosures of all aspects of its programmes for weapons of mass destruction and ballistic missiles with a range greater than 150km and verification by the Special Commission of the accuracy of these disclosures;

- complete verification of Iraq's declaration of 19 March concerning items it destroyed unilaterally;

- declarations by Iraq required under resolution 715 (1991), which are to include dual capability plants used for permitted purposes but which could be used for prohibited purposes;

- the initiation and smooth functioning of the plans for future ongoing monitoring and verification to ensure that Iraq does not reacquire prohibited capabilities;

- acceptance by Iraq of the Special Commission's aircraft landing rights.

360-6-6

'92-04-08 10:52 ☎202 797 0595 EMBASSY OF KOREA --- WOIMUBU ☑009

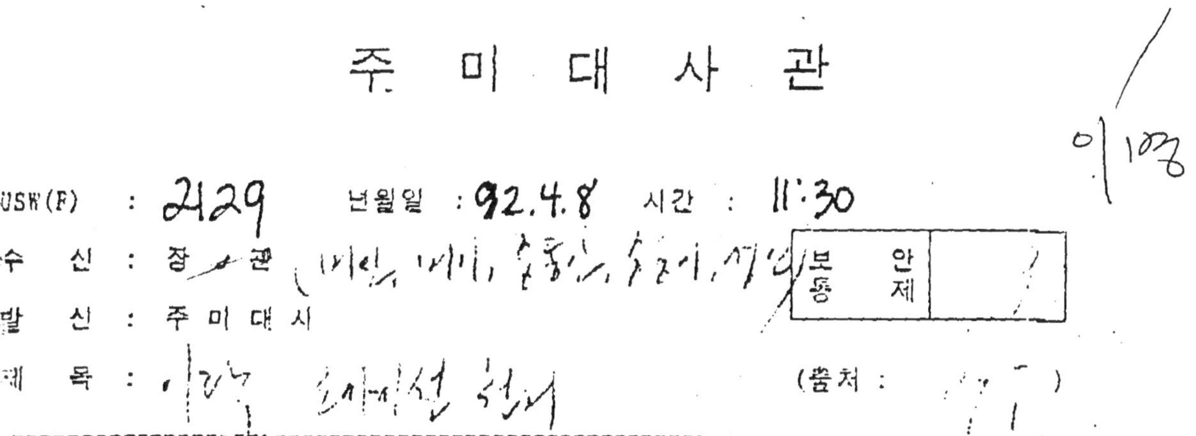

주 미 대 사 관

USW(F) : 2129 년월일 : 92.4.8 시간 : 11:30

수 신 : 장 관 (미원, 미이, 중동일, 중근이, 기정)

발 신 : 주 미 대 사

제 목 : 이라크 핵시설 현황 (출처 : )

보안 통제

# Iraq Agrees to Begin Destruction Of a Nuclear Complex, U.N. Says

Special to The New York Times

VIENNA, April 7 — Iraq has told a United Nations inspection team that it will begin on Wednesday to destroy what the United Nations says is the technical heart of the Iraqi nuclear weapons program at Al Atheer, an official at the International Atomic Energy Agency said today.

"They told us they would comply, but certainly they are not happy about it," said Maurizio Zifferero, who heads an agency team investigating Iraq's nuclear program.

After the revelation last year that it was working on a clandestine program to develop nuclear weapons in violation of international agreements, Iraq was ordered by the United Nations Security Council to destroy its weapons of mass destruction.

Iraq had resisted destruction of the Al Atheer installation, 20 miles southwest of Baghdad, maintaining that it was a civilian research center. But at a meeting here two weeks ago, Iraq was unable to convince the agency of that and was ordered to demolish it.

**Demolition Methods**

"Al Atheer was our priority target because of the danger of their resuming at an early stage the weapons production," Mr. Zifferero said.

At a meeting today with agency inspectors in Baghdad, Iraq first proposed destroying the bunker-like buildings by filling them with cement. But inspectors insisted that they be blasted or bulldozed. Iraq finally agreed and presented a 10-day plan for their destruction by army engineers, Mr. Zifferero said, adding that the time frame was "optimistic."

Agency inspectors are to stay in Iraq for 10 days to oversee the destruction, he said.

The huge Al Atheer installation, which was barely grazed by allied bombings during the Persian Gulf war, consists of more than 100 buildings worth several hundred million dollars, agency officials say. The agency seeks the demolition of 6 to 10 buildings that it says were used to test explosive charges that could be used to detonate a nuclear weapon.

Agency inspectors have already monitored the destruction of other components of Iraq's nuclear program. Earlier this year they verified that Iraq had destroyed large quantitites of maraging steel, a special hard steel used in centrifuges that were used to enrich uranium. Calutrons, also used for uranium enrichment, have been destroyed, too.

92.4.8 NYT

외신 1과 통 제

(2129 - 1 - 1)

| 배부처 | 장관실 | 차관실 | 一차보 | 二차보 | 외정실 | 분석관 | 아주국 | 미주국 | 구주국 | 중아국 | 국기국 | 경제국 | 통상국 | 문협국 | 외연원 | 청와대 | 안기부 | 공보처 | 경기원 | 상공부 | 재무부 | 농수부 | 동자부 | 환경처 | 과기처 | | | |
|---|---|---|---|---|---|---|---|---|---|---|---|---|---|---|---|---|---|---|---|---|---|---|---|---|---|---|---|---|
| 처 | /2 | / | / | | / | / | | /2 | | /2 | | | | | / | / | / | | | | | | | | | | | |

0012

원 본

# 외 무 부

이명, 한

종 별 :

번 호 : UNW-1079 일 시 : 92 0411 1530

수 신 : 장 관(연일,중동이,기정)

발 신 : 주 유엔 대사

제 목 : 걸프사태(유엔안보리 비공식 회의)

1. 4.10. 저녁 유엔안보리는 이락정부가 요청한 유엔의 이락영공 정찰비행 중지에 대 하여 비공식협의를 갖고 하기 요지의 안보리 의장명의 성명을 발표함

가. 유엔의 정찰비행은 안보리결의 687,707 및 715호에 근거하여 수행되고 있음

나. 유엔특별위원회는 이락영공 정찰비행의 권리가 있음을 재확인하면서 이락정부는 이락군이 동정찰비행에 간섭하거나 안전을 위협하지 않도록 보장하고 유엔 정찰기 및 승무원의 안전을 확보하도록 모든 조치를 취할것을 요청함

다. 안보리 회원국들은 이락정부가 상기의무를 이행치 않음으로서 발생하는 심각한 결과에 대하여 경고함

2. 이락정부는 유엔특별위원회(이락무기폐기위원회) EKEUS 위원장앞 4.9자 서한을통하여 4.4. 이란의 대이락 공습의 결과로 유엔 정찰기를 공습기로 오인, 격추가능성이 있어 정찰기와 조종사에 위험이 되고 있음을 언급하고 동정찰비행 중지를 요청하면서, 동정찰비행이 위협의 목적으로 수행되고 있으며 특별위원회의 임무와 전혀 관계없는 임무를 수행하고 있다고 항의하였다함

(대사 유종하-국장)

첨부 UNW(F)-0380

---

국기국 중아국 안기부 외감실 보석관 1차관

PAGE 1 92.04.12 06:54 DS

외신 1과 통제관

0013

APR 11 '92 14:04 KOREAN MISS P.1

UNW(F)-0380 20411 1530 UNW-1079 의 첨부

The members of the Security Council have learnt with grave concern from the Executive Chairman of the Special Commission of recent developments which appear to call for a halt in and constitute a threat to the safety and security of the Special Commission's aerial surveillance flights over Iraq. The members of the Council wish to point out that the surveillance flights are carried out under the authority of Security Council resolutions 687, 707 and 715 (1991).

Reaffirming the right of the Special Commission to conduct such aerial surveillance flights, the members of the Council call upon the Government of Iraq to take all the necessary steps to ensure that the Iraqi military forces will not interfere with or threaten the security of the flights concerned and to comply with its responsibilities to secure the safety of the Special Commission's aircraft and personnel while flying over Iraq. The members of the Council warn the Government of Iraq of the serious consequences which would ensue from any failure to comply with these obligations.

380-1-1

0014

# UN의 이라크 대량살상무기폐기 특별위원회(UNSCOM)

92. 4. 14

## 1. 활동근거

가. UN 안보리 결의 687(91.4.3)

o 이라크는 국제적 감시하에 모든 생화학무기 및 사정거리 150km 이상의 탄도미사일과 이들의 저장, 연구, 개발, 지원 및 제조시설들을 파기, 철거 또는 무력화해야 함.

o 이라크는 핵무기 또는 핵무기 가용물질의 연구, 개발, 지원시설 및 생산시설의 확보, 개발포기를 수락하여야 함.

나. UN 안보리 결의 707 (91.8.15) 및 715(91.10.11)

o 안보리 결의 687호의 이행방안
- 이라크의 의무이행 및 시설 감시 및 검증
- UN 특별위원회 및 IAEA의 관련활동에 관한 특권과 면제

다. UN 안보리 결의 699(91.6.17)

o 상기 UN 사찰관련 제반경비는 이라크가 부담

## 2. 관련 분야별 진전사항

가. 생·화학무기

o UN 안보리 특별위원회는 현재까지 이라크내 43개 화학무기 관련시설에 대한 사찰을 실시하였고 나머지 장소에 대한 사찰도 곧 실시예정

o UN은 그간의 사찰과정에서 이라크가 자체 개발했거나 개조한 10개 유형의 화학무기를 발견하였음.

o 생물무기에 대해서 이라크는 당초 보유치 않고 있다고 선언하였으나, 사찰 과정에서 이라크 관리들은 방어 및 공격용 생물무기 개발계획을 시인한 바 있음.

나. 탄도미사일 및 장거리포

o UN 안보리 특별위 사찰팀은 71개 장소에 대한 사찰실시

o UN 사찰팀은 사찰과정에서 구경 1,000㎜이상의 슈퍼건, 이동식 스커드 미사일 발사대를 발견, 대부분 관련시설을 파기함.

o UN은 동 분야에서는 대체적으로 만족할 만한 성과가 있었다고 분석하고 있으나 아직도 이라크가 개조형 스커드등을 보유하고 있을 가능성도 배제치 않고 있어 각국과의 정보교환등을 통한 완전한 사찰 노력 경주중

다. 핵 무 기

o 그간의 이라크측 부인에도 불구하고 UN 사찰팀은 핵사찰 과정에서 이라크의 핵무기 제조계획을 발견

o UN은 그간 이라크가 명확한 증거 발견시까지 핵무기 개발노력을 부인해온점등을 고려, 계속적인 사찰 실시예정

라. UN의 지속적 감시 및 검증

o UN은 이라크의 결의안 687 준수에 대한 국제적 감시를 위해 검사 및 답사, 대량파괴무기 및 생산시설의 파괴, 지속적 감시 및 검증을 실시하고 있음.

o UN은 92.1 현재까지의 진전사항으로 보아 탄도미사일, 화학무기 및 핵연료등의 제거외에는 만족할만한 성과가 없었다고 분석하고 있음.

## 3. 최근 동향

### 가. 안보리 동향

o 92.2.15. 안보리는 이라크의 안보리 결의상 제반의무 불이행과 관련, 최후 통첩성격의 결의안 또는 의장 성명발표 검토

o 2.19. 안보리는 안보리결의 이행에 불성실한 것으로 판단되는 이라크에 대하여 UN의 단호한 조치가 필요하다는 특별위 보고서를 청취하고 R. Ekeus 특위의장의 이라크 파견을 결정(2.21-24)

o 2.28. UN 안보리는 Ekeus 특위의장의 이라크 방문에도 불구, 이라크가 성실한 의무이행 자세를 보이지 않고 있음을 지적, 이라크의 의무 불이행 비난 및 조속한 이행 촉구 내용의 안보리 의장성명을 발표

o 3.11-12. 이라크측 제의하 이라크 정부대표단(단장 : 티릭 아지즈 부수상) 참석하 안보리 공식회의 개최
  - 이라크측 후속태도를 보아가며 대응방향 강구 예정
  - IAEA 및 SCOM과 이라크측과의 협력과정 당분간 관망 예정

o 3.21. SCOM 이라크 방문(제9차 미사일 폐기 검증단 활동 개시)

o 3.27. 안보리 비공식회의 개최, 의장명의 성명 발표
  - 이라크의 안보리결의 687호 이행을 위한 최근 조치에도 불구 재재결의 해제에는 아직 미흡함.

o 4.3자 UNSCOM 위원장의 안보리 의장앞 서한 요지

- 이락 외무장관이 UNSCOM 위원장앞 92.3.19자 서한을 통하여 최초로 밝힌바에 의하면

  · 이락은 유엔감시하에 91.7월 폐기된 미사일 62기외에 92기를 보유하고 있었으나, 91년 여름 일방적으로 폐기하였다 함. (UNSCOM에 폐기잔재 확인)

  · 또한 이락정부는 유엔에 통보하지 않는 45개의 화학탄두를 포함한 135개의 미사일탄두와 8개의 이동 미사일 발사대를 보유하고 있었으나, 91.7월 이를 일방적으로 폐기하였으며 (UNSCOM에서 확인불가) 다량의 화학무기도 일방적으로 폐기 하였다 함.

- 상기와 같은 이락의 일방적 폐기는 국제감시하에 폐기토록 되어 있는 안보리결의(687)를 위반하는 것이며 이락이 최근까지도 보유한 무기관련 정보를 UN에 숨기고 있었음.

- 이락은 유엔이 요청한 미사일관련 폐기대상물중(S/23673 ANNEX A) 최초로 92.3.21. 309개 대상물을 폐기하였으며 여타 폐기대상물의 폐기계획안을 UNSCOM에 제출하였음.

- 유엔감시하에 화학무기 2.5톤을 2.21-3.24중 폐기하였음.

- 유엔조사단이 4월초순 이락을 방문, AL ATHEER소재 핵무기 생산 관련 시설 및 장비의 파괴를 감독, 확인 예정이며 파괴방법은 IAEA가 현재 검토중임.

- 이락의 상기 조치는 유엔결의 이행의 진전이나 이락의 유엔결의를 충실히 이행할지는 좀더 두고 보아야 함.

o UNSCOM 위원장, 주유엔대사에게 Muthanna State Establishment 소재 화학무기 폐기 위한 작업단 설치계획 설명 및 우리나라 참여 타진 서한 송부(4.3자)

o 4.8. IAEA - 이라크간 Al Atheer 소재 핵무기 시설 파괴 합의

나. 주요이사국 태도

o 미, 영, 불은 일단 관망하겠다는 자세이나 새로운 대응 조치를 취해야할 경우 제한적 군사행동도 포함될 것으로 보임.

o 비동맹 국가그룹은 이라크가 명백히 안보리 결의안을 위반하고 있으므로 안보리 이사국들의 강경조치에 동의할 수 밖에 없다는 입장임.

## 第11次 IAEA 이락 核査察 結果

1. 第11次 IAEA 核査察團(團長 :「페레이코스」IAEA檢査官) 26명이 4.7 - 15간 이락의 「알 아티르」核工團(바그다드 西南方 40km 所在)査察을 實施하여

   가. 鐵製壁을 絶斷하는 方法으로「알 아티르」內 小型 發破室을 破壞(4.9)하고

   나. 3단계의 다이너마이트 爆破作業을 통한 大型鐵製 建物(1萬 5,000㎡) 파괴 및 核實驗 用途의 大型방커를 콘크리트와 古鐵로 채우는 作業을 實施(4.13)한 가운데

   다. 「페레이코스」團長은 記者會見을 통해 「알 아티르」內 主要建物의 2/3 破壞를 監視함으로써 이락 核武器 計劃의 核心을 除去했다고 發表(4.14)했음.

2. IAEA의 이락 核査察 動向을 보면

   가. 걸프戰 停戰決議 687호(91.4 採擇)에 따라 UN大量破壞武器 廢棄 特別委의 協調하에 투와이다 등 이락內 主要 核關聯 施設에 대한 査察 및 廢棄作業을 專擔해 왔는 바

   나. 그간 10次에 걸친 査察團 파견을 통해 濃縮우라늄 25kg 封印(91.5), 核關聯 書類 押收(91.9) 및 遠心分離器를 破壞(91.10)한바 있으나

다. 최근 이락 核計劃의 中樞神經 役割을 수행해 온 것으로 알려진「알 아티르」內 核施設 廢棄問題와 관련

○ IAEA측은 6次 査察團(91.9)入手資料 및 8차 査察團(91.11)의 査察結果를 바탕으로「알 아티르」內 施設一部가 核武器 開發 및 製造에 필요한 特殊設備로 考案된 것으로 判斷, 이락側에 無條件 破壞를 命令(3.25)한데 대해

○ 이락側은 同 施設이 産業 및 技術分野 관련 資料生産을 연구하기 위한 國立硏究所라고 주장, 廢棄를 拒否함에 따라 IAEA·이락間 摩擦이 노정된 바 있음.

3. 이번 第11次 IAEA 이락 核査察과 관련

가.「알 아티르」核施設 破壞는

○ 이락側이 IAEA의 同施設에 대한 無條件 破壞要求를 受容(4.7)한데 따라 이루어진 것으로서

○ UN의 對이락 核査察이 濃縮우라늄 등 核物質과 濃縮部品에 이어 核施設 破壞로 發展되었다는 점에서 意義가 있으나

나. 基本的으로 이락側은 査察 妨害·遲延을 통해 軍事潛在力을 保存하려는 原則을 견지하고 있는데 대해

다. 이번에 廢棄對象으로 選定된 建物이「알 아티르」所在 100개 이상의 建物중 일부분(8 - 10개)인데다가 IAEA側이 核施設 破壞 및 査察過程에 있어 이락側의 協調가 불충분한 것으로 評價하고 있다는 점에서

※「페레이코스」團長은 이락이 査察官들이 발견해 낸 것만 보여주고 核計劃의 主要 要素들은 뒤로 숨기고 있으며 이락이 우라늄 濃縮을 위한 遠心分離器 및 地下 플루토늄 原子爐를 隱匿하고 있는 것으로 推定된다고 言及(4.14)

라. 5월 중순으로 豫定된 第12次 核査察團의「알 아티르」殘餘 核施設에 대한 破壞 및 隱匿 核施設 査察이 계속되면서 이락의 反撥 등에 따른 緊張은 持續될 것으로 보임.

24-24

0022

# 주 국 련 대 표 부

주국련 2031- 628 1992. 6. 5.

수신 장 관

참조 국제기구국장, 중동아프리카국장 朱

제목 이락무기 폐기

연 : UNW - 1620

1. 유엔 UNSCOM의 이락무기 폐기활동과 관련, UNSCOM의 활동내용, 방향, 대금약품 목록등이 포함된 "이락의 안보리결의 687 이행의 사찰 및 검증 계획"에 관한 유엔 사무총장의 보고서를 별첨 송부합니다.

2. UNSCOM이 요청한 정보제공과 관련하여, UNSCOM은 이락이 안보리 결의에 의해 관련정보를 제출해야 함에도 불구하고 이를 이행치 않음으로써 일부 유엔 회원국에게 관련 정보제공을 요청하는 것인바, UNSCOM이 필요로 하는 화학, 생물 및 미사일관련 정보는 별첨 보고서 P8-P11 및 관련 부록(AAnnex II, III, IV)에 포함되어 있음을 첨언합니다.

첨 부 : 91.10.2자 유엔 사무총장 보고서(S/22871/Rev.1) 1부. 끝.

발 송 No. 1992. 6. 5 주유엔대표부

주 국 련 대 사

| 선 길 | | | 공 람 | | |
|---|---|---|---|---|---|
| 접수일시 | 1992. 6. 8 | | | | |
| 처리과 | | 32346 | | | |

0023

UNITED
NATIONS

**S**

**Security Council**



Distr.
GENERAL

S/22871/Rev.1
2 October 1991

ORIGINAL: ENGLISH

Plan for future ongoing monitoring and verification of Iraq's compliance with relevant parts of section C of Security Council resolution 687 (1991)

Report of the Secretary-General

## I. GENERAL

### A. Introduction

1. The present report is submitted in pursuance of Security Council resolution 687 (1991). In paragraph 10 of section C of that resolution, the Security Council requested the Secretary-General, in consultation with the Special Commission, to develop and submit for approval a plan for the ongoing monitoring and verification of Iraq's compliance with its obligations under that paragraph. The Plan is contained in section II of the present report.

2. As outlined in my report to the Security Council of 17 May 1991 (S/22614), the provisions of section C of resolution 687 (1991) lend themselves to a three-stage implementation procedure: gathering and assessment of information; disposal of weapons and facilities and all other items specified in paragraphs 8 and 12 of resolution 687 (1991); and ongoing monitoring and verification of Iraq's compliance. The first two stages are currently being implemented and will continue until their objectives are fully achieved.

3. The Plan submitted in the present report addresses the third stage, i.e. ongoing monitoring and verification of Iraq's compliance with its unconditional obligation not to use, retain, possess, develop, construct or otherwise acquire any weapons or related items prohibited under paragraphs 8 and 9 of resolution 687 (1991). Thus, monitoring and verification will need to cover not only military but also civilian sites, facilities, material and other items that could be used or activities that could be involved in contravention of Iraq's obligations under resolution 687 (1991). The Plan incorporates the additional obligations of Iraq under Security Council resolution 707 (1991) and the corresponding monitoring and verification activities.

91-32425 2644f (E)

/...

0024

4. The Plan should enter into force directly upon its approval by the Security Council, which means that the early stages of its implementation and the later stages of the disposal of existing prohibited weapons, facilities and related items would take place simultaneously. This would, at an early stage, prevent Iraq from developing new capabilities regarding the relevant weapons categories, thus already closing a potential loophole during the first stages of the implementation of section C of resolution 687 (1991). Carefully managed use of available resources would make it possible to carry out the dual tasks in parallel, to great effect. With the gradual completion of the disposal of Iraq's present weapons capabilities, resources can gradually be transferred and streamlined without therefore, at any stage, compromising the efficiency of the verification of Iraq's compliance with its obligations under resolutions 687 (1991) and 707 (1991). In paragraph 14 of its resolution 687 (1991) the Security Council noted that the actions to be taken by Iraq in paragraphs 8, 9, 10, 11, 12 and 13 of that resolution "represent steps towards the goal of establishing in the Middle East a zone free from weapons of mass destruction and all missiles for their delivery and the objective of a global ban on chemical weapons". The implementation of the Plan, developed pursuant to paragraph 10 of resolution 687 (1991), will contribute to an environment conducive to achieving the above-mentioned goal and objective.

## B. Institutional and organizational aspects

5. Bearing in mind that resolutions 687 (1991) and 707 (1991) were adopted by the Security Council acting under Chapter VII of the Charter of the United Nations, it is assumed that the task of carrying out the monitoring and verification provided for under the Plan should be entrusted to an executive body under the authority of the Security Council. This is particularly important should any situation arise of non-compliance by Iraq with its obligations under section C of resolution 687 (1991) and under resolution 707 (1991).

6. The intrinsic interrelationship between paragraphs 8, 9 and 10 of resolution 687 (1991) requires that this body make direct use of the expertise, the information gathered and assessed and the experience gained by the Special Commission established as a subsidiary organ of the Security Council pursuant to paragraph 9 of resolution 687 (1991).

7. In view of these considerations, it would appear most practical and efficient that a compliance unit be organized under the Special Commission in order to carry out the monitoring and verification tasks provided for under the Plan. The present arrangements for staffing would continue on a revised scale, with appropriate support from the Department for Disarmament Affairs. The financing of the Plan would have to be determined by the competent United Nations organs, possibly in the same way as the arrangements agreed upon for the present phase of the Special Commission's work.

/...

## II. THE PLAN

### A. Scope

13. In accepting unconditionally Security Council resolution 687 (1991), Iraq has undertaken not to use, retain, possess, develop, construct or otherwise acquire:

(a) Any chemical or biological weapons or any stocks of agents or any related subsystems or components or any research, development, support or manufacturing facilities;

(b) Any ballistic missiles with a range greater than 150 kilometres or any related major parts, including launchers, or any repair or production facilities.

14. In order to ensure Iraq's compliance with these undertakings, the Special Commission, pursuant to resolutions 687 (1991) and 707 (1991), shall, through inspections and through aerial overflights, as well as through the provision of information by Iraq, monitor and verify that activities, sites, facilities, material and other items, both military and civilian, are not used by Iraq in contravention of its obligations under resolutions 687 (1991) and 707 (1991).

15. To this end, the provisions set forth in the Plan and its annexes, which constitute an integral part of the Plan, shall apply.

### B. General provisions

#### 1. Information

16. Iraq shall:

(a) Provide to the Special Commission, on a regular basis, full, complete, correct and timely information on activities, sites, facilities, material and other items, both military and civilian, that might be used for purposes prohibited under paragraph 10 of resolution 687 (1991);

(b) Provide to the Special Commission full, complete, correct and timely information on any additional activities, sites, facilities, material or other items that the Commission may designate for provision of information on a regular basis;

(c) Provide to the Special Commission, fully, completely, and promptly, any additional information or clarification that the Commission may request and respond fully, completely and promptly to any questions or requests from the Special Commission.

Further provisions related to the submission of information are set forth in sections C, D and E and in annexes II, III and IV of the Plan.

/...

(e) Accept unconditionally the Special Commission's determinations regarding use of the Commission's aircraft with appropriate sensors as necessary and airfields in Iraq for such aircraft;

(f) Not obstruct aerial overflights or take concealment measures at any area, location, site or facility designated by the Special Commission for inspection or overflight;

(g) Accept unconditionally the inspectors and all other personnel designated by the Special Commission and ensure the complete implementation of the privileges, immunities and facilities of the personnel of the Special Commission and their complete safety and freedom of movement;

(h) Cooperate fully with the Special Commission and facilitate its inspections, overflights and other activities under the Plan;

(i) Accept unconditionally the rights of the Special Commission under the Plan and not take any action to interfere with, impede, or obstruct the exercise by the Special Commission of its functions and rights under Security Council resolutions 687 (1991), 707 (1991) and the Plan;

(j) Designate its Inspection Representative for each inspection to accompany the inspection team in Iraq;

(k) Invite and accept unconditionally the decision of the Special Commission on any requests by Iraq to move or destroy any material, equipment or item relating to its nuclear, chemical or biological weapons or ballistic missile programmes, or material, equipment or any item relating to its other nuclear activities.

19. Further provisions on inspections, aerial overflights, security, privileges and immunities and related provisions are set forth in annex I.

### 3. National implementation measures

20. Iraq shall adopt the necessary measures to implement its obligations under section C of resolution 687 (1991), resolution 707 (1991) and the Plan, in particular:

(a) To prohibit all natural and legal persons under Iraq's jurisdiction or control from undertaking anywhere any activity that is prohibited for Iraq by resolutions 687 (1991), 707 (1991), by other related Security Council resolutions or by the Plan;

(b) To enact penal legislation which, in conformity with international law, shall extend to the activities referred to under subparagraph (a) above undertaken anywhere by any natural or legal persons under Iraq's jurisdiction or control.

/...

C. Provisions related to chemical items

28. Chemicals, equipment and facilities set forth herein and in annex II could be used for purposes related to chemical weapons. They shall therefore be subject to monitoring and verification in accordance with the following additional provisions in order to ensure that Iraq does not use, develop, produce or otherwise acquire chemical weapons or related items prohibited under resolution 687 (1991).

29. Chemicals that could be used for the development, production or acquisition of chemical weapons but which also have significant uses for purposes not prohibited by resolution 687 (1991) are set forth in list A in annex II. These chemicals may be used, developed, produced, stored or acquired solely for purposes not prohibited by resolution 687 (1991), subject to the provisions under paragraphs 30 and 31 below, and annex II.

30. Iraq shall, not later than 30 days after the adoption of the Plan by the Security Council, and on a regular basis thereafter, provide to the Special Commission information in accordance with annex II regarding:

(a) The total national quantity of the production, processing or consumption of any chemical specified in list A of annex II and of the import and export of any of these chemicals specifying the supplier or recipient countries involved;

(b) Any site or facility that is involved in production, processing, consumption, storage, import or export of one tonne or more per year of any chemical specified in list A of annex II or that at any time has been involved in activities with any of these chemicals for chemical weapons purposes;

(c) Any site or facility that is involved in production or processing of organophosphorus chemicals or is involved in production of organic chemicals by chlorination;

(d) Any site or facility where production, processing, consumption, storage, import or export of one tonne or more per year of any chemical specified in list A of annex II, or where production or processing of organophosphorus chemicals or where production of organic chemicals by chlorination is planned;

(e) Any import or any other acquisition of equipment or technologies intended for production and processing of any chemical specified in list A of annex II, of any organophosphorus chemical or for production of organic chemicals by chlorination.

31. Should Iraq plan any production, processing, consumption, storage, import or export not notified under paragraph 30 (d) above, it may begin such an activity only after providing to the Special Commission a special notification in accordance with annex II.

/...

0028

(e) Any site or facility for the production of vaccines;

(f) Any research, development, testing or other support or manufacturing facility for equipment and other items specified in paragraph 1 of annex III;

(g) Any imports, other acquisition or exports of micro-organisms meeting the criteria for risk groups IV, III and II, toxins and vaccines, as well as related equipment and facilities, specifying the supplier or recipient countries involved.

36. Iraq shall, not later than 30 days after the adoption of the Plan by the Security Council, and on a regular basis thereafter, provide to the Special Commission:

(a) A list of all documents of a scientific and technical nature published or prepared by any site or facility engaged in work relating to toxins or micro-organisms meeting the criteria for risk groups IV, III and II, including those of a theoretical nature. Full copies of such documents shall be made available by Iraq to the Special Commission upon request. Documents of a purely diagnostic nature relating to risk group II micro-organisms are excepted;

(b) A description of all work on toxins or micro-organisms meeting the criteria for risk groups IV, III or II as well as of all work being conducted on the dissemination of micro-organisms or toxins into the environment or on processes that would lead to such dissemination, specifying the site or facility involved.

37. Iraq shall provide to the Special Commission in accordance with annex III information on all cases of infectious diseases affecting humans, animals or plants, that deviate, or seem to deviate, from the normal pattern or are caused by any micro-organism meeting the criteria for risk groups IV and III and on all cases of similar occurrences caused by toxins.

38. Iraq shall not:

(a) Import items referred to in paragraph 35 (g) above without giving prior notice to the Special Commission in accordance with annex III. As an exception, the emergency import of vaccines may take place with simultaneous notification to the Special Commission;

(b) Conduct any activities in the field of micro-organisms and toxins except by civilian personnel not in the employ of any military organization. Such activities shall be conducted openly; no classified or secret programmes or activities shall be permitted. The sites or facilities engaged in such activities shall not be under the control of, or owned by, any military organization. Should any military organization need to be involved in such activities for prophylactic or therapeutic purposes, Iraq shall submit a request to the Special Commission specifying precisely the toxins, micro-organisms and the quantities required, the site or facility where they

/...

42. Iraq shall not construct, otherwise acquire or operate sites or facilities for the use, development, production, training or other support of ballistic missiles capable of a range greater than 150 kilometres, including sites or facilities for research, development, modification, manufacture, assembly, testing, storage, repair, training, flight simulating and operational use of such missiles, nor acquire related major parts specified in paragraph 41 and the items listed in paragraph 1 of annex IV for such missiles.

43. Iraq shall, not later than 30 days after the adoption of the Plan by the Security Council, and on a regular basis thereafter, provide to the Special Commission the following:

(a) A list of all its missiles designed for use, or capable of being modified for use, in a surface-to-surface role with a range greater than 50 kilometres, specifying their name and type, type of propulsion, number of stages and/or boosters, guidance systems, payload, warhead and re-entry vehicle types, launcher types, airframe and warhead transporter, ground support equipment and the sites or facilities where these missiles, items or equipment are located;

(b) Information on any project and on any site or facility for such missiles, including sites or facilities for production, assembly, repair and maintenance, storage and operational bases, specifying their locations;

(c) Information on any project and on any site or facility for missile research, development, modification or testing, specifying its locations;

(d) Information on the development, production, export, import or other acquisition, training or other services related to the items, equipment and technologies listed in annex IV, specifying sites or facilities where such items, equipment and technologies are located, the purposes and the projects for which they are being used and the supplier or recipient countries involved.

44. Iraq shall notify the Special Commission in accordance with annex IV of the developmental or test launch of any missile, specifying where and when the launch is to take place.

45. Further provisions related to missiles are set forth in annex IV.

/...

0030

4. Iraq shall, upon receipt of the name of the Chief Inspector for an inspection, immediately inform the Special Commission of the name of the individual who will be the Iraqi Inspection Representative for the inspection.

## Conduct of inspections or aerial overflights

5. The Special Commission shall have the right:

(a) To request, receive, examine, copy and remove any record, data, information or documentation and to verify inventories;

(b) To examine, retain, move or photograph, including by videotaping, any activity or item;

(c) To conduct interviews with any personnel at a site or facility under inspection, or with any Iraqi official;

(d) To install containment, surveillance and other equipment and devices and to construct facilities for inspection, observation, testing, verification or monitoring activities;

(e) To take samples of any kind and perform on-site analyses of the samples using its own equipment;

(f) To remove and transfer samples outside Iraq for analyses off-site at laboratories of its choice;

(g) To mark, tag or otherwise identify any material or other item;

(h) To use its own instrumentation to collect data during inspections and aerial overflights, including photographic, video, infrared and radar data.

6. Iraq shall:

(a) Provide clarification or explanation of any ambiguity that might arise during an inspection;

(b) Perform, upon request by the Special Commission, analyses of samples in the presence of inspectors, including on-site;

(c) Perform, upon request by the Special Commission, any additional task.

/...

(c) Provide priority clearance, as well as the basing and all necessary facilities as determined by the Special Commission for any fixed- or rotary-wing aircraft used by the Commission;

(d) Provide, upon the request of the Special Commission, the means of transport, maps or other information needed;

(e) Take every necessary measure to ensure that the inspection team arrives at the site or facility to be inspected by the time notified by the Special Commission;

(f) Provide, upon the request of the Special Commission, appropriate means of communication;

(g) Provide, upon request of the Special Commission, appropriate escort and/or support personnel;

(h) Provide, upon request of the Special Commission, medical, logistical and/or technical support;

(i) Not interfere with or censor any communication to or from the Special Commission or its personnel;

(j) Permit, without delay or hindrance, the Special Commission to remove from Iraq any material or other item, including any documentation, acquired by the Commission during inspection or other monitoring and verification activities.

<u>Security, privileges and immunities</u>

9. The Special Commission shall have the right to make its own arrangements to ensure the safety and security of its personnel and property and to take custody of any material or other item, including documentation.

10. Iraq shall ensure the safety and security of the personnel and property of the Special Commission and shall provide the arrangements to this end when so requested by the Special Commission.

11. In addition and without prejudice to the foregoing provisions, the Special Commission and any agency of the United Nations system participating in the carrying out of the Plan, its property, funds, assets and personnel shall enjoy the facilities, privileges and immunities provided for in the applicable convention or agreement, namely the Convention on the Privileges and Immunities of the United Nations, the Agreement on the Privileges and Immunities of the International Atomic Energy Agency (IAEA) and the Convention on the Privileges and Immunities of the Specialized Agencies.

/...

0032

upon the rights, facilities, privileges and immunities provided for in the exchange of notes between the Secretary-General of the United Nations and the Minister for Foreign Affairs of Iraq, which entered into force on 14 May 1991, regarding the status, privileges and immunities of the Special Commission as originally established pursuant to paragraph 9 of Security Council resolution 687 (1991).

/...

0033

| List A | Chemical Abstracts Service (CAS) registry No. |
|---|---|
| 12. Cyanogen chloride | (506-77-4) |
| 13. Hydrogen cyanide | (74-90-8) |
| 14. Trichloronitromethane (chloropicrin) | (76-06-2) |
| 15. Phosphorus oxychloride | (10025-87-3) |
| 16. Phosphorus trichloride | (7719-12-2) |
| 17. Phosphorus pentachloride | (10026-13-8) |
| 18. Trimethyl phosphite | (121-45-9) |
| 19. Triethyl phosphite | (122-52-1) |
| 20. Dimethyl phosphite | (868-85-9) |
| 21. Diethyl phosphite | (762-04-9) |
| 22. Sulphur monochloride | (10025-67-9) |
| 23. Sulphur dichloride | (10545-99-0) |
| 24. Thionyl chloride | (7719-09-7) |
| 25. Cyclohexanol | (108-93-0) |
| 26. Hydrogen fluoride | (7664-39-3) |
| 27. Ortho-chlorobenzylidenemalononitrile (CS) | (2698-41-1) |
| 28. Potassium fluoride | (7789-23-3) |
| 29. Ammonium bifluoride | (1341-49-7) |
| 30. Sodium bifluoride | (1333-83-1) |
| 31. Sodium fluoride | (7681-49-4) |
| 32. Sodium sulphide | (1313-82-2) |
| 33. Chloroethanol | (107-07-3) |
| 34. Dimethylamine | (124-40-3) |

/...

0034

| List B | Chemical Abstracts Service (CAS) registry No. |
|---|---|
| 4. Sulphur mustards: | |
| 2-Chloroethylchloromethylsulphide | (2625-76-5) |
| bis(2-chloroethyl)sulphide: | |
| Mustard gas (H) | (505-60-2) |
| bis(2-chloroethylthio)methane | (63869-13-6) |
| 1,2-bis(2-chloroethylthio)ethane: | |
| Sesquimustard (Q) | (3563-36-8) |
| 1,3-bis(2-chloroethylthio)-n-propane | (63905-10-2) |
| 1,4-bis(2-chloroethylthio)-n-butane | |
| 1,5-bis(2-chloroethylthio)-n-pentane | |
| bis(2-chloroethylthiomethyl)ether | |
| bis(2-chloroethylthioethyl)ether: | |
| O-Mustard (T) | (63918-89-8) |
| 5. Lewisites: | |
| Lewisite 1: 2-chlorovinyldichlorarsine | (541-25-3) |
| Lewisite 2: bis(2-chlorovinyl) chloroarsine | (40334-69-8) |
| Lewisite 3: tris(2-chlorovinyl)arsine | (40334-70-1) |
| 6. Nitrogen mustards: | |
| HN1: bis(2-chloroethyl)ethylamine | (538-07-8) |
| HN2: bis(2-chloroethyl)methylamine | (51-75-2) |
| HN3: tris(2-chloroethyl)amine | (555-77-1) |
| 7. 3-Quinuclidinyl benzilate (BZ) | (6581-06-2) |
| 8. Saxitoxin | (35523-89-8) |
| 9. Ricin | |
| 10. Alkyl (Me, Et, n-Pr or i-Pr) phosphonyldihalides | |
| e.g. methylphosphonyldifluoride | (676-99-3) |
| methylphosphonyldichloride | (676-67-1) |
| 11. Dimethylmethylphosphonate | (756-79-6) |
| 12. O-Alkyl (H or $\leq C_{10}$, incl. cycloalkyl) O-2-dialkyl (Me, Et, n-Pr or i-Pr)-aminoethyl alkyl (Me, Et, n-Pr or i-Pr) phosphonites and corresponding alkylated salts and protonated salts | |
| e.g. QL: O-ethyl O-2-diisopropylaminoethyl methylphosphonite | (57856-11-8) |

/...

0035

(c) A general description of all types of activities at the site or facility;

(d) The sources and amounts of the financing of the site or facility, and of its activities.

7. The location of a site or facility shall be specified by means of the address and a site diagram. Each diagram shall be drawn to scale and shall indicate the boundaries of the site or facility, all road and rail entrances and exits and all structures on the site or facility, indicating their purpose. If the site or facility is located within a larger complex, the diagram shall specify the exact location of the site or facility within the complex. On each diagram, the geographic coordinates of a point within the site or facility shall be specified to the nearest second.

8. In addition to information specified in paragraph 6 of this annex, the following information shall be provided for each site or facility that is or will be involved in production, processing, consumption, storage, import or export of chemicals specified in list A of this annex:

(a) A detailed description of activities related to these chemicals including, as applicable, material-flow and process-flow diagrams, chemical reactions and end-use;

(b) A list of equipment used in activities related to these chemicals;

(c) The production capacity for these chemicals.

9. In addition to information specified in paragraph 6 of this annex, the following information shall be provided for each site or facility that is or will be involved in production or processing of organophosphorus chemicals or in production of organic chemicals by chlorination:

(a) A detailed description of activities related to the relevant chemicals, and the end-uses for which the chemicals are produced or processed;

(b) A detailed description of the processes used in the production or processing of organophosphorus chemicals or in the production of organic chemicals by chlorination, including material-flow and process-flow diagrams, chemical reactions and list of equipment involved.

10. The information on each import to be provided under section C of the Plan shall include:

(a) Specification of each item and the quantity imported and the purpose of its use in Iraq;

(b) Country from which the item is imported and the specific exporter;

(c) Point or port and time of entry of the item into Iraq;

/...

0036

## Annex III

### Provisions related to biological items

1. The following list contains equipment and other items relevant to the acquisition of biological and toxin weapons or biological and toxin weapons capability:

(a) Detection or assay systems specific for risk groups IV, III and II micro-organisms and toxins;

(b) Biohazard containment equipment;

(c) Equipment for the micro-encapsulation of living micro-organisms;

(d) Complex media for the growth of risk groups IV, III and II micro-organisms;

(e) Bio-reactors and fermentation vessels;

(f) Recombinant deoxyribonucleic acid (DNA), equipment and reagents for its isolation, characterization or production and equipment and reagents for the construction of synthetic genes;

(g) Equipment for the release into the environment of biological material;

(h) Equipment for studying the aerobiological characteristics of micro-organisms or toxins;

(i) Equipment for breeding of vectors of human, animal or plant diseases.

2. The initial information under paragraphs 35 and 36 of the Plan to be provided not later than 30 days after the adoption of the Plan by the Security Council shall cover the period from 1 January 1986. Subsequent information shall be provided each 15 January and 15 July and shall cover the six-month period prior to the provision of the information. Notifications under paragraph 38 (a) of the Plan shall be provided not later than 60 days in advance.

3. Whenever the information that Iraq is required to provide under section D and this annex is equal to nil, Iraq shall provide nil returns.

4. The information on each site or facility to be provided under section D of the Plan shall include the following:

(a) The name of the site or facility and of the owner, company, or enterprise operating the facility;

/...

(c) Country from which the micro-organisms, toxins, vaccines or items are imported and the specific exporter;

(d) Point or port and time of entry into Iraq;

(e) Site or facility where it is to be used and purpose of its use.

(f) Name of the specific importing organization in Iraq.

6. The information under paragraph 37 of the Plan shall be provided within seven days of the occurrence and the standardized form contained in section III of the annex on confidence-building measures in document BWC/CONF.III/23/II shall be utilized as appropriate.

7. Iraq shall, not later than each 15 April, provide to the Special Commission the copies of the declarations, information and data that Iraq has sent to the United Nations Department for Disarmament Affairs pursuant to the agreements on confidence-building measures, including the exchange of information and data, reached at the Third Review Conference of the Parties to the Convention on the Prohibition of the Development, Production and Stockpiling of Bacteriological (Biological) and Toxin Weapons and on Their Destruction (document BWC/CONF.III/23/II and its annex on confidence-building measures).

/...

(i) Gyroscopes, accelerometers and inertial equipment and software therefor;

(ii) Flight control systems usable in missile systems;

(iii) Avionics equipment specially designed or modified for use in unmanned air vehicles or rocket systems and software and components therefor usable in missile systems;

(d) Equipment and technical data for the production of structural composites usable in missiles and components, accessories and software therefor that could be used in the development and manufacture of ballistic missiles capable of a range greater than 150 kilometres;

(e) Pyrolytic deposition and densification equipment and technology that could be used in the development and manufacture of ballistic missiles capable of a range greater than 150 kilometres;

(f) Launch and ground support equipment and facilities usable for missile systems that could be used in the development and manufacture of ballistic missiles capable of a range greater than 150 kilometres;

(g) Analog computers, digital computers or digital differential analysers usable in air vehicles, rocket systems or missile systems that could be used in the development and manufacture of ballistic missiles capable of a range greater than 150 kilometres;

(h) Test facilities and equipment usable for missile systems, to include vibration test equipment using digital control techniques, wind tunnels and test benches for solid- or liquid-fuel rockets that could be used in the development and manufacture of ballistic missiles capable of a range greater than 150 kilometres;

(i) Specially designed software or components for missile design, production or operation that could be used in the development and manufacture of ballistic missiles capable of a range greater than 150 kilometres;

(j) Materials and devices for reduced observables in missile systems that could be used in the development and manufacture of ballistic missiles capable of a range greater than 150 kilometres;

(k) Material and devices for protecting missile systems against nuclear effects that could be used in the development and manufacture of ballistic missiles capable of a range greater than 150 kilometres.

2. The initial information under paragraph 43 of the Plan to be provided not later than 30 days after the adoption of the Plan by the Security Council shall cover the period from 1 January 1988. Subsequent information shall be provided each 15 January and 15 July and shall cover the six-month period

/...

(d) Project and site or facility where it is to be used;

(e) Name of the specific importing organization in Iraq.

-----

0040

# 외 무 부

원 본

종 별 :

번 호 : UNW-1865 일 시 : 92 0706 2000

수 신 : 장 관(연일,중동일,기정)

발 신 : 주 유엔 대사

제 목 : 유엔 안보리(이락무기 폐기)

1.금 7.6 유엔 안보리 비공식 회의는 7.5 이락정부가 유엔 안보리 이락무기 폐기 특별위원회 사찰반의 이락 농업성 청사 현장사찰을 거부한 사건을논의, 하기요지의 안보리 의장명의 성명을 채택하고 안보리 의장이 주 유엔 이락대사 대리를 초치하여 전달하기로함

- 안보리 결의 687 에 의거, 이락은 특별위원회와 사찰반의 무조건적, 무제한적인 사찰을 허용해야함

- 이락이 특별위원회 사찰반의 사찰을 거부한 것은 용납할수 없는 안보리 결의위반임

- 안보리 이사국들은 이락 정부가 유엔 사찰반의 동청사 사찰에 즉각 동의할것을 요청함

2. 7.5 유엔 이락무기 폐기 특별위원회 사찰반은 이락 농업성 청사 사찰을 위하여 동청사에 도착하였으나, 이락정부는 동청사가 화생무기나 미사일의 제조 또는 보관과는 아무런 관계가없다는 이유로 동사찰반의 농업성 청사입장을 거부하였는바, 유엔 안보리는 금일 성명을 통하여 안보리 결의 687 과 707 에 의해 이락은 안보리 특별위원회와 동사찰반이 원하는 모든지역, 건물, 장비, 기록등의 사찰을 허용하여야 함을 재확인한 것임

(대사 유종하-국장)

첨부UNW(F)-0579

국기국 중아국 외정실 안기부

PAGE 1 92.07.07 09:07 WG

외신 1과 통제관

0041

UNW(F)-0579 20706 2000 — UNW-1864 외첨부

Revised

DRAFT STATEMENT BY THE PRESIDENT OF THE SECURITY COUNCIL

The members of the Security Council have learnt with concern of the refusal of the Government of Iraq to permit a team of inspectors sent to Iraq by the Special Commission to enter certain premises designated by the Special Commission for inspection.

The members of the Council recall that, under paragraph 9 (b) (i) of section C of Security Council resolution 687 (1991), Iraq is required to permit the Special Commission to undertake immediate on-site inspection of any locations designated by the Commission. This obligation is imposed as a result of a decision of the Council, taken under Chapter VII of the Charter. Furthermore, Iraq has agreed to such inspections as a condition precedent to the establishment of a formal cease-fire between Iraq and Kuwait and the Member States cooperating with Kuwait in accordance with Security Council resolution 678 (1990). The members of the Council further recall that by paragraph 2 (ii) of resolution 707 (1991) the Council has reaffirmed the relevant provision of resolution 687 (1991) and expressly demanded that Iraq "allow the Special Commission ... and their Inspection Teams immediate, unconditional, and unrestricted access to any and all areas, facilities, equipment, records, and means of transportation which they wish to inspect".

Iraq's present refusal to permit access to the Inspection Team currently in Iraq to the premises designated by the Special

579-2-1

0042

Commission constitutes a material and unacceptable breach by Iraq of a provision of resolution 687 which established the cease-fire and provided the conditions essential to the restoration of peace and security in the region. The members of the Council demand that the Government of Iraq immediately agree to the admission to the premises concerned of the inspectors of the Special Commission as required by the Chairman of the Special Commission, so that the Special Commission may establish whether or not any documents, records, materials, or equipment relevant to the responsibilities of the Commission are located therein.

5?8-2-2

대 한 민 국

주 오스트리아 대사관

오스트리아 20300-671　　　　　　　　　　　　　　1992 . 7 . 9 .

수 신 : 장관　　　　　　　　　　　　　　　　　(보존기간 :　　 )

참 조 : 국제기구국장, 과기처장관(원자력실장)

제 목 : 제 12차 대 이락 핵사찰 보고

표제 보고서를 별첨과 같이 송부합니다.

첨부 : GOV/INF/662 (92.6.29) 끝.

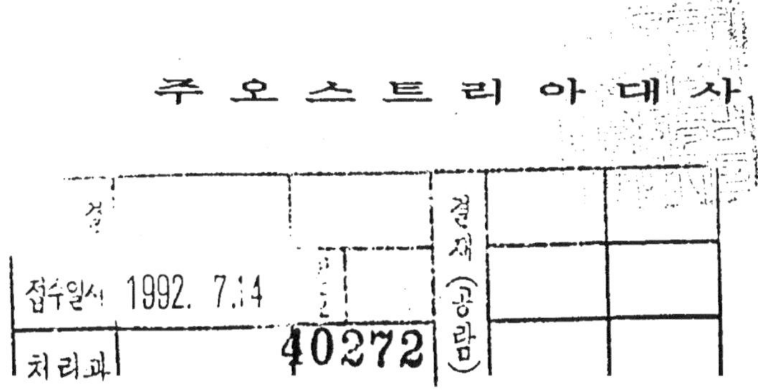

주 오스트리아 대사

| 접수일시 1992. 7.14 | 40272 | 결재 (공람) | | |
|---|---|---|---|---|
| 처리과 | | | | |

0044

International Atomic Energy Agency
# BOARD OF GOVERNORS

GOV/INF/662
29 June 1992

RESTRICTED Distr.
Original: ENGLISH

For official use only

# REPORT ON THE TWELFTH IAEA ON-SITE INSPECTION IN IRAQ UNDER SECURITY COUNCIL RESOLUTION 687 (1991)

26 May - 4 June 1992

INTERNATIONAL ATOMIC ENERGY AGENCY

92-02345

0045

REPORT ON THE TWELFTH IAEA ON-SITE INSPECTION IN IRAQ
UNDER SECURITY COUNCIL RESOLUTION 687 (1991)

26 May - 4 June 1992

**SALIENT POINTS**

- The destruction of key technical installations and equipment at the Al Atheer-Al Hatteen site, begun during the eleventh IAEA inspection mission to Iraq, was completed in the course of the twelfth mission. Three more buildings, with a combined surface area of approximately 11 000 square meters, and the remaining equipment items were destroyed.

- At the request of the inspection team, the Iraqi side has begun preparations for the destruction of selected buildings at the Tarmiya and Ash Sharqat EMIS sites. Related actions associated with the dismantling of utilities and ventilation systems and the reduction in delivered electrical power to the sites are also under way. Progress was monitored throughout the inspection mission. More than 50% of the necessary work has been done. The actions will be finished during the next mission.

- As was the case at the Al Atheer-Al Hatteen site, the Iraqi side is providing all equipment, materials and manpower necessary for the efficient fulfillment of the destruction plan under the supervision of the inspection teams.

- Despite repeated requests for information by inspection teams, the Iraqi side has implemented a government decision not to identify the suppliers of the maraging steel, the carbon fibre centrifuge tubes and technical advice regarding centrifuge technology. This "grey area" will persist as the IAEA Action Team continues to seek this information through other avenues.

0046

- The work to identify the machine tools and better understand the overall capabilities existing in facilities declared by the Iraqi side to have been involved in the Iraqi Atomic Energy Commission programme was completed. The purpose was directly related to establishing the basis for the longer-term monitoring programme.

- The amount of undeclared nuclear material processed in a safeguarded fuel fabrication facility, in violation of the safeguards agreement between Iraq and the IAEA, has been revised upward by the Iraqi side from 19 kilograms to approximately 60 kilograms of natural uranium dioxide. This non-compliance with the safeguards agreement was first communicated to the IAEA Board of Governors in July and August 1991.

- The last quantity (473 grams U235) of fresh highly enriched uranium fuel remaining in Iraq was removed by the twelfth inspection team.

- Through written questions, meetings and interviews, some clarification of issues related to Iraqi work on weaponization and uranium enrichment and to Iraqi nuclear material declarations was obtained. Open issues related to the centrifuge enrichment programme and the extent of the chemical enrichment work remain.

- The Iraqi side's co-operation in implementing destruction plans at Al Atheer-Al Hatteen, Tarmiya and Ash Sharqat cannot be faulted and should be noted. However, in the course of the twelfth mission there was a definite stiffening in the Iraqi attitude to working with the inspection team. There were numerous attempts to prohibit or limit the taking of photographs and the placing of seals. Meetings, transportation and other activities were often slow to be organized. The Iraqi explanation was that the active co-operation extended during previous inspections had not resulted in an improvement in the sanctions situation.

0047

**INTRODUCTION**

1. This report summarizes the findings of the twelfth inspection mission carried out by the IAEA under United Nations Security Council resolution (UNSCR) 687 (1991) with the assistance and co-operation of the Special Commission of the United Nations. The mission took place from 26 May to 4 June 1992 and was headed by Mr. Demetrius Perricos of the IAEA as Chief Inspector. The team consisted of 21 inspectors and 6 supporting staff; it comprised 17 nationalities.

The objectives of the inspection mission were broadly

- to supervise the completion of the destruction of key technical installations comprising buildings and equipment at the Al Atheer-Al Hatteen site.
- to supervise the destruction of key technical installations at the Tarmiya and Ash Sharqat sites.
- to clarify issues arising from nuclear material accountancy questions and to visit related facilities.
- to further investigate the work done in enrichment, particularly in the areas of centrifuge and gaseous diffusion methods, and to assess procurement data in the centrifuge area.
- to assess the Iraqi answers to questions related to experiments and studies in the area of weaponization and to inspect related facilities.
- to continue field activities related to the identification and cataloguing of equipment used or capable of use in Iraq's nuclear programme.
- to remove from Iraq the remaining quantity (473 grams) of fresh highly enriched uranium.

These objectives were assigned to three groups within the overall team, with a group leader responsible for co-ordinating the work of each group. A total of 23 facilities and sites were inspected. These are shown in Table 1. All of these facilities and sites had been inspected previously by an IAEA team.

0048

## Table 1

### List of facilities and sites inspected during the twelfth inspection mission

1. Tuwaitha site and associated locations (Locations A, B, C, Ash Shakyli storage, Al Nafad storage)
2. Tarmiya site
3. Al Atheer site
4. Al Qa Qaa site
5. Ash Sharqat site
6. Al Jesira site, including uranium waste location and equipment storage
7. Al Furat project site
8. State Enterprise for Heavy Engineering Equipment (Daura)
9. Badr General Establishment
10. Auqba Bin Nafi State Establishment
11. Al Radwan
12. Al Ameer
13. Nassr Establishment (Taji)
14. Saladdine Establishment (SAAD-13)
15. Al Dijjla site
16. Saddam State Establishment
17. Dhu Al Fiqar Establishment
18. National Computer Centre, Baghdad
19. Iskandariyah State Enterprise for Mechanical Industries
20. Al Qaim site
21. Geological Survey Institute, Baghdad
22. Al Hadre explosive test site
23. Nassariya Ur Establishment

**SUMMARY**

2. The Al Atheer-Al Hatteen complex, located approximately seventy kilometers south-west of Baghdad, has been identified by the IAEA as the site where Iraq had planned to locate its nuclear weapons development effort. The destruction of key technical installations and equipment at the Al Atheer-Al Hatteen site, begun during the eleventh IAEA inspection mission to Iraq, was concluded in the course of the twelfth mission.

Three large buildings (the carbide, powder and polymer buildings), with a combined surface of approximately 11 000 square meters, and two equipment items (large, hot and cold isostatic presses) were completely destroyed with explosive charges. Eight buildings, covering a surface of approximately 35 000 square meters, and equipment items that together constituted a major portion of the Al Àtheer-Al Hatteen complex have now been destroyed.

As was the case in the eleventh mission, the Iraqi side provided all equipment, materials and manpower necessary for efficient implementation of the destruction plan under the supervision of the IAEA team.

3. A list of actions to be undertaken pursuant to UNSCR 687 with respect to the facilities at the Tarmiya and Ash Sharqat sites (see Annex 1) had been communicated to the Iraqi side on 15 May 1992. The Iraqi side responded with an energetic and well organized effort to carry out the required actions. The progress of the work at Tarmiya was inspected three times in the course of the twelfth mission. The work at Ash Sharqat was inspected twice. Overall, the work is more than 50% complete and the actions detailed in the 15 May 1992 letter, including the destruction of eight buildings (four at each site), will be concluded during the next mission.

0050

4. The verification of Iraqi declarations regarding quantities of maraging steel and carbon fibre centrifuge rotors procured for Iraq's centrifuge programme and the identification of the source(s) of technical advice remain as open issues. A political decision by the Iraqi Government not to provide specific information on suppliers has been taken and formally communicated to UNSCOM. Resolution of these issues will be delayed while information is sought through Member States' Governments.

5. The work to identify the machine tools and better understand the related capabilities existing in facilities declared by the Iraqi side to have been involved in the IAEC programme was completed. The purpose was directly related to establishing the basis for the longer-term monitoring programme. This work was a source of contention with the Iraqi side throughout the inspection. Attempts were made to limit the placing of identification seals on selected pieces of equipment and the taking of photographs. The Iraqi argument was that they believed that these activities were being carried out with the goal of destroying the industrial base of Iraq. The Iraqi side requested and received clarification from the IAEA Action Team regarding the intended use of the machine tool inventory (Annex 2).

6. In July and August 1991, the IAEA Board of Governors was informed of the non-compliance of Iraq with its obligations under the safeguards agreement concluded by Iraq with the Agency. Continuing work with the Iraqi side to resolve inconsistencies in Iraq's nuclear material declarations have resulted in revisions that indicate that amounts of unsafeguarded material processed in the safeguarded fuel fabrication facility had been understated by the Iraqi side. Specifically, the Iraqi authorities had stated that they had fabricated five fuel assemblies containing approximately 19 kilograms of natural uranium dioxide pellets. The revised declaration is that an additional 26 kilograms of natural uranium dioxide pellets and 14 kilograms of natural uranium dioxide pellets in fresh fuel rods had been fabricated using unsafeguarded material.

7. The last quantity (473 grams U235) of fresh highly enriched uranium fuel (93% plates and 36% pins) remaining in Iraq was removed by the twelfth inspection team. The removal from Iraq of the remaining 36 kilograms of U235 contained in the irradiated fuel elements of the Tamuz 2 and IRT 5000 research reactors is a major task still pending.

0051

8. As has been the case throughout recent inspections, a number of meetings took place with the Iraqi side to clarify issues related to Iraqi work on weaponization and uranium enrichment and Iraq's nuclear material declarations. In general terms, a more consistent picture as regards the work on weaponization and gas diffusion enrichment technology has emerged. Some inconsistencies in the Iraqi nuclear material declarations were resolved, but the Iraqi side indicated its unwillingness to meet further on this subject and requested that all further questions be put in writing. Open issues relating to the centrifuge enrichment programme and the extent of the chemical enrichment work remain.

9. The long awaited "full, final and complete" declaration from the Iraqi side regarding all activities involving weapons of mass destruction covered by UNSCR 687 was delivered on 4 June. A copy of the nuclear portion is currently being translated. No judgement can yet be made regarding the completeness and accuracy of the report.

10. A full record of the correspondence between the Chief Inspector of the twelfth inspection team and the Iraqi counterpart is given in Annex 3.

**DESTRUCTION OF KEY TECHNICAL INSTALLATIONS AND EQUIPMENT**

11. The destruction of buildings and equipment at the Al Atheer-Al Hatteen site specified in a communication transmitted to the Iraqi authorities on 25 March 1992 has been completed. The destruction of three major buildings (the carbide, powder and polymer buildings) and of remaining equipment items (the hot and cold isostatic presses) and the removal of the protective berm from around the Building 33 firing site were observed during the twelfth inspection.

12. The status as of 4 June 1992 is given below. A line drawing of the Al Atheer-Al Hatteen site is provided in Figure 1.

1. Building 33 - The high explosives test bunker was destroyed by filling it with concrete and scrap metal. The protective berm has been removed.

0052

**Figure 1**

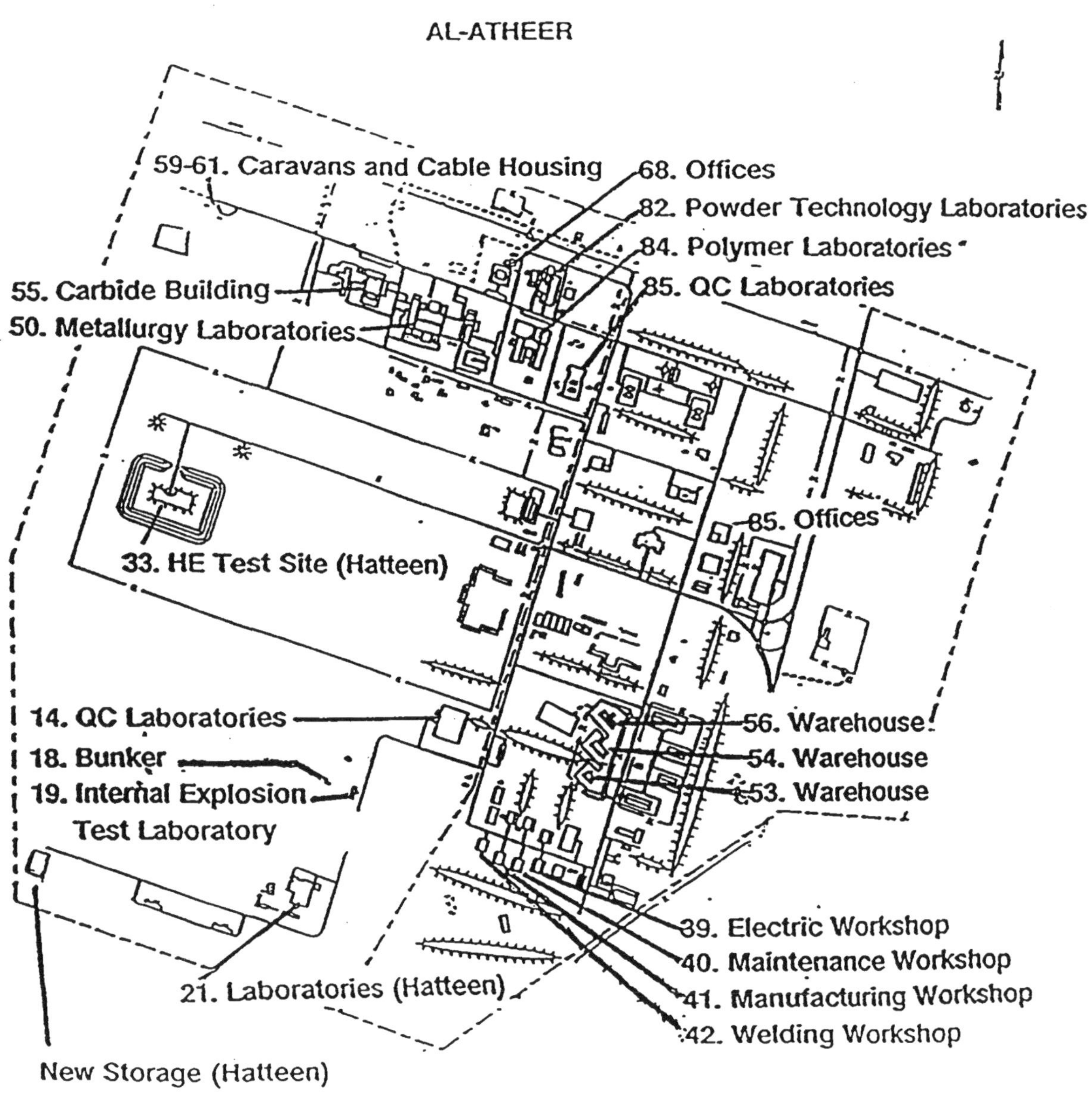


0053

2. Building 18 - Explosion chamber destroyed with cutting torch.

3. Building 19 - Control building destroyed by explosives.

4. Building 21 - Physics building destroyed by explosives. Cell foundation destroyed with cutting torch.

5. Building 50 - Casting building destroyed by explosives.

6. Building 55 - Carbide building destroyed by explosives.

7. Building 82 - Powder building destroyed by explosives.

8. Building 84 - Polymer building destroyed by explosives.

The combined surface area of the eight destroyed buildings was approximately 35 000 square meters. An updated list of destroyed equipment is given in Table 2. The hot and cold isostatic presses were destroyed with explosives. The destruction of specified ventilation and process equipment left in the buildings was verified by the inspection team.

As has been stated previously, the Iraqi side provided all equipment, materials and manpower necessary for efficient implementation of the destruction plan. The actual destruction of buildings and equipment took place under the supervision of the inspection team.

13. A list of actions to be undertaken pursuant to UNSCR 687 with respect to the facilities at the Tarmiya and Ash Sharqat EMIS sites (see Annex 1) had been communicated to the Iraqi authorities on 15 May 1992. The Iraqi side responded with a large and well organized effort to carry out the required actions. The progress of work at both sites was monitored in the course of the inspection mission. The work is more than 50% complete. The actions detailed in the 15 May 1992 letter, including the destruction of eight buildings (four at each site), will be completed during the next mission.

## Table 2

### List of type of equipment destroyed at the Al Atheer-Al Hatteen Site

| Equipment | Manufacturer | Status |
|---|---|---|
| Large cold isostatic press | ASEA-Brown Boveri | Completed |
| Large hot isostatic press and two associated furnaces | ASEA-Brown Boveri | Completed |
| Cold isostatic press | ABRA | Completed |
| Hot isostatic press | ABRA | Completed |
| Resistance furnaces | Pfeiffer | Completed |
| Induction furnace | Pfeiffer | Completed |
| Vacuum furnaces | Pfeiffer | Completed |
| Vacuum plasma spray system | Plasmatechnik | Completed |
| Atmospheric plasma spray system | Plasmatechnik | Completed |
| Precision turning machine | Schäublin | Completed |
| Superprecision lathe | Hardinge Brothers | Completed |
| Jig grinding machine | Waida | Completed |
| 3-axis coordinate measuring machine | Leitz | Some key components removed by IAEA; manufacturer has confirmed that this equipment is rendered harmless |
| Viewing windows for high explosives test bunker | not determined | Completed |

0055

14. The Tarmiya site was inspected three times in the course of the twelfth mission. The purpose was to monitor the preparations being made by the Iraqi side to meet the requirements of the 15 May 1992 letter. The work force at Tarmiya consisted of some 700 people on an around-the-clock basis. The situation as it existed on 4 June 1992 vis-à-vis the various requirements is summarized below:

- The electric substation serving the site is part of the national grid. It serves a number of local users in addition to the Tarmiya site. Representatives from the site worked with technical people from the State Electric Establishment to develop a proposal for reducing the delivered power to the site by an order of magnitude. The proposal was delivered to the inspection team on the last day of the inspection and is currently being evaluated.

- The horizontal return iron installed in Building 33 has been completely removed. There is a total of 51 identical pieces (~30 tonnes each). They are currently in front of the building, and will later be moved to a nearby open storage area (named Al Nafad II).

- All transformers and switchgear have been removed from Buildings 5, 38 and 243 to nearby storage areas. About 50% of the electrical cable connecting Buildings 5 and 38 to Building 33 and Building 243 to Building 245 has been removed.

- The equipment installed in the Building 248 (general utilities) is essentially disassembled. Connecting flanges for the main pumps have been removed. The equipment will be stored in situ.

- At the request of the inspection team, the Iraqi side had concentrated a large effort on preparing Building 245 for destruction. The work was more than 50% complete by the conclusion of the inspection.

All preparations will be completed prior to the next inspection, scheduled for mid-July. Buildings 5, 38, 243 and 245 will be destroyed during that inspection. With the

0056

exception of Building 245, all buildings in the main process area (particularly Building 33) were damaged during the war. All high-efficiency particulate air filters (HEPAs) and activated charcoal filter elements from the high-efficiency exhaust air filtration units installed in chemistry Buildings 46, 57 and 225 have been removed and inventoried and are awaiting destruction as requested by the twelfth inspection team.

15. The Ash Sharqat facility was severely damaged during the war. This, together with Iraqi salvage efforts that had begun prior to the first inspection of the site in July 1991, has resulted in a situation where the work necessary to meet the requirements of the 15 May 1992 letter is much less here than at Tarmiya. The status as of 3 June 1992 is summarized below:

- The substation serving the Ash Sharqat site has been completely dismantled. All that remains are two badly damaged step-down transformers.

- Rubble has been removed from Building 51 to the extent necessary for the inspection team to confirm previous judgements that no horizontal return iron had ever been installed there.

- All transformers and switchgear have long since been removed from Buildings 27, 29 and 20. Approximately 90% of the electric cable connecting Buildings 27 and 29 to Building 51 and Building 20 to Building 21 has been removed.

- The general utilities in Building 31 had been dismantled during the period between the third and seventh inspection missions (July-October 1991). Most of the equipment is sitting in a nearby open storage area.

- Building 21 was damaged during the war, but the basic structure is still intact. Preparations to complete the destruction of this building are nearly complete.

As is the case for Tarmiya, all preparations at Ash Sharqat will be completed prior to the next inspection mission. The destruction of Buildings 27, 29, 20 and 21 will be completed at that time. A portion of the high-efficiency exhaust air filtration systems in the chemistry buildings had been installed. Action that parallels that to be carried out at Tarmiya has been initiated.

0057

**ACTIVITIES RELATED TO NUCLEAR MATERIAL**

16. In the report on the eleventh inspection mission, an evaluation of the changes in the nuclear material balance included in Iraq's "final and revised chart" received by the IAEA in Vienna on 22 April 1992 was presented. In that report, the differences between declared and verified amounts and categories of nuclear material were identified. One of the objectives of the twelfth team was to clarify these differences. The Iraqi side indicated that it was not willing to discuss any differences further and that its "final and revised chart" was to be regarded as its final declaration. After several meetings, however, changes were made; they are reflected in the chart included in the "full, final and complete" report (Figure 2). The changes are summarized below. The declarations regarding the processing of material in the Building 73 complex are presented in detail because of the connection with the statements of Iraq's non-compliance with the safeguards agreement made to the IAEA Board of Governors in July and August 1991.

- The amounts of EMIS solutions produced at Al Tuwaitha and presented to the IAEA were modified so as to be in agreement with those declared in the letter of 31 May 1992 from the Iraqi counterpart to the Chief Inspector of the twelfth IAEA team. The changes related to the amounts of enriched and depleted uranium, but the 782 grams of natural uranium declared in the above-mentioned declaration were not included in the revised chart.

- The processes involved and the nuclear material produced in Building 73 in Tuwaitha (Figure 3) have been redistributed. In the "final and revised chart" of 22 April 1992, the nuclear material processed in the Building 73 complex was divided into two categories, one corresponding to material of Italian origin which was under safeguards and the other to material which was not under safeguards: 9.1 tonnes of natural uranium and $UO_4$ from Al Qaim, 375.2 kilograms of natural uranium and $UO_2$ from Al Jesira and 220 kilograms of natural uranium (as $UO_2$) from Brazil.

  During the twelfth inspection mission, the Iraqi side explained that "Building 73" referred to a complex of buildings (see Figure 4). Of this complex, Buildings

0058

73A and 73B were under safeguards. In addition, the Iraqi side declared that the activities involving the unsafeguarded material had taken place in Building 73C except for the production of 18.9 kilograms of natural uranium as five fuel elements, of 26 kilograms of natural uranium as pellets and of 14 kilograms of natural uranium as 46 fresh fuel pins; these had been produced in Building 73A using $UO_2$ from Al Jesira. The production of the five fuel elements, their irradiation in the IRT 5000 reactor and the reprocessing of three of them had been previously declared and the corresponding non-compliance with the safeguards agreement between Iraq and the IAEA communicated to the IAEA Board of Governors. Figure 5 includes the processes declared as having taken place in Building 73C. Building 73C had been declared in the past as containing only utilities and a mechanical workshop (including the electron beam welder).

- The Iraqi side indicated that no filtration system had been installed in Building 73C. Thirty-seven filters containing 50 kilograms of natural uranium as $UO_4$ were declared as belonging to Building 73B and the nuclear material present in them as being of Italian - instead of Al Qaim - origin. Additional samples have been taken with a view to clarifying this matter.

17. Several questions about remaining inconsistencies (see Table A4-1) in the Iraqi nuclear material flow chart were put to the Iraqi side in writing. The Iraqi side's response was that "any differences in weights existing in the chart of nuclear material as verified by the Agency are attributed to either losses of the material during the bombing or mixing of the material during the evacuation or the inaccuracy of the analysis of the samples". According to the statements of the Iraqi side, it considers that the "nuclear material file is closed".

18. Other nuclear-material-related inspection activities carried out during the twelfth IAEA inspection mission were:

- Inspection and sampling of the waste tanks belonging to the Building 73 complex. There is a rectangular concrete tank beside the complex. Inside this concrete tank there is a cylindrical steel tank with a capacity of approximately

0059

0060

**Figure 2**

**Nuclear material flow chart as included in the "full, final and complete" report**

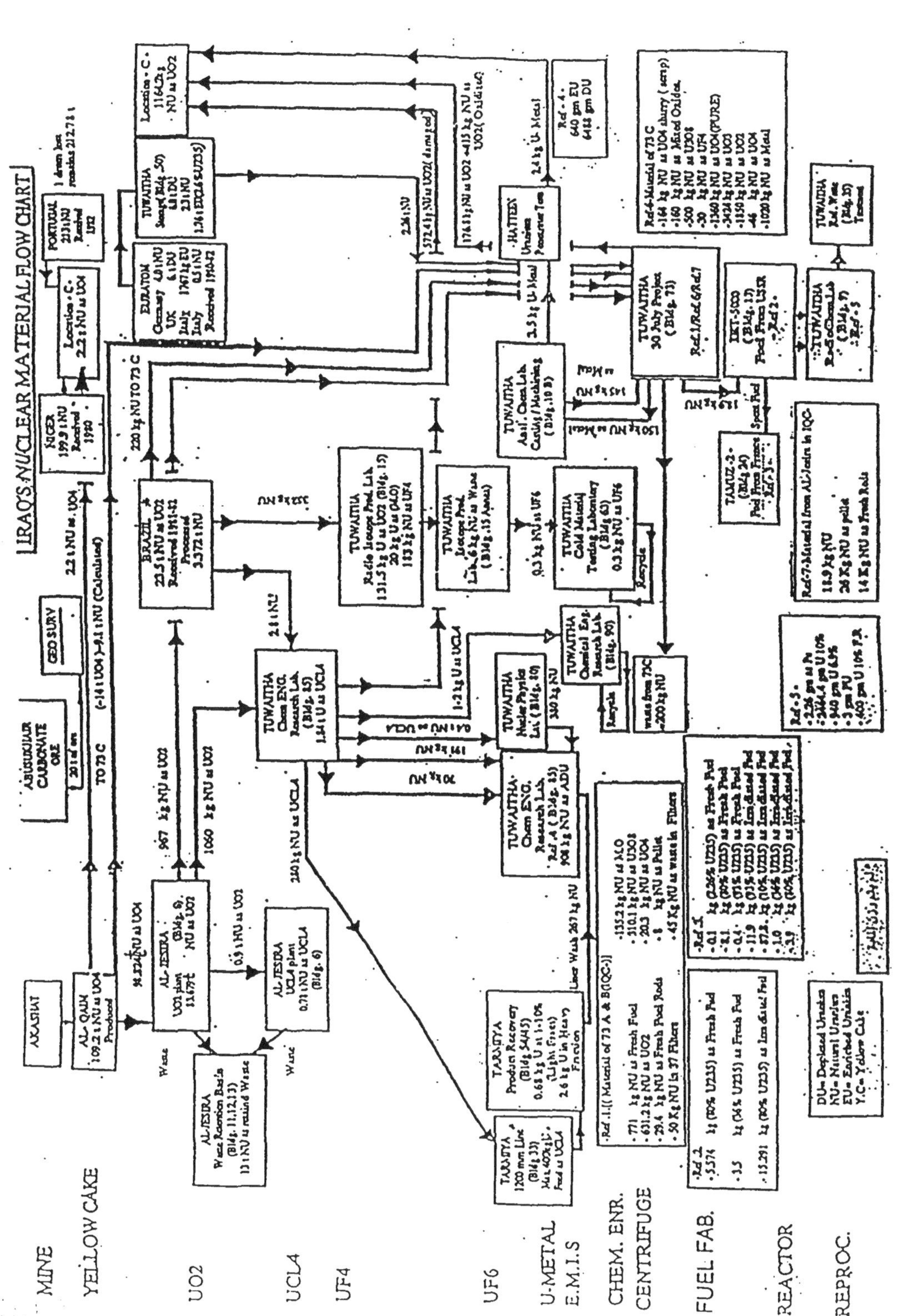

## Figure 3

### Tuwaitha Nuclear Research Centre

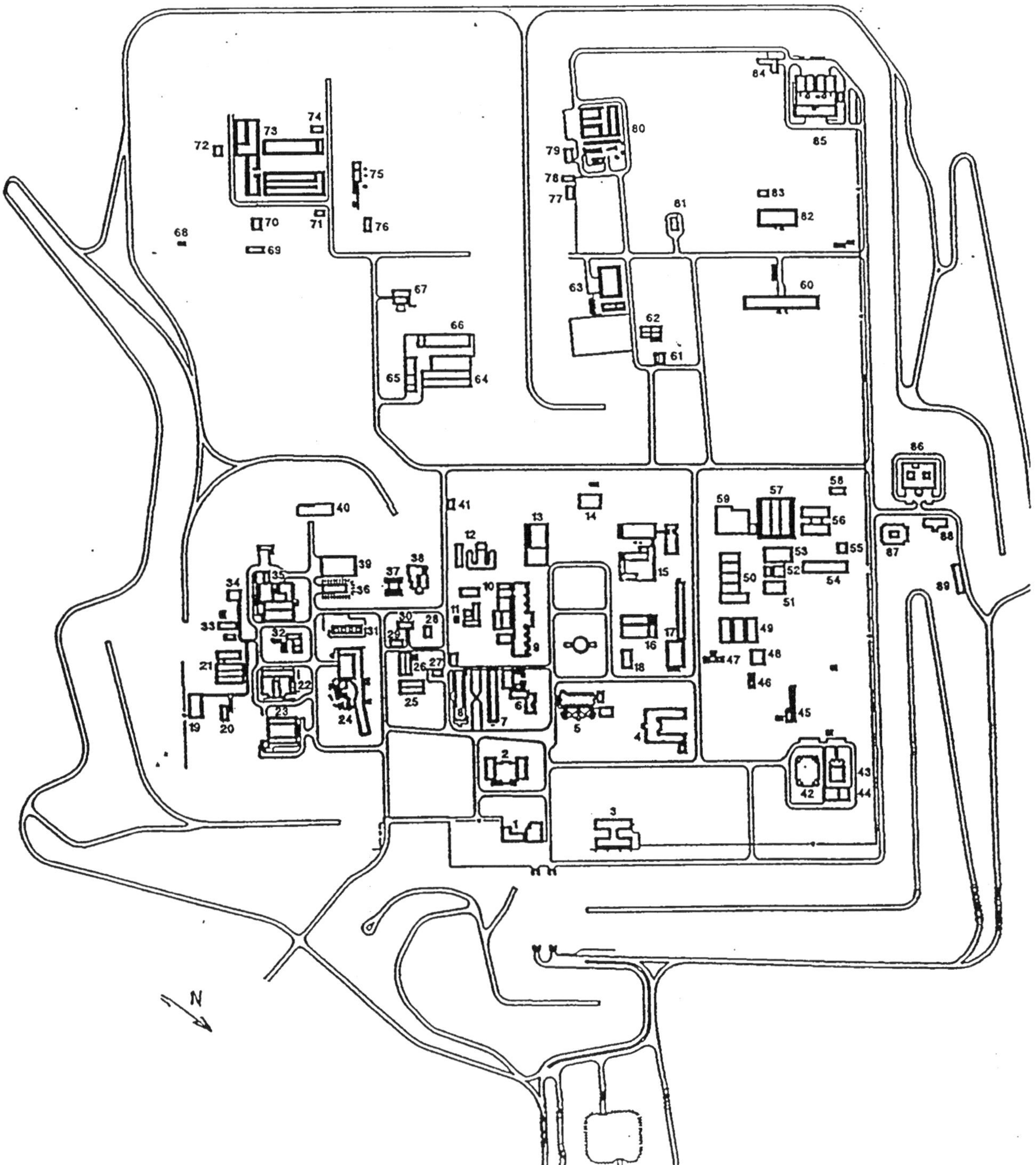

0061

0062

**Figure 4**

**Layout of the Building 73 complex presented by the Iraqi authorities**

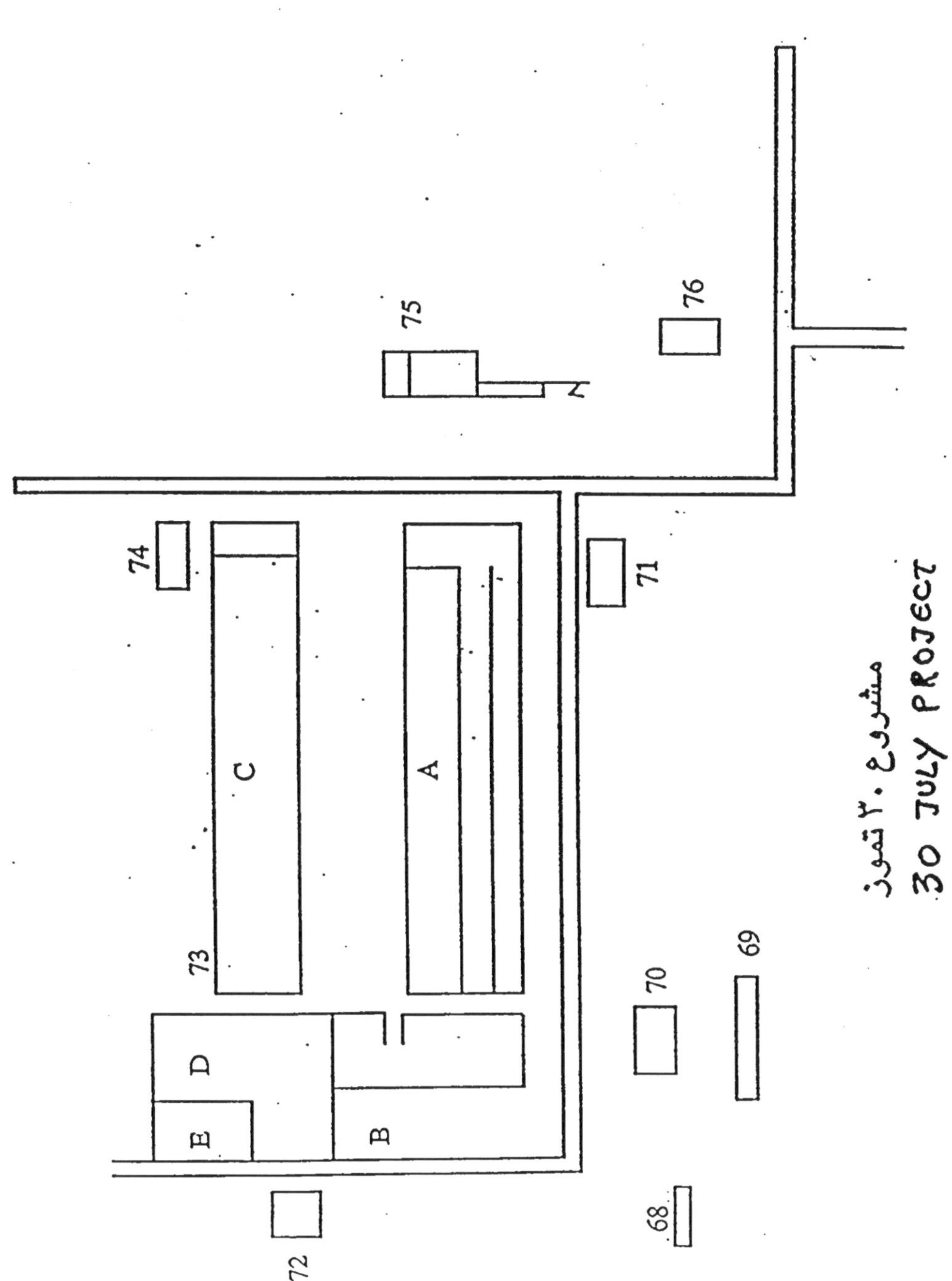

0063

Figure 5

**Layout of Building 73C as presented by the Iraqi authorities**

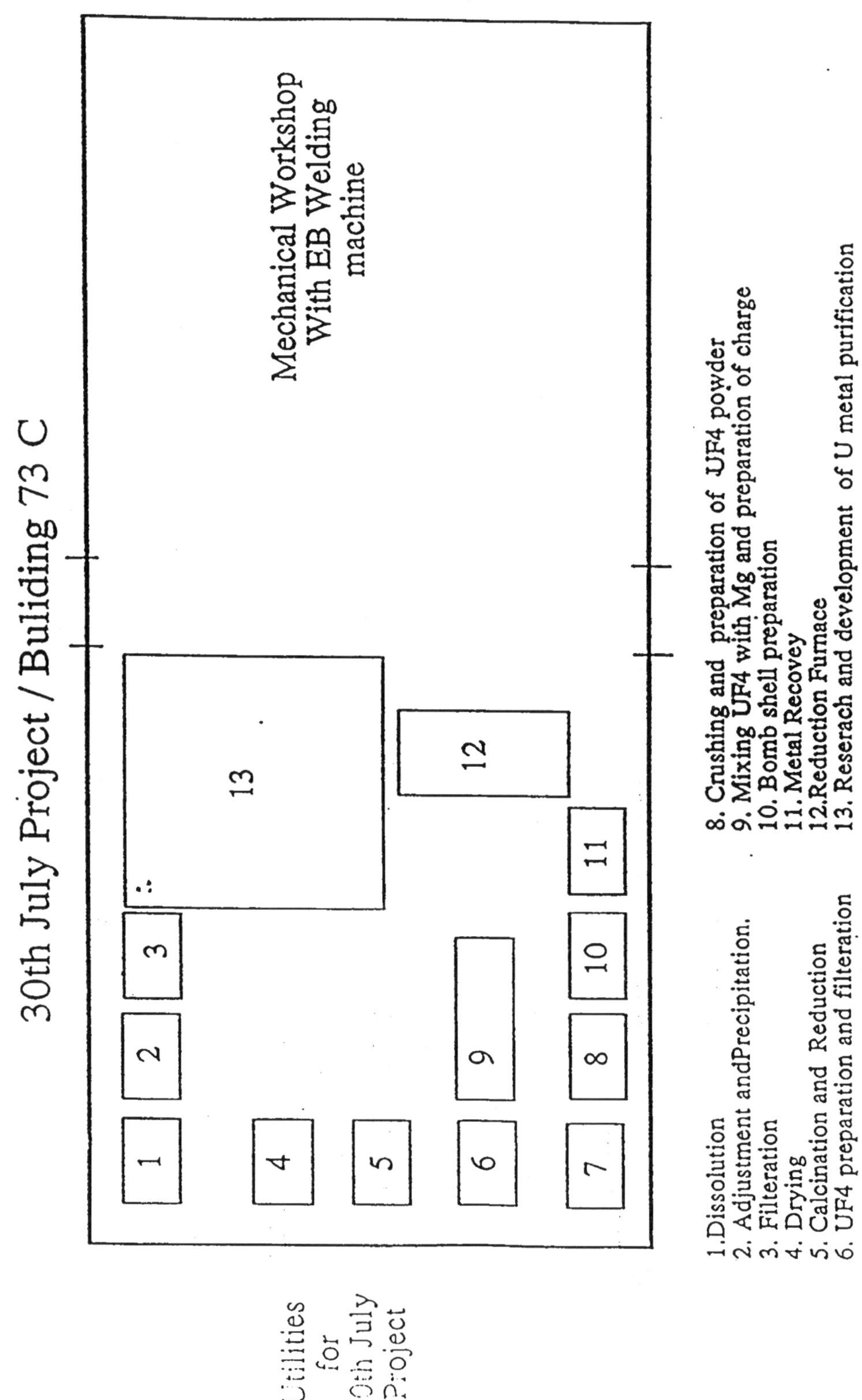

7m$^3$. The Iraqi side declared that the content of the steel tank belongs to Buildings 73A and B and that the content of the concrete tank belongs to Building 73C. Samples were taken from both tanks to confirm the declared origins and the amounts of uranium contained in them.

- EMIS solutions containing highly-enriched uranium produced in Al Tuwaitha Building 80 was diluted using nuclear material of Brazilian origin. The dilution was performed in order to downgrade the highly-enriched uranium present in the solutions to low-enriched uranium.

- The remaining unirradiated highly enriched uranium was removed from Iraq. It included 14.5 pins of 36%-enriched uranium (332.6 grams uranium, 116.1 grams U235) and 23 plates of 93%-enriched uranium (383 grams uranium, 356.5 grams U235).

- A drum containing 163 grams of enriched uranium (5.8%) in solution form (145 litres) was moved from Tarmiya to location C and placed under IAEA seal. The remaining low-enriched uranium and depleted uranium solutions are still in Tarmiya.

- The nuclear material stored at location C has been reconfigured in line with new Iraqi declarations (see Figures A4-1 and A4-2). Monitoring activities (seals check and item counting) were carried out on the irradiated fuel located in the IRT 5000 reactor and in the tanks at location B.

A complete summary of the declared amounts and the corresponding verification results for nuclear material stored at locations B and C and in the IRT 5000 reactor are presented in Annex 4.

**ACTIVITIES RELATED TO THE ENRICHMENT PROGRAMME**

19 On the last day of the eleventh inspection mission a meeting was arranged with the Chairman of the IAEC to discuss the Iraqi position that the suppliers of the maraging steel, carbon fibre rotor tubes and technical advice (centrifuge technology) would not be disclosed. The Chairman indicated that the matter was being discussed at the highest levels of the Iraqi Government and requested that the inspection team regard

it as an "open issue" that would be resolved during the next inspection mission. At a meeting held early during the twelfth mission, the Iraqi side described a political decision of the Government not to provide specific information on suppliers. The decision reflected inter alia "a position based on moral grounds which Iraq is not prepared to abandon". The necessary information continues to be sought through other sources, and in the meantime these aspects of the Iraqi centrifuge programme remain open issues.

20. A list of questions calling for additional details about various aspects of the Iraqi enrichment programme was given to the Iraqi side on the first day of the inspection mission. These questions were discussed and further clarifications offered during subsequent meetings. A written response to the questions, although often promised, was not received. In several instances the Iraqi side referred the team to the "full, final and complete" report as containing the requested information. Throughout the discussions, the Iraqi side took the position that Iraq's enrichment programme had been fully disclosed and that the inspection team's efforts to obtain additional details were a form of harrassment that would not add to the overall assessment.

21. Nevertheless, in spite of the above, a number of meetings between Iraqi technical experts and uranium enrichment experts from the inspection team did result in an improved understanding of Iraqi efforts in both centrifuge and gaseous diffusion. Detailed technical statements regarding such things as the method used to assemble the extraction system, the effect of the choice of wall velocity on the overall centrifuge design and the method of manufacturing the bottom bearing cup were credible and further convinced the team that the Iraqi side had received significant advice from abroad. Similarly, the Iraqi experts' description of their attempts to develop gaseous diffusion barrier was technically credible and consistent with information contained in the PC-3 reports.

**ACTIVITIES RELATED TO THE WEAPONIZATION PROGRAMME**

22. The Iraqi side responded to a number of written questions regarding weaponization issues. The information is still being analyzed, but the answers appear to be consistent with previous declarations, seized documentary evidence and direct inspection results. More than before, the Iraqi side seems anxious to end this process.

23. A follow-up inspection was conducted at the Al Qa Qaa facility, south of Baghdad. The Iraqi side had presented to the eleventh team a die set declared to have been used for pressing high explosive lenses. However, further evaluation suggested that this die set could not have been used to produce the described high explosive components. Iraqi engineers met with the twelfth inspection team and provided a detailed decription of a manufacturing process that appears consistent with both the declared components and the observed equipment. The team went on to inspect two areas consisting of small-scale testing and research buildings. One area contains a number of test facilities that could be adapted to machining and manufacturing. The other area was declared to be a quality control facility serving the whole Al Qa Qaa high explosive component manufacture operation. Construction is still under way. Al Qa Qaa's role in the weapons development programme appears to have been that of a service organization. The inspection process has not identified a facility uniquely associated with the Iraqi nuclear programme.

24. Buildings 66 and 73C at Tuwaitha were again inspected as a result of changed Iraqi declarations regarding the location of uranium metallurgy work and detonator development tests. Both buildings were badly damaged during the war and by subsequent cleanup operations. They have continued to deteriorate since then. Little can be done to verify the Iraqi declarations that Building 73C was the location of the uranium metal production (approximately one tonne) and that Building 66 had been planned for this activity in the future. Building 66 was declared as the location of the detonator development work. Samples taken from waste tanks adjacent to Building 73C may provide some clues. Both buildings lack the appropriate filtered ventilation systems for long-term work with uranium metal.

25. The Al Hadre munitions testing site, first inspected in October 1991 by the seventh inspection team, was visited again by the twelfth team. The judgement that the site is convertible to nuclear hydrodynamic testing was confirmed. The facility has not been used, and the war damage observed during the October visit has not been repaired.

0066

**ACTIVITIES RELATED TO EQUIPMENT AND MATERIALS**

26. The team visited the Nassr State Establishment (Taji), the State Enterprise for Heavy Engineering Equipment (Daura), the Badr General Establishment, Al Ameen, the Al Ameer and Al Radwan factories of the Auqba bin Nafi Establishment, the Saddam State Establishment (Al Ameer) and the Saladdine State Establishment to inventory machine tools and other relevant equipment. With these visits, the inventory of machine tools at facilities related to the nuclear programme declared in July 1991 has been completed. The current inventory of machine tools is shown in Table 3. According to the declaration, the involvement of some of these facilities in the nuclear programme was only slight. Key machines are those which have technical characteristics required for producing key components needed in a nuclear programme. Key machines have been identified (to the extent possible) by type, serial number and manufacturer, and in some cases an IAEA seal has been applied for identification purposes (see Annex 2). Such key machines include high-precision milling and turning machines (Schäublin, Matrix Churchill), large turning and milling machines (SHW, Zayer, Innocenti, Dorries, Schiess Froriep), turning and milling machines with special fixtures (MAHO, Magdeburg), jig bores (SIP), and flow forming machines (H & H Metallform). Key machines include also electron beam welders (Leybold, Heraeus, Sciaky) and precision measurement machines (Leitz, DEA). The Iraqi side attempted to limit the placing of identifying seals and the taking of photographs on numerous occasions throughout these inspections.

27. The team inspected the Ash Shaykhili warehouses of the Ministry of Industry to identify, photograph and inventory. The items of interest included those brought back by the 93-truck convoy during the third IAEA inspection mission. Additional items of interest were discovered during this inspection. They included ten pieces of small EMIS discs (880 mm pole diameter) which probably belonged to the R-24 experiment, a small EMIS coil winding machine for these discs, and two large vacuum valves. The Iraqi side promised to move items of interest to the area of warehouse 13B at Ash Shaykhili, where there are other items under IAEA control. The remaining equipment was judged to be of general use and was released.

0067

28. The team visited the Ur State Establishment (Nassariya), where melted aluminium components of centrifuge housings are stored. Material which had been presented to the tenth IAEA team, was declared to contain 84 tons of aluminium tubing for centrifuge molecular pumps and 300 tons of aluminium tubing for centrifuge housings. These have been melted together into large blocks; according to Iraqi declarations, it was done prior to the start of UNSCR 687 inspections. During the tenth IAEA inspection mission, the total weight was estimated and samples were taken. The twelfth IAEA team took additional samples (total 15) to confirm the analytical results. It found partially melted blocks which were sampled selectively. The tenth IAEA team was presented with a batch of smaller blocks, which was declared to contain the melted remains of aluminium forgings for 9000 upper flanges, 9000 jacket rings and 200-250 disk-shaped lower flanges. The total weight of 126 tons had been confirmed by the tenth team. An intact top flange from a poorly melted block was removed. The twelfth team took five additional samples for chemical analysis. In some poorly melted blocks, identification marks and components were detected which could be of help in confirming manufacturer information.

29. The team revisited the Iskandariya foundry to take additional samples from the maraging steel blocks, which again, according to Iraqi declarations, had been melted unilaterally by Iraq prior to the start of UNSCR 687 inspections. During the eleventh IAEA inspection mission, two blocks of maraging steel were rendered harmless by remelting with an equal amount of scrap carbon steel. The analytical results indicate that this action renders the material harmless. The Iraqi side has located a foundry in Basra which is capable of completing the destruction in a few days. This activity will therefore be completed during a future mission.

**TABLE 3**

**UPDATED LIST OF IDENTIFIED EQUIPMENT - BASED ON RESULTS OF THE TWELFTH INSPECTION MISSION**

| Type of Machine | Total | Key Machines |
|---|---|---|
| Milling, 5 axes | 32 | 32 |
| Milling, 4 axes | 62 | 0 |
| Milling, 3 axes | 214 | 10 |
| Turning | 148 | 71 |
| Grinding | 21 | 0 |
| Jig grinding | 8 | 0 |
| Jig boring | 7 | 3 |
| Electric discharge, RAM or wire type | 15 | 0 |
| Precision measurement | 16 | 3 |
| Cutting | 7 | 0 |
| Boring | 4 | 0 |
| Electron beam welding | 5 | 5 |
| Flow or spin forming | 16 | 14 |
| Press | 16 | 0 |
| **TOTAL** | **571** | **138** |

0069

**OTHER ACTIVITIES**

30. Inspection at Al Qaim - Al Qaim, located about 300 kilometers north-west of Baghdad, near the Syrian border, is the site of a yellow cake ($UO_4$) production facility co-located with a very large superphosphate fertilizer plant. This plant was badly damaged during the Gulf War. The yellow cake facility was particularly hard hit. Portions of the fertilizer plant have been repaired. The yellow cake facility remains in the condition it was in when first inspected, in July 1991, by the third IAEA inspection team. The team was given a complete description of the construction history (including contractors), processes and operational history of the plant.

    The yellow cake facility is located within the site boundary in a separately secured area. Construction began in 1982. The design capacity was 103 tonnes/year, the second cycle and refinery sections being built with an overcapacity of 100%. The capacity is based on a feed concentration of 75ppm and a minimum recovery rate of 93%. The plant was planned for commissioning in the first half of 1984. Operating records show that 20 514 kilograms of $UO_4$ had been produced by 1 October 1984. The team was presented with daily production records. Copies of the records have been requested for review at Tuwaitha.

31. Inspection at the Geological Survey Institute, Baghdad - This is the location of process development and pilot plant operation intended to recover uranium (as $UO_4$) from carbonate ore from the Abou-Sukhair mine. The team received a complete description of the process. The pilot plant was completed in June 1990 and 20 tonnes of ore were received from Abou-Sukhair in July 1990. Ten tonnes were processed, producing 500 grams of $UO_4$, and the remaining 10 tonnes was sent back to the mine. The processing capacity of the plant was 200 kilograms of ore per hour. At present the plant is being used for aluminium extraction. Equipment located at the Institute was inspected by the fifth IAEA inspection team.

32. Follow-up inspection at Al Jesira - The transfer of uranium waste from the oil tank to the open-air settling tanks at Al Jesira, begun during the tenth mission, is complete. It is expected that the solutions will evaporate during the summer; the solid deposit will

0070

then be collected into drums and transferred to location C at Tuwaitha. The team performed a seal check on the equipment items stored in an open area adjacent to the facility. The search for additional manufacturer information was not successful.

33. Follow-up inspections were carried out at Al Furat, Dijjla and the National Computer Centre (NEC-750) during the twelfth inspection mission. A second and again unsuccessful attempt was made to operate the NEC-750 computer.

34. The second version of the Iraqi "full, final and complete" report (dated May 1992) regarding all activities relating to weapons of mass destruction covered by UNSCR 687 (the Iraqi Nuclear Programme Before and After UNSCR 687 (1991)), was provided on 4 June for onward transmission. The Minister of State for Foreign Affairs - Mr. Al-Sahaf - requested in the covering letter that the report be treated as confidential because of the nature of the contents. The nuclear portion of the report is currently being translated. No judgement can yet be made regarding the completeness and accuracy of the report.

## ANNEX 1

### Actions required regarding Tarmiya/Ash Sharqat sites

The actions identified below apply to both sites and should be undertaken only in the presence of the IAEA inspection team.

Requested actions:

(1) Reduce delivered electrical power to the Tarmiya and Ash Sharqat sites by approximately an order of magnitude. Proposals are expected from the Iraqi side on how this could be done such that (i) it can be monitored, and (ii) has minimum impact on other users in the area).

(2) Remove the 1200mm system horizontal return iron from Building 33, Tarmiya and Building 51, Ash Sharqat to the Al Nafad storage area.

(3) Remove the electrical cables connecting Buildings 5 and 38 to Building 33, Tarmiya; Buildings 27 and 29 to Building 51, Ash Sharqat; Building 243 to Building 245, Tarmiya; and Building 20 to Building 21, Ash Sharqat.

(4) Dismantle and remove the general utilities infrastructure from Buildings 248, Tarmiya and 31, Ash Sharqat.

(5) Buildings 5, 38, 243, 245 - Tarmiya and Buildings 27, 29, 20, 21 - Ash Sharqat are to be destroyed.

(6) Building 33, Tarmiya and Building 51, Ash Sharqat are not to be re-built.

Equipment and other useable materials, with the exception of the ventilation systems in Building 245, Tarmiya and Building 21, Ash Sharqat, may be salvaged, but should be stored at the site for inspection prior to removal.

Additional actions covering equipment at either or both sites may be required.

0072

Tarmiya

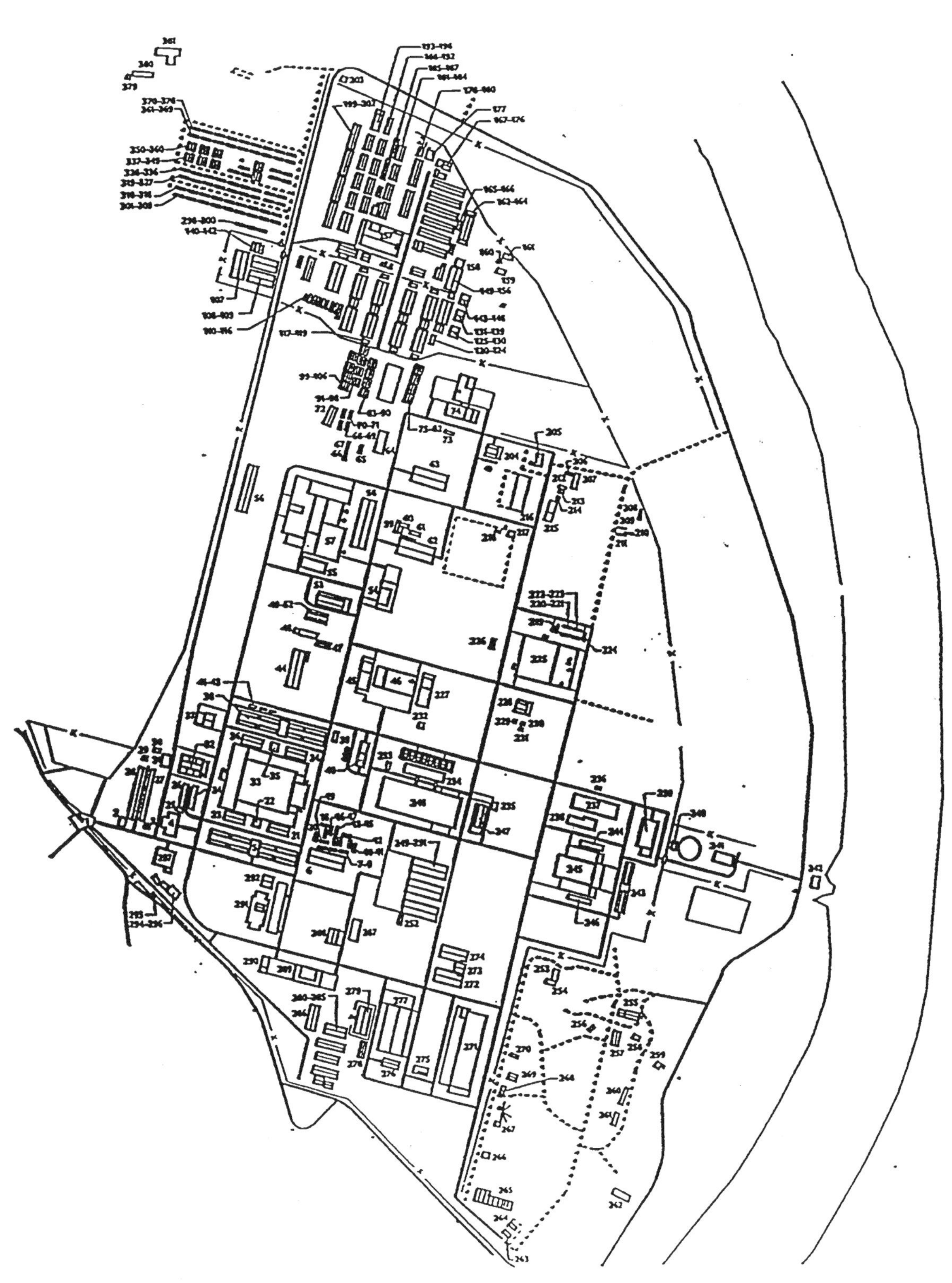

0073

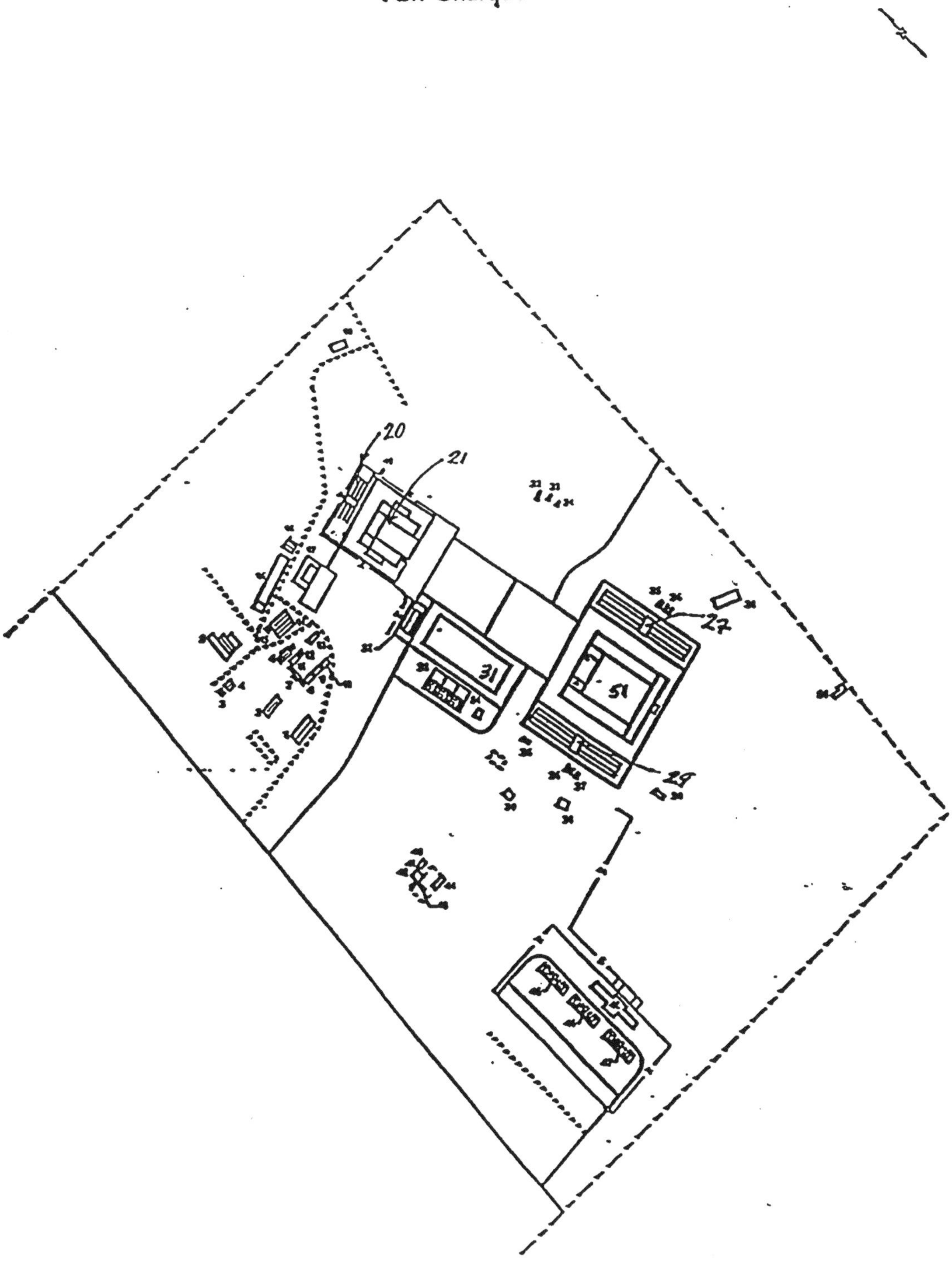

0074

INTERNATIONAL ATOMIC ENERGY AGENCY
AGENCE INTERNATIONALE DE L'ENERGIE ATOMIQUE
МЕЖДУНАРОДНОЕ АГЕНТСТВО ПО АТОМНОЙ ЭНЕРГИИ
ORGANISMO INTERNACIONAL DE ENERGIA ATOMICA

WAGRAMERSTRASSE 5, P.O. BOX 100, A-1400 VIENNA, AUSTRIA
TELEX: 1-12645, CABLE: INATOM VIENNA, FACSIMILE: 43 1 234564, TELEPHONE: 43 1 2360

IN REPLY PLEASE REFER TO:
PRIERE DE RAPPELER LA REFERENCE:

DIAL DIRECTLY TO EXTENSION:
COMPOSER DIRECTEMENT LE NUMERO DE POSTE:

**ANNEX 2**

1 June 1992

Dear Dr. Al Hajjaj,

1. The Chief Inspector of IAEA-12 informed me that you request clarification as to the purpose of the current inventorying/seals application activity on certain equipment and machine tools located at different facilities.

2. As communicated to you by the Chief Inspector, these measures are chiefly meant to facilitate the identification of items, particularly those associated with the implementation of the long-term monitoring plan, and save time in subsequent inspections.

3. In more general terms, the application of seals does not prejudge the final disposal of the item in question, i.e., the decision to release the sealed items for general use under the long-term monitoring plan or to destroy, remove or render harmless the item in question, under UN Security Council resolution 687 (1991).

4. Items which are prohibited under UN Security Council resolution 687 (1991) are identified for destruction, removal or rendering harmless. The application of seals to such items found in Iraqi facilities is to prevent their use or movement prior to their destruction, removal or rendering harmless, as appropriate.

5. Dual-use items, for which there is no evidence of use in activities prohibited under UN Security Council resolution 687 (1991), are sealed for identification and will be considered for release under the long-term monitoring plan, or allowed to be used pending the implementation of such a plan. The definition of dual-use items, the procedure for release and the modalities of the long-term plan are established in UN Security Council resolutions 707 (1991) and 715 (1991).

6. Hence, acceptance of these resolutions by the Iraqi authorities and full compliance with their provisions will greatly facilitate the orderly processing of requests for re-use of facilities and equipment, including machine tools and materials.

Sincerely,

Maurizio Zifferero
Leader
UNSC 687 Action Team

Dr. Al Hajjaj
Directorate for International Organizations
Baghdad

0075

## ANNEX 3

List of Documents Received or Sent

12-01 Mr. Zifferero to Mr. Al Hajjaj on 920515 regarding actions to be taken for the destruction of buildings and equipment at Al Atheer/Al Hatteen complex, Tarmiya and Ash Sharqat

12-02 Mr. Muhammad Said Al-Sahaf, Minister of State for Foreign Affairs, to Mr. R. Ekeus, Executive Chairman of UNSCOM, on 920524 stating among other things the reasons for not providing procurement information related to the Iraqi centrifuge programme.

12-03 Mr. Al Hajjaj to Mr. Perricos on 920527 providing a response to questions concerning the plutonium line asked on 920414 (IAEA-11)

12-04 Mr. Al Hajjaj to Mr. Perricos on 920527 providing a response to questions regarding Al-Rabee and Al Dijla factories, centrifuge programme and weaponization asked on 920414 (IAEA-11)

12-05 Mr. Perricos to Mr. Al Hajjaj on 920527 clarifying the purpose of attaching IAEA seals to equipment.

12-06 Mr. Perricos to Mr. Al Hajjaj on 920527 reminding the Iraqi side that there were still open questions - such as the procurement of carbon fibre rotors and maraging steel and source(s) of technical advice on the centrifuge programme - and asking for additional information on EMIS 1200-mm iron cores, light metal collectors used for EMIS, properties and current location of some HV DC power supply cabinets for EMIS, identification of gaseous diffusion projects 304 and 305 (including siting information on various gaseous diffusion projects), location of frequency converters, list and sources of imported chemical enrichment equipment, installation diagram for Building 90 at Al Tuwaitha, purpose of "paper plant", and locations of Khairat collection and Al Khayrat assembly points.

12-07 Mr. Perricos to Mr. Al Hajjaj on 920528 clarifying the criteria and specifications on the basis of which machine tools would be considered by the IAEA inspection team to be key equipment and have IAEA seals applied to them.

12-08 Mr. Perricos to Mr. Al Hajjaj on 910528 asking for clarifications regarding nuclear material balance and production at Abu Sukhair, Al Qaim and Al Jesira, processing of material of Brazilian origin, $UCl_4$ production in Building 85 at Tuwaitha, inconsistencies in U235 and U236 content of some samples, discrepancies in depleted uranium and enriched uranium recovered from the EMIS programme at Tuwaitha, and exact location and description of flows and dates of various activities performed in building complex 73 at Tuwaitha.

12-09 Mr. Perricos to Mr. Al Hajjaj on 920530 asking for clarifications and additional information on IAEC/PC-3 projects, code names and PC-3 organization chart.

12-10 Mr. Perricos to Mr. Al Hajjaj on 920530 requesting a special meeting on the activities performed in Building 73 "30 July project" at Tuwaitha.

0076

12-11 Mr. Perricos to Mr. Al Hajjaj on 920531 asking for explanations regarding the Iraqi nuclear material flow chart sent to IAEA on 920422, the activities in Building 73 at Tuwaitha and the origin of materials in a batch of ADU.

12-12 Mr. Perricos to Mr. Al Hajjaj on 920601 confirming the removal of MTR fuel plates containing 93% and pins containing 36% enriched uranium.

12-13 Mr. Perricos to Mr. Al Hajjaj on 920601 requesting presentation of the daily production records of the yellow cake plant at Al Qaim.

12-14 Mr. Perricos to Mr. Al Hajjaj on 920602 asking for information on the feasibility studies on underground nuclear reactors, including siting studies, type(s) of reactor, and procurement information related to reactors and reprocessing.

12-15 Mr. Al Hajjaj to Mr. Zifferero on 920602 providing information on the planned use of some radioisotopes in Iraq.

12-16 Mr. Zifferero to Mr. Al Hajjaj on 920601 clarifying the purpose of the inventorying/seals application activities involving certain equipment and machine tools.

12-17 Mr. Al Hajjaj to Mr. Perricos on 920602, in response to the request of 920528 (item 12-08 above), providing information on the production at Abou-Sukhair mine, Al Qaim and Al Jesira and discrepancies observed by the inspection teams.

12-18 Mr. Al Hajjaj to Mr. Perricos on 920528, in response to the request made by IAEA-11 on 920407, providing information on the inventory of nuclear material mentioned in an Al Atheer plan progress report, deliveries from Akashat/Al Qaim to Tuwaitha and Al Jesira, materials lost during bombing, shipments of $UO_2$ from Brazil, and EMIS washing solutions.

12-19 Mr. Perricos to Mr. Al Hajjaj on 920604 regarding the destruction activities at Tarmiya and Ash Sharqat and requesting the destruction of high-efficiency and activated charcoal filters and actions to be taken with regard to filter housings during IAEA-13.

12-20 Mr. Perricos to Mr. Al Hajjaj on 920604 agreeing to the removal and demolition of the two hot cells in Building 15 at Tuwaitha and requesting the presentation of manipulators, leaded glass windows etc, to the IAEA-13 team.

12-21 Mr. Perricos to Mr. Al Hajjaj on 920604 agreeing to release the general-purpose equipment and utilities stripped from the destroyed buildings at Al Atheer/Al Hatteen site and the destroyed equipment (IAEA-12).

12-22 Mr. Perricos to Mr. Al Hajjaj on 920604 requesting the presentation of missing parts (such as power supply, control unit, mandrels and rollers) of a flow forming machine inspected by the team at Iskandariya on 920601.

0077

12-23 Mr. Perricos to Mr. Al Hajjaj on 920604 asking about the original purpose of the design workshop, the designer and the intended user, and requesting information on the contracts of Dijla with foreign firms.

12-24 Mr. Perricos to Mr. Al Hajjaj on 920604 reminding the Iraqi side about the remaining open questions relating to the hydrodynamic codes and NEC 750 computer used in the weaponization studies.

12-25 Mr. Al Hajjaj to Mr. Perricos on 920604 providing some information on the studies and experiments related to weaponization.

12-26 Mr. Al Hajjaj to Mr. Perricos on 920604 providing a list of $UO_2$ shipments received from Brazil in 1981.

12-27 Mr. Al Hajjaj to Mr. Perricos on 920604 regarding proposals to retain two generators in Building 243 at Tarmiya, and tasks and power requirements for Tarmiya site.

12-29 Mr. Al Hajjaj to Mr. Zifferero on 920603 reminding the Iraqi side that the irradiated fuel, which has not yet been removed form Iraq, is causing a potential environmental hazard.

12-30 Mr. Al Hajjaj to Mr. Perricos on 920603 providing two additional diskettes containing codes and data used by Group IV of PC-3.

0078

## ANNEX 4

**Tables A4-1, A4-2 and A4-3 provide a complete description of the nuclear materials and the declared and verified inventories stored at location C, location B and the IRT 5000 reactor respectively. Figures A4-1 and A4-2 give a description of the physical configuration of the nuclear material stored at location C.**

0079

# SUMMARY OF INSPECTION RESULTS

12th On-Site Inspection

Table 1

Location C

| ORIGIN | Processing Site | Material Type | | Presented to Team No. | DECLARED INVENTORY No. of Items | Compound Weight (kg) | Element Weight (kg) | $U_{235}$ (kg) | VERIFIED INVENTORY No. of Items | Compound Weight (kg) | Element Weight (kg) | $U_{235}$ (kg) | Verification Activities I | NDA | B | D |
|---|---|---|---|---|---|---|---|---|---|---|---|---|---|---|---|---|
| Niger | - | NU | Yellow Cake | 1,3,8 | 858 | 276844 | 199934 | - | 858 | 276844 | 199934 | - | 858 | 329 | 122 | 41 |
| Portugal | - | NU | Yellow Cake | 1,3 | 916 | 286435 | 213016 | - | 916* | 286435 | 213016 | - | 916 | 322 | 127 | 48 |
| Italy | Al Tuwaitha Bldg. 73 A & B | NU | $UO_2$ Pellets | 1,3 | 1 | - | 8 | - | 1 | 9.272 | 8.17 | - | 1 | 1 | 1 | 1 |
| | | | $U_3O_8$ Powders | 1,3 | 10 | 366.58 | 310.1 | - | 10 | 366.58 | 309.75 | - | 10 | 6 | 3 | 3 |
| | | | $UO_2$ Powders | 1 | 22 | 721.43 | 631.2 | - | 22 | 721.43 | 624.54 | - | 22 | 18 | 7 | 3 |
| | | | $UO_4$ Powders | 1 | 1 | 29.71 | 20.3 | - | 1 | 29.5 | 20.14 | - | 1 | 1 | 1 | 1 |
| | | | Mix U Oxides | 1 | 6 | 166.77 | 135.2 | - | 6 | 166.77 | 135.51 | - | 6 | 6 | 3 | 2 |
| | | | FF Bundles | 3 | 4 | - | 771 | - | 4 | 876.1 | 771 | - | 4 | 4 | 4 | 1 |
| | | | FF Rods | 1,3 | 55 | - | 29.96 | - | 54** | 33.82 | 29.42 | - | 54 | 4 | 54 | - |
| | | | $UO_4$ in Filters | 4 | 37 | - | 50 | - | 37 | - | 50 | - | 37 | - | - | 6 |
| | - | | $UO_2$ Powders | 1 | 68 | - | 2253.6 | - | 68 | 2620.5 | 2253.6 | - | 68 | 68 | 14 | 10 |
| | - | LEU (2.6%) | $UO_2$ Powders | 1 | 75 | - | 1767 | 45.82 | 75 | 2031 | 1767 | 45.82 | 75 | 75 | 23 | 10 |
| | - | DU | $UO_2$ Powders | 1 | 183 | - | 6005 | - | 183 | 7007 | 6005 | - | 183 | 183 | 16 | 7 |
| U.K. | Al Tuwaitha Bldg. 9 | DU | Metal | 4 | 2 | 2 | 2 | - | 2 | 2 | 2 | - | 2 | 1 | 2 | - |
| | | NU | $UO_2(NO_3)_2$ Solution | 4 | 4 | - | 0.4 | - | 4 | 0.54 | 0.4 | - | 4 | 1 | 1 | - |

I = item counting, B = weighing, D = sample analysis, NDA = non-destructive analysis
LEU = Low Enriched Uranium, DU = Depleted Uranium, NU = Natural Uranium, FF = Fresh Fuel

* Drum #MHI contains about 150 kgs Yellow Cake from Portugal and 217 kgs from Al Qaim origin and purified in Bldg. 73C (30 July Project)
** 1 FF Rod containing 0.54 kg NU was declared lost during bombing

0080

# SUMMARY OF INSPECTION RESULTS

12th On-Site Inspection

## Table 1 (cont. 1)

Location C

| ORIGIN | Processing Site | Material Type | | Presented to Team No. | DECLARED INVENTORY | | | | VERIFIED INVENTORY | | | | | | | |
|---|---|---|---|---|---|---|---|---|---|---|---|---|---|---|---|---|
| | | | | | No. of Items | Compound Weight (kg) | Element Weight (kg) | $U_{235}$ (kg) | No. of Items | Compound Weight (kg) | Element Weight (kg) | $U_{235}$ (kg) | Verification Activities | | | |
| | | | | | | | | | | | | | I | NDA | B | D |
| Brazil | | NU | $UO_2$ Powders | 3 | 201 | - | 20128 | - | 201 | 20731 | 18036 | - | 201 | 37 | 201 | 7 |
| | Al Tuwaitha Bldg. 15 | | $UF_6$ | 3 | 1 | 0.465 | 0.3 | - | 1 | 0.6 | 0.4 | - | 1 | 1 | 1 | 1 |
| | | | Liquid Waste | 4 | 4 | - | 6 | - | 4 | - | 6 | - | 4 | - | - | 5 |
| | | | Mix U Powders | 1,3,4 | 1 | - | 20 | - | 1 | 30 | 13.9 | - | 1 | 1 | 1 | 6 |
| | | | $UF_4$ Powders | | 1 | - | 183 | - | 1 | 227 | 170.2 | - | 1 | 1 | 1 | 3 |
| | | | $UO_2$ Powders | | 3 | - | 131.5 | - | 3 | 150.8 | 131.2 | - | 3 | 3 | 3 | 2 |
| | Al Tuwaitha Bldg. 85 | | $UCL_4$ | 3,4 | 33 | - | 1840 | - | 33 | 2996.1 | 1917 | - | 33 | 33 | 33 | 17 |
| | | | ADU Powders | 3 | 13 | - | 717 | - | 13* | 1140 | 545.04 | - | 13 | 13 | 13 | 15 |
| | Al Tuwaitha Bldg. 80 | | EMIS Solutions | 3 | 19 | - | 0.783 | - | 5** | - | 0.393 | - | 5 | 5 | 5 | 3 |
| | | EU | | | | - | 0.322 | 0.050 | | - | 0.278 | 0.044 | | | | 10 |
| | | DU | | | | - | 2.438 | - | | - | 1.746 | - | | | | [illegible] |
| | | EU | EMIS Powders | 10 | 8 | 0.398 | 0.318 | 0.021 | 8 | 0.411 | 0.308 | 0.020 | 8 | 8 | 8 | 8 |
| | | DU | | | 13 | 5.063 | 4.050 | - | 13 | 5.150 | 4.120 | - | 13 | 13 | 13 | 11 |
| | Tarmya Bldg. S4/46 | EU | EMIS Solutions | 3 | 1 | - | 0.146 | 0.009 | 1 | - | 0.163 | 0.010 | 1 | 1 | 1 | 5 |
| Denmark | Tamuz-2 Bldg. 24 | LEU (2.26%) | FF Rod | 1 | 1 | - | 0.080 | 0.002 | 1 | - | 0.080 | 0.002 | 1 | 1 | 1 | - |

I = item counting, B = weighing, D = sample analysis, NDA = non-destructive analysis
HEU = High Enriched Uranium, LEU = Low Enriched Uranium, NU = Natural Uranium, EU = Enriched Uranium
DU = Depleted Uranium, FF = Fresh Fuel
* Drum #1 among ADU from Al-Jesira (contains 95.8 kg NU) is a mixture of Brazilian and Akashat powder
** Since part of the solutions were HEU. All mixed to change category to LEU (~1% U-235)

0081

12th On-Site Inspection

# SUMMARY OF INSPECTION RESULTS

## Table 1 (cont.2)

Location C

| ORIGIN | Processing Site | | Material Type | Presented to Team No. | DECLARED INVENTORY No. of Items | DECLARED INVENTORY Compound Weight (kg) | DECLARED INVENTORY Element Weight (kg) | DECLARED INVENTORY $U_{235}$ (kg) | VERIFIED INVENTORY No. of Items | VERIFIED INVENTORY Compound Weight (kg) | VERIFIED INVENTORY Element Weight (kg) | VERIFIED INVENTORY $U_{235}$ (kg) | Verification Activities I | Verification Activities NDA | Verification Activities B | Verification Activities D |
|---|---|---|---|---|---|---|---|---|---|---|---|---|---|---|---|---|
| USSR | IRT-5000 | - | Beryllium Cell | 4 | 1 | - | - | - | 1 | - | - | - | 1 | 1 | - | - |
| Akashat | Al Qaim | Natural Uranium | Yellow Cake | 3 | 12 | - | 2200 | - | 12 | 3008 | 2023 | - | 12 | 12 | 12 | 9 |
| | Al Jesira | | $UO_2$ Powders | 3 | 410 | - | 84843.2 | - | 410 | 97331 | 84680 | - | 410 | 308 | 98 | 47 |
| | | | $UCL_4$ | 3 | 8 | 1207 | 780 | - | 8 | 1156 | 747 | - | 8 | 8 | 8 | 1 |
| | | | Retained Waste | 3 | - | - | 13000 | - | - | - | - | - | - | - | - | 10 |
| | Al Tuwaitha Bldg. 85 | | ADU Powders | 4 | 2 | 219 | 191.4 | - | 2 | 92 | 53.34 | - | 2 | 2 | 2 | 3 |
| | Al Tuwaitha Bldg. 73 A&B | | FF Pins | 4 | 46 | - | 14 | - | 46 | - | 14 | - | 46 | 10 | 46 | - |
| | | | $UO_2$ Pellets | 4 | 1 | - | 26 | - | 1 | 29.25 | 25.8 | - | 1 | 1 | 1 | 3 |
| Akashat & Brazil | Al Tuwaitha Bldg.73C (30 July Project) | | $UO_4$ Slurry | 4 | 8 | - | 164 | - | 8 | 1181.5 | 206.15 | - | 8 | 8 | 8 | 10 |
| | | | $UO_2$ Powders | 3 | 23 | - | 1850 | - | 23 | 2024.4 | 1755.15 | - | 23 | 23 | 23 | 2 |
| | | | Mix U Oxides | 3 | 19 | - | 160 | - | 19 | 200.5 | 172.21 | - | 19 | 19 | 19 | 2 |
| | | | $U_3O_8$ Powders | 3,4 | 5 | - | 500 | - | 5 | 154.9 | 130.99 | - | 5 | 5 | 5 | 2 |
| | | | $UF_4$ Powders | 3,4 | 2 | - | 30 | - | 2 | 78.2 | 56.18 | - | 2 | 2 | 2 | 2 |

I = item counting, B = weighing, D = sample analysis, NDA = non-destructive analysis
FF = Fresh Fuel

0082

12th On-Site Inspection

## SUMMARY OF INSPECTION RESULTS

Table 1 (cont.3)

Location C

| ORIGIN | Processing Site | Material Type | | Presented to Team No. | DECLARED INVENTORY | | | | VERIFIED INVENTORY | | | | | | | |
|---|---|---|---|---|---|---|---|---|---|---|---|---|---|---|---|---|
| | | | | | No. of Items | Compound Weight (kg) | Element Weight (kg) | $U_{235}$ (kg) | No. of Items | Compound Weight (kg) | Element Weight (kg) | $U_{235}$ (kg) | Verification Activities | | | |
| | | | | | | | | | | | | | I | NDA | B | D |
| Akashat & Brazil | Al Tuwaitha Bldg. 73 C (30 July Project) | NU | $UO_4$ Purified | 3 | 9 | - | 1360 | - | 9 | 1991.5 | 1314.4 | - | 9 | 9 | 9 | 2 |
| | | | $UO_3$ Powders | 3,4 | 24 | - | 3424 | - | 24 | 4599.3 | 3187.8 | - | 24 | 24 | 24 | 34 |
| | | | U Metal | 4 | 21 | - | 1020 | - | 21 | - | 1023.4 | - | 21 | 21 | 21 | 5 |
| | | | $UO_4$ Powder | 3 | 4 | - | 46 | - | 4 | 146.2 | 73.73 | - | 4 | 4 | 4 | 5 |
| | | | Waste | 12 | 1 | - | 200 | - | 1 | - | - | - | 1 | - | - | 1 |
| USSR (Exempted) | Al Tuwaitha Bldg. 9 | LEU (10%) | U-oxides & ADU | 1,4,10 | 11 | - | 2.464 | 0.246 | 11 | - | 1.949 | 0.190 | 11 | 11 | 11 | 13 |
| | | LEU (6.9%) | ADU Powder | | 1 | - | 0.940 | 0.065 | 1 | 1.373 | 0.934 | 0.064 | 1 | 1 | 1 | 1 |
| | | LEU (10%) | FF Pins | | 5 | - | 0.400 | 0.040 | 5 | - | 0.400 | 0.040 | 5 | 5 | - | - |

I = item counting, B = weighing, D = sample analysis, NDA = non-destructive analysis
NU = Natural Uranium

0083

UNSC 687

12th On-Site Inspection

## SUMMARY OF INSPECTION RESULTS

Table 2

Location B

| ORIGIN | Processing Site | Material Type | | Presented to Team No. | DECLARED INVENTORY | | | | VERIFIED INVENTORY | | | | | | | |
|---|---|---|---|---|---|---|---|---|---|---|---|---|---|---|---|---|
| | | | | | No. of Items | Compound Weight (gm) | Element Weight (gm) | $U_{235}$ (gm) | No. of Items | Compound Weight (gm) | Element Weight (gm) | $U_{235}$ (gm) | Verification Activities | | | |
| | | | | | | | | | | | | | I | NDA | B | D |
| France | Tamuz-2 Bldg. 24 | HEU (93%) | Irradiated Fuel | 1 | 38 | - | 11874 | 11050 | 38 | - | 11874 | 11050 | 38 | 98 | - | - |
| USSR | | HEU* (80%) | | 1 | 20 | - | 3933 | 3165 | 20 | - | 3933 | 3165 | 20 | 20 | - | - |
| | | HEU (36%) | | 1 | 3 | - | 1002 | 360 | 3 | - | 1002 | 360 | 3 | 3 | - | - |
| | | LEU (10%) | | 1 | 69 | - | 87760 | 8776 | 69 | - | 87760 | 8776 | 69 | 69 | - | - |
| Al Qaim | | NU | | 4 | 2 | - | 7900 | - | 2 | - | 7900 | - | 2 | 2 | - | - |
| France | | - | Beryllium blocks | 1 | 7 | - | - | - | 7 | - | - | - | 7 | - | - | 1 |

I = item counting, B = weighing, D = sample analysis, NDA = non-destructive analysis
HEU = High Enriched Uranium, LEU = Low Enriched Uranium, NU = Natural uranium
* Six elements in tank no. 14 contain control rods

0084

## SUMMARY OF INSPECTION RESULTS

12th On-Site Inspection

Table 3

IRT-5000 Reactor

| ORIGIN | Processing Site | Material | Type | Presented to Team No. | DECLARED INVENTORY | | | | VERIFIED INVENTORY | | | | | | | |
|---|---|---|---|---|---|---|---|---|---|---|---|---|---|---|---|---|
| | | | | | No. of Items | Compound Weight (kg) | Element Weight (kg) | $U_{235}$ (kg) | No. of Items | Compound Weight (kg) | Element Weight (kg) | $U_{235}$ (kg) | Verification Activities | | | |
| | | | | | | | | | | | | | I | NDA | B | D |
| USSR | IRT-5000 Reactor | HEU (80%) | Irradiated Fuel | 1 | 76 | - | 15291 | 12232 | 76 | - | 15291 | 12232 | 76 | 68 | - | - |
| | | - | Beryllium Blocks | 1 | 17 | - | - | - | 17 | - | - | - | 17 | - | - | - |

I = item counting, B = weighing, D = sample analysis, NDA = non-destructive analysis
HEU = High Enriched Uranium

(NOT UNDER IAEA SEALS)

0085

## FIGURE 4: LEFT SIDE STORAGE OF LOCATION C

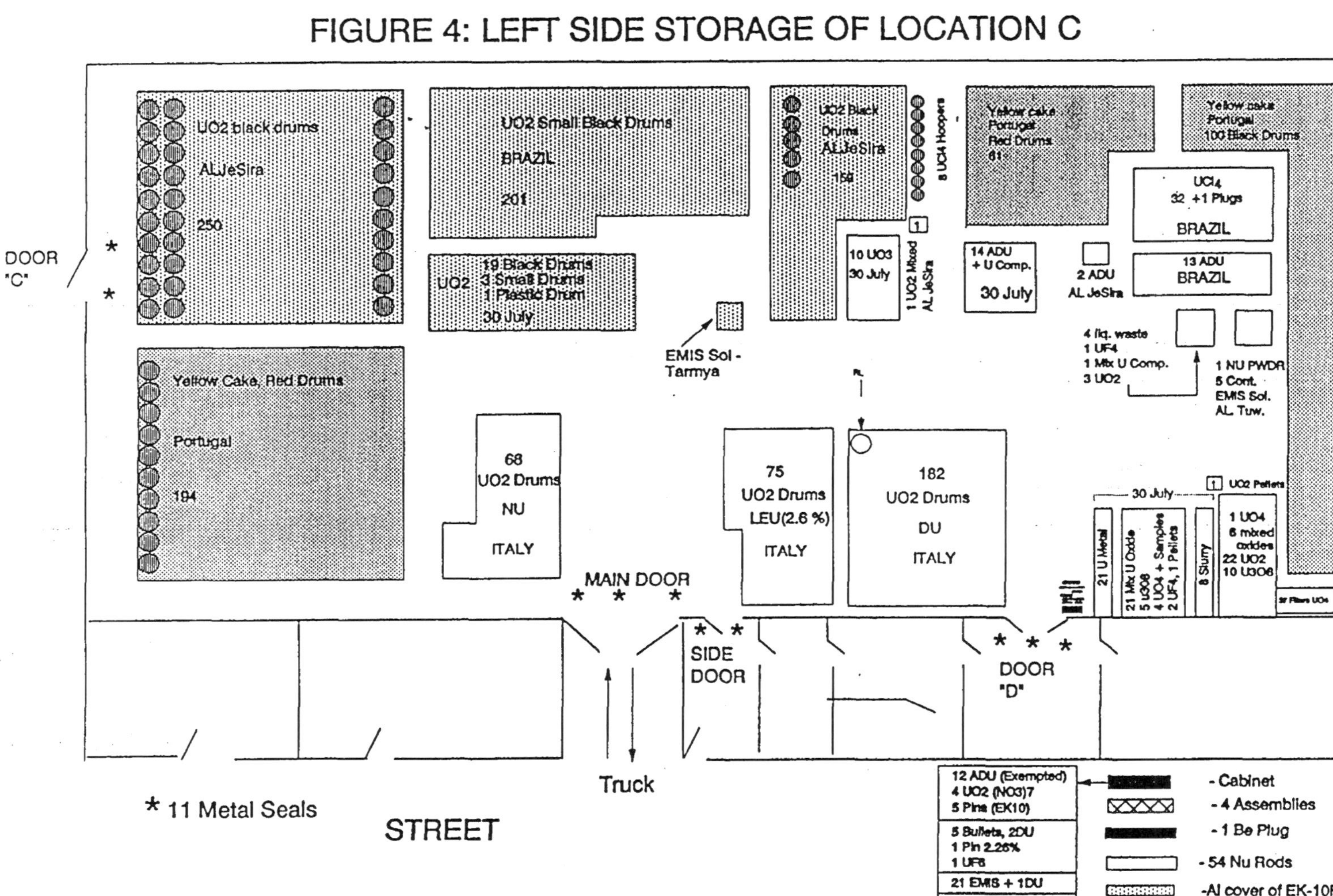


0086

FIGURE 5: RIGHT SIDE STORAGE OF LOCATION C

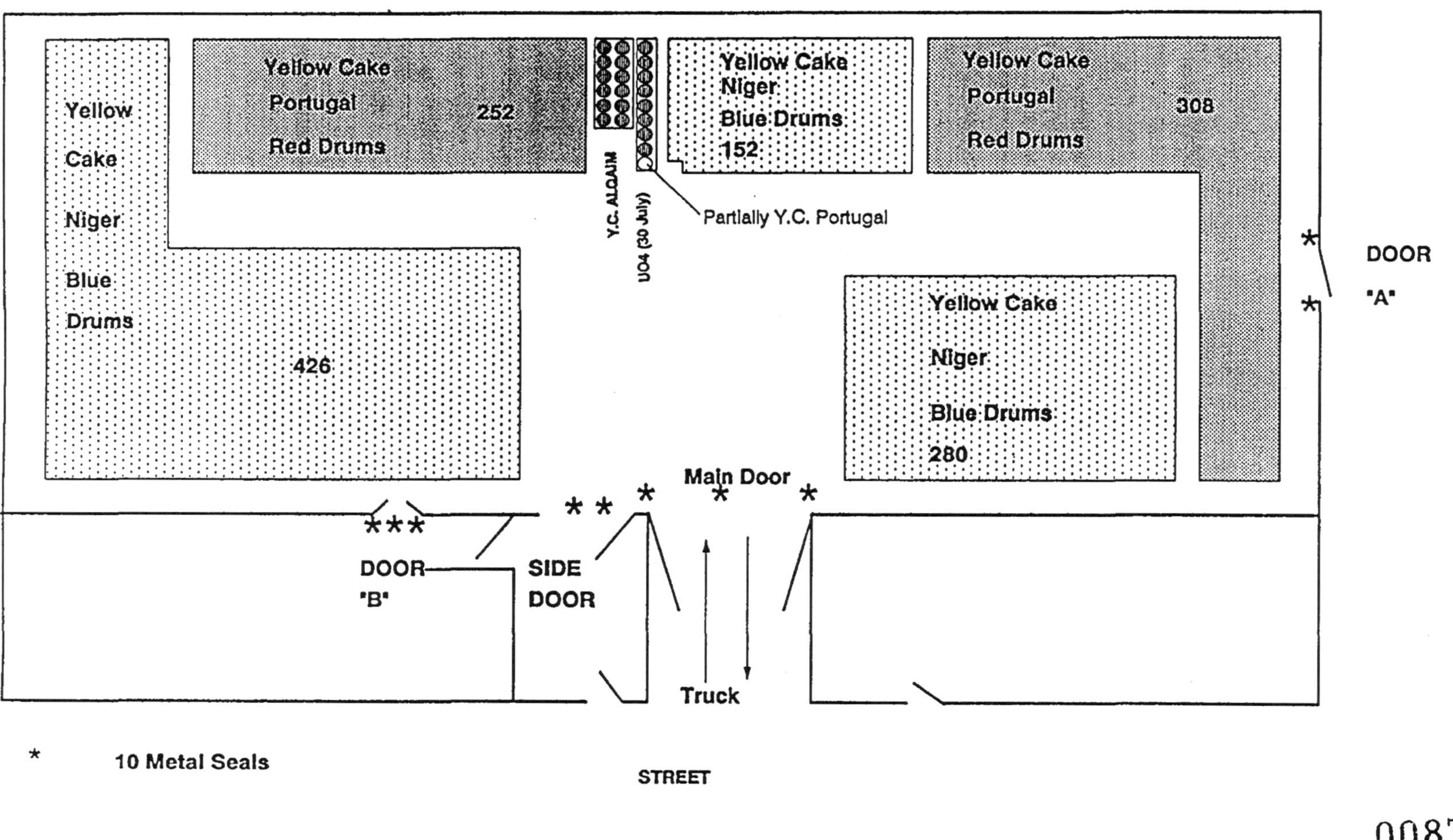


0087

지원할 것이며 인는 재래진
전과 군비감축등 책임있는
협상에 맞춰 이뤄질것이다.
7
자유안전보장선을 위해 다
국간 협력계획에 의한 지원
을 제의한다.

틀으로 아태평양협력기구 그리고유
만들고 럽안보협력기구참여등 광범
。 한 문제를 이슈화, 이를 관
언등에 철함으로써 신질서주도권경
민족분규 쟁에 성큼 뛰어들었다.
력을 거 소련붕괴에 따른 진정한
실체로 냉전종식후 최초의 G7정
주도권 상회담으로 표현된 이번 회
럽대륙 담의 결과는 결국 동서대결
실효성 종식후의 세계가 새로운 동
못했 반협의질서와는 거리가 먼
열강의 치열한 대결구도속
북방영 에 표류하고 있음을 입증했
제판만 다.
一아시

회원국 자격을 잠정 정지키
로 합의했다.•

## 日參議院선거전 돌입
## PKO등 주요이슈로

【東京=文昌宰특파원】 제16회 일본참의원통상선거가 8일 공고돼 18일간의 선거전이 시작됐다.

34개정당에서 6백29명의 입후보자가 출마한 이번 선거는 상원인 참의원 의석의 50%인 1백27석을 개선하는 것으로 PKO협력법과 경기대책, 정치개혁이 3대 이슈로 부상했다.

참의원의 여야역전을 재역전시키려는 집권자민당은 경제정책을 간판으로 내세웠으나 社會·共産양당은 PKO법안의 국민심판을 받겠다는 전략으로 현재의 與小野大현상지속을 목표로하고있다.•

율 위 이와관련 CSCE는 8
-본격 일 유고슬라비아 내전의 책
전해졌 임을 물어 세르비아가 주도
하고 있는 신생 유고연방의

## 국청 경고

앞서 동안 강산처럼 아무런 변화
없이 통치해온 사람들, 그리
고 조상들이 이룩한부를 탕
행방 진한 사람들이 발붙일 자
고방 리를 없앨것」이라고 말한
제하 것으로 이 신문은 보도했
발언 다.
하고 이 신문은 鄧小平이 지난
해나 5월22일 北京의 철강공업
적인 단지 순시중 행한 발언을
버려 처음으로 전하고 올해말로
다. 예정된 제14차 공산당대회
경경 를 앞두고 개혁지지파 지도
한편 자들을 가려뽑는데 있어서
득하 의 명확한 지침을 밝혔다고
말했다.•

## 유엔 이라크査察團
## 시위대에 봉변당해

【바그다드·유엔본부 外電綜合】=이라크내 은닉무기 색출을 위한 유엔사찰단이 7일 시위대로부터 계란과 과일등을 투척당하는등 봉변을 당했다.

이라크 당국은 바그다드 농무부 청사 밖에서 철야대기하며 청사내 수색작업 허용을 요구하고 있는 유엔사찰단 보호를 위해 사건발생후인 8일 경비병력을 증원했다.•

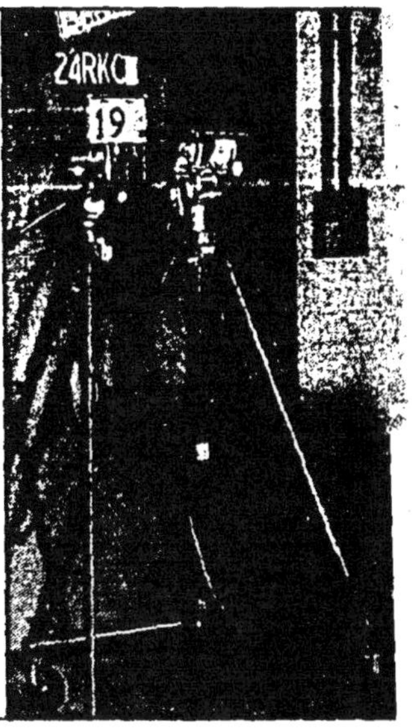

기 시베리아 톰스크市의 前 국우회합 권한이 없다고
당 공산당 제1서기인 비크토 강변했다.
13 르 조르갈체프 의원은 「우 또다른 대표인 드미트리
리 나라가 70여년동안에 산 스테파노프는 「공산당이 작
업생산에 있어서 유럽에서 년 8월 발생한 강경파의

7. 9. 한국일보 4면

라빈 당수는 이식 조멧당등 일부 우파정당들을 연정에 끌어들이기 위한 방안을 모색하고 있으나 각료직 인배문제등으로 에이탄 조멧당 당수와의 협상이 성공하지 못할 경우 對아랍정책등에서 좌파노선이 특히 두드러지게될 것으로 보인다.

라빈당수는 팔레스타인 사람들에게 내년초까지 제한된 자치를 허용할 방침임을 거듭 천명해왔으며 다음달 미국을 방문해 조지 부시 美대통령과 아랍.이스라엘 간 평화협상의 향후 전개방향등을 논의할 예정이다.(끝)

이라크,유엔 사찰 최종시한까지 거부

(바그다드.니코시아 AFP.AP=聯合) 이라크는 화학무기 관련자료등이 보관돼있는 것으로 의심을 받아온 이라크 농무부청사 에 대한 유엔의 개방요구 최종시한인 9일 저녁까지 유엔 사찰팀의 농무부청사 사찰을 거부했다고 유엔의 이라크 대량살상무기 파괴 특별위원회 지역책임자인 더글라스 엥글룬드씨가 밝혔다.

엥글룬드씨는 기자회견에서 16명의 유엔 화학무기 사찰팀이 5일째 농무부청사 바깥에서 머물며 조사를 요구했으나 이라크측은 끝내 이에 응하지 않았다고 말했다.

이에 앞서 압델 와하브 마무드 알-사바 이라크 농무장관은 이날 아침 회견을 갖고 이라크는 "유엔 결의와 아무런 관계가 없는 민간 부서"에 대한 조사를 결코 허용치 않을 것이라는 기존 입장을 재천명했다.

그는 미국이 對이라크 전쟁을 도발하기 위해 유엔 사찰팀들을 이용하고 있다고 주장했다.

한편 사찰팀들이 머물고 있는 농무부청사 주변에서 일단의 이라크人들이 유엔의 사찰 요구에 항의하는 시위를 벌였다고 관영 이라크통신(INA)이 보도했다.(끝)

(YONHAP) 920710 1026 KST

신

원 본

# 외 무 부

종 별 :

번 호 : AVW-1145 일 시 : 92 0717 1200

수 신 : 장 관(국기,중동일)

발 신 : 주 오스트리아 대사

제 목 : 대이락 국제핵사찰단의 태도에 대한 이락 정부의견

당지 이락 대표부는 안전보리 결의 687에 따른 대이락 국제핵사찰단의 태도에 대한 이락정부의 의견서를 배포하였는바, 동 의견서를별첨 FAX 송부함.끝.

(대사 이시영-국장)

별첨:AVW(F)-0172 3 매.

국기국 중아국

PAGE 1

92.07.17 22:11 FO

외신 1과 통제관

0090

EMBASSY OF THE REPUBLIC OF KOREA

Praterstrasse 31, Vienna
Austria 1020 (FAX : 2163438)

| No : AVW(F) - 0122 | Date : 20212 1200 |
|---|---|
| To : 장 관(국기. 중동일)<br>(FAX No : ) | |
| Subject : AVW - 1145의 첨부 | |

표지포함 4 매

Total Number of Page :

4 - 1

0091

PERMANENT MISSION
OF THE REPUBLIC OF IRAQ
TO THE INTERNATIONAL
ORGANIZATIONS

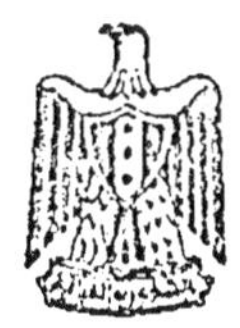

JOHANNESGASSE 26
A-1010 VIENNA

The following are observations on the behaviour of the International Inspection Teams conveyed by the Iraqi authorities to the IAEA

1 - The teams kept asking questions which we have previously answered; this means that the inspection teams had plenty of time which they wanted to fill by any means, including repeating the same questions over and over again. This causes serious damage to Iraq in two ways: firstly, the non-completion of the inspections which subsequently means the prolongation of the embargo; secondly, the increase in the expenses which Iraq will be requested to pay to cover the inspection teams in the future;

2 - There is an attempt to make believe that the information presented by the Iraqi side is not true and to cast doubts about the credibility of such information, especially that relating to nuclear material;

3 - Many items which are needed by the teams (such as drinking water) are bought from outside Iraq with hard currency although such items are available in Iraq. Spending these burdensome funds is bound to damage the Iraqi economy since Iraq will be requested to pay them in the future;

4 - The emergence of a provocative, unfriendly and inappropriate attitude on the part of some members of the inspection teams (e.g. one team member wore a T-shirt with anti-Iraqi cericatures and captions);

. . ./ 2

4-2

0092

PERMANENT MISSION
OF THE REPUBLIC OF IRAQ
TO THE INTERNATIONAL
ORGANIZATIONS

JOHANNESGASSE 26
A-1010 VIENNA



5 - Some members of the teams ask questions as if they were police investigators in an attempt to provoke Iraqi officials;

6 - The inspection teams involved some persons in their support services, whose names are not included in the lists of inspection team members;

7 - We have information that some members of the inspection teams exploit their travel by a special UN plane and buy personal items (such as rare carpets and antiques etc.) from Iraqi markets and carry these items outside Iraq, thus violating Iraqi customs regulations which currently prohibit the export of such items;

8 - We often noticed that UN cars used by the inspection teams do not observe Iraqi traffic laws, which constitutes unacceptabl behaviour;

9 - During the visit of the Twelfth Inspection Team a request was made to hold a meeting with Dr. Mahdi El Ubaydi in order to discuss some technical issues concerning the enrichment by gas diffusion. At the beginning of that meeting, Mr. Nichols indicated that he would like to discuss some technical issues with Dr. Mahdi for evaluation purposes which concern the United States in respect of the release of information about the gas diffusion technology which is owned by the US. As you know, the Agency's mandate, according to Security Council resolution 687, has nothing to do with such action;

. . . / 3

4-3

0093

PERMANENT MISSION
OF THE REPUBLIC OF IRAQ
TO THE INTERNATIONAL
ORGANIZATIONS

JOHANNESGASSE 26
A-1010 VIENNA



10 - During the visits made to the Al Qa Qaa and Al Kaim sites, some Inspectors took charts and drawings of buildings and sites that are not related to the nuclear field. This in itself constitutes a clear act of espionage practised under the umbrella of the International Organizations.

We could go on enumerating other examples and observations but we shall confine ourselves to the above examples which demonstrate how it has become increasingly difficult to deal with the Inspection Teams.

4-4

| 관리번호 | 92-857 |
|---|---|

원 본

# 외 무 부

종 별 :

번 호 : UNW-1962　　　　일 시 : 92 0720 2030

수 신 : 장 관(연일,중동일,기정)

발 신 : 주 유엔 대사

제 목 : 대 이락 제재

연:UNW-1865

1. 금 7.20 안보리는 비공식 회의를 개최하고 7.17 이락을 방문하고 금일 귀임한 UNSCOM(이락무기 폐기위원회) EKEUS 위원장으로 부터 연호 이락무기 폐기위원회 작업반의 이락 농업성 청사 사찰거부사건에 관해 보고를 청취함. 금일 보고에게서 EKEUS 위원장은 7.5 이락정부가 유엔 작업반의 농업성 사찰을 거부한 이래 금일 현재까지 동 작업반의 농업성 청사밖에서 24 시간 대기 상태에 있으나금번 방문에서 이락정부측과 협의결과 이락측의 입장 변화는 기대하기 어려운 상태임을 보고 하였다고함

2. 금일 회의에서 EKEUS 위원장은 동건과 관련하여 이락측과의 타협은 금후유엔의 이락무기 폐기활동에 많은 영향을 미칠수 있으므로 강력한 대응이 필요하다는 의견을 개진하였다고 하는바 유엔이 구체적으로 동건에 관해 어떤 조치를취할지는 상금 미정임. 당관이 탐문한바에 의하면 미.영. 불등 3 개국은 최근 이락의 대유엔 강경입장(농무성 사찰불허, 이락-쿠웨이트 국경 획정 거부, 구호활동을 위한 유엔 직원체류 연장거부, 식량수입을 위한 석유수출 조건 합의 거부등)에 대응하기 위하여 무기제조소등 특정건물에 대한 폭격을 은밀히 검토하고 있다고함

3.UNSCOM 이락 농부성 청사내에 미사일제조 관련 서류가 보관되어 있다는 정보에 따라 동청사를 시찰코자하고 있는바, 유엔 안보리는 7.6 성명을 채택하고이락 처사를 비난한바, 있음. 이락측이 상기 농무성 사찰을 거부하고 있는 이유는 동 청사사찰을 허용할 경우 여타 정부건물과 궁극적으로는 후세인 대통령 사무실까지도 사찰대상이 될것을 우려하고 있기 때문인것으로 보도되고 있음

(대사 유종하-국장)

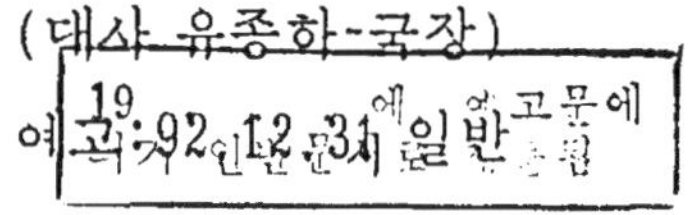


| 국기국 | 장관 | 차관 | 1차보 | 중아국 | 분석관 | 청와대 | 안기부 |
|---|---|---|---|---|---|---|---|

PAGE 1　　　　92.07.21 09:33

외신 2과 통제관 BX

0095

관리 번호 92-866

원 본

# 외 무 부

종 별 :

번 호 : UNW-1979　　　　일 시 : 92 0721 2100

수 신 : 장 관(연일,중동일,기정)

발 신 : 주 유엔 대사

제 목 : 대이락 제재

연:UNW-1962

1. 연호 이락의 최근 대유엔 강경입장에 대한 미, 영, 불의 대응과 관련, 당관 이수혁 참사관이 불란서 및 일본대표부를 접촉, 추가 탐문한바에 의하면 미,영, 불 3 개국은 하기 4 가지 방안을 논의하고 있다함.

-안보리는 60 일마다 이락의 결의안 이행결과를 정기적으로 검토하도록 되어있는 조항을 삭제하여 대이락 제재조치를 무기한 지속시킬 것임을 천명

-페트리엇 미사일을 이락-쿠웨이트 국경에 배치

-이락 항공기의 이락 영공내 비행금지

-특정 이락 무기시설의 폭격

2. 작 7.20 안보리 비공개 협의에서 미국 PERKINS 대사는 미국정부는 이락에 대한 대응조치를 관계 당사국과 협의중에 있다고 간략히 발언하여 미, 영, 불 3 개국간에 모종의 대응책을 검토하고 있음을 암시하였다함

3. 한편 7.20 안보리는 비공식회의에서 이락정부의 유엔 이락무기 폐기위원회(UNSCOM)의 농무성 사찰불허와 관련하여 유엔 사찰대신 비동맹국가와 중국, 오지리, 스웨덴의 전문가를 초청, 사찰을 하도록 하겠다는 이락측의 제의를 받아드릴수 없는것으로 결정하고 안보리의장이 동내용을 이락측에 전달하기로 하였다함

4. 동건 진전사항 탐문되는대로 추보위계임.끝.

(대사 유종하-차관)

예고:92.12.31 일반에 의거 일반문서로 재분류

첨부:UNW(F)-0612

국기국　장관　차관　1차보　중아국　문석관　정와대　안기부

PAGE 1　　　　92.07.22　14:58

외신 2과 통제관 BS

0096

UNITED NATIONS

**S**

Security Council

Distr.
GENERAL

S/24321
20 July 1992
ENGLISH
ORIGINAL: ARABIC

LETTER DATED 19 JULY 1992 FROM THE PERMANENT REPRESENTATIVE OF IRAQ TO THE UNITED NATIONS ADDRESSED TO THE PRESIDENT OF THE SECURITY COUNCIL

With a view to dealing with the predicament relating to the building of the Ministry of Agriculture and Irrigation, my Government makes the following proposal:

"Iraq shall invite a group of experts from the States of the Non-Aligned Movement and possibly from other States, such as China, Austria and Sweden, to visit the building of the Ministry of Agriculture and Irrigation and to inspect its contents in order to ascertain that no materials or documentation relevant to resolution 687 (1991) are present. Such visit shall be outside the mandate of the Special Commission."

I should be grateful if you would have this letter circulated to the members of the Security Council as a document of the Security Council, and I shall be glad to convey to my Government any clarifications that you may seek, regarding the implementation of the above-mentioned proposal.

(Signed) Abd al-Amir AL-ANBARI
Ambassador
Permanent Representative

-----

92-32597 3313h (E) 200792 200792

200792

6/2-1-/

0097

92- 7-20 : 17:05 ; #18

주 미 대 사 관

USR(F) : 4757 년월일 : 92. 7. 20 시간 : 16:40

수 신 : 장 관 (미일, 연일, 중동일)

발 신 : 주미대사

제 목 : 이락의 유엔결의 준수

| 보 안 | |
|---|---|
| 통 제 | |

(출처 : )

# U.N. Aide Quits Iraq After Failing To Gain Access for Arms Inquiry

By PAUL LEWIS

Special to The New York Times

BAGHDAD, Iraq, July 19 — Iraq sent a senior United Nations envoy away empty-handed today, citing sovereignty and security as reasons for its latest refusal to allow United Nations arms inspectors into its Agriculture Ministry.

"The Iraqi position is fundamentally unchanged," Rolf Ekeus, head of the commission to eliminate Iraq's weapons of mass destruction, said before he left the country.

When Mr. Ekeus arrived on Friday, he said he would warn Iraq that it faced the risk of attack if it did not comply fully with the terms of the cease-fire that ended the Persian Gulf war.

After two days of talks with Iraqi officials here, Mr. Ekeus left for Bahrain before returning to New York to [illegible] of the United Nations Security Council [illegible] his discussions.

Col. Douglas England of the United States Army, who heads the United Nations arms inspectors here, said, "There was nothing I could characterize as progress."

U.N. Team Sits in Jeeps

A team of United Nations inspectors has been sitting in white jeeps outside the Agriculture Ministry since July 5, when they were first refused permission to search the building after receiving a tip from a Western intelligence agency that documents relating to Iraq's banned ballistic missile program might be hidden there.

The United States, Britain and France are becoming increasingly irritated over Iraq's stand against the inspectors and a number of other quarrels with the United Nations. Diplomats say they are considering methods of dealing with President Saddam Hussein, including the possibility of an air strike.

On July 6, the Security Council issued a statement calling for the inspectors to be given "immediate access" to the ministry and saying Baghdad is guilty of "a material and unacceptable" breach of its obligations under the gulf war cease-fire agreement.

United Nations officials said the Iraqi Deputy Prime Minister, Tariq Aziz, showed some slight flexibility when he met with Mr. Ekeus today. But they said they were uncertain whether this indicated that Iraq was considering a change of position.

United Nations officials said the Iraqis appeared worried that granting this request might set a precedent that would allow the inspectors to poke around in other ministries and offices of President Hussein's secretive bureaucracy.

These officials speculated that the Iraqis' real fear might be that the inspectors would find clues to Mr. Hussein's personal movements and pose a threat to his security.

The standoff with the inspectors is only the latest in a series since inspectors began seeking information on Iraq's weapons of mass destruction so they could be disabled.

In all such previous confrontations, Iraq has backed down in the end, under pressure from the Security Council. But on this occasion, the quarrel is only one of a number of disputes, which suggests Baghdad may be adopting a tougher line toward the United Nations.

The work of relief agencies is being hampered by Baghdad's refusal to renew an agreement with the United Nations on humanitarian aid that expired last month. Iraq has turned down a

**Baghdad's defiance seems to be hardening.**

Security Council offer to let it sell some oil to pay for imports of food and medicine and start compensating victims of the Kuwait invasion.

Iraq has also refused to accept the new boundary the United Nations has demarcated with Kuwait. And it continues its economic blockade of Kurdish-controlled northern parts of the country, denying them food and fuel from the south and refusing to pay civil servants and pensioners living there.

At the same time, United Nations workers here have started to come under attack for the first time.

A United Nations guard protecting relief workers in the northern region was shot dead Thursday and earlier this month two others were wounded in attacks by unknown assailants.

( 4757 - 1 - 1 )

| 외신 1과 | |
|---|---|
| 통 제 | |

NYT 92.7.20.

| 배부처 | 장관실 | 차관실 | 1차보 | 2차보 | 의전실 | 외정실 | 분석관 | 아주국 | 미주국 | 구주국 | 중아국 | 국기국 | 경제국 | 통상국 | 문협국 | 외연원 | 청와대 | 안기부 | 공보처 | 경기원 | 상공부 | 재무부 | 농수부 | 동자부 | 환경처 | 과기처 |
|---|---|---|---|---|---|---|---|---|---|---|---|---|---|---|---|---|---|---|---|---|---|---|---|---|---|---|
| | | | / | | / | / | 0 | | / | / | | | | | | | / | / | | | | | | | | |

0098

京鄕新聞

1992. 7. 22. 수, 4면

# "유엔 10일內 이라크공습"

## 농무부 사찰거부따라 불가피

【유엔본부=AP연합】이라크가 농무부청사에 대한 사찰을 계속 거부함에 따라 美·英·佛등 다국적군의 이라크공습이 불가피하게 됐다고 유엔 안전보장이사회의 한 외교관이 20일 말했다.

익명을 요구한 이 외교관은 이라크가 휴전협정 준수의사를 전혀 보이지않고 있어 유엔이 더이상 농락당할 수 없음을 보여주기 위해서라도 소규모 공습은 이제 선택의 여지가 없는 것으로 安保理회원들은 대체로 생각하고 있다고 전했다.

이같은 공습은 10일이내에 이루어질 것이며 미국을 포함한 영국·프랑스·사우디아라비아 등이 가담할 것이라고 익명을 요구한 수명의 다른 외교관들이 확인했다.

이들 외교관은 사담 후세인 이라크 대통령이 유엔사찰단의 이라크 농무부청사 진입을 계속 거부할 경우에만 이같은 공습이 실천에 옮겨질 것이라고 덧붙였다.

세계일보

1992. 7. 22. 수, 4면

# "다국적軍, 이라크공습불가피"

## 安保理관계자 "査察계속거부로 선택여지 없다"

【유엔본부=AP연합】이라크가 농무부 청사에 대한 사찰을 계속 거부함에 따라 美-英-佛등 다국적軍의 이라크 공습이 불가피하게 됐다고 유엔 안전보장이사회의 한 외교관이 20일 말했다.

익명을 요구한 이 외교관은 이라크가 휴전협정 준수 의사를 전혀 보이지 않고 있어 유엔이 더이상 농락당할 수 없음을 보여주기 위해서라도 소규모 공습은 이제 선택의 여지가 없는 것으로 安保理회원국들은 대체로 생각하고 있다고 전했다.

이같은 공습은 10일 이내에 이루어질 것이며 美國을 포함한 英國 프랑스 사우디아라비아 등이 가담할 것이라고 익명을 요구한 수명의 다른 외교관들이 확인했다.

한편 20일에 열렸던 유엔 안보리 비공개회의에 참석했던 한 외교관은 쿠웨이트와 터키가 對이라크 공습을 위해 자국 공군기지를 제공하겠다고 제의했으며, 사우디아라비아도 공중조기경보기(AWACS)를 제공하겠다는 뜻을 표명했다고 말했다.

0099

韓國日報
1992. 7.22. 수, 4면

# 多國軍 곧 이라크 공습

## 査察거부따라 10일내 강행전망

【유엔본부AP=聯合】이라크가 농무부 청사에 대한 사찰을 계속 거부함에 따라 美·英·佛등 다국적군의 이라크 공습이 불가피하게 됐다고 유엔 안전보장이사회의 한 외교관이 20일 말했다。

익명을 요구한 이 외교관은 이라크가 휴전협정 준수 의사를 전혀 보이지 않고있어 유엔이 더이상 농락당할 수 없음을 보여주기 위해서라도 소규모공습은 이제 선택의 여지가 없는것으로 安保理 회원들은 대체로 생각하고 있다고 전했다。

이같은 공습은 10일 이내에 이루어질 것이며 미국을 포함한 영국 프랑스 사우디아라비아 등이 가담할 것이라고 익명을 요구한 수명의 다른 외교관들이 확인했다。

이들 외교관은 사담 후세인 이라크 대통령이 유엔사찰단의 이라크 농무부 청사 진입을 계속 거부할 경우에만 이같은 공습이 실천에옮겨질 것이라고 덧붙였다。

한편 20일에 열렸던 유엔 안보리 비공개회의에 참석했던 한외교관은 쿠웨이트와 터키가 對이라크 공습을 위해 자국 공군기지를 제공하겠다고 제의했다。

0100

世界日報
1992. 7. 23. 화, 4면

# 이라크 「유엔査察」 계속거부

## 武力사용경고 불구

## 美, 對이라크제재 無期연장

【워싱턴·유엔본부=AFP연합】 이라크 정부는 바그다드에 폭격이 가해지는 한이 있더라도 유엔무기사찰단의 요구를 받아들이지 않을 것이라고 압둘 알 안바리 유엔주재 이라크대사가 21일 말했다.

안바리대사는 유엔의 對이라크 사찰을 관철하기 위해 무력사용도 배제하지 않겠다는 美英佛 3국의 경고와 관련, 「바그다드市에 폭탄 한두발이 떨어지더라도 이라크 정부의 입장은 변하지 않을 것」이라면서 이같이 밝혔다.

이라크 정부는 유엔무기사찰단의 농무부 청사 사찰을 거부, 지난 5일이래 계속 대치중이다. 유엔사찰단측은 이라크 정부가 은닉무기에 관한 비밀자료를 농무부 청사내에 숨겨놓고 있다고 믿고 있다.

한편 조지 부시 美대통령은 이날 이라크가 중동지역에서 미국의 이익을 위협하는 활동을 계속해서 벌이고 있기 때문에 이라크의 쿠웨이트 침공직후인 지난 90년 8월2일을 기해 취해진 이라크에 대한 무역제재와 이라크 資産에 대한 동결조치를 무기한 연장한다고 발표했다.

### 유엔사찰팀 철수

【바그다드·유엔본부=AFP 연합특약】 바그다드에서 核사찰활동을 벌이고 있는 유엔사찰단은 22일 이라크 농무부에 대한 사찰노력을 중단하고 숙소로 철수했다.

0101

## 最近 이락 大量破壞武器 査察을 둘러싼 緊張 動向

1. 최근 美·英·佛등 西方圈은 이락當局이 化學武器등 大量破壞武器 關聯資料의 隱蔽處로 알려진 이락 農務部에 대한 UN 化學武器査察團의 搜索을 계속 妨害하고 있는데 따라 對應措置로 武器製造所를 비롯한 特定建物爆擊 등의 軍事制裁問題를 檢討하고 있음.

2. 關聯 動向

가. UN의 對이락 査察動向

○ 6.27부터 化學武器 生産關聯 裝備破壞作業을 監督하고 있는 UN 化學武器査察團은 이락 農務部내 化學武器 및 大量破壞武器 關聯資料가 隱匿되어 있다는 情報에 따라 7.5 搜索作業에 着手하려 했으나 이락當局의 妨害로 中斷되었으며

○ UN安保理 議長은 이락側에 대해 UN 査察團 活動에 協調해 주도록 促求(7.6)하고 「에케우스」UN 이락武器 廢棄 特別委員會 委員長을 이락에 派遣(7.15 - 17), 이락側을 說得했으나 失敗하였음

※ 「에케우스」委員長은 安保理에서 이락側의 農務部 査察 許容은 기대할 수 없으므로 강력한 對應이 必要하다고 報告(7.20)

26-20

0102

나. 이락의 對應動向

○ UN査察團의 이락 公共機關 搜索은 主權侵害 行爲로서 바그다드가 爆擊을 당하더라도 이를 받아들일 수 없다는 強硬態度를 堅持(7.21 「안바리」駐UN 이락大使)하는 한편

※ 7.7이래 4차례에 걸쳐 이락 住民들을 動員, 農務部를 監視중인 UN 査察團員들에 대해 抗議示威 展開

○ 「갈리」UN事務總長에게 이락은 安保理 決議에 따른 責任을 완수했으므로 經濟制裁 등의 對이락 決議를 取消해 주도록 要求(7.15)하면서 UN 安保理所屬 中立國 專門家들에게 農務部 搜索 許容 用意를 表明(7.19 「아지즈」副總理)하였음

다. 西方측 動向

○ 美·英·佛등 西方측은 이락이 UN의 權威에 도전, 계속 査察團 活動을 妨害할 경우 이락 武器製造所등 特定建物에 대한 爆擊이 불가피하다는 점을 이락側에 通報할 것을 고려중인 바

○ 美國은

- 對이락 貿易制裁와 이락資産 凍結措置(90.8.2)를 無期限 延長한다고 發表(7.21 「부시」大統領)하고

- 英·佛등 多國籍軍 參與 主要國家들과 UN 査察團의 이락 農務部 査察實現 方案을 協議(7.20)한 가운데

○ 英國은 이락이 UN 安保理 權威에 계속 도전할 경우 軍事措置도 排除되지 않는다고 警告(7.20 「하네이」駐UN 大使)하였음.

3. 評價 및 展望

가. UN의 이락 保有 大量破壞武器 廢棄 查察活動은

○ 걸프戰 終戰 決議(91.4)에 따라 核·化學武器·生物武器·미사일등 4개 查察團을 構成하여 사찰을 수행하여 왔는 바

○ 核 查察團은 13차례에 걸쳐 核物質 및 濃縮施設 廢棄, 核硏究 中樞施設인 「알 아티르」工團내 核施設 破壞등 이락內 核關聯 施設 破壞作業을 監督했고

※ 이락은 91.9 바그다드市內 核硏究施設에서 4상자의 秘密書類 搬出을 試圖한 查察團을 強制 抑留한 바 있으나 美國의 軍事 再攻擊 警告로 查察에 동의

○ 미사일 查察團은 11차례에 걸친 活動으로 수퍼건, 스커드미사일 등을 破壞한데 이어 2.21 - 29간 스커드미사일 部品과 生產設備 등을 破壞하였음

※ 이락은 同 生產設備가 石油產業등 民需用으로 轉用이 可能하다고 查察에 不應했으나 UN의 軍事 再攻擊 警告에 따라 查察을 許容

나. 이락의 農務部 查察拒否는

○ 農務部內에 化學武器등 大量破壞武器 關聯資料를 보관하고 있어 이를 隱匿할 수 있는 시간을 確保하려는 試圖에서 비롯되었을 可能性이 농후하나

26-22

0104

○ 餘他 政府機關 建物은 물론 「후세인」大統領 事務室도 査察對象으로 擴大되는 것을 미연에 방지함과 아울러

○ UN이 貿易監視團의 요르단 派遣計劃을 推進(6.16 美 國防部 代辯人)하는 등 對이라 經濟封鎖를 強化할 움직임을 보이고 있는데 대응하여, UN과의 協商 계기를 조성하려는 底意로 評價됨

다. 앞으로 이락內 大量破壞武器 査察을 둘러싸고

○ 이락側으로서는 UN의 經濟封鎖 持續·強化시 「후세인」政權의 存立基盤을 威脅받을 수 있어 査察協調를 代價로 經濟封鎖 緩和를 최대한 確保해야 할 立場인 반면

○ 西方측으로서는 이락의 戰爭賠償등 UN 終戰決議를 履行시키고 「후세인」의 退陣 雰圍氣를 조성해야 할 立場이기 때문에

○ 이락側의 査察拒否가 長期 持續되면서 UN安保理 決議 707號(91.8)에 근거한 西方圈의 制限的인 對이락 軍事膺懲 可能性도 커질 것으로 展望됨.

※ 安保理決議 707號는 UN憲章 7章(平和破壞·侵略行爲에 대한 措置)에 입각하여 이락에 대해 모든 地域·施設·裝備·技術에의 接近·調査를 無條件·無制限 許可하도록 요구

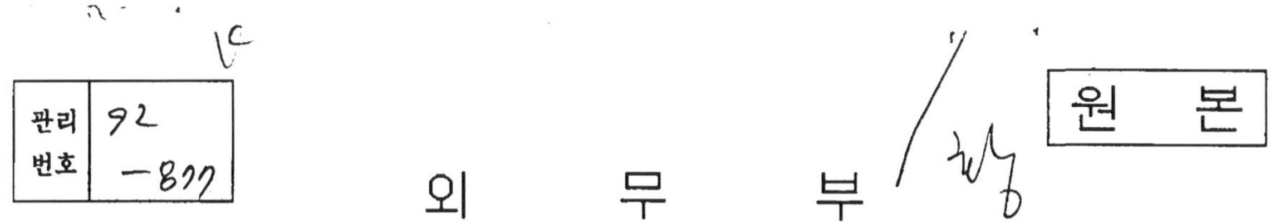

종 별 :

번 호 : UNW-2002 일 시 : 92 0723 2030

수 신 : 장관 (연일,중동일,기정)

발 신 : 주 유엔 대사

제 목 : 이락 무기폐기 활동

1.7.23. 안보리 비공개 회의는 UNSCOM (유엔 이락무기 폐기위원회)의 EKEUS위원장으로 부터 유엔 사찰반의 이락 농무성 철수와 관련한 보고를 청취하였는바 동 위원장은 주유엔 이락대사와 접촉하여 이락 정부의 입장을 파악한후 안보리에 재보고 키로 함. 금일 회의에서 미국대사는 EKEUS 위원장의 재보고를 일단 기다려 보겠으며 미국은 관계국과 이락에 대한 대응책을 계속 논의중에 있음을 재차 언급하였다함.

2.7.5. 이래 이락 농무성 앞에서 대기해온 UNSCOM 사찰반은 7.22. 이락 시민들의 폭력위협과 유엔 사찰반원에 대한 이락 정부의 신변보호 의무 불이행을 비난하고 농무성 앞에서 철수하였는바 7.22. 이락 외무부는 성명을 통하여 이락은 유엔 사찰반에 대해 모든 보호조치를 하여왔음을 주장하면서 UNSCOM 의 신변위협 주장은 이락에 적대감을 가지고있는 안보리의 일부 이사국으로 하여금 비합리적 간섭을 유도하기 위한 구실이라고 반박함. 끝

(대사 유종하-국장)

예고: 92.12.31. 일반

첨부: 이락외무부 성명 (FAX (UNW(F)-619)

국기국 장관 차관 1,2차보 중아국 분석관 청와대 안기부

PAGE 1 92.07.24 09:47

외신 2과 통제관 BX

0106

UNITED NATIONS UNW(F끼)-619 20723 2030 정무물 S

총204

**Security Council**

Distr.
GENERAL

S/24336
22 July 1992
ENGLISH
ORIGINAL: ARABIC

LETTER DATED 22 JULY 1992 FROM THE PERMANENT REPRESENTATIVE OF IRAQ TO THE UNITED NATIONS ADDRESSED TO THE SECRETARY-GENERAL

On instructions from my Government, I enclose herewith a statement delivered on Wednesday, 22 July 1992, by the official spokesman of the Ministry of Foreign Affairs of the Republic of Iraq concerning the decision to withdraw the inspection team from in front of the building of the Ministry of Agriculture and Irrigation.

I should be grateful if you would have this letter and its annex distributed as an official document of the Security Council.

(Signed) Abd al-Amir AL-ANBARI
Ambassador
Permanent Representative

619-2-1

92-33333 3458d (E) 220792 220792 220792 /...

Annex

Statement by the spokesman of the Ministry for Foreign Affairs

The leader of the inspection team positioned in front of the building of the Ministry of Agriculture and Irrigation announced on the morning of Wednesday, 22 July 1992 that he had decided to withdraw the members of the inspection team from outside the building on the grounds that they had been threatened with physical violence and that the Government of Iraq had failed to fulfil its commitment to ensure the safety of the inspectors of the Special Commission.

Commenting on this statement, an authorized source in the Ministry of Foreign Affairs stated the following:

Since the beginning of the work of the United Nations Special Commission in Iraq in April 1991 right up to now, the commitment of the Iraqi side has been to provide complete protection and security for the inspectors and members of the Special Commission working in Iraq. No member of the Special Commission or inspector has been exposed to any bodily harm or dangers of that kind throughout this period, even though some leaders and members of the inspection teams, including the Americans, tried in every way to incite and provoke the Iraqi officials and citizens, and these attempts at provocation were even reported in the world press. The French newspaper Libération on 22 October 1991 carried a statement by a French expert member of an inspection team of the Special Commission to the effect that the American inspectors had deliberately sought a confrontation with the Iraqi side, even hoping that one of the members of the mission would be killed, thereby justifying American intervention.

As regards the present inspection team that has been positioned since 5 July 1992 in front of the building of the Ministry of Agriculture and Irrigation, the Iraqi side has provided it with all the protection requested, and we challenge the leader of the inspection team to mention a single incident in which any member of his team has been exposed to bodily harm, even though the team has been located in a street in the centre of Baghdad both day and night, and has sorely provoked the feelings of Iraqi citizens by taking up a position in front of the Ministry building, a symbol of the national sovereignty of the Iraqi people.

The decision to withdraw the inspection team stems from the dilemma in which the Special Commission found itself after Iraq had expressed its readiness to accept the formation of a neutral team to inspect the Ministry in order to ascertain the falsity of allegations concerning the presence of prohibited materials on its premises. The pretext of bodily harm is an idle one: it seems clear that the underlying intention is to create a situation enabling the influential members of the Security Council harbouring hostility towards Iraq to commit unlawful intervention, thereby achieving their political aims through aggression.

----- 618-2-2

0108

연합 H1-086 S06 외신(664)

PLO 라빈의 평화제안 거부

(튀니스 AP=聯合) 팔레스타인해방기구(PLO) 지도부는 23일 이스라엘 점령지내 유태인 정착촌 건설을 일부 중단한다는 이츠하크 라빈 이스라엘 총리의 제안에 대해 대책회의를 갖고 이를 거부하기로 결정했다.

PLO지도부는 이날 3일간의 회의를 마치고 가진 AP통신과의 회견에서 정착촌 건설 전면중단과 요르단강 서안 및 가자지구 등 이스라엘 점령지역에서의 철수를 요구한다는 종전의 입장을 고수할 것을 재확인했다.

이들은 또 이스라엘이 정착촌 건설을 전면 중단할 때까지 미국은 주택건설 자금을 위한 차관 지급 보증을 유보해 줄 것을 촉구했다.

지도부는 이어 안보목적의 정착촌 건설은 계속되어야 한다는 라빈의 제안은 "유엔중전안을 회피하는 것이며 이스라엘의 점령을 영구화하려는 구실에 불과하다"고 주장했다.

한편 팔레스타인 망명의회격인 팔레스타인 민족평의회의 소베이드 사무총장은 "라빈이 진정 평화를 원한다면 리쿠드 정권하에 15년간 무너져온 신뢰의 다리를 재건해야 할 것"이라고 말했다.

라빈총리의 건설 중단 제안발표 이후 시리아는 방문중인 제임스 베이커 美국무장관에게 "완전한 건설중단만이 평화로 나아가는 길"이라고 말하고 "정치적인 것이건 안보적인 것이건 정착촌 건설은 불법이며 현재와 장래의 평화협상에 주요한 장애물"이라고 주장했다.

한편 이스라엘 정부는 이날 유태인 정착촌 건설계획중 공사계약을 이미 체결했으나 착공되지 않은 총 6천6백81채분의 주택 건설계약을 취소하고 이 지역의 도로신설 계획도 대부분 중단할 것이라고 발표했다.(끝)

(YONHAP) 920724 0818 KST

a6186ALL r
u i BC-IRAQ-USA-POST 24-07 0281
BC-IRAQ-USA-POST
U.S., ALLIES AGREE ON ULTIMATUM FOR IRAQ - POST

WASHINGTON, July 24, Reuter - The United States, Britain and France plan to give Iraq several days at most to end its confrontation with U.N. weapons inspectors, The Washington Post said on Friday.

If it fails to do so they could take military action, the Post said, citing unidentified senior officials.

The newspaper said the ultimatum could be issued in the name of the U.N. Secretary-General or the head of the U.N. Security Council and that other countries may join the effort.

It also said the United States had been trying to get other countries to back an allied bombing campaign against Iraqi military targets.

A similar report was broadcast on Thursday by NBC News.

It quoted a senior administration official as saying that President George Bush supported an allied attack unless Iraq allowed United Nations inspectors to enter the agriculture ministry in Baghdad to look for records on weapons programmes.

A White House spokeswoman declined to comment.

The current two-and-a-half-week confrontation is the latest of several standoffs between Saddam Hussein and the U.N. since Iraqi troops were driven from Kuwait by a U.S.-led military coalition in the Gulf War in February last year.

The inspections are required by U.N. resolutions issued after the war that order Iraq to destroy its weapons of mass destruction.

Iraq says the search of the agriculture ministry is beyond the scope of U.N. resolutions.

The United States and Britain have refused to rule out the use of force to enforce the U.N. resolutions. The Pentagon said an aircraft carrier battle group had cancelled Mediterranean port calls to remain at sea.

REUTER ABM SM
Reut05:49 24-07

19

0110

| 관리 번호 | 92 -732 |
|---|---|

# 외 무 부

종 별 : 지 급

번 호 : USW-3704 일 시 : 92 0724 1859

수 신 : 장관(미일,중동일,연일)

발 신 : 주 미 대사

제 목 : 대이락 군사제재 동향

연: USW(F)-4708, 4860, 4864

1. 연호 관련, 금 7.24 자 주재국 언론은 미.영. 불 등 3 국이 빠르면 금주말경 이락정부가 대량 살상무기 관련 비밀문서를 은폐중인 것으로 알려진 농무부청사등에 대한 유엔 사찰팀의 조사활동을 조속 허용토록 촉구하기 위한 최후통첩을 보내기로 합의하였다고 보도함.

2. 이와관련, FITZWATER 백악관 대변인은 금일 특별 브리핑을 통해 부쉬대통령이 작일에 이어 명 7.25(토) 오전, 체니국방자오간, 파웰 합참의장등 안보보좌관들과 재차 회도, 이락사태에 대한 대응방안을 논의할 예정이며 최후 통첩발송 여부는 현재 진행중인 유엔안보리협의 결과를 보아가며 결정할 (STILL OPEN AND UNDER DISCUSSION) 문제라고 답변하고, 그 시기에 관하여는 즉답을 회피함. 한편, CLINTON 민주당 대통령 후보는 작 7.23 성명을 통해 이락이 종전협정을 준수토록 하기 위해 유엔이 무력사용을 결의할 경우 자신은 미국이 여사한 조치에 동참하는 것을 지지할 것이라고 언명함.

3. 상기 관련동향에 대해 금일 당관 조태열 서기관이 접촉한 DAVID REUTHER국무부 이란. 이락과 부과장은 아래 요지로 답변함.

가. 금번 유엔 사찰팀의 조사활동에 대한 이락의 거부 및 방해 행위는 이락이 그동안 유엔결의 의무를 이행치 않은 수많은 사례중 일례(ONLY ONE CHALLENGE) 에 불과함. 금번 행위는 종전협정에 관하 유엔결의 687 호를 위반한 것이나, 이외에도 이락은 이락. 쿠웨이트간 국경선 위원회 불참, 쿠웨이트 자산반환 및 억류자 송환의무 불이행, 유엔 인도적기구의 활동방해등 거의 모든 유엔결의를 위반해 왔음(ATTACKING EVERY APSECT OF UN RESOLUTIONS). 미국의 상기와 같은 움직임은 이락이 계속 유엔결의를 위반할 경우 미국과 유엔의 강경조치를 감내해야 할 것임을 명백히

미주국 장관 차관 1차보 2차보 중아국 국기국 외정실 분석관
청와대 안기부

PAGE 1

92.07.25 08:40
외신 2과 통제관 BN

0111

하기위한 것임.

나. (최후 통첩 계획 및 시기에 대해) 상기 언론 보도의 진위여부를 확인할입장에 있지 않음. 다만, 현재 유엔안보리에서 모든 가능한 대응방안을 협의중이며, 여하한 조치를 취하든 간에 그 시기는 안보리 협의가 종료된 이후의 시점이 될 것임.

다. (후세인이 과거와는 달리 강경한 자세로 나오고 있는 배경에 대해) 아마도 미국은 국내선거로, 구주제국은 유고사태로 여념이 없어 효율적으로 대응하지 못하래란 판단이 섰을 것임. 미국등이 설사 강경대응을 한다 하더라도 걸프전의 경우와 같이 지속적인 대규모 공격 보다는 제한된 범위의 공습에 불과할 것이라는 판단도 작용하였을 수 있음. 또한 최근 유엔이 이락 난민구호등을 위한 각종 인도적 사업 실천을 위한 재원확보에 큰 어려움을 겪고 있음에 비추어 유엔이이락사태 개입의지(WILL POWER)를 상실해 가고 있다고 판단했을 지도 모름.(후세인 암살기도설 이후 자신의 건재를 과시할 필요에 따른 책략일지도 모른다는 일부 언론분석에 대해 동인은 재미있는 관찰이라는 반응을 보임.)

4. 상기와 같은 미행정부 인사들은 이락에 대한 최후통첩 계획여부 및 시기에 관해 확인을 거부하고 있으나, 대이락 군사조치 및 이를 위한 초후통첩 문제는 미행정부내에서 심각히 검토중인 것으로 보이며, 유엔안보리 협의가 순조로울경우 빠르면 수일내 최후통첩 조치가 이루어질 가능서도 있는 것으로 감지됨. 동건 진전사항 추보위계임.

(대사 현홍주-국장)



PAGE 2

0112

# 주 미 대 사 관

USW(F) : 4404 년월일 : 92.7.24 시간 : 18:59

수 신 : 장 관 (미일, 중동일, 연일)

발 신 : 주 미 대 사

제 목 : 대 이락 군사제재 동향 (백악관 및 국무부 브리핑)

| 보 안 통 제 | |
|---|---|

(출처 : FNS )

SPECIAL BRIEFING BY MARLIN FITZWATER
WHITE HOUSE PRESS SECRETARY
DAYTON, OHIO FRIDAY, JULY 24, 1992

Q Marlin, does this mean that an ultimatum is in the wind, that the President will be joined by Major, by Mitterrand in issuing an ultimatum to Saddam?

MR. FITZWATER: Well, we're still in the process of reviewing the entire situation. As you know, the President met with his national security advisers yesterday and discussed this situation. In addition, the UN Security Council is considering the matter. I think they just -- Mr. Ekeus just completed a press conference in New York in which he described the current status of events with regard to the inspectors in Baghdad.

So our deliberations in Washington are in concert with those that are going on at the UN. The question of an ultimatum is one that's still open and under discussion.

Kathleen?

Q What's changed since yesterday that made him cancel the rest of his trip?

MR. FITZWATER: The situation is that we continue to find a pattern of defiance in Iraq by Saddam Hussein and his regime to the UN resolutions. We continue to see a situation in which they are not making satisfactory efforts to comply with the inspections. There have been attacks on their own citizens by aircraft bombing in the south. There has been ignoring of other resolutions -- the oil-for-food resolution and others. So the situation that we are considering is the across-the-board defiance that we see in Iraq of the UN resolutions.

( 4404 - 4 - 1 )

| 외신 1과 통 제 | |
|---|---|

| 배부처 | 장관실 | 차관실 | 一차보 | 二차보 | 외정실 | 분석관 | 아주국 | 미주국 | 구주국 | 중아국 | 국기국 | 경제국 | 통상국 | 문협국 | 외연원 | 청와대 | 안기부 | 공보처 | 경기원 | 상공부 | 재무부 | 농수부 | 동자부 | 환경처 | 과기처 | | |
|---|---|---|---|---|---|---|---|---|---|---|---|---|---|---|---|---|---|---|---|---|---|---|---|---|---|---|---|
| | / | / | / | | / | / | | ○ | | / | / | | | | | / | / | | | | | | | | | | |

0113

Yes, Kathleen?

Q Marlin, I'm still not clear what changed, what has changed since yesterday to make him decide to do this?

MR. FITZWATER: There is nothing -- there is nothing specifically that's changed in the field, it simply is a natural sequence of our deliberations and the feeling by the President that we needed to have another meeting tomorrow morning in concert with the UN deliberations.

Doug?

Q Marlin, we've seen a series of stand-offs between the administration and Iraq since the end of the war. But would you say now that the United States is closer to using force than it has been at any time since the war ended?

MR. FITZWATER: I would say that this is probably the most serious situation that we've faced in terms of edging up on that deadline. We have had a series of efforts to seek enforcement. We have had to make certain threats in the past, but in the past Iraq has continued progress towards complying with the UN resolutions. However, the pattern of defiance here and the widespread nature of their violation of the resolutions suggests this may be a more difficult situation, and we are prepared to act accordingly to enforce the resolutions.

Frank?

Q Yeah, Marlin, can you tell us if there have already been any ship movements or any changes in defense posture in the region?

MR. FITZWATER: I don't have to report that haven't been already outlined by the Pentagon in recent days.

Q Who specifically will be at the meeting tomorrow morning? Which advisors?

MR. FITZWATER: It'll be essentially the same group that meets with the President regularly. I can't say specifically because I don't know that they're all available, but, as you know, that's the Secretary of Defense, Chairman of the Joint Chiefs, Secretary of State or his designate if Secretary Baker is not back, the National Security Advisor, the Deputy National Security Advisor, Chief of Staff. Those are the principal --

Q And the Vice President?

MR. FITZWATER: And the Vice President, if he's here as well.

Charles?

Q Marlin, you talked of a deadline. Exactly what kind of a deadline are you considering? What timeframe are we operating on?

MR. FITZWATER: Well, we wouldn't comment on any specifics,

4404-4-2

0114

Q     Does the NSC put any credence in the theory is goading us, goading the allies for his own political purposes? I mean, for his own internal political purposes?

MR. FITZWATER: Well, I think it's pretty hard for us to judge what Saddam Hussein's motives are. When you have a man who has invaded another country and engaged in the slaughter that he did -- suffice to say he is not complying, and what his motives are are not really relevant.

Craig?

Q     You used the phrase "edging up on a deadline." Is that the deadline that has been set or one that will be set or -- I mean, deadlines in the past have been spelled out.

MR. FITZWATER: Well, the issue under consideration is enforcement action. And so, there's no timetable at this point, but, obviously, as you consider the matter, there has to be some point at which final judgments are made.

41 04-4-3

0115

STATE DEPARTMENT REGULAR BRIEFING BRIEFER: JOE SNYDER
S-5-1 page# 1 FRIDAY, JULY 24, 1992

Q Do you have any update on the situation concerning Iraq?

MR. SNYDER: Yes, George, I do. As you know, of course, Marlin was just on and spoke to that question as well, but let me give you what I've got. Particularly on this question of consultations and so forth, there's been a great deal of press speculation. Let me put the issue into context.

Iraq is steadily expanding its confrontation with the UN. It has refused to comply with Security Council obligations, including UN Security Council Resolution 687 and 707, by denying the UN Special Commission team access to the Agricultural Ministry building. But it should be emphasized that Baghdad's defiance is not limited to its obstruction of the UN Special Commission.

The Baghdad regime continues to try to starve the Iraqi people in the north and to attack those in the south in flagrant violation of UN Security Council Resolution 688. A new military offensive against its own people is now underway in the south.

The Baghdad regime is steadily increasing its harassment of UN officials, humanitarian agencies, and nongovernmental organizations in Iraq.

It has formally withdrawn from the deliberations of the boundary commission and has sent a letter on July 13 to the Secretary-General calling into question its willingness to honor its commitment to the UN to respect the Iraq-Kuwait border.

And it has formally refused to implement Security Council Resolution 706 and 712, which allows an exemption of the embargo on the sale of Iraqi oil to facilitate the purchase of food and humanitarian supplies, finance UN operations, and require the equitable distribution of food and medicine throughout the country under UN supervision.

All of these actions constitute a clear, systematic policy of defying the range of UN Security Council resolutions imposed upon Iraq since its invasion of Kuwait. These challenges to the UN and international community cannot be allowed to stand. The United States and other members of the Council have warned Iraq that it risks serious consequences if it does not live up to its obligations under relevant UN resolutions.

Q Joe, you say that this defiance cannot be allowed to stand. Is there any time limit to the patience of this government?

MR. SNYDER: I'm just not going to get into that. We are -- we've spoken, I think, fairly clearly both here and at the White House, at the Defense Department. I'm just not going to get into any time limit.

YP04-4-4

0116

관리번호 92-730

원 본

# 외 무 부

종 별 :

번 호 : UNW-2026 일 시 : 92 0724 2130

수 신 : 장 관(연일,중동일,기정)

발 신 : 주 유엔 대사

제 목 : 이라크 제재

연:UNW-2002

1. 연호 유엔의 이라크 농무성 사찰과 관련, 금 7.24 안보리 비공개회의에서 안보리 의장(JESUS 카프 베르데 대사)은 주이라크 대사가 이라크 정부의 입장을 명 7.25 유엔에 회보해 주겠다고 통보하여 왔음을 보고하여 금일 회의에서는 동건에 관한 협의가 없었음

2. 금일 EKEUS 유엔 이라크 무기 폐기 위원회 위원장은 기자회견에서 작 7.23 AL-ANBARI 이라크 대사를 접촉, 농무성 사찰의 MODALITY 를 협의하였으며 이에 대한 이라크측은 회신을 대기중에 있다고 언급함

3. 안보리는 명일 이라크측의 회보를 받으면 7.27(월) 동건에 관해 협의를 계속할 예정임

(대사 유종하-국장)

예고:92.12.31 까지

19 . . . 에 문에 의거 일반문서로 재분류됨

국기국 장관 차관 2차보 중아국 분석관 청와대 안기부

PAGE 1

92.07.25 11:07

외신 2과 통제관 FK

0117

원 본

# 외 무 부

종 별 :

번 호 : UNW-2029 일 시 : 92 0726 1800

수 신 : 장 관(연일,중동일,미일,정보,기정)

발 신 : 주 유엔 대사

제 목 : 유엔.이라크 사찰 문제 합의

1.유엔 사찰단의 이라크 농무성 건물 사찰허용문제에 대하여 유엔.이라크간 합의가 이루어졌다고 EKEUS 유엔 특별위원회 의장이 금 7.26 오후기자회견에서 밝혔음(별 첨 PRESS RELEASE 참조)

2.동의장은 양측이 사찰 형식에 대하여 만족스럽게 합의하였으며 동사찰은 UNSCOM 사찰팀의 SOP 에 따라 수행될것이 고동사찰의 중요성에 비추어 동의장이 직접 7.28바그다드를 방문하게 될것이라고 말하였음

3.한편 BUSH 미 대통령은 이번에 이라크가국제사회의 압력에 굴복, 농무부 건물에 대한사찰을 허용하였으나 앞으로 이라크의 진정한 협력여부가 중요한 문제라고 말하고, 후세인 대통령의종래 태도를 비난하면서 이라크측의 여타 유엔 결의내용 준수를촉구하였음

(대사 유종하-차관)

첨부:UNW(F)-0630

국기국 미주국 중아국 외정실 안기부 차관

PAGE 1

92.07.27 07:24 FX

외신 1과 통제관

0118

UNW(5)-1630 20726 1800 UNW-2029의 첨부

(26 July 1992) PRESS RELEASE

On 24, 25 and 26 July 1992, the Executive Chairman of the Special Commission, Mr. R. Ekeus, had the series of meetings with the Permanent Representative of Iraq to the United Nations, Ambassador Abd al-Amir Al-Anbari.

The modalities of the inspection of the building of the Ministry of Agriculture were discussed and arrived at to the satisfaction of both sides. Because of the importance of the current inspection and future inspection operations under the Security Council mandate given to the Special Commission, the Executive Chairman of the Special Commission will go to Baghdad on 28 July 1992.

* * *

The Special Commission will conduct a full inspection of the building of the Ministry of Agriculture as previously designated for inspection by the Commission. This inspection under the terms of the Security Council resolution 687 (1991) will be carried out in accordance with the standard operational procedures for UNSCOM inspection teams. The inspectors to conduct this inspection have been appointed by the Executive Chairman of the Special Commission. These inspectors possess necessary expertise in all relevant area covered by section C of Security Council resolution 687 (1991). The Chief Inspector is Mr. Achim Biermann. The inspection team will arrive at Baghdad on 28 July 1992.

630-1-1

0119

| 관리번호 | 92-740 |
|---|---|

# 외 무 부

종 별 :

번 호 : UNW-2039 일 시 : 92 0727 2030

수 신 : 장 관(연일,중동일,기정)

발 신 : 주 유엔 대사

제 목 : 이라크 농무성 사찰

연:UNW-2029

1. 연호 7.26 유엔-이라크간 농무성 사찰 합의와 관련, 금 7.27 안보리 비공개 협의회에서 안보리의장이 설명한 유엔특별위(UNSCOM), EKEUS 위원장의 보고내용은 아래와 같음(동 위원장은 7.28 농무성 사찰을 위하여 7.26 뉴욕을 출발함)

2. 보고내용

-EKEUS 위원장은 7.24-26 간 AL-ANBARI 주 유엔 이라크 대사와 일련의 회합을 갖고 농무성 사찰의 MODALITY 를 협의, 양측에 만족할만한 합의를 하였음

-7.28 부터 동 농무성을 철저히 사찰할 예정이며 동사찰은 안보리 결의 687호에 의거 수행될것임

-금번 사찰은 안보리 결의 678 에 의해 금지된 무기, 시설, 품목및 활동의 유무를 확인하는 임무를 포함하며 이를 확인하는 자료가 발견될 경우 UNSCOM 이 지정하는 장소로 옮겨놓도록 사찰반에 훈령하였음. 지정장소에서 자료에 대한 철저한 검토와 조사가 진행될것임

-EKEUS 위원장은 이라크 당국에 UNSCOM 요원의 신변보호 문제를 제기하고 이에관한 이라크의 책임을 상기시켰음

3. 금번 이라크 농무성의 사찰허용 합의와 관련, 미, 영, 불등 다국적군 참가 국가 특히 미국이 새로 구성된 농무성 사찰반(독일 2, 스위스, 스웨덴, 핀랜드, 러시아 각 1 인 계 6 인)에 포함되지 않은것을 이라크측은 성공적인 타협으로 주장하고 있는데 대하여 안보리 이사국들은 대부분 UNSCOM 에 의한 사찰 관철을 높이 평가하고 사찰반의 구성은 전적으로 UNSCOM 이 결정할 사항으로 인식하고 오히려 사찰을 관철시키기 위한 EKEUS 위원장의 재량으로 평가하고 있는 분위기임. 또한 현실적으로도 이미 이라크측이 농무성내의 자료를 파기 또는 이동시켰을 가능성이

국기국 장관 차관 1차보 중아국 분석관 청와대 안기부

PAGE 1 92.07.28 10:47

외신 2과 통제관 BX

0120

높다는 점을 감안할때 유엔에 의한 사찰 자체가 의미가 있으며 사찰반의 구성 자체에 대하여는 큰 관심의 대상이 아니라는 것이 일반적 분석임

(대사 유종하-국장)

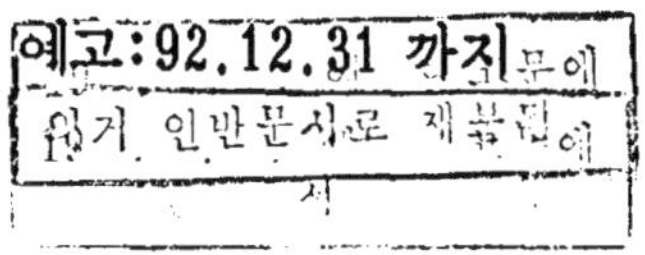
예고:92.12.31 까지 무에
일반문서로 재분류 예

| 관리번호 | 92-744 |
|---|---|

# 외 무 부

종 별 :

번 호 : USW-3765 일 시 : 92 0729 1850

수 신 : 장 관 (미일, 중동일, 연일)

발 신 : 주 미 대사

제 목 : 이락 제재 동향

연 : USW-3704

유엔 사찰팀의 이락 농무부 청사 조사 문제로 긴장이 고조되었던 이락사태는 7.26. 이락측과 유엔간 협상타결에 따라 7.28-29 양일간 동 청사에 대한 사찰이 이루어짐으로써 일단 진정 국면에 들어선 것으로 보이는 바, 현 상황에 대한 미 행정부 반응과 동향 및 언론의 분석을 아래 요약 보고함.

1. 미 행정부 반응 및 동향

가. FITZWATER 백악관 대변인은 7.28. 정례브리핑에서 급박한 위기는 일단 해소되었음을 인정하나 이로써 긴장이 완전히 해소된 것은 아니며, 미국은 향후 사탈팀의 조사활동과 이락의 유엔결의 준수 여부를 계속 예의 주시할 것이라고 말하고 사태진전 여하에 따라 군사조치를 포함, 여하한 대응방안도 배제하지 않고 있다는 기존입장은 분명히 함.

나. 부쉬 대통령은 지난주와 금주초에 있었던 안보보좌관들과의 연쇄회동에 이어 7.28. 오전에는 공화, 민주 양당의 의회지도자들을 백악관에 초치, 이락사태에 대한 대응방안을 논의하고 유엔결의 이행과 유엔 평화유지군의 능력강화를 위한 확고한 결의를 표명함. 이와관련, FITZWATER 대변인은 동 모임에 참석한 의회인사 대부분이 유엔결의 이행을 위해 향후 행정부가 취할 조치에 대해 적극적인 지지입장 (HIGH DEGREE OF GENERAL SUPPORT)을 표명하였다고 밝힘.

다. 미국의 일방적인 조치 검토 여부에 대해, FITZWATER 대변인은 상기 모임에 참석한 일부 의회인사들로 부터 미국이 일방조치를 취할 경우에도 이를 지지할 것이라는 입장 표명이 있었으나 미국은 여하한 조치를 취하든간에 여타 우방국들과의 공동행동 (COALITION)을 추구할 것이라고 답변, 독자 행동 가능성을 부인함.

라. 금번 농무부 청사 사찰팀 구성에서 미국을 포함한 걸프전 참전국 사찰관이

미주국 장관 차관 1차보 2차보 중아국 국기국 외연원 외정실
분석관 청와대 총리실 안기부

PAGE 1 92.07.30 08:49

* 원본수령부서 승인없이 복사 금지 외신 2과 통제관 FS

0122

배제된 것과 관련, 미 행정부내 이에 대한 불만과 이견이 있었다는 보도에 대해 동 대변인은 이를 부인하고, 금번 사탈팀은 향후 사탈팀 구성시 선례가 되는것이 아니며 (NO PRECEDENT-SETTING), 앞으로 계속될 사찰팀 구성에서 미국인이 베제되지 않을 것임을 분명히함.

(금번 사찰팀 구성이 선례를 만든 것이라는 이락측 주장을 정치선전에 불과하다고 일축)

마. 한편, 베이커 장관은 금 7.29. 오전 이락내 쿠르드족 및 시아파, 수니파등 회교 반군지도자들을 면담한 바, 베이커 장관이 전례없이 직접 반군 지도자들을 접촉한 것은 금번 사태와 관련, 이락에 대한 압력을 가중시키기 위한 전략의 일환으로 분석되고 있음.

2. 미 의회 및 언론의 반응

가. 금번 사태에 대한 부쉬 행정부의 대응과 향후 대처 방향에 대해 민주당 지도부인사중 FOLEY 하원의장과 MITCHELL 상원 원내총무등은 협력적인 태도를 보이고 있는 것으로 알려지고 있으나 ASPIN 하원 군사위원장과 GORE 부통령 후보등은 부쉬 행정부의 미온적 대응으로 후세인의 입지만 강화시켜준 결과를 초래하였다고 공개적인 비판 입장을 취하고 있음.

나. 당지 언론에서도 부쉬 행정부가 공개적으로는 금번 사태가 후세인의 굴복 (CAVE-IN)으로 수습되었다고 주장하고 있으나 실질적으로는 후세인이 사찰팀 구성에서 일종의 거부권을 행사하였을뿐 아니라 사찰이 지체된 동안 이락측이 관련 비밀문서들은 여타 장소로 은닉할 수 있는 시간적 여유를 부여함으로써 오히려 잃은 것이 많으며, 따라서 후세인 정권이 부쉬 행정부를 상대로 한 심리전에서 소기의 성과를 거둔 결과가 되었다는 비판적 시각을 보이고 있음. (단, NYT 지 7.28. 자 사설은 사태 수습결과에 호의적 논조)

3. 당관 관찰

가. 현시점에서 부쉬 행정부가 대이락 군사조치를 취하는데에는 국내선거라는 기본적 제약 요인이외에도 이를 정당화할 만한 여건에 대한 판단이나 시기선택의 문제에 있어 우방국들간에도 콘센서스가 이루어져 있지 않은 것으로 알려지고 있어 당분간은 이락에 대한 압력의 강도를 유지하면서 사태의 추이를 지켜보는 소극적 대응에 머무를 수밖에 없을 것으로 봄.

나. 그러나, 국내문제로 인한 지지도 하락으로 고심하고 있는 부쉬 행정부로서는

국내외적인 여건만 허락한다면 대 이락 군사조치를 통해 국내정치적인 전기를 마련코자 시도할 것이며, 따라서 현재 그 적절한 시기를 기다리고 있다는 분석도 있는 바, 경우에 따라서는 국내선거 정국이 오히려 대 이락 강경책을 촉진하는 요인으로 작용할 가능성도 배제할 수는 없음. (최근 미측이 유엔에 대해 사찰팀의 조사활동 강화를 촉구한 것도 여사한 구실을 찾기 위한 전략의 일환이라는 분석도 있음)

다. 미국이 대 이락 군사조치 여부를 결정함에 있어서는 상기와 같은 국내외적인 여건과 동 조치로 인한 이해득실 여부가 중요한 고려 요소가 될 것이나, 결국은 향후 이락의 태도 여하가 무엇보다 중요한 변수가 될 것인 바, 이락이 계속 강경태도를 굽히지않고 이에 대한 국내외 여론이 유리한 국면으로 전개될 경우 미국이 군사조치를 선택할 가능성은 있다고 봄. 다만, 이 경우에도 미국의 독자행동은 어려울 것으로 보며, 여타 우방국의 충분한 지지를 확보한 연후에나 가능할 것으로 보임.끝.

(대사 현홍주-국장)

예고:1992.12.31. 일반 ...에 의거 일반문서로 ...

PAGE 3

0124

# 외 무 부

종 별 :

번 호 : SZW-0421　　　　일 시 : 92 0730 1700

수 신 : 장관(연이,구이,정보)

발 신 : 주 스위스 대사

제 목 : 유엔 특위 이라크 조사반 (자료응신 28호)

1. 주재국 외무성은 유엔 특위 이라크 조사반에 동국인 생물무기 전문가 1 명을 7.26 자로 파견하였다고 발표함.

2. 외무성은 이와관련, 상기인이외에 스위스의 화학무기 전문가 1 명이 이라크 화학무기 제거목적을 위해 UN 대표단에 참가 활동하고 있으며, 1991.8 월이래 스위스 국방성 산하 연구소 'SPIEZ LABORATORY AC' 소속 전문가들이 10 여건에 이르는 유엔 대이라크 조사활동에 참가하여 왔다고 밝힘. 끝

(대사 강대완-국장)

국기국　차관　1차보　구주국　외정실　분석관　청와대　안기부

PAGE 1

92.07.31　04:30

외신 2과　통제관 EC

0125

UNSCOM file

| 관리번호 | 92-751 |
|---|---|

원 본

# 외 무 부

종 별 :

번 호 : UNW-2067　　　　일 시 : 92 0730 1930

수 신 : 장 관(연일,중동일,기정)

발 신 : 주 유엔 대사

제 목 : 안보리 비공개회의(이라크 무기사찰)

연:UNW-2039

1. 금 7.30 안보리 비공개회의에서 이락무기 폐기사찰 유엔 특별위원회(UNSCOM) EKEUS 위원장은 7.28-29 간 실시된 이라크 농무성 사찰 결과, 안보리 결의687 에 저촉되는 아무런 자료를 발견하지 못하였으며 농무성에 보관되었을 것으로 믿었던 무기관련 자료들을 이라크측이 사찰직전 옮긴흔적을 조사하였는바 농무성 내부의 가구재배치등의 흔적이 있어 동조사결과를 검토한후 자료가 옮겨졌는지 여부를 결정할수 있을것이라고 보고함

2. 또한 동위원장은 이라크 AZIZ 부수상과 헬리콥터를 이용한 항공사찰등 금후 사찰 방식에 관하여 협의를 하였으며 동부수상은 금후 유엔 사찰에 대한 협조를 약속하였다고 보고함

(대사 유종하-국장)

예고:92.12.31 까지

| 국기국 | 장관 | 차관 | 1차보 | 중아국 | 분석관 | 청와대 | 안기부 |
|---|---|---|---|---|---|---|---|

PAGE 1　　　　92.07.31 09:05

외신 2과 통제관 CE

0126

대 한 민 국

주 오스트리아 대사관

오스트리아 20300-768 　　　　　　　　　　　　1992 . 8 . 5 .

수 신 : 장관 　　　　　　　　　　　　　　　(보존기간 : 　　)

참 조 : 국제기구국장, 중동아국장

제 목 : 대이락 유엔 조사단에 대한 이락 외무부 대변인 성명

당지 이락대표부는 유엔 안보리 결의 687에 의한 유엔조사단 활동과 관련한 92.7.30.자 이락 외무부 대변인 성명을 송부하여 왔는 바, 동 성명을 별첨 송부합니다.

첨부 : 상기 성명 및 관련 자료 　　끝.

주 오스트리아 대사

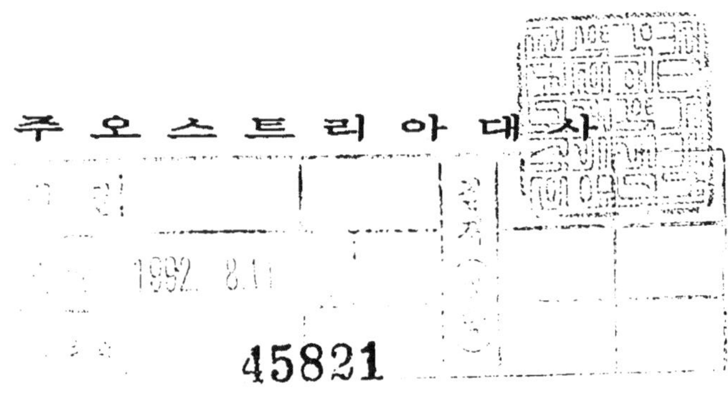

45821 　　　　　　0127

PERMANENT MI ON
OF THE REPUBLIC OF IRAQ
TO THE INTERNATIONAL
ORGANIZATIONS

JOHANNESGASSE 26
A-1010 VIENNA

Statement by the Spokesman of the Foreign Ministry
of the Republic of Iraq issued on 30th July 1992

---

When Mr. Ekeus went back to New York, a new phase begun in attempting to find an appropriate solution, and in order to avoid the embarrassment that might have resulted from solving the inspection problem, in one way or another, and allowing the team to visit the Ministry of Agriculture building, which would have confirmed that it did not contain any material related to RES 687, thus enhancing the credibility of the Iraqi position. To find that appropriate cover up, Mr. Mark Silver, an American national, who headed the team after the departure of Major Karen Jensen, was asked to fabricate a story and declare that the inspection team was exposed to a dangerous situation as a pretext to withdraw the team from the Ministry of Agriculture's site without consulting the Iraqi authorities about that presumed danger. The withdrawal occured despite the fact that the popular protests against the American conspiracy continued for several days before, and the fact that not one team member complained about any threats or dangers. The team was in fact safe and the public was behaving rationally and the Iraqi authorities took all the necessary measures to ensure the safety of the inspection team. The team's safety issue was only raised when a solution was being sought in New York and Baghdad, a solution which could have uncovered the embarassing situation the special commission found itself in by relying on false information provided by the American intelligence.

Twelve hours after the withdrawal of the team from the Ministry's site on 22/7, Mr. Mark Silver, the team head, contacted the Iraqi side and requested to go back to the site. The team head was told that it was up to him to go back because it was him who took the decision to withdraw in the first place. At that point, the team head again raised the safety issue and was told that the Iraqi authorities were completely responsible at all times for the team's safety as long as it remained in Iraq. Still, the team head was not convinced and did not return to the site but left for Bahrain instead on the 14th of July when contacts between New York and Baghdad were producing some results.

It was clear that the withdrawal of the team from the Ministry's site and its departure to Bahrain were aimed at creating an atmosphere of mystery and suspicion as a pretext to claim that certain material or documents were removed from the building when the commission's experts enter the building and do not find what they were looking for.

When the group of experts visited the Ministry of Agriculture and Irrigation building on 28 and 29 July and did not find any of the items that some claimed were hidden in that building, Mr. Rolf Ekeus, head of the Special Commission and the group of experts stressed that the building did not contain any material related to resolution 687. However, the team head added "that there are some points that remained to be studied by the team members". Again, statements were made in Bahrain and in New York to create suspicions and give the impression that certain material were removed from the building before the expert team entered it. In response to these allegations, a spokesman of the Ministry for Foreign Affairs issued the following statement:

0128

Claims that items were removed from the building were an ill-organized attempt to cover up the difficult situation in which the Commission found itself in, when it listened to false reports from the American Intelligence Community that material related to resolution 687 were hidden in the building. Accordingly, Major Karen Jensen, an American national and Mr. Mark Silver, also an American national, were entrusted with implementing that American plan.

Concrete facts however, point out that the whole thing was an American ploy from beginning to end. Thus, the team headed by Mr. Karen Jensen arrived at the building's entrance on the 5th of July and stayed there until the 22nd of July. When Mr. Ekeus arrived in Baghdad, he met the deputy prime minister on the 19th of July who requested from him to select a group of experts from neutral countries such as India and China to enter the building and proceed with its inspection to confirm the Iraqi position that no material was hidden in that building as he was made to believe. Prior to that, the Iraqi authorities invited journalists and news agencies and TV personnel into the building on 25/7/1992. In addition, heads of diplomatic missions residing in Baghdad were also invited to visit the building on 2/7/1992. All this was happening in front of the team which was still monitoring the building round the clock from outside. These Iraqi initiatives represent concrete evidence as to the truthfulness of the Iraqi position that no material or documents related to resoltuion 687 were kept at any time in that building.

The spokesman added that the building was under surveillance by the special commission's inspectors and that the commission's officials confirmed that, at the time.

The spokesman also said that this was not the first time special commission experts made surprise or planned visits and did not find anything. In the last seventeen months, for example, inspection teams made about 200 inspection visits, half of them were made by surprise and some even used surveillance aircraft, but the teams found nothing on the visited sites.

The spokesman further added that the whole thing was a ploy initiated by the American intelligence community to achieve certain political goals and help president Bush in his election campaign.

In response to statements made by Mr. Ekeus that Iraq has promised to cooperate, the spokesman said that the discussions in Baghdad focused on the work methods, and the composition of the inspection teams. He said that Mr. Ekeus, during his meetings with Iraqi officials, promised that he will take into consideration aspects related to sovereignty, dignity and internal security which were repeatedly stressed by Iraq. The Iraqi side was satisfied with these assurances. The discussions also dealt with the fact that Iraq met its obligations in accordance with resolution 687 and the Iraqi side requested from the Head of the special commission to confirm that fact at the Security Council especially that he himself has previously declared in New York that Iraq did indeed honour most of these obligations.

Vienna 1/8/1992

# Part I

**Iraq's Deputy Prime Minister Tareq Aziz appeared on television on Monday to cast light on the Iraq-UN agreement that ended a three-week crisis ignited by a demand of the UN inspection team 39 to inspect the Ministry of Agriculture and Irrigation. Following is the first part of the text of the TV interview with Mr Aziz:**

Question: Iraq is reported to have reached an agreement with Rolf Ekeus (Head of the UN Special Committee) on the inspection of the Ministry of Agriculture and Irrigation by a number of experts. What is this agreement and how was it concluded?

Aziz: As it is known, on July 5, an inspection team headed by an American Karen Jansen, tried to enter the building of the Ministry of Agriculture and Irrigation to inspect it allegedly for material and documents related to issues covered by Resolution 687. We immediately informed this team that we reject to give it access to the Ministry's premises because it is a civilian government building and as a ministry headquarters, it represents a symbol of national sovereignty. We do not allow this building and other similar ones to be treated like industrial sites or other facilities which inspection teams wanted to inspect because of the difference in nature between this building and other facilities which are likely to be covered by Resolution 687. As known to all, we have accepted this resolution despite being unjust for reasons known which were explained in the letter by the Foreign Minister in April 1991. In accordance with our acceptance of the Resolution, we have dealt with it and inspection teams in a practical way. These teams visited, before this incident, scores or perhaps more of the sites covered by the provisions of Resolution 687 including establishments, industrial facilities, warehouses and some military sites. However, no problem had arisen. In this regard, some problems of a difficult nature did happen and I explained to them at the time.

But this time, the demand by American Major Karen Jansen is strange. It is aimed at violating Iraq's dignity and sovereignty. That's why we prevented her from the beginning and maintained our position. This state of affairs continued until mid-July. We were informed that Ekeus wanted to come to Baghdad and he really did. On July 18, he met twice with Minister of State for Foreign Affairs Mohammed Sa'eed al-Sahhaf and a number of Iraqi experts. Aspects of this issue were discussed and also the nature of relationship between Iraq and Special Committee and also the conduct of inspection teams and the behaviour of some of these teams especially when headed by an American. You remember the famous stories of American spy David Kay for the reason we have mentioned, that he is a CIA officer. This team is headed by an officer in the US army, Major Karen Jansen. We raised this point with Mr. Ekeus during the meeting with the State Minister.

On the next day, he (Ekeus) met the Foreign Minister Ahmed Hussein and came to meet me. I told him, "Listen very well, I'll sum up to you our position. We don't hide in this building material or documents related to Resolution 687. It is not logical for an Iraqi official who is concerned with this issue to hide such things in the build-

(1)

0130

ing of a ministry which has hundreds of civil servants and which is frequented daily by hundreds or perhaps thousands of people. This plan or perception by the Special Committee or the inspection, let me say, is silly. This is the reality. Therefore, we don't have any objection to having people entering this building to ascertain this fact but the problem lies with the objective. What is it that prompted Karen Jansen to demand access to this building? We assume the objective is to affront Iraq and this we cannot accept."

He said the Special Committee is authorised to enter and inspect any facility or building in Iraq. He also reminded me of the provisions of the resolutions which give sweeping powers saying they did not apply these powers always but these are the powers, he said.

I told him that I am fully aware of this and I know the texts of UN resolutions. "But you remember, and you were present during my meeting with the Security Council last March. I said yes, we are ready to cooperate with the Special Committee to facilitate its missions as defined by Resolution 687. I said we are ready to cooperate with the Special Committee. This happened but on the basis of respect to the principles of the country's sovereignty and not jeopardizing its internal security and not intervening in its internal affairs."

"Therefore, there is nothing new about our position. The position which we have adopted vis-a-vis this issue is already announced and reported to the Security Council. However, if there are doubts that we are hiding in this building material or things which have to do with your specialisation, I may make a proposal that we chose experts from Non-aligned and neutral states and I gave him examples like India, China or others which are members of the Security Council. They can enter the building to see for themselves what it houses then come out and talk to the press about what they have seen in the building. I told him I was sure that if they entered the building, and searched its papers, and rooms, they would not find anything because it would be illogical as I said before, for this building to be used for purposes which head of the team has alleged. He (Ekeus) did not accept the proposal saying it was a hard one and that if those experts have come, and we have chosen them, they would be people untrained for inspection work. They might be experts in their own fields but they are ignorant of the procedure and nature of the work done by inspection teams."

I told him it was not an essential issue for us. "At any rate I ask you to adopt this proposal and I would tell our ambassador in New York to inform members of the Security Council of it." He said, and this is an important point, these are my observations about the proposal but he would not act against the proposal. But he failed to keep this pledge because when he returned to New York he announced that Iraq's proposal was unacceptable. Here there is contradiction and descrepancies between what Ekeus had told me and the State Minister for Foreign Affairs here in Baghdad and what he announced later.

There are descrepancies and sometimes contradiction, different tone between what he said to Dr Al-Anbari (Iraq's permanent UN ambassador) and what he declared at press conferences. Here appears the American influence. America always steps in and pressurise Ekeus and seeks the support of the British and sometimes the French to pressurise Ekeus to adopt tougher attitude. The Iraqi proposal was presented to the Security Council with the Americans and Westerners taking a very negative attitude towards it. Regrettably, other delegations did not speak and they made so much fuss about the alleged threats to the inspection team before members of the Security Council without allowing Dr.al-Anbari to explain facts as they are at the Council's meeting.

In this artificial, fervent hostile atmosphere created by the Americans and their agents, the Iraqi proposal was rejected.

(To be continued)

0131

# Part II

**Iraq's Deputy Prime Minister Tareq Aziz appeared on television on Monday to cast light on the Iraq-UN agreement that ended a three-week crisis ignited by a demand of the UN inspection team 39 to inspect the Ministry of Agriculture and Irrigation. Following is the second part of the text of the TV interview with Mr Aziz**

Later, Ekeus met Dr al-Anbari and proposed some solutions to the problem. We learned at the time from sources in New York that the three westerners met Ekeus and warned or censured him because he was dealing with Iraq in a relatively lenient way. He met al-Anbari on July 22 and aired ideas and proposals to defuse the crisis. We, on Thursday, July 23, sent our reply to Ekeus's ideas in the form of an integrated proposal which contained the following:

1. A group of experts should be selected from states that did not take part in the aggression on Iraq. This is to be done jointly by Iraq and the Special Committee.

2. These experts should not be from among those who have already carried out inspection work in Iraq. In this regard, we stressed our previous proposal or desire that experts from India or China take part. If these experts were not specialised or unfamiliar with the tactics of the Special Committee, Iraq would have no objection to them being technically briefed by the Committee.

3. The Special Committee should inform the team of experts in a precise and written form about what it looks for in the Ministry's building and that they should not come to inspect everything and ask about everything. He (Ekeus) should instruct them that they have information the building contains this and that, some well defined things. When the team enters, and let's suppose, finds in the building documents or other suspicious things which it believes related to what it was instructed to look for and which it cannot give a verdict on it through local observation, these documents or things should be carried away after they are sealed to a place to be agreed upon outside the building where they are checked by the team. We do not have any objection to having other inspectors to be chosen joining the checking provided that these would remain outside the building, work in the outer site and do not enter it.

The other point is that the group is not to be allowed into the Minister's office or the offices of the undersecretaries. They should not be allowed to take any data related to the dossiers of civil servants and data about the stockpiles of grain, foodstuffs, the cultivated area in Iraq or any other information having to do with agricultural or irrigation plans in Iraq because this is related to Iraq's national security and because Iraq is under embargo.

This proposal was sent on July 23 and al-Anbari reported it to Ekeus who in turn made some positive remarks about the Iraqi proposal. However, he wanted one amendment. He said experts who have not taken part in inspection missions are not known and we have to choose a convenient number and if they are not good we have to train them and this is a procedure that may take a long time.

He said, "I'm coming under great pressure over this problem." In the meantime, as you know, he withdrew the

0132

( )

know time difference between Baghdad and New York is eight hours and it is nightime. It means when Al-Anbari meets Ekeus at 5 p.m., we have to add eight hours and it will be night when the reply gets through the next day. We got a reply from Ekeus on Friday. The reply contained a piece of information that China and India are not immediately ready or ready at all in principle to take part in this operation. We wanted to make sure of this. Upon receiving the reply, brothers in the Foreign Ministry summoned in the morning the Chinese and Indian ambassadors to officially sound out. They were asked whether that was the position of their respective governments. They were told Iraq would like them to be involved in this process.

team from the Ministry and they created the story of threats made to the team. They also created a frenzied climate to push us around. We said OK. This is a practical aspect which can be considered. Whether they (inspectors) have already participated or not, the main important condition is that these experts should not be from the states that took part in the aggression on Iraq and must be from neutral states, states whose attitude can be deemed neutral or relatively objective. All things are relative in the world and it is not always true that all people are neutral or objective. However, they should be from states whose representatives are expected to behave in an acceptable manner. Moreover, we were concerned with names also, not only with states because we have full information about those who have participated in inspection work. We know the behaviour of some of them. Some behaved as professionals and technicians while others as spies, behaving in a provocative manner like David Kay and Karen Jansen.

We also informed Ekeus that China does not want to be involved in inspection work while India is normally cooperating with the Special Committee in this respect.

Ekeus send us a reply. You

We were following this issue at night and on Friday afternoon. Ekeus's proposal got relatively closer to our basic proposal on July 23. This situation has remained unchanged. Suddenly, Ekeus announced he had a press conference. He appeared on American TV saying time is running short...the situation is serious and critical and the Special Committee is invested with powers...the inspection team was subject to physical threats...and all that...there was an obvious escalation...it was different from the talk that took place between him and Dr Al-Anbari the day before.

Interviewer: On the measures taken, i.e. the process of wresting an accord was disrupted by the press conference.

Aziz: No, it did not disrupt it. But it was obvious that it was a stage-managed move to escalate the situation. We were watching American TV. After Ekeus had finished his press conference, Fitzwater,

0133

( )

the White House spokesman appeared and started talking in a rude language of threats. His talk was full falsifications. He announced that Bush had changed his mind. Instead of heading for his private retreat, he went to Washington and then to Camp David and he would meet his advisors...etc. What matters most is that they created a certain climate to justify a rush to handle the issue. Even the objective debate we were conducting with Ekeus failed to run its full course and did not get through to the Security Council.

Interviewer: James Baker was in the midst of his tour and he was also yelling.

Aziz: Baker is the echo of what Bush and his aides had said in America. In this atmosphere, they tried to create a situation where they can pressurise the Special Committee and the Security Council. Its members according to reports by diplomats in New York were excluded from contacts.

We were the only party to report to them as much as time would allow our ambassador there who is busy following up the issue and to inform this or that ambassador of the situation and likely developments. Regardless of the escalation that took place and the ridiculous threats made and in line of our proposal which was a balanced and logical one to handle the issue and in line with our proposal we said OK. If the quest for new experts would take a long time and in order to deny George Bush the opportunity to this time for his election campaign and stage managing which he is carrying out let it be so. What matters most is that experts are from states that have not taken part in the aggression on Iraq. We would consider the list of experts. If China they are welcome, we can add them to the list. If they tell us they don't want, we can exclude them. But there are Russians in Baghdad two of those working with Ekeus and we propose that they join the experts who would enter the Ministry's building.

This was reported and the Chinese came later and said China regretted it could not take part and they had a special attitude vis-a-vis this issue. He said we originally do not participate in work like this. Indians did not reply.

Over this period of deliberations and name checking of the list Ekeus had sent to us. We made some observations about some of them. He started taking an illogical tough attitude, for instance, he insisted that this expert is unique. How could he be unique? We know him, our colleagues who work in this field know these people very well. They know their standards. It was obvious that there were political demands being imposed on Ekeus. These negotiations continued until Saturday.

On Saturday we reported to them and the situation became very dense because Ekeus was artificially and illogically getting tougher.

After that there were no contacts... The talks between us who were in Baghdad following up New York and them.

0134

# Part III

**Iraq's Deputy Prime Minister Tareq Aziz appeared on television on Monday to cast light on the Iraq-UN agreement that ended a three-week crisis ignited by a demand of the UN inspection team 39 to inspect the Ministry of Agriculture and Irrigation. Following is the third part of the text of the TV interview with Mr Aziz:**

A proposal was made that Ekeus come. The purpose of the visit by Ekeus as our ambassador in New York told me was to guarantee a responsible conduct by the team that enters the building in his presence and not to have any conduct of the type we have complained about which is not governed by the agreement.

Those who would enter the building are a German, a Swede, a Swiss, another German, a Finn, and a Russian. Those six were the people who would enter the building. Their entrance would be carried out in the way I have explained.

Interviewer: American circles following the announcement of the agreement between Iraq and the Special Committee said they had achieved their announced basic objective to inspect the building. Meanwhile, Ekeus announced it would be a normal inspection operation. How does your excellency evaluate these stage managed American statements and the commitment of the Special Committee.

Aziz: As I said the team's head was an American and the provocative attitude she and a number of American members of the team pursued is an American attitude. Therefore now and after we have concluded this accord, they want to give the impression that the objective they sought from entering the building had been achieved. This is not true. This is American fuss and uproar. To say that the operation is a normal inspection work is also inaccurate. The inspection work of facilities included in Resolution 687 was of a different nature.

First, we would not block the access of a team seeking to enter a factory. Normally we say OK. They ask so many questions and try to acquaint themselves accurately with the contents. They look into files and information related to their field of specialisation. This was going on and we did not intervene in the makeup of those who entered (the facilities) or their nationalities. This is a different operation as I have explained. This is an operation according to an agreement between us and head of the Special Committee on every step. It was therefore not a normal inspection process as claimed. The American objective of provoking Iraq or affronting it was not realised.

Interviewer: Would the inspection work be carried out in a different manner?

Aziz: Yes, like I said. This procedure is entirely different from start to end. This is a special case handled in a special way. It was unprecedented in inspection operations. As I said Iraq took part in picking up the experts or made some remarks about them. In the past we did not make conditions about certain states or certain nationalities. It is unprecedented that head of the Special Committee himself comes to Baghdad to oversee or make sure and we too secure through him the pledges he made. All these are new formulas that correspond to the nature of the issue itself.

Interviewer: Let's talk frankly about the crisis which tarted on July 5 when Iraq decided to block the inspection team's access to an Iraqi Ministry building which represents national sovereignty. Does your excellency view the administration of this crisis has underlined Iraq's positions, or the ensuing results have led to some retreat in this regard?

Aziz: I'm pleased that you ask this open question because this issue must be made clear. Resolution 687 was imposed on Iraq. As known, our position towards this resolution is already known but for considerations known to our people, this resolution was accepted and Iraq has dealt with it. Following two years of an unjust embargo on Iraq and following an unprecedented aggression, after Bush has dropped more than 100,000 tonnes of bombs and explosives on the people of Iraq, what does Iraq's rejection of Karen Jansen's demand on July 5 mean? And what doesn't mean that Iraq insists on the rejection and forces the Special Committee to conclude a balanced agreement to handle this issue. Over 22 days of the crisis, there were military threats, threats to hit Iraq again, threats to tighten the embargo and an intensive prop-

0135

aganda campaign. Half of this or even a quarter of it could have intimidated a major power. But people are [illegible] pened. What has happened is that neither the people of Iraq nor the government of Iraq was shaken before these threats. The Iraqi people have demonstrated their genuine position when they took to the streets to give their verdict. This is an extremely important factor, very important to the issue... The people reject the American plan and objectives and support the decision of the leadership. They have voiced their anger at and denunciation of the American scheme to affront Iraq.

Interviewer: And their readiness to defend the homeland and sovereignty..

Aziz: Absolute readiness. There was anger in the eyes of Iraqi women, men and children who saw Mark Silver, the second head of the team and Karen Jansen and others. They saw the wrath of Iraqis in the people's eyes, those who were manifesting their attitude before the inspection team. They claimed people had come to physically threaten them. This is not right. Iraqis behaved in a civilised manner. True, their expression of anger was one of determination but their [illegible] was quite civilised. Also security authorities took all the precautions lest an evil-intentioned one might carry out something artificial. All measures were taken to protect these inspectors.

I can affirm that Iraq has through this confrontation achieved some positive objectives. I can safely say much of this can be attributed to the people of Iraq who were an element of support for the leadership in confronting this issue with firmness and resolution. When dealing with the practical side of thing, it does not mean retreat because it is the leadership's duty to weigh all things and act in a way that makes the enemy's goal un- [illegible] affair was created, it was designed to affront Iraq, jeopardise its sovereignty. When the people of Iraq rejects, when the leadership rejects and when the UN and the Special Committee are forced to negotiate with us on the handling of this crisis in a different way, this is a positive progress. When we measure this by the scale of aggression against Iraq and the nature of the embargo imposed on Iraq, political topics are relative. Like I said a little while before this pressure, if exercised on a major power it would have forced it to accept so many things. As you see we have the international arena before us where we can see what happens. The American side did not want us to conclude an agreement with the Special Committee. The American scenario... which was on TV had an upturn trend. They have [illegible] objectives which they themselves have declared. We were not afraid of the confrontation with America because this confrontation has already occurred. Iraq is no more in need to prove its bravery. It has become well known and Iraq's bravery has [illegible] this world.

This is beside the topic. The main issue is thwarting the enemy's scheme. What did he want out of this operation? When you discover his real objectives how would you behave to drop these objectives and handle the issue in the balanced manner as the one concluded with head of the Special Committee.

Interviewer: Your Excellency Deputy Prime Minister, despite the conclusion of an accord between Iraq and the Special Committee on the problem we still hear mass media carrying insolent threats by Bush and his aides who claim that Iraq has at last [illegible] threat. What do you think? How do you appraise the American position throughout this crisis?

Aziz: Before coming to this meeting with you I watched US President George Bush on American TV making a statement yesterday, given the difference of time as I said. I watched George Bush this morning and he looked

unhappy and dissatisfied with the agreement judging by the press statement he made. This indicates that he was seeking a different development of the issue not the one concluded yesterday. That is why he is still threatening. This American threat is no longer only insolent because insolence has become a feature characteristic but this threat has also become one characterised more often than not with silliness. The American game has become so public and so ridiculous

and muddled up. Now and according to the latest statistics, Bush has secured only 22 per cent according to opinion polls. He is trying with these artificial acts of muscle flexing to boost public support of him and to give the impression that he fits for a second term as the general commander who can move fleets and troops. So this language which the Americans used before the conclusion of the accord is political and media language.

(To be continued)

(7)

0136

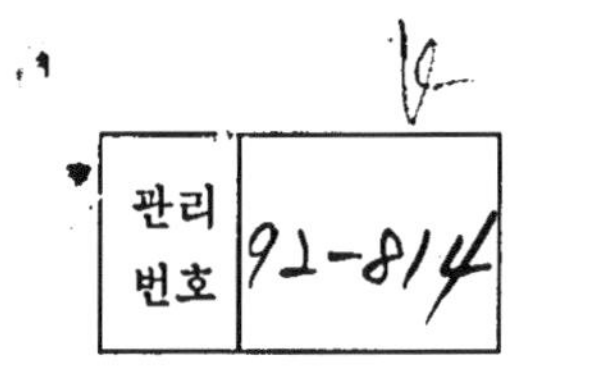


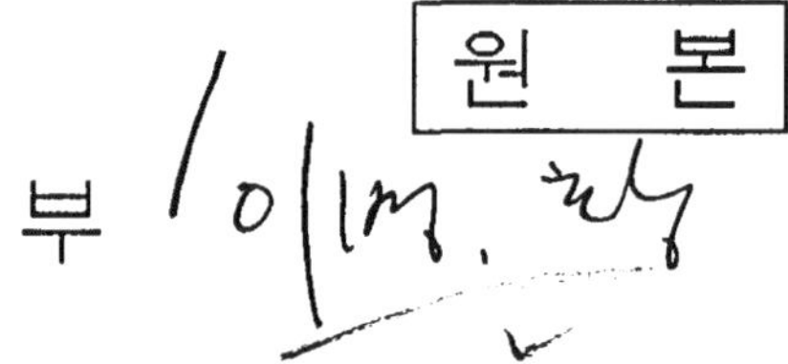


# 외 무 부

종 별 :

번 호 : UNW-2241 일 시 : 92 0818 1900

수 신 : 장 관 (연일,중동일,미일,기정)

발 신 : 주 유엔 대사

제 목 : 대 이라크 사찰

1. 유엔 특별위원회 (UNSCOM)의 대 이라크 무기사찰과 관련, 금 8.18 자 NYT는 유엔사찰반의 8.17 이라크 국방성 사찰계획이 마지막 순간에 취소되었다고 보도하였는바, TIM TREVAN UNSCOM 대변인이 작 8.17 기자회견에서 언급한 내용을아래 보고함.

0 (이라크 정부부처 사찰계획 유무에 대하여) 사찰반의 활동에 관한 정보는 공개할 수 없음. 유엔사찰반은 이라크내 어느 장소든지 UNSCOM 에 위임된 사항과 관련된 정보가 있을 수 있다고 믿을만한 이유가 있으면 언제든지 사찰 할수있음

0 (이락 정부부처를 사찰하는데 이라크측으로부터 아무문제가 없다는 보장을받았느냐는 질문에 대하여) 이라크측이 그와같이 시사한바 없음. 사찰 장소를 선택하는것은 이라크 정부가 아님. UNSCOM 의 권한은 유엔 안보리가 부여한 것이므로 이러한 권한을 변경할 수 있는것은 이라크나 UNSCOM 이 아니라 안보리임.

0 (농무성사찰 불허사건의 재발방지를 이라크로부터 확약받았느냐는 질문에 대하여) 이라크 정부와의 논의된 내용을 구체적으로 밝힐 수 없으나 정부부처건물 사찰과 관련하여 두개의 선례가 있음. 즉 지난 2 월 산업 및 광업성 방문과 7 월 농업성 방문임. 유엔의 사찰권리는 부인될 수 없음

0 (금번 사찰반의 이라크 정부부처 사찰여부에 대하여) 금번 사찰반은 정부 부처를 방문한바 없음. 동사찰반이 사찰을 계획하였던 모든 장소에 대하여 성공적인 사찰을 수행하였음. 어느장소도 동사찰반의 사찰이 거부된 바 없음. UNSCOM 은 이라크의 무기계획에 대해 보다 잘 파악하게 되어 사찰 빈도가 줄어들 것임.

0 (사찰반 활동 공개와 관련) 지난번 농무성 사찰때에는 대치상태로 긴장이 고조되어 사찰반의 활동이 공개되었으나 통상 UNSCOM 은 사찰반의 파견일등 활동에 관한 정보는 공개하지 않음이 원칙임. 금번사찰반은 한장소에서 미사일계획에 관한 정보를

국기국 장관 차관 1차보 미주국 중아국 분석관 청와대 안기부

PAGE 1 92.08.19 08:59

외신 2과 통제관 FS

0137

발견한후 동건과 관련하여 이라크 당국과 대화를 가진바 있음.

0 (미국 정부로부터 산업성 사찰을 요청받았느냐는 질문에 대하여) 사찰장소와 관련한 정보와 제의는 개인, 기관, 정부등 다양한 소스로부터 제공되고 있음. 미국정부가 유엔사찰반의 활동에 주요 지원자임은 비밀이 아님. 그러나 정보를 분석하고 사찰 여부와 장소, 일자를 결정하는 것은 UNSCOM 의 책임임.

0 (금번 사찰반의 사찰 계획변경 여부에 대하여) 사찰반은 사찰 목표 (TARGETS)가 있으나 그 일정은 융통성이 있음. 예정대로 사찰이 실시되지 못할 수도있으나 이는 이라크 사정때문일 수도있고 사찰반의 형편상 실시되지 못할 수도있음. 금번 사찰반은 계획했던 모든 장소를 성공적으로 사찰했음.

2. 지난 주말이후 대이라크 사찰을 위요한 미국언론의 보도에도 불구하고 안보리 및 UNSCOM 은 이에 관한 특이동향 없음. UNSCOM 의 EKEUS 위원장은 현재 휴가중임

(대사 유종하 - 국장)

예고: 92.12.31 일반 고문에 의거 일반문서로 재분류

첨부: UNW(F)-0675

PAGE 2

0138

UNW(G)-0615 20818 1900

# U.N. Calls Off Inspection Of Iraqi Military Ministry

## Confrontation Postponed, but Reason Is Unclear

By ERIC SCHMITT
Special to The New York Times

WASHINGTON, Aug. 17 — Acting at the last minute, United Nations inspectors in Baghdad canceled a visit today to a military ministry considered off-limits by Iraq, apparently abandoning for now a United States plan to demand access to sensitive sites.

American officials had said over the weekend that Washington and its allies might renew bombing raids on Baghdad if inspections were blocked.

The United Nations team, which made one inspection today but did not disclose where, plans to leave Iraq Tuesday. The next round of inspections has not yet been scheduled, leaving uncertain when the United Nations might test Iraq's threat to bar access to military ministries.

### Reasons Unclear

It was not immediately clear why the planned inspection of an Iraqi military ministry this morning was postponed. Some Bush Administration officials said the inspectors abandoned the plans out of concern they would appear to be pawns in Washington's effort to confront Saddam Hussein.

Other Administration officials said the White House itself had second thoughts after a report Sunday in The New York Times that described a plan to force inspections. The Times also reported that some officials had said the timing appeared calculated to give President Bush a boost during the Republican National Convention.

Mr. Bush and others have angrily denied any political motivations.

### The 'No Fly' Zone

As the possibility of a confrontation over the inspections seemed to recede, Washington continued discussions with Britain, France, Saudi Arabia and Kuwait on creating new safeguards to protect Shiite Muslims in southern Iraq from Iraqi air attacks.

Under the plan, the United States and its allies would declare a "no fly" zone, roughly below the 32d parallel in Iraq, from which Iraqi aircraft would be barred. The proposal came as intelligence reports indicated that President Hussein's Government is preparing to renew an air and ground offensive against the Shiites, Administration officials said today. [Page A6.]

Regarding the inspection today in Baghdad, which was supposed to include the Ministry of Military Industrialization, it was not clear whether any last-minute misgivings originated with the inspectors in Baghdad, at higher levels of the United Nations or among the members of the Security Council.

"After the publicity, they decided it wouldn't be good to continue on," a Defense Department official said. "The publicity killed the idea of any confrontation."

### 'We Retain the Right . . .'

Defense Secretary Dick Cheney today sharply criticized the New York Times article on forcing inspections. "I think it's a new low in political reporting," he said in an interview on "The MacNeil-Lehrer Newshour" on PBS. "I'm outraged by it."

Tim Trevan, a spokesman for the United Nations special commission in charge of destroying Iraq's major weapons, said at a news conference at the United Nations headquarters in New York that the 22-member team did not visit a ministry "because this time round we didn't have the need to."

"Of course, we retain the right to designate any location in Iraq," Mr. Trevan said. "And when we have the need to, we shall visit any location."

Administration officials said again today that Washington was not calling the shots for the inspectors, although

Continued on Page A6, Column 1

675-2-1

0139

# U.N. Team Cancels Inspection Of a Military Ministry in Iraq

Continued From Page A1

many sites visited were selected based on tips from United States intelligence sources.

"What they elect to inspect and when they do these inspections is strictly for their decision," said Richard A. Boucher, a State Department spokesman.

**Trying to Protect Shiites**

The plan to protect the Shiites in southern Iraq could lead to allied air patrols over the area with authority to shoot down Iraqi aircraft. Iraqi helicopters and, in at least one instance, fixed-wing aircraft have attacked the Shiite areas, Administration officials said.

In an interview today with the Cable News Network, President Bush referred to the Iraqi flights, saying of President Hussein: "He has been using air power to go after the Shiites in the south and regrettably the Kurds in the north, both regrettable. And so if there is some edict that keeps him from flying, clearly that would deny him one way of harassing his own people."

**The question is, Who's in charge? The answer is still in doubt.**

At the State Department, Mr. Boucher elaborated, saying, "The situation is that over the past several days there's been a significant amount of fixed-wing aircraft and helicopter activity in the south.

"The Iraqi army's pressure against the people in the marshes continues," he continued. "There have been skirmishes that continue to occur. So the military pressure on the population in the south has continued."

**If Shiites Get Stronger**

In London today, British military officials told reporters that after a special meeting of military and foreign policy advisors that Prime Minister Minister John Major is to convene on Tuesday, British air forces would be put on alert, ready to participate in any patrols over southern Iraq.

The proposal to support and protect the Shiites was adopted only after some sharp disagreement among allied military planners. Some Administration officials, for example, have voiced concern since the gulf war that a resurgent fundamentalist Shiite force in southern Iraq, backed by Iran, could destabilize the region.

Countering this argument, Western officials said that creating a security zone in the south, as the coalition did in the Kurdish area in northern Iraq after the gulf war, would hurt Mr. Hussein politically without significantly strenghthening the military hand of the Shiites.

With the focus of attention shifting to the protection of the Shiites, the end of a 10-day inspection by the United Nations weapons experts became a bit of an anticlimax.

**Lesser Facility Visited**

The team's leader, Nikita Smidovich of Russia, declined to identify the site visited today or to describe the mission's findings. But he said Iraq had not interfered. Senior Defense Department officials said the building inspected today was a "military facility, but not one of any great consequence."

Mr. Trevan, the United Nations spokesman, said that during the 10 days of inspections, the team "found significant additional information concerning the ballistic missiles programs."

"We have learned things that will be very useful and very helpful now in future inspections," Mr. Smidovich said in Baghdad.

The main drama, however, had been reserved for the visits to places identified by officials earlier as Baghdad's most closely guarded ministry buildings. A Defense Department official said today that the principal aim of those visits was to re-establish "who's in charge."

**A Question of Precedent**

After the three-week standoff at the Agriculture Ministry last month, which ended when the United Nations agreed not to include experts from countries that had attacked Iraq in the gulf war, diplomats and Administration officials said the United Nations teams had to reaffirm their right to go anywhere they wanted in Iraq and to select team members without Baghdad's veto.

"Re-establishing that precedent was the main goal," the Defense Department official said. "Whatever they found inside the buildings was secondary."

Indeed, the genesis for several Administration decisions in recent weeks was the standoff at the Agriculture Ministry, Administration officials said.

Days after the Administration was widely criticized for allowing Baghdad a say in the makeup of the inspection teams, Washington began pursuing three options.

One included having the United Nations speed up inspections to show that Iraq had to submit to the will of the international organization. Administration officials also said they would press Iraq to end attacks against the Shiites. Finally, Washington began taking steps to elevate the status of opposition groups inside and outside of Iraq.

The possibility of a confrontation over U.N. inspections in Baghdad seems to have receded.

## British Consider Bombing

Special to The New York Times

LONDON, Aug. 17 — The British Government said today that it was discussing with the United States and other allies whether to resort to force, including bombing missions, to protect the Shiites in southern Iraq.

In what appeared to be a sharp change in the tone of public statements, the Foreign Office characterized the situation in southern Iraq as "shocking" and "intolerable," and said it might be necessary once again to force Iraq to comply with the cease-fire imposed by the United Nations at the end of the Persian Gulf war.

British officials referred specifically to Iraq's use of aircraft against the Shiites. The Foreign Office spokesman said President Hussein's Government appeared to have embarked on a military campaign in recent weeks "to systematically wipe out" civilian opposition in southern Iraq.

**'Have Not Ruled Out' Planes**

A senior British official, describing options to enforce the cease-fire, said Britain and its allies "have not ruled out the use of British aircraft."

The Foreign Office said the Iraqi assault on the Shiites was the most recent instance of what it described as a pattern of systematic defiance of the cease-fire, which was imposed after Baghdad's forces were defeated in March 1991.

That includes the obstruction of aid shipments to Iraqi civilians, the refusal to take part in talks about the disputed border with Kuwait and the refusal to allow inspections of buildings in which Iraq is believed to be maintaining records or research on weapons of mass destruction.

615-2-2

0140

| 관리번호 | 92-1249 |
|---|---|

원 본

# 외 무 부

종 별 :

번 호 : UNW-2347 일 시 : 92 0827 2000

수 신 : 장 관 (연일,중동일,기정,국방부)

발 신 : 주 유엔 대사

제 목 : 대 이라크 무기사찰

연 : UNW - 1649

1. 유엔의 대 이라크 무기사찰과 관련, 금 8.27 당관 이수혁 참사관은 8.7-18간 이라크에서 사찰을 실시한 UNSCOM(유엔특별위) 미사일 사찰반 반장 SMIDOVICH (러시아인)을 접촉, 파악한 동 사찰반의 활동내용을 아래보고 함.

가. 사찰반 구성

0 오지리, 불란서, 독일, 러시아, 여어국 및 미국등 6 개국 전문가 22 인

나. 사찰 주임무

0 미사일 유도(GUIDANCE)및 제어(CONTROL) 시스템 생산능력 조사

다. 사찰 방법

0 8 개장소를 방문, 서류 및 컴퓨터 조사

0 현장에 설치된 시설 및 기계등의 생산 국가 및 내용 파악

라. 확인사항

0 이라크가 미사일의 유도 및 통제 시스템을 생산할수 있는 능력을 가지고있다는 증거는 발견되지 않음.

0 안보리 결의에 의해 생산 및 보유 금지된 무기나 주요 부품도 발견 되지않음.

0 8 개 사찰대상중에는 미사일 연구, 개발을 위하여 지난 4 월 바그다드 북쪽에 새로이 건설한 시설물도 사찰을 하였는바, 이라크측은 동 시설물은 안보리 결의의 금지 대상이 아닌 사정거리 150KM 미만의 미사일, 로켓트등의 개발 연구소라고 하나 동 시설물이 장차 사정거리 150KM 이상의 미사일 생산을 하지 않도록 사찰, 확인해야 할 과제가 제기됨.

0 금번 사찰을 통하여 컴퓨터에 의한 미사일 조작과 미사일 연료생산 계획에 관한 정보를 처음으로 입수하였으며, 여타 미사일 및 부품 획득과 생산에 관한 사업

| 국기국 | 장관 | 차관 | 1차보 | 중아국 | 분석관 | 청와대 | 안기부 | 국방부 |
|---|---|---|---|---|---|---|---|---|

PAGE 1

92.08.28 09:55
외신 2과 통제관 FS

0141

계획서도 입수하였음.

0 미사일 개발 계획과 관련된 이라크내의 각종기관을 파악하는데 도움이 되는 정보도 입수됨.

0 특히 이라크의 미사일 개발계획에 관련(참여, 부품수출 또는 시설물 설치등)된 외국 업자들에 관한 정보도 다량 입수됨.

마. 성 과

0 금번 사찰반이 마지막 순간에 사찰 계획을 포기하였다는 일부 보도가 있었으나, 이는 사실이 아니며, 당초 계획했던 8 개 대상장소를 철저히 사찰하였음.

0 금번 사찰을 통하여 이라크의 미사일 개발계획의 전모를 파악하는데 필요한 정보를 많이 입수하였으며, 금후 유엔의 사찰, 확인작업 계획 수립에 큰 도움이 되었음.

0 금번 사찰은 농무성 사찰거부 사건 직후의 사찰이었던 관계로 매우 긴장된 가운데 사찰이 진행되었으나, 이라크측의 의도적인 방해는 없었음.

2. 동인 접촉시 이 참사관은 이라크 남부 비행금지 조치와 관련, 이라크에서 금명 작업을 개시할 아국인 2 명을 포함한 화학무기 사찰반의 신변안전을 문의하였는 바 UNSCOM 으로서는 향후 수일이 매우 중요한 시기로 보아 동 사찰반에게 신변 안전에 각별주의하고 필요시 이라크측에게 신변보호 강화를 요청토록 조치하였다하고 현 상황에 큰 변화가 없는한 9 월중에도 2-3 개 사찰반이 파견될 것이라함

3. SMIDOVICH 는 UNSCOM 이 주요국가에 요청한 연호 정보제공 요청과 관련하여 바그다드에서 북서쪽 155KM 지점에 있는 SALAHADIN 단지(ESTABLISHMENT)에 현대건설이 현지 기술자들의 주택을 건설하였는바, 동 주택이외에 혹시 지하 시설물을 건설한 실적이 있으면 관계정보를 제공하여 주기를 희망하였음. (동 SALAHADIN 단지는 전자, 전기제품 생산 공단으로서 SAAD 13 으로 지칭된다 하며 불란서 회사가 공장을 건설하였다 함.) 이에 대하여 이 참사관은 구체적인 정보가 없어 현지에 진출하였던 기업들에게 자료제공을 요청하기가 어려운 사정일 것이므로 UNSCOM 이 파악하고 있는 아국기업 관계자료가 있으면 제공 하여 줄 것을 요청하였는 바, 동인은 한국건설 기업들의 시설물 공사, 특히 지하시설물 내용 파악이 UNSCOM 의 관심사항이라 하고 현재로서는 구체적 자료가 없으나 파악되는자료가 있으면 제공하겠다 함.

(대사 유종하 - 국장)

예고 : 92.12.31 일반

PAGE 2

0142

이라크 화학폐기반 file
1 황

# 외 무 부

종 별 :

번 호 : JOW-0625 일 시 : 92 0907 1315

수 신 : 장관(중동일,국연,기정)

발 신 : 주요르단대사

제 목 : 이락 핵사찰

이락내 핵사찰과 관련, 9.7.자 요르단 타임지는 바그다드발 외신인용 아래와 같이보도함.

1.이락 남부지방의 비행금지 구역설정 이후 1주일간 이락내 핵사찰을 마친 MAURIZIO ZIFFERERO 단장이 9.6. 밤 바그다드를 출발하면서 기자단에게 밝힌바로는 이락이아 직도 핵무기 개발을 지원하는 해외 공급자를 밝히지 않고 있다함.유엔안보리 결의의 충분한 이행을 위해서는 동정보가 필요하나 이락은 이를 밝히기를 거절하였다함.금번 조사에서 이락내 핵 처리에 관한 아무런사실도 밝혀낼수가 없었다함. 핵처리에관한정보를 캐내는것이 금번 사찰중에 가장애로였으며 앞으로도 동 정보를 수집하도록 계속노력할 것이라함.

2.ZIFFERERO 단장은 또 금번 사찰시 이락의 관계당국이 잘협조해 주었고 이락이사찰에임하는 분위기는 매우 긍정적이어서 사찰을하는측이나 받는측 모두에게 건설적이였다함.

3.한편 BRITON RON MANLEY 를 단장으로 한 3명으로구성된 화학무기 폐기반도 바그다드 북서쪽 130KM지점인 MUTHANA 지역에서 독가스 군수공장실험단지 조사를 마치고돌아왔다함.끝.

(대사 이한춘-국장)

중아국 국기국 외정실 분석관 안기부 차관 1차보

PAGE 1 92.09.07 20:44 CJ

외신 1과 통제관

0143

원 본

# 외 무 부

종 별 :

번 호 : AVW-1341 일 시 : 92 0908 0900

수 신 : 장 관(국기,과기처)

발 신 : 주오스트리아대사

제 목 : 이라크 핵사찰 문제

1. IAEA 사무국은 ZIFFERERO IAEA 이락 핵사찰단장이 현재 이라크의 핵무기 개발 계획관련 모든 시설이 모두 파괴되었다고 언급한것으로 보도한 9.3자 HERALD TRIBUNE보^도에 대하여 9.3.자로 별첨(FAX)PRESS RELEASE 를 통해 걸프전쟁시 폭격및 그간수차의 IAEA 핵사찰단의 활동으로 지금까지 드러난 이락의 핵무기 개발 계획과 관련한 시설은 모두 파괴되었으나 그렇다고 새로운사실의 발견 가능성을 배제하는것은 아니라고 해명하였음

2. 당지 이라크 대표부는 상기 9.3.자 HERALD TRIBUNE보도를 COVERING NOTE 없이당지 주재외교공관에 FAX 로 송부한바 있음.

첨부:상기 FAX 1 매( AVWF-0206). 끝

(대사 이시영-국장)

국기국 1차보 외정실

PAGE 1

92.09.08 19:56 CM

외신 1과 통제관

0144

# EMBASSY OF THE REPUBLIC OF KOREA

Praterstrasse 31. Vienna
Austria 1020 (FAX : 2163438)

| No : AVW(F)-0206 | Date : 20908 0900 |
|---|---|
| To : 장 관( 국기, 과기처 ) (FAX No : ) | |
| Subject : 첨부 | |

표지포함 2 매

Total Number of Page :

0145

INTERNATIONAL ATOMIC ENERGY AGENCY
WAGRAMERSTRASSE 5, P.O. BOX 100, A-1400 VIENNA, AUSTRIA,
TELEPHONE: 1 2360, TELEX: 1-12645, CABLE: INATOM VIENNA,
TELEFAX: 431 234564

3 September 1992
PR 92/31
FOR IMMEDIATE RELEASE

PRESS RELEASE FOR USE OF INFORMATION MEDIA • NOT AN OFFICIAL RECORD

## STATUS OF IRAQ NUCLEAR PROGRAMME: CLARIFICATION OF IAEA POSITION

Recent news agency messages quoting the leader of the current IAEA inspection team in Iraq, Mr. Maurizio Zifferero, as saying that Iraq's nuclear programme is "at zero" have given a misleading impression of his understanding of the situation. He has not intended to issue a "clean bill of health" for Iraq in the nuclear sphere. He has asked that the following clarification be issued by the IAEA:

IAEA inspectors have repeatedly visited Iraq's known nuclear-related sites. Buildings or specialized equipment which were not destroyed during the war and which the inspectors considered to be directly relevant to sensitive nuclear, or especially military nuclear activity have been destroyed on their instruction. However, this does not exclude the possibility of further discoveries in the future. The mapping of the Iraqi clandestine nuclear programme, which has involved fieldwork by fourteen IAEA teams over many months, has been based on a compilation of intelligence information from various sources, including satellites and defectors, supplied to the IAEA via the UN Special Commission on Iraq in New York. While no new knowledge has come to hand recently, it is still too early to conclude that such will not be the case. In addition, the Security Council has mandated the IAEA in the nuclear sphere to conduct long-term surveillance in Iraq, and this will be done.

0146

화학무기폐기반 file

## UN化學武器 査察團, 이락 訪問

1. 제13차 UN 化學武器 査察團(「베르나르트 브룬너」團長 포함 6명)이 9.21 부터 8일간 日程으로 이락을 訪問중임.

2. UN의 이락 化學武器 査察은

가. 91.5이후 걸프戰 終戰 UN 決議(91.4)에 의거, 이락의 大量破壞武器를 廢棄하기 위해 化學·生物·核·미사일등 4개 分野로 나누어 實施되어 오고 있는 査察의 일환으로서

나. 그간 12차에 걸쳐 무타나團地(바그다드 北西쪽 80km)등 化學武器 관련 시설에 대한 査察活動을 전개해 오고 있는 바

○ 제1차 査察團이 91.6 무타나團地에서 이락이 UN에 公表한 양보다 4배 많은 4萬 6,000여개의 化學彈 및 化學物質을 보유하고 있고 이락 內에서 化學武器의 破壞가 가능함을 확인하였고

○ 2차(91.8), 3차(91.8), 4차(91.9), 5차(91.10), 6차(91.10), 7차 (92.1)에 걸쳐 하바니아 空軍基地, 무하마디야트 兵器貯藏所 및 무타 나團地 등에서 化學彈頭(6,420개) 및 겨자가스 爆彈 8,200발 등을 發見하였으며

○ 8차 査察(2.21 - 3.24)시 神經가스化學彈 500개를 破壞하고 殘餘化學武器를 93년 중반까지 무타나團地에서 廢棄하기로 이락측과 합의 하고

29-25

0147

○ 9차(4.5 - 14), 10차(4.15 - 29)査察을 통해 무타나의 化學武器 廢棄專擔 工場建立을 감독하고 이락이 自體 破壞했다고 主張한 場所 및 埋沒地域을 訪問하였으며

다. 특히 11차 査察(6.26 - 7.29)에서는

○ 化學彈 製造 工作機械類 및 압착기등 化學武器 製造裝備의 破壞 作業을 監視(7.4) 한 반면

○ 이락이 農務部내에 大量破壞武器 關聯書類를 隱匿해 놓고 있다는 情報에 따라 7.5부터 同 廳舍를 査察할 計劃이었으나 이락측이 主權侵害라는 理由를 들어 妨害함으로써 査察計劃이 中斷된데 대해

○ 美國을 中心으로 한 UN安保理가 對이락 軍事攻擊 斷行意志를 보임으로써 이락이 査察團에서 美國人 除外條件으로 査察을 許容(7.26)함에 따라 農務部 査察을 實施(7.28 - 29)하였으나 새로운 資料確保에 失敗한 한편

라. 최근 12차 査察(9.4 - 12)을 통해

○ 이락이 建設한 무타나團地내 2개 化學武器 廢棄工場을 試驗 稼動하고

○ 「론 맨리」團長은 記者會見(9.11)을 통해 빠르면 9月末부터 神經·겨자가스의 廢棄가 본격 着手될 豫定이며 이락 全體 保有推定 140톤의 神經가스와 400톤의 겨자가스를 모두 除去하는데 6個月내지 1年이 소요될 것이라고 發表한 바 있음.

※ 現在 이락內에는 化學武器 査察團과는 別途로 化學武器 廢棄를 專擔한 作業團(13個國 39명)이 同 廢棄工場에서의 作業開始를 위해 8.31 이래 바그다드 滯留중

29-26

0148

3. 이번 13차 化學武器 査察團은

가. 무타나 團地내 化學武器 廢棄 專擔工場의 本格 稼動을 推進하면서 化學武器의 무타나團地 移動與否 確認과 함께 여타 化學武器 貯藏所에 대한 索出作業을 實施하기 위한 것으로서

나. 최근 UN의 査察活動과 關聯하여 美國등 西方측의 對이라 飛行禁止區域 設定(8.26)에 이락측이 反撥하면서 UN의 査察活動을 妨害, UN權威에 挑戰하다가 美國과 UN의 軍事制裁 강행 순간에 양보하는 등 査察活動을 遲延 또는 隱蔽하려는 戰略을 고수하고 있어

다. 앞으로 UN의 査察 및 廢棄活動 過程에서 美·이락間 摩擦이 再燃될 可能性은 尙存해 있는 것으로 평가됨.

29-27

0149

주 오스트리아 대사관 겸
주 비인 국제기구 대표부

Praterstrasse 31,
A-1020 Vienna, Austria 전화 (0222) 2163441 FAX NO. (0222) 2163438

문서번호 : 오스트리아 20300-
시행일자 : 92. 10 . 8 . 1007
수 신 : 장관
참 조 : 국제기구국장, 과기처장관 (원자력실장)
제 목 : 대이락 IAEA사찰보고

| 선결 | | | 지시 | |
|---|---|---|---|---|
| 접수 | 일자 시간 | . . : | 결재 | |
| | 번호 | 57197 | | |
| 처리과 | | | 공람 | |
| 담당자 | | | | |

제14차 대이락 IAEA 사찰보고서등 이락 사찰 관련 자료를 별첨과 같이 송부합니다.

첨부: 1. GOV/INF/667

2. IAEA INSPECTIONS AND IRAQ'S NUCLEAR CAPABILITIES. 끝.

주 오스트리아 대사관 겸
주비인 국제기구대표부 대사

0150

International Atomic Energy Agency

# BOARD OF GOVERNORS

For official use only

GOV/INF/667
30 September 1992

RESTRICTED Distr.
Original: ENGLISH

# REPORT ON THE FOURTEENTH IAEA ON-SITE INSPECTION IN IRAQ UNDER SECURITY COUNCIL RESOLUTION 687 (1991)

31 August - 7 September 1992

INTERNATIONAL ATOMIC ENERGY AGENCY

92-03839

0151

REPORT ON THE FOURTEENTH IAEA ON-SITE INSPECTION IN IRAQ
UNDER SECURITY COUNCIL RESOLUTION 687 (1991)

31 August - 7 September 1992

**SALIENT POINTS**

- The completion of the destruction by the Iraqi side of selected buildings at the two EMIS (Electro Magnetic Isotope Separation) sites at Tarmiya and Ash Sharqat was verified by the inspection team. The two sites will in future be inspected under the long-term monitoring plan.

- In the context of the long-term monitoring plan, a project has started aiming at the periodical control of radionuclides and other selected, stable nuclides of the main water bodies in Iraq. An adequate number of sites has been established covering the whole territory of Iraq, where water and sediment samples will be periodically collected. Very sensitive analytical techniques will enable information on any sizable nuclear activity carried out in the area to be obtained. The first collection of water and sediment samples, which started in the course of IAEA-14 and will be completed during IAEA-15, will provide the baseline against which future sampling results will be compared.

- The identification and tagging of a number of high-temperature laboratory furnaces and other non-released equipment kept at the Ash Shaykilii warehouse was completed. These items had been removed from Tuwaitha prior to the beginning of inspections under UNSC resolution 687 (1991), and at the request of the Agency had been collected and stored at the Ash Shaykilii warehouse.

0152

- Several sites already inspected in previous IAEA missions have been revisited for monitoring purposes. These visits have included Al Atheer, Hatteen, Al Qa Qaa, Rashdiya, Bilat Ash Shuhada, Al Mansour and the Al Hamath "date palm tree factory". One of the two buildings at Al Hamath has been selected by the IAEC for eventual storage of the irradiated fuel elements now placed in location B in temporary makeshift containers.

- All follow-up activities from previous inspections assigned to the team as e.g. the transfer of maraging steel to a foundry in Basra for future destruction by melting, the monitoring of uranium containing wastes at Al Jezira and of the water level in the spent fuel containers stored in location B were executed.

- The team inspected an underground facility near Ash Sharqat. The facility proved to be an underground oil refinery now undergoing extensive repair and maintenance works.

- Several meetings were held with Iraqi authorities on the radiometric hydrologic survey as a component of the long-term monitoring plan, on the completeness of the "full, final and complete" Iraqi report and on Annex 3 of the long-term monitoring plan.

- The Iraqi authorities extended full co-operation to the Agency team in fulfilling the objectives of the mission.

**INTRODUCTION**

1. This report summarizes the activities of the fourteenth inspection mission carried out by the IAEA under United Nations Security Resolution 687 (1991), with the assistance and cooperation of the Special Commission of the United Nations. The mission took place from 31 August to 7 September 1992 and was headed by Professor Maurizio Zifferero of the IAEA as Chief Inspector. The team consisted of 15 inspectors of 10 nationalities.

The objectives of the mission were:

- to verify the completion of destruction of key technical installations at the Tarmiya and Ash Sharqat sites;
- to begin a comprehensive radiometric hydrologic survey of the surface waters of Iraq to look for possible signs of prohibited activities;
- to carry out monitoring inspections at a number of sites previously visited;
- to conduct follow-up activities such as taking confirmatory samples of nuclear materials, item counting of nuclear fuel in IRT-5000 elements, replacing water in spent fuel storage tanks; and
- collecting detailed technical data on equipment under Agency control.

0154

2. The Iraqi side indicated during this visit that they wanted to work in a co-operative and professional way. There had also been many security incidents involving UNSCOM personnel in the previous weeks following the Ministry of Agriculture episode. The Iraqi counterparts knew of these problems and pledged support and increased protection. The team did not face civil demonstrations either in Baghdad or during field trips. The Iraqi side took note of earlier problems with timing of meetings and transportation. The meetings on technical subjects started on time without repeated cancellations. Transportation was provided as scheduled and was sometimes arranged at short notice. The counterparts were flexible and helpful in this sort of planning.

## Table 1

## List of facilities and sites inspected during the fourteenth inspection mission

1. Tuwaitha

    1a. Al Hamath
    1b. Location B
    1c. Location C

2. Ash Shaykilii
3. Al Qa Qaa
4. Tarmiya
5. Ash Sharqat
6. K-2 Facility
7. Al Mansour
8. Rashdiya
9. Al Jezira
10. Bilat ash Shuhada
11. In addition, water and sediment samples were taken at 15 sites indicated in Figure 1.

0155

**DESTRUCTION OF KEY TECHNICAL INSTALLATIONS AND EQUIPMENT**

3. A list of actions to be undertaken pursuant to Security Council resolution 687 (1991) with respect to the facilities at the site of Tarmiya and Ash Sharqat had been communicated to the Iraqi authorities on 15 May 1992. Relevant activities began during the twelfth IAEA inspection mission and continued during the course of the thirteenth mission. At the end of the fourteenth mission all destruction of EMIS facilities at Ash Sharqat has been completed. Transformer and process buildings have all been destroyed in accordance with Agency instructions. The main electrical supply to the EMIS process was destroyed during the war. A water treatment plant some 9 km north of the main plant has been inspected. This plant was built to supply Ash Sharqat with water nearly ten years ago when a nuclear reactor was being planned there. Today it only supplies the water needs of the now destroyed EMIS site.

4. Destruction of the EMIS facility at the Tarmiya site was also completed. All transformer sheds for the main EMIS process building were destroyed. The destruction of all HEPAs (High Efficiency Particulate Air filters) and exhaust air filtration units was completed. The EMIS buildings have been destroyed, either by the war or by the Iraqi side under Agency supervision. The delivered power to the site has now been reduced by a factor of three. Further reductions in delivered power will depend on an evaluation of the Iraqi proposals for an alternative use of the Tarmiya site. The EMIS capability at Tarmiya can now be considered to be completely destroyed. As was the case in previous missions, the Iraqi side provided all equipment, material and manpower to efficiently implement the destruction plan under the supervision of the Agency teams.

**ACTIVITIES RELATED TO LONG-TERM MONITORING**

5. Discussions with the Iraqi side were held on the new Annex 3 of document S/22872/Rev.1/Corr.1, that lists and describes materials and equipment that are either prohibited to Iraq or that must be declared and monitored. The contents of this list have been approved by the Security Council and are non-negotiable. The Iraqi side asked clarification on some items, the definitions of which were, in their opinion, not sufficiently detailed. Clarifications were provided by the team. It was, however, agreed that another round of talks was needed to finally dispose of this issue.

6. Al Atheer was visited as part of the long-term monitoring program. Most of the large industrial processing buildings here were destroyed by the Iraqis under the supervision of the eleventh and twelfth IAEA inspection teams. The remaining buildings consist of offices, warehouses, and characterization and quality control laboratories. The site has been handed over to the joint use of the Ministry of Industry and Minerals, and the Military Industrial Corporation. The extant buildings are being used for non-nuclear industrial activities, including light machine shops, material characterization, and reverse engineering for spare parts production.

7. The Al Qa Qaa site has been visited many times by IAEA teams investigating links to the nuclear program. In preparation of the long-term monitoring plan at Al Qa Qaa, the team visited machine shops, testing areas, and high-explosives synthesis facilities. No nuclear-related activities were observed. The Iraqi capability to produce RDX was destroyed in the war. The relevant building has been rebuilt but the equipment has not been replaced because of the embargo. Only ordinary machine tools were found in the machine shops. Activities in the high explosive test area were found to be ordinary munitions tests.

8. South of Ash Sharqat is a heavily defended facility built into the side of a hill. It has thick concrete bunker buildings covered with several meters of earth. It had previously been visited by UNSCOM but there have been information linking it to nuclear activities. The fourteenth IAEA team also visited this site and confirmed that the facility is an underground petroleum facility (oil refinery) as declared with no nuclear function.

9. The Al Mansour Electronics Plant was visited by the fourth IAEA inspection team and was inspected as part of the long-term monitoring plan on this visit. The IAEA had information obtained after the fourth visit that Al Mansour produced some electronic components as part of the weaponization feasibility study. The Iraqis denied this and described some similar, but non-nuclear, electronics activities. The team toured the plant to establish a better baseline of its activities. No nuclear-related work was observed.

10. The team visited the Engineering Design Centre at Rashdiya as part of the long-term monitoring program. No centrifuge or nuclear-related activities were observed.

**ACTIVITIES RELATED TO THE RADIOMETRIC HYDROLOGIC SURVEY**

11. The purpose of this survey is to establish a radionuclide and stable isotope composition baseline in the major watershed regions of Iraq in order to detect changes resulting from aqueous effluents of nuclear related facilities. This survey will provide information in several areas: first, the data will measure the impact of present nuclear related facilities in Iraq on surface water systems receiving their aqueous effluents: second, possible unknown nuclear facilities may be detected; third, a set of data will be provided, from which changes in composition can be easily detectable for interpretation.

0158

12. The sampling network is based upon a detailed hydrologic survey compiling the water discharges in the Tigris and Euphrates basins for selected gaging stations in Iraq. Sampling points were selected along the Tigris and Euphrates rivers and their major tributaries. Also, the New River (Canal) and selected lake basins are additional sampling points. A total of 43 sampling sites were selected. During this mission fifteen sites (fig. 1) were visited and samples were taken. The remaining sites will be sampled during the next IAEA inspection.

13. Three types of samples were collected, a filtering column used to concentrate for dissolved and particulate matter from a large volume of water (~300 l), a sediment core and a 100 ml water sample. A comprehensive sample analysis of the water filters and sediment cores will include high sensitivity gamma spectrometry, radiochemical separations of the actinides (primarily U, Pu) followed by alpha spectrometry, high sensitivity multistage surface ionization mass spectrometry (SIMS), ultralow background gas proportional counting for tritium and Inductively Coupled Plasma Mass Spectrometry (ICP/MS) for stable isotopes. Physical measurements including water and air temperature, barometric pressure, water conductivity, surface water elevations, and accurate locations description were also made.

14. The samples analysis data will be coupled with the physical measurements to establish a baseline of the present hydrologic and radiometric conditions from which present and future indications of sizable nuclear activity in Iraq can be determined.

0159

**Figure 1**

**The black triangles give the approximate locations of the sampling sites.**

0160

**ACTIVITIES RELATED TO MATERIALS AND EQUIPMENT**

15. In response to requirements of Annex 3 of the long-term monitoring plant, the Iraqi side has declared 16 high temperature furnaces. Two are visible in the debris of building 73A at Tuwaitha where they are badly damaged. Two more are declared as having been at Al Jezirah and are lost or destroyed. One is in working condition at building 12 at Tuwaitha. The others were all located in the warehouse at Ash Shaykilil and they were examined and catalogued. All except one fall outside the specifications listed in Annex 3. This is the induction furnace used for experiments in uranium metal casting.

16. The level of water in the spent fuel container stored in location B had decreased as a consequence of evaporation. The team supervised Iraqi activities to restore the required water level. New seals were applied to each container. The IAEA team reviewed a proposed change in the storage containers that will allow addition of water without disturbing seals. This will aid in reducing radiation exposure significantly and permit further addition of water without Agency presence. One of the two buildings at the Al Hamath site near Tuwaitha has been selected by the IAEC for storage of the irradiated fuel elements now placed in location B in temporary makeshift containers. Experience of the past seventeen months has shown that this situation entails excessive radiological risks and if removal of this fuel is delayed beyond the coming winter, a more suitable albeit temporary solution has to be found. The building at Al Hamath could be a reasonable choice.

17. The IAEA has placed approximately 250 tonnes of HMX high explosive under seal at Al Qa Qaa. The Iraqi authorities have requested that this material be released to them for civil blasting applications. The IAEA team checked the seals of the explosive storage buildings and found them to be in order.

18. Part of the IAEA team travelled to the Al Jezira site to check the volume reduction of uranium containing wastes in the evaporation tanks. Summer heat has evaporated the waste to dryness and plans are in progress to place the solid waste in drums and remove them to location C at Tuwaitha.

19. The maraging steel ingots have been removed from Iskandariya at the request of the Agency and are now ready for melting with an equal amount of high carbon steel at a foundry in the Basra area. This operation will be performed under the supervision of the next IAEA inspection mission.

20. Despite repeated questioning, the Iraqi side remained unwilling to disclose important procurement-related information and the foreign sources of technical advice. Once again the team renewed its request for documents which were not returned to the sixth inspection mission.

## Annex 1

### List of documents received or sent

14-01 Mr. Zifferero to Mr. Al Hajjaj on 920827 regarding the release of additional items relating to the 92-truck convoy.

14-02 Mr. Zifferero to Mr. Al Hajjaj on 920831 requesting written confirmation of a previous oral statement made by the Iraqi authorities that no quantities of uranium was ever introduced in buildings 14 and/or 85 of the Al Atheer site.

14-03 Mr. Al Hajjaj to Mr. Zifferero on 920906 confirming that no quantities of uranium have ever been introduced in buildings 14 and/or 85 of the Al Atheer site.

14-04 Mr. Dorn (Specom) to Mr. Zifferero and from Mr. Zifferero to Mr. Al Hajjaj on 920831 requesting clarifications on use of integrated hydrodynamic-neutronic codes.

14-05 Mr. Al Hajjaj to Mr. Zifferero on 920906 giving answers to the queries contained in 14-04.

14-06 Mr. Zifferero to Mr. Al Hajjaj on 920902 concerning the removal from Iraq of samples of depleted uranium, pellets of 10% enriched uranium oxide and of a pin containing 2.26% enriched uranium oxide.

14-07 Mr. Al Hajjaj to Mr. Zifferero on 920905 stating that the material listed in 14-06 had been removed by the IAEA-14 team.

14-08 Mr. Al Hajjaj to Mr. Zifferero on 920906 providing an explanation on the intended use of some equipment contained in the list of the 92-truck convoy for which the Iraqi side had requested release.

0163

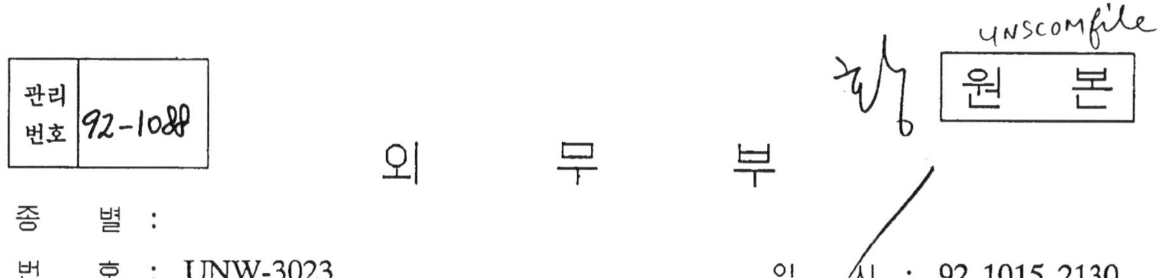

| 관리 번호 | 92-1088 |
|---|---|

원 본

# 외 무 부

종 별 :

번 호 : UNW-3023 일 시 : 92 1015 2130

수 신 : 장 관 (연이)

발 신 : 주 유엔 대사

제 목 : 이락사태 (무기사찰반 파견)

1. 금 10.15 안보리 비공개회의에서는 이락무기 폐기사찰 유엔특위(UNSCOM) EKEUS 위원장의 보고를 청취한바, 동위원장은 이락측이 금번 사찰팀의 파견을지연시키려는 요청을 해왔으나, 금번 사찰이 포괄적 성격을 갖고 있음을 감안,계획대로 파견키로 결정, 명 10.16 바그다드에 도착할 것이라고 말하고, 무기사찰팀에 대한 전화협박, 장비제공 거절등 각종 위협이 이락내에서 계속되고 있음을 상기시켰음. 또한 동위원장은 이락측이 동위원장을 금번 사찰팀과 함께 오도록 초청했으나, 이락내에 뚜렷한 상황변화가 없는 점을 감안, 추후에 합류키로 했다고 하면서 UNSCOM 활동에 대한 안보리의 계속적인 협조를 요청함

2. 이에대해 안보리는 동 의장의 활동이 올바른 방향으로 진행되고 있다고 지적하고, 별첨 내용의 안보리 의장 명의의 PRESS STATEMENT 를 발표키로함

3. 금번 파견되는 사찰팀은 10 개국 50 명으로 구성되었으며, 반장은 SMIDOVITCH (러시아인)로서 10.17 부터 사찰을 개시할 예정임

(대사 유종하-국장)

예고:92.12.31까지

첨부;UNW(F)-0867

국기국 차관 1차보 분석관 청와대 안기부

PAGE 1 92.10.16 11:58

* 원본수령부서 승인없이 복사 금지

외신 2과 통제관 FR

0164

UNW(번)-0267 210/5 2130 # 3매목

**STATEMENT TO THE PRESS**
**OF THE PRESIDENT OF THE SECURITY COUNCIL**

THE SECURITY COUNCIL HAS RECEIVED THIS AFTERNOON AN INTERESTING BRIEFING FROM THE EXECUTIVE CHAIRMAN OF THE SPECIAL COMMISSION.

ON THIS OCCASION, AMBASSADOR EKEUS INFORMED US ON THE UNSCOM 45'S GENERAL FRAMEWORK AND PURPOSES.

IN HIS BRIEFING, THE EXECUTIVE CHAIRMAN CONFIRMED HIS DECISION TO MAINTAIN THIS INSPECTION ACCORDING TO THE SCHEDULED TIMETABLE. THE SECURITY COUNCIL EXPRESSED ITS SUPPORT TO THIS DECISION.

PRESIDENT EKEUS ALSO DREW ATTENTION TO PRESS REPORTS OF A HIGH LEVEL STATEMENT MADE IN IRAQ WHICH WOULD CONSTITUTE A THREAT TO THE SECURITY OF THE UNITED NATIONS INSPECTORS. ON THIS OCCASION, THE SECURITY COUNCIL STRESSED ITS PARTICULIAR CONCERN FOR THE SAFETY OF THE UN INSPECTORS.

FINALLY, THE COUNCIL EXPRESSED THE WISH THAT IRAQ WILL FULLY COOPERATE WITH UNSCOM 45 AND, BY THAT MEAN, WILL SEIZE THE OPPORTUNITY TO DEMONSTRATE ITS WILLINGNESS TO COMPLY FULLY WITH THE COUNCIL'S RESOLUTIONS.

867-1-1

0165

## UN 混成 武器査察團, 이락訪問

1. 50여명으로 構成된 核·化學·生物武器 및 미사일 分野를 망라한 UN 混成 武器査察團(團長 : 니키타 스미도비치)이 2주간 豫定으로 10.16 이락을 訪問함.

2. 關聯 動向

가. UN의 對이락 査察活動 推移

○ 걸프戰 終戰(91.2)이후 採擇된 UN 決議 687호 (91.4)가 이락의 核·化學·生物·미사일 武器등 大量破壞武器를 廢棄토록 규정함에 따라

○ 核査察團은 14차에 걸쳐 核關聯 施設·物質에 대한 査察을 實施하여

- 濃縮우라늄 25kg 封印(91.5 1차), 우라늄 濃縮을 위한 遠心分離器를 발견(91.7 4차)하여 遠心分離器 및 그 부품과 플루토늄 3g의 再處理 裝備를 破壞(91.10 7차)하고

- 高濃縮 우라늄(12.5kg)과 燃料捧 47개의 IAEA로 搬出(91.11 8차) 및 「알 아티르」核工團(바그다드 西南方 40km)내 核實驗用 大型방카와 鐵製建物(1萬 5,000平方M)을 破壞했으며(91.4 11차)

- 13차 査察(92.7)시 「타르미야」와 「아쉬 샤르카트」에서 EMIS(電氣磁石式 同位元素 분리장치)가 설치된 건물을 破壞하고 14차 査察(9.1 - 7)시 核關聯 施設의 完全 破壞를 확인하였고

29-26

0166

○ 化學武器 査察團은 13차에 걸쳐 무타나 團地(바그다드 北西쪽 80㎞)를 중심으로 査察活動을 전개하여

- 이락이 UN에 報告한 量보다 4배나 많은 4萬 6,000여개의 化學彈 및 化學物質의 保有를 확인(91.6 1차)하고

- 2차(91.8) - 7차査察(92.1)을 통해 하바니아 空軍基地, 무하마디야트兵器 貯臧所, 무타나 團地 등에서 6,000여개의 化學彈頭와 8,200여발의 겨자가스 폭탄을 비롯한 化學武器들을 발견, 8차査察시(92.2)부터 93년 중반까지 무타나團地에서 廢棄하기로 이락側과 合意한 바 있으며

- 이락보유 化學武器(신경가스 140톤, 겨자가스 400톤 推定) 除去에는 6個月 내지 1년이 소요될 것으로 推定하고 最近 11차(92.6) - 13차査察(92.9)을 통해 化學彈 제조관련 시설의 破壞作業의 감독과 化學武器 廢棄工場의 試驗 稼動을 시작하였으며

※ 현재 이락內에는 化學武器 査察團과는 별도로 化學武器 廢棄專擔班(13個國 39명)이 8.31이래 바그다드 滯留 作業中임

○ 生物武器 査察은 2차에 걸쳐 실시, 生物武器 製造 증거는 入手하지 못했으나 86년부터 生物武器 研究計劃이 진행된 사실은 確認(91.8 이락측 是認)하는 成果를 거둔 한편

○ 미사일査察團은 11차례의 査察을 통해

- 1차(91.6) - 5차査察(91.10)기간중에 「알 타지」미사일 發射基地(바그다드 北西쪽 45㎞)에서 改良型 스커드미사일(알 후세인)과

29-27

0167

彈道미사일등 80여기를 廢棄한 것을 비롯하여 슈퍼건(口徑 350mm 砲身 30m) 및 그 製造基地를 發見, 廢棄하였으며

- 6차(91.12) - 8차査察(92.2)기간중에 이락의 隱匿 스커드미사일 索出에 주력하고

- 최근 10차(92.4), 11차査察(92.5)을 통해 스커드미사일 製造裝備 및 施設의 破壞作業을 추진하고 있음

나. 이락의 對應動向

○ 이락은 6차 核査察(91.9)시에 核硏究 施設에서 발견한 4박스의 祕密書類를 搬出하려는 査察團을 強制 抑留하고 서류를 몰수하였으며

○ 8차 미사일査察(92.2)시에는 스커드미사일 部品 및 生產設備 破壞要請에 대해 民間施設로 轉用 可能한 것임을 이유로 거부하였고

○ 核武器 製造에 필요한 特殊設備로 고안된「알 아티르」工團내 시설 일부의 破壞 要求를 거부(92.3)한 바 있으며

○ 최근 제11차 化學武器 査察(92.6)시에는 査察團의 농업부 청사내 査察要求를 主權侵害라는 이유로 拒否하고 群衆을 동원 抗議示威를 전개하기도 하였으나

○ UN側의 對이락 軍事攻擊 可能性을 示唆하는 경고와 安保理 聲明 및 IAEA의 강경한 査察活動 준수 요구 등에 의해 결국은 査察에 응하여 왔음.

3. 이번의 UN 混成 武器査察團의 이락 訪問은

가. UN이 지난 7월 이락의 農務部 廳舍 査察 거부이후 混成査察團을 派遣(8.9 - 17)한데 이어 두번째로서

나. 이락이 UN에 대해 美國의 大統領選擧 이용을 이유로 査察團 入國을 3주 延期하도록 要請(10.9)했음에도 불구하고 強行된다는 점에서 注目되는 바

다. UN의 對이락 査察이

○ 그간 査察活動으로 색출한 核·化學·미사일등 大量破壞武器 製造施設·裝備 破壞 및 破壞作業 確認 등에 주력하고 있고

○ 제14차 核査察 團長인 「마우리오 지페레로」(IAEA 事務次長)가 이락의 核開發計劃이 無力化되어 제로상태에 있다고 言及(9.2)한바 있다는 점에서

라. UN 終戰決議 678호(91.4)에 規定된 이락의 義務履行 상태를 包括的으로 점검하여 향후 査察方向을 摸索하는 데 重點을 둘 것으로 豫想됨.

이락사찰

## UN 混成 武器査察團, 이락 訪問 終了

1. 核·化學·生物武器 및 미사일 分野 專門家 50명으로 構成된 UN 混成 武器査察團(團長:「니키타 스미도비치」)이 10.16 - 30간 이락을 訪問, 大量破壞武器에 대한 査察을 實施하였음.

2. 關聯 動向

가.「스미도비치」査察團長은

○ 이락이 安保理 決議 687호(91.4)가 금지하는 彈道미사일을 隱密히 보유해 왔다는 情報를 入手했으며 이번 任務는 매우 重要하다고 強調(10.16)하면서

○ 이락軍需品 備蓄基地 등에 대한 査察 및 化學武器 廢棄實態 點檢活動을 시작했으며, 政府 및 大統領官을 포함, 疑心이 가는 모든 地域을 訪問할 것이라고 言及(10.17)하고

○ 10.18 - 19간 바그다드 周邊地域을 대상으로 스커드미사일등 大量殺傷 武器 保有與否 및 長距離 미사일 잔류에 대한 檢證을 實施했다고 밝히는 한편(10.19)

○ 이락 官吏들과 11시간에 걸친 會談(10.25)을 가진 바 있으며 UN 査察團이 任務를 거의 完遂했을 뿐 아니라 目的도 達成했다고 闡明(10.28)하면서도

30-25

0170

○ 査察團이 이락 當局의 安全保障 主張에도 불구하고 査察活動을 방해받았으며 심지어 殺害威脅까지 받기도 했다고 暴露(10.30)

나. UN 側에서는

○ 安保理가 이락當局에 대해 UN 武器査察團員들의 安全을 保障하고 全幅的인 協力을 해달라는 聲明을 發表(10.15)한 데 이어

※ 이락은 UN 査察團의 保護를 위해 필요한 모든 措置를 취할 것이라고 言及(10.17 「하마디」이락 公報長官)

○ 「갈리」事務總長이 이락에 관한 定期報告書(10.21)를 통해 이락이 UN의 大量破壞武器 廢棄計劃을 철저히 遵守하지 않고 있다고 밝혔으며

○ UN의 對이락 大量破壞武器 廢棄特委 委員長인 「에케우스」는 「후세인」이락大統領이 大量破壞武器를 모두 없애는 데 同意하거나 權座에서 물러나야 할 것이라고 主張(10.22)했고

○ 秘密 核基地로 의심받아 온 이락內 核施設에 대한 衛星寫眞을 확보함에 따라 11월中旬 國際原子力機構(IAEA) 專門家들이 이락內 核施設을 조사하기 위해 바그다드를 訪問할 것이라고 言及(10.26 UN 官吏).

3. 評 價

가. 이번 UN 混成 武器査察團의 對이락 査察은

○ 同 査察團이 걸프戰 이후 最大規模로서 16명의 美國人을 비롯 러시아·英國·佛蘭西·이탈리아·獨逸·濠洲 등의 50명에 달하는 專門家로 構成되어 있다는 점과 「스미도비치」査察團長의 言及內容 등을 勘案할 때

○ 그간 4개分野(核·化學·生物武器 및 미사일)에 대한 査察活動을 통해 索出한 大量破壞武器 製造施設·裝備 破壞現況 및 破壞作業 確認과 아울러 새로운 武器製造施設 및 隱匿 스커드미사일 摘發등 包括的 點檢을 實施함으로써

○ 向後 이락에 대한 査察方向을 摸索하는 데 주력할 것으로 보임

나. 앞으로 UN의 對이락 査察은

○「스미도비치」査察團長이 査察結果에 대해 特異한 發見事項을 밝히지 않고 있으나, 이는 그간 査察結果 公開로 이락政府의 査察活動 妨害 등 摩擦을 惹起한 점을 고려한 것으로 보이며

○ 이락의 大量破壞武器 廢棄 履行에 대한「갈리」UN事務總長의 不信表明, 核 査察團의 이락訪問 計劃 등을 勘案할 때 UN 終戰決議(91.4)에 따른 對이락 經濟制裁 및 大量破壞武器 廢棄査察은 持續될 것으로 豫想됨.

30-27

0172

## UN核査察團, 이락訪問 豫定

< 1992 >

1. UN의 제15차 核査察團이 11.6 이락을 訪問할 豫定임.

2. UN의 對이락 核査察은

가. 걸프戰 終戰決議(687호, 91.4)에 의거 化學·生物·미사일 등 4개 분야 大量破壞武器 廢棄活動의 일환으로 실시되는 것으로

나. 1차(91.5) - 6차 査察(91.9)까지는 이락이 UN에 보고한 核關聯 事項의 진위여부 및 核武器 製造施設 確認에 주력하여 濃縮우라늄(25kg)의 압수, 우라늄 濃縮을 위한 원심분리시설 및 전기분리식 플랜트와 建設중인 EMIS(전기자석식 동위원소분리기) 施設을 發見·確認하였고

다. 7차(91.10) - 11차 査察(92.4)에서는 그간 發見·確認한 核武器 製造關聯 主要施設의 破壞作業을 실시하여 원심분리기와 그 부품, 플루토늄 再處理 裝備의 파괴, IAEA(國際原子力機構)로 高濃縮우라늄(12.5kg) 및 연료봉(42개) 반출, 대형방카 등 主要建物을 破壞하였으며

라. 12차(5.26 - 6.5) - 14차 査察(9.1 - 7)시에는 殘存 核施設의 破壞確認 및 核關聯 技術과 主要物質 調達루트의 發見에 주력하여 왔음.

28-27

0173

3. 이번 核査察은

가. 최근 混成武器査察團의 査察(10.16 - 30)에 뒤이은 것으로 「갈리」 UN事務總長(10.21)과 「에케우스」 UN大量破壞 武器廢棄 特委 委員長(10.22)은 이락이 UN決議에 의한 核開發計劃 抛棄를 비롯하여 大量破壞武器 廢棄를 철저히 이행하지 않고 있다고 비난한 바 있고

나. 人工衛星 사진을 분석한 美 物理學者들이 이락 北部 자브강地域에 秘密 核武器 製造工場으로 추정되는 2개建物이 있다고 주장한 것으로 보도(10.23, 美 CBS 放送報道)된데 이어 플루토늄(80kg)의 이락 搬入企圖 沮止說(11.1 英國 선데이 익스프레스지)도 유포되는 등 이락의 核潛在力 隱匿疑惑이 지속되는 가운데 實施된다는 점에서

다. 核關聯 施設의 破壞確認과 더불어 이락 核開發 計劃 관련 資料 索出, 이락 北部의 2개 建物 確認 등에 중점을 둘 것으로 豫想됨.

# 第15次 UN 이락 核査察 結果

1. 32명의 專門家로 구성된 제15차 UN核査察團(團長:「드미트리 페리코스」)이 11.8 - 18간 이락을 訪問, 核關聯 시설의 殘存與否 및 技術·部品의 調達經路 糾明 등을 위한 査察을 실시하였음.

2. 査察團의 活動內容

가. 核武器 製造關聯 시설 및 물질의 殘存與否 확인을 위해 투와이다(바그다드 東南 25km)의 核硏究施設등 20여개소 이상의 關聯施設들에 대한 再査察을 실시하여

○ 모술(바그다드 北西 350km)에서 200드럼의 우라늄 含有物質이 核廢棄物로 적재되어 있는 것을 發見(11.10)한 데 이어

○ 이락 南部의 바스라에서 우라늄 濃縮에 사용되는 特殊鋼鐵(Maraging Steel) 100톤을 解體(11.14)하였고

나. 核開發 關聯 技術 및 部品供給 국가와 企業의 糾明을 위해

○ 査察團측이 이락 政府官吏, 核專門家들과의 회담을 통해 關聯資料의 공개를 要求했음에도 불구하고 이락側은 道義的 責任을 이유로 명단 提出을 拒否하였으나

○ 核關聯 장비들의 調査를 통해 數個 外國企業의 명단을 파악하는 한편 核物質의 형태 등에 대한 精密分析으로 상당수의 外國 支援業體들을 把握할 수 있을 것이라고 發表(이상 1.18,「페리코스」團長)했으며

28-22

0175

다. 核開發 추진의 長期的 監視를 위해 水質과 土壤에 대한 기초조사를 실시하고 이락 全域에서 放射性 檢査를 위한 표본을 채취하였음.

3. 評　價

가. 이번 核査察은

○ 査察團 構成에 있어 92年중 실시된 7回의 核査察중 最大規模(18個國 출신 32명의 專門家들로 구성)로 編成되었고

○ 이락의 農務部 査察拒否(7.5)이후 摩擦을 憂慮하여 공개하지 않던 核査察의 진척상황을 상세히 發表한 가운데

○ 이락에 核技術과 裝備 등을 供給한 數個의 외국기업의 명단을 把握하게 되었다는 점에서 重要한 成果를 거둔 것으로 評價됨

나. 앞으로 UN의 査察活動은

○ 最近 이락側이 對外的으로 査察活動에 협조하겠다고 公言하면서 UN 監督下에 이루어지고 있는 主要 核關聯 施設의 파괴확인과 化學武器 廢棄등 自國의 UN결의 이행을 부각시켜 UN의 經濟制裁 解除를 要求하고 있음에도 불구하고

○ UN측은 이락이 核開發 지원국가에 대한 資料提供을 拒否, 核開發 疑惑을 解消하지 못하고 있는 등 UN決議에 의한 大量破壞武器 廢棄關聯 UN決議(687호, 92.4)를 履行하지 않고 있는 것으로 보고 있어

○ 이락의 核開發을 支援한 外國과 企業들에 대한 資料確保와 調達루트 糾明을 통해 核開發 全貌를 把握하는 데 重點을 두고 繼續될 것으로 豫想됨.

28-23

0176

이/

# 주 오스트리아 대사관 겸
# 주 비인 국제기구 대표부

Praterstrasse 31,
A-1020 Vienna, Austria    전화 (0222) 2163441    FAX NO. (0222) 2163438

문서번호 : 오스트리아 20300-31

시행일자 : 93. I. 4.

수신 : 장관

참조 : 국제기구국장

제목 : 이락 핵사찰 관계 자료

| 선결 | | | 지시 | |
|---|---|---|---|---|
| 접 | 일자 시간 | . . : | 결 | |
| 수 | 번호 | 01661 | 재 | |
| 처리과 | | | 공 | |
| 담당자 | | | 람 | |

제 I5차 대이락 핵사찰 결과 보고 (92.II.8-I8) 등 표제 자료를 별첨 송부합니다.

첨부 : I. 제I5차 이락 핵사찰 결과 보고 (GOV/INF/677, 92.I2.I7)

2. 대이락 사찰 단장 비방기사 관련 IAEA 서한 등 I건    끝.

주오스트리아 대사관 겸
주비인 국제기구대표부

0177

INTERNATIONAL ATOMIC ENERGY AGENCY
AGENCE INTERNATIONALE DE L'ENERGIE ATOMIQUE
МЕЖДУНАРОДНОЕ АГЕНТСТВО ПО АТОМНОЙ ЭНЕРГИИ
ORGANISMO INTERNACIONAL DE ENERGIA ATOMICA

WAGRAMERSTRASSE 5, P.O. BOX 100, A-1400 VIENNA, AUSTRIA
TELEX: 1-12645, CABLE: INATOM VIENNA, FACSIMILE: (+43 1) 234564, TELEPHONE: (+43 1) 2360

IN REPLY PLEASE REFER TO:
PRIERE DE RAPPELER LA REFERENCE:

DIAL DIRECTLY TO EXTENSION:
COMPOSER DIRECTEMENT LE NUMERO DE POSTE:

1992-12-22.

The Secretariat of the International Atomic Energy Agency presents its compliments to the Permanent Mission of the Republic of Korea and, wishes to draw to the Mission's attention the attached exchange of correspondence between the Director General and the Editor of the Sunday Telegraph concerning an article in its edition of December 13 which is appended for ease of reference.

The Secretariat of the International Atomic Energy Agency avails itself of this opportunity to renew to the Permanent Mission of the Republic of Korea the assurances of its highest consideration.

David R. Kyd
Director
Division of Public Information

H.E. Mr. See Young Lee
Ambassador
The Resident Representative of the
Republic of Korea to the International
Atomic Energy Agency
Praterstrasse 31
A-1020 Vienna

0178

INTERNATIONAL ATOMIC ENERGY AGENCY

THE DIRECTOR GENERAL

N7.51

16 December 1992

Sir,

I have rarely been so outraged and disgusted by a press article as I was in reading that which appeared in your newspaper on 13 December concerning one of my senior staff, Professor Maurizio Zifferero.

Mr. Zifferero has served the International Atomic Energy Agency as a Deputy Director General with great distinction and loyalty for almost a dozen years. His most recent duties have been as head of the IAEA's Action Team established to carry out the Security Council-mandated nuclear inspection activities in Iraq. No one could have done more in mapping, skilfully and independently, Iraq's clandestine nuclear capability and in supervising its dismantling. This work has been commended not only by our own governing bodies but also by the United Nations and the Members of the Security Council, which have given unremitting support to the IAEA's efforts in Iraq.

It surprises and dismays me that you would quote an unnamed former staff member as claiming that Mr. Zifferero had been "involved in selling nuclear weapons to Iraq". This is totally untrue and I look to you to set the record straight on this matter which calls into question Mr. Zifferero's integrity.

.../2

The Editor
SUNDAY TELEGRAPH
181 Marsh Wall
London E14 9SR
fax 987-8787

0179

Mr. Zifferero did indeed work for the Italian Nuclear Energy Commission during the period 1975-76 when it was negotiating bilaterally with Iraq and other developing nations on peaceful nuclear co-operation agreements, and this has been a matter of public record. To portray this involvement in the way your newspaper chose to do is irresponsible and highly regrettable.

On one point of detail, I have never issued a statement contradicting an assessment by Mr. Zifferero. The statement apparently referred to was a clarification issued when he himself wished to correct a false impression that had arisen from comments he had made while in Baghdad concerning the status of Iraq's known nuclear capability.

On another point, the recent, ultimate admission by the Iraqi authorities of a connection between the Rashidiya site and the Iraqi nuclear weapons programme was a direct result of Mr. Zifferero's unrelenting insistence in the course of an inspection mission led by him in Iraq.

The statement that regular contacts with Iraqi representatives took place outside IAEA offices is false in fact and the innuendo that such contacts might have influenced Professor Zifferero's judgment in favour of the Iraqi Government is outright defamatory.

I urge you to publish this letter prominently and in full in your next edition, while reserving the right to consider options for seeking redress.

Yours sincerely,

Hans Blix

Drafted by: DKyd/imk 9432x
Cleared by: WWSturms

cc.: DGO
Mr Sturms
Mr Zifferero
RCS

0180

The Sunday Telegraph

1 CANADA SQUARE CANARY WHARF LONDON E14 5DT
TELEPHONE: 071-538 5000 TELEX: 22874 TELLDN G
DX42657 ISLE OF DOGS

DIRECT LINE: 071 538 7305 FAX: 071 538 7872



18th December 1992

Hans Blix Esq
The Director General
International Atomic Energy Agency
Wagramerstrasse 5
PO Box 100
A-1400 Vienna
Austria

Dear Mr Blix,

Thank you for your letter. I regret that it has only just reached me because it was sent to the wrong part of our organisation. I am, therefore, not able to deal with it in time for our edition this Sunday, but I can assure you of giving it our proper attention next week.

Yours sincerely,

CHARLES MOORE
Editor

0181

# UN nuclear inspector had links with Iraq

by John Bulloch and Con Coughlin

MAURIZIO Zifferero, the Italian leader of the team of UN inspectors searching for nuclear weapons in Iraq, himself played a key role in building Iraq's nuclear arsenal, it has been revealed.

Zifferero worked for the Italian atomic energy authority in the mid-1970s. He was directly involved in the sale of sophisticated nuclear technology which was later used by Saddam Hussein for extracting plutonium, the key ingredient in an atomic bomb.

The sale of the equipment went ahead in spite of a strong protest from Washington. The Americans opposed the sale of nuclear technology which might lead to the proliferation of nuclear weapons in the Third World.

Zifferero later moved to the International Atomic Energy Authority (IAEA) in Vienna. Earlier this year he was placed in charge of the United Nations inspection team checking that Iraq destroyed its nuclear weapon-making potential, in accordance with the UN resolutions which ended the 1991 Gulf war.

Zifferero's involvement in selling nuclear weapons to Iraq has prompted many of his colleagues to question whether he is the right man for the job.

"I would have a great deal more confidence in his judgment if he had not been involved in selling nuclear weapons to Iraq," commented one of his former colleagues at the IAEA. "Because of that there will always be the suspicion that he has been influenced in favour of the Iraqis."

The Italian scientist provoked a strong protest last September when he declared that Iraq's nuclear capability had been reduced to zero by Allied bombing during the Gulf War and subsequent inspections.

David Kay, an American nuclear expert who headed the earlier UN inspection teams, condemned Zifferero's assessment as "naive".

Hans Blix, the IAEA director, also issued a statement contradicting Zifferero's assessment.

He said that Iraq had still not complied fully with UN resolution 687, requiring Iraq to give full disclosure of its nuclear programme and to produce any components left. Two weeks later another UN team led by a different inspector, Demetrios Pericos, a Greek, visited a site at Rashidiyah, near Baghdad, which Zifferero had declared clean.

They found evidence that centrifuges for uranium enrichment had been built there. This was later confirmed by the Iraqis.

Zifferero has hotly denied any involvement in building up the Iraqi arms industry.

In a statement issued at the IAEA headquarters in Vienna, he claimed he was only working as an adviser to the Italian government, that he only visited Iraq a couple of times and that his involvement pre-dated Saddam's emergence as the undisputed head of Iraq.

While it is technically correct to claim that Saddam was not the undisputed ruler of Iraq in 1976, the time of the Italian deal, he was Iraq's vice-president then and became the architect of his nation's nuclear weapons project.

Zifferero: key role

As deputy director of research at the IAEA between 1980-88, the period of the Iran-Iraq war, Zifferero was regularly consulted by Iraqi scientists and engineers.

He is also said to have had regular meetings in Vienna, but outside the IAEA offices, with Rahim Abdullah Abdel-Kital, the Iraqi in charge of the fuel fabrication laboratory supplied from Italy. Abdel-Kital was later appointed Iraq's ambassador to Austria and its representative on the IAEA.

A spokesman for the Foreign Office in London, which has pressed the UN inspection team to be rigorous in its search for Iraqi nuclear weapons, said it had no comment to make about Zifferero's past involvement in Iraq. The British Government was satisfied with the work being carried out by the IAEA in Iraq.

Sunday Telegraph 13 Dec 92

0182

| 정 리 보 존 문 서 목 록 | | | | | |
|---|---|---|---|---|---|
| 기록물종류 | 일반공문서철 | 등록번호 | 2020110024 | 등록일자 | 2020-11-09 |
| 분류번호 | 731.33 | 국가코드 | IQ | 보존기간 | 30년 |
| 명 칭 | 유엔이라크대량살상무기폐기특별위원회(UNSCOM)의 화학무기폐기작업단 참여 요청, 1992. 전2권 | | | | |
| 생 산 과 | 국제연합1과 | 생산년도 | 1992~1992 | 담당그룹 | |
| 권 차 명 | V.1 4월-6.9 | | | | |
| 내용목차 | * 국방부 요원 2명 파견(기간 : 8.24-12.4)<br>* 이라크 지하시설물 건조, 지상건물 신축 등의 공사실적 정보 제공 요청 포함 | | | | |

0001

원 본

| 관리번호 | 92-337 |
|---|---|

# 외 무 부

종 별 :

번 호 : UNW-1030 일 시 : 92 0407 1930

수 신 : 장 관(연일,중동일,기정)

발 신 : 주 유엔 대사

제 목 : 걸프사태(이락 대량무기 폐기 유엔특위)

1. 이락 대량무기 폐기유엔특위(UNSCOM) EKEUS 위원장은 4.3. 본직앞 서한을 통하여 이락의 화학무기 폐기를 위한 UNSCOM 작업단 설치계획을 통보하고 동작업단에 아국의 참여를 요청하여 왔는바 동서한을 별첨 송부하니 검토후 회시바람

2. 서한내용

가. UNSCOM 은 92.6-12 월간 이락 MUTHANNA STATE ESTABLISHMENT 에 있는 화학무기 폐기를 위한 작업단을 구성키로 하였음

나. 작업단의 규모는 추후결정 예정이나 영어를 구사하는 자로서 화학무기에 관한 지식을 갖춘 민간인이나 군인및 기술자, 화학무기 탐지전문가, 의료인, 건물철거기술자들로 구성됨

다. 필요장비는 방독의복, 화학무기제거및 탐지장비, 폐쇄회로 TV 등임

라. 동화학무기폐기 작업단 설치에 한국정부의 참여를 희망함

3. 동위원회측에 문의한바에 의하면 동작업단은 약 30-35 명으로 구성 예정이며 현재 안보리 상임이사국을 포함 27 개국(아시아에서는 호주, 인도, 일본, 뉴질랜드, 파키스탄, 중국, 태국포함)에 작업단 참여를 요청하였으며 각국이 1-2 명의 화학무기 제거 전문가를 파견하여 줄것을 희망하고 있음

(대사 유종하-국장)

예고:92.12.31 일반

첨부:UNW(F)-0365

검 토 필(1992.6.30.)

| 국기국 | 장관 | 차관 | 1차보 | 2차보 | 중아국 | 외정실 | 분석관 | 청와대 |
|---|---|---|---|---|---|---|---|---|
| 안기부 | | | | | | | | |

PAGE 1 92.04.08 09:25

외신 2과 통제관 BZ

0002

IHW(under)-0365 20407 1930 #원본

UNITED NATIONS  NATIONS UNIES

Amb. Shin.

POSTAL ADDRESS—ADRESSE POSTALE UNITED NATIONS, N.Y. 10017
CABLE ADDRESS—ADRESSE TELEGRAPHIQUE: UNATIONS NEWYORK

REFERENCE:

3 April 1992

Excellency,

I have the honour to advise you that with the deployment of UNSCOM 29/CD1 on 18 February 1992 the formal programme for the destruction of Iraq's Chemical Warfare capability has commenced. Shortly, following the soon-to-be completed construction of a nerve agent hydrolysis plant and mustard incinerator, we will initiate the destruction of the bulk of Iraq's CW agents which are either stored or have been relocated to the Muthanna State Establishment. This chemical destruction programme will continue concurrently with other Special Commission activities, and will require substantial personnel and other resources. To carry out this task I must yet again turn to your Government for support.

I have decided to establish a team comprising personnel serving on a 3-6 monthly basis, at the Muthanna State Establishment, from June 1992 until the end of 1992 at least. The exact size and detailed composition of the team is yet to be determined; however, it will require English speaking civilians or military officers and technicians with appropriate chemical defence and destruction process knowledge, decontamination and detection experts, medical personnel, technical storemen and occasional short tour calls on structural engineers, demolition engineers, EOD personnel and analytical experts. There will also be requirements for protective clothing, decontamination, detection, agent monitoring, closed circuit television equipment and possibly analytical instruments in support of this operation.

The establishment of this standing team will not preclude occasional requests for personnel and equipment for chemical destruction operational requirements at other locations.

Inevitably, as the programme evolves, there will be modifications. You will be advised promptly of any changes.

/...

H.E. Mr. Chang Hee Roe
Ambassador Extraordinary and Plenipotentiary
Permanent Representative of the Republic
of Korea to the United Nations
New York, New York

0003

UNITED NATIONS  NATIONS UNIES

- 2 -

It would be appreciated if your Government could contribute to the establishment of the UNSCOM programme at the Muthanna State Establishment. In the event you are prepared to participate in this important task, kindly inform UNSCOM of the nature of your contribution.

Accept, Excellency, the assurances of my highest consideration.

Rolf Ekéus
Executive Chairman
Office of the Special Commission

0004

관리 92 — 326

# 외 무 부

110-760 서울 종로구 세종로 77번지 / (02) 720-2334 / (02) 723-3505

문서번호 연일 2031-358
시행일자 1992. 4. 13.
(경유)
수신 국가안전기획부장, 국방부장관
참조 (군수국장) 군비통제관

| 취급 | | 장 관 |
|---|---|---|
| 보존 | | |
| 국 장 | 전 결 | |
| 심의관 | | |
| 과 장 | 김수석 | |
| 기안 | 황준국 | 협조 |

제목 의견 문의

1. 걸프전 종전에 관한 유엔 안전보장이사회 결의(결의 687호, 91.4.3)에 따라 설치된 이라크 대량살상무기폐기 특별위원회(UNSCOM)의 Ekeus 위원장은 이라크의 화학무기 폐기를 위해 설치예정인 작업단에 한국의 참여를 요청하여 왔습니다.

2. 상기 화학무기 폐기 작업단 구성 및 관련사항은 아래와 같으며, 동 위원회 측은 각국이 1-2명의 화학무기 폐기 전문가를 파견해 줄 것을 희망하고 있다고 하는바, 우리의 동 작업단 참여문제에 대한 귀부의 의견을 지급 ~~회시하여~~ 알려 주시기 바랍니다.

가. 작업단 규모 : 추후 결정예정이나 30-35명 규모 예상

나. 구 성 : 영어를 구사하는 민간인 또는 군인으로서 화학무기의 탐지 및 폐기전문가, 의료진, 건물철거 전문가등으로 구성

/ 계속 /

군비통제관실
검증과 조이석중령
793 4772

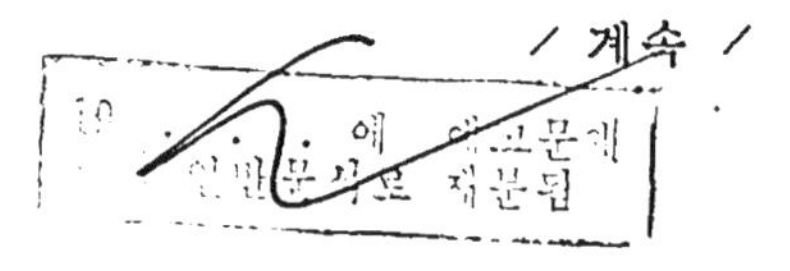

0005

다. 참여요청 대상국 : 안보리 상임이사국을 포함한 27개국
(아시아에서는 호주, 인도, 일본, 뉴질랜드, 파키스탄, 중국, 태국등 포함)

3. Ekeus 위원장의 요청서한과 동 위원회 활동관련 자료를 별첨 송부하니 본건 검토에 참고하시기 바랍니다.

첨 부 : Ekeus 위원장 서한 및 이라크 대량살상무기 폐기 특별위원회 관련 참고자료. 끝.

예 고 : 92.12.31.일반
19 . . . 에 예고문에 의거 일반문서로 재분류됨

0006

UNW(F)-0365 20407 1930 # 친북문

UNITED NATIONS  NATIONS UNIES

Amb. Shin.

POSTAL ADDRESS · ADRESSE POSTALE UNITED NATIONS, N.Y. 10017
CABLE ADDRESS—ADRESSE TELEGRAPHIQUE UNATIONS NEWYORK

REFERENCE:

3 April 1992

Excellency,

I have the honour to advise you that with the deployment of UNSCOM 29/CD1 on 18 February 1992 the formal programme for the destruction of Iraq's Chemical Warfare capability has commenced. Shortly, following the soon-to-be completed construction of a nerve agent hydrolysis plant and mustard incinerator, we will initiate the destruction of the bulk of Iraq's CW agents which are either stored or have been relocated to the Muthanna State Establishment. This chemical destruction programme will continue concurrently with other Special Commission activities, and will require substantial personnel and other resources. To carry out this task I must yet again turn to your Government for support.

I have decided to establish a team comprising personnel serving on a 3-6 monthly basis, at the Muthanna State Establishment, from June 1992 until the end of 1992 at least. The exact size and detailed composition of the team is yet to be determined; however, it will require English speaking civilians or military officers and technicians with appropriate chemical defence and destruction process knowledge, decontamination and detection experts, medical personnel, technical storemen and occasional short tour calls on structural engineers, demolition engineers, EOD personnel and analytical experts. There will also be requirements for protective clothing, decontamination, detection, agent monitoring, closed circuit television equipment and possibly analytical instruments in support of this operation.

The establishment of this standing team will not preclude occasional requests for personnel and equipment for chemical destruction operational requirements at other locations.

Inevitably, as the programme evolves, there will be modifications. You will be advised promptly of any changes.

/...

H.E. Mr. Chang Hee Roe
Ambassador Extraordinary and Plenipotentiary
Permanent Representative of the Republic
of Korea to the United Nations
New York, New York

0007

UNITED NATIONS  NATIONS UNIES

- 2 -

It would be appreciated if your Government could contribute to the establishment of the UNSCOM programme at the Muthanna State Establishment. In the event you are prepared to participate in this important task, kindly inform UNSCOM of the nature of your contribution.

Accept, Excellency, the assurances of my highest consideration.

Rolf Ekéus
Executive Chairman
Office of the Special Commission

0008

# UN의 이라크 대량살상무기 폐기 특별위원회(UNSCOM)

## 1. 활동근거

가. UN 안보리 결의 687(91.4.3)

o 이라크는 국제적 감시하에 모든 생화학무기 및 사정거리 150km 이상의 탄도미사일과 이들의 저장, 연구, 개발, 지원 및 제조시설들을 파기, 철거 또는 무력화해야 함.

o 이라크는 핵무기 또는 핵무기 가용물질의 연구, 개발, 지원시설 및 생산시설의 확보, 개발포기를 수락하여야 함.

나. UN 안보리 결의 707 (91.8.15) 및 715(91.10.11)

o 안보리 결의 687호의 이행방안
- 이라크의 의무이행 및 시설 감시 및 검증
- UN 특별위원회 및 IAEA의 관련활동에 관한 특권과 면제

다. UN 안보리 결의 699(91.6.17)

o 상기 UN 사찰관련 제반경비는 이라크가 부담

## 2. 관련 분야별 진전사항

가. 생·화학무기

o UN 안보리 특별위원회는 현재까지 이라크내 43개 화학무기 관련시설에 대한 사찰을 실시하였고 나머지 장소에 대한 사찰도 곧 실시예정

o UN은 그간의 사찰과정에서 이라크가 자체 개발했거나 개조한 10개 유형의 화학무기를 발견하였음.

o 생물무기에 대해서 이라크는 당초 보유치 않고 있다고 선언하였으나, 사찰 과정에서 이라크 관리들은 방어 및 공격용 생물무기 개발계획을 시인한 바 있음.

나. 탄도미사일 및 장거리포

o UN 안보리 특별위 사찰팀은 71개 장소에 대한 사찰실시

o UN 사찰팀은 사찰과정에서 구경 1,000mm이상의 슈퍼건, 이동식 스커드 미사일 발사대를 발견, 대부분 관련시설을 파기함.

o UN은 동 분야에서는 대체적으로 만족할 만한 성과가 있었다고 분석하고 있으나 아직도 이라크가 개조형 스커드등을 보유하고 있을 가능성도 배제치 않고 있어 각국과의 정보교환등을 통한 완전한 사찰 노력 경주중

다. 핵 무 기

o 그간의 이라크측 부인에도 불구하고 UN 사찰팀은 핵사찰 과정에서 이라크의 핵무기 제조계획을 발견

o UN은 그간 이라크가 명확한 증거 발견시까지 핵무기 개발노력을 부인해온점등을 고려, 계속적인 사찰 실시예정

2

0010

## UN의 이라크 대량살상무기폐기 특별위원회(UNSCOM)

92. 4. 14

### 1. 활동근거

가. UN 안보리 결의 687(91.4.3)

o 이라크는 국제적 감시하에 모든 생화학무기 및 사정거리 150km 이상의 탄도미사일과 이들의 저장, 연구, 개발, 지원 및 제조시설들을 파기, 철거 또는 무력화해야 함.

o 이라크는 핵무기 또는 핵무기 가용물질의 연구, 개발, 지원시설 및 생산시설의 확보, 개발포기를 수락하여야 함.

나. UN 안보리 결의 707 (91.8.15) 및 715(91.10.11)

o 안보리 결의 687호의 이행방안

- 이라크의 의무이행 및 시설 감시 및 검증
- UN 특별위원회 및 IAEA의 관련활동에 관한 특권과 면제

다. UN 안보리 결의 699(91.6.17)

o 상기 UN 사찰관련 제반경비는 이라크가 부담

### 2. 관련 분야별 진전사항

가. 생·화학무기

o UN 안보리 특별위원회는 현재까지 이라크내 43개 화학무기 관련시설에 대한 사찰을 실시하였고 나머지 장소에 대한 사찰도 곧 실시예정

1

0011

o UN은 그간의 사찰과정에서 이라크가 자체 개발했거나 개조한 10개 유형의 화학무기를 발견하였음.

o 생물무기에 대해서 이라크는 당초 보유치 않고 있다고 선언하였으나, 사찰 과정에서 이라크 관리들은 방어 및 공격용 생물무기 개발계획을 시인한 바 있음.

나. 탄도미사일 및 장거리포

o UN 안보리 특별위 사찰팀은 71개 장소에 대한 사찰실시

o UN 사찰팀은 사찰과정에서 구경 1,000mm이상의 슈퍼건, 이동식 스커드 미사일 발사대를 발견, 대부분 관련시설을 파기함.

o UN은 동 분야에서는 대체적으로 만족할 만한 성과가 있었다고 분석하고 있으나 아직도 이라크가 개조형 스커드등을 보유하고 있을 가능성도 배제치 않고 있어 각국과의 정보교환등을 통한 완전한 사찰 노력 경주중

다. 핵 무 기

o 그간의 이라크측 부인에도 불구하고 UN 사찰팀은 핵사찰 과정에서 이라크의 핵무기 제조계획을 발견

o UN은 그간 이라크가 명확한 증거 발견시까지 핵무기 개발노력을 부인해온점등을 고려, 계속적인 사찰 실시예정

라. UN의 지속적 감시 및 검증

o UN은 이라크의 결의안 687 준수에 대한 국제적 감시를 위해 검사 및 답사, 대량파괴무기 및 생산시설의 파괴, 지속적 감시 및 검증을 실시하고 있음.

o UN은 92.1 현재까지의 진전사항으로 보아 탄도미사일, 화학무기 및 핵연료등의 제거외에는 만족할만한 성과가 없었다고 분석하고 있음.

## 3. 최근 동향

### 가. 안보리 동향

o 92.2.15. 안보리는 이라크의 안보리 결의상 제반의무 불이행과 관련, 최후 통첩성격의 결의안 또는 의장 성명발표 검토

o 2.19. 안보리는 안보리결의 이행에 불성실한 것으로 판단되는 이라크에 대하여 UN의 단호한 조치가 필요하다는 특별위 보고서를 청취하고 R. Ekeus 특위의장의 이라크 파견을 결정(2.21-24)

o 2.28. UN 안보리는 Ekeus 특위의장의 이라크 방문에도 불구, 이라크가 성실한 의무이행 자세를 보이지 않고 있음을 지적, 이라크의 의무 불이행 비난 및 조속한 이행 촉구 내용의 안보리 의장성명을 발표

o 3.11-12. 이라크측 제의하 이라크 정부대표단(단장 : 티릭 아지즈 부수상) 참석하 안보리 공식회의 개최
  - 이라크측 후속태도를 보아가며 대응방향 강구 예정
  - IAEA 및 SCOM과 이라크측과의 협력과정 당분간 관망 예정

o 3.21. SCOM 이라크 방문(제9차 미사일 폐기 검증단 활동 개시)

o 3.27. 안보리 비공식회의 개최, 의장명의 성명 발표
  - 이라크의 안보리결의 687호 이행을 위한 최근 조치에도 불구 제재결의 해제에는 아직 미흡함.

o 4.3자 UNSCOM 위원장의 안보리 의장앞 서한 요지

- 이락 외무장관이 UNSCOM 위원장앞 92.3.19자 서한을 통하여 최초로 밝힌바에 의하면
  - 이락은 유엔감시하에 91.7월 폐기된 미사일 62기외에 92기를 보유하고 있었으나, 91년 여름 일방적으로 폐기하였다 함. (UNSCOM에 폐기잔재 확인)
  - 또한 이락정부는 유엔에 통보하지 않는 45개의 화학탄두를 포함한 135개의 미사일탄두와 8개의 이동 미사일 발사대를 보유하고 있었으나, 91.7월 이를 일방적으로 폐기하였으며 (UNSCOM에서 확인불가) 다량의 화학무기도 일방적으로 폐기 하였다 함.
- 상기와 같은 이락의 일방적 폐기는 국제감시하에 폐기토록 되어 있는 안보리결의(687)를 위반하는 것이며 이락이 최근까지도 보유한 무기관련 정보를 UN에 숨기고 있었음.
- 이락은 유엔이 요청한 미사일관련 폐기대상물중(S/23673 ANNEX A) 최초로 92.3.21. 309개 대상물을 폐기하였으며 여타 폐기대상물의 폐기계획안을 UNSCOM에 제출하였음.
- 유엔감시하에 화학무기 2.5톤을 2.21-3.24중 폐기하였음.
- 유엔조사단이 4월초순 이락을 방문, AL ATHEER소재 핵무기 생산 관련 시설 및 장비의 파괴를 감독, 확인 예정이며 파괴방법은 IAEA가 현재 검토중임.
- 이락의 상기 조치는 유엔결의 이행의 진전이나 이락의 유엔결의를 충실히 이행할지는 좀더 두고 보아야 함.

o UNSCOM 위원장, 주유엔대사에게 Muthanna State Establishment 소재 화학무기 폐기 위한 작업단 설치계획 설명 및 우리나라 참여 타진 서한 송부(4.3자)

o 4.8. IAEA - 이라크간 Al Atheer 소재 핵무기 시설 파괴 합의

나. 주요이사국 태도

o 미, 영, 불은 일단 관망하겠다는 자세이나 새로운 대응 조치를 취해야할 경우 제한적 군사행동도 포함될 것으로 보임.

o 비동맹 국가그룹은 이라크가 명백히 안보리 결의안을 위반하고 있으므로 안보리 이사국들의 강경조치에 동의할 수 밖에 없다는 입장임.

92-356

# 외 무 부

110-760 서울 종로구 세종로 77번지 / (02) 720-2334 / (02) 723-3505

문서번호 연일 2031- 124
시행일자 1992. 4. 14.
(경유)
수신 중동아프리카국장
참조

| 취급 | | 장 관 |
|---|---|---|
| 보존 | | |
| 국 장 | 전 결 | |
| 심의관 | | |
| 과 장 | | |
| 기안 | 황준국 | 협조 |

제목 UNSCOM 작업단 참여문제

이라크 화학무기폐기 작업단 설치와 관련한 유엔특별위원회(UNSCOM)의 대아국 요청사항(관련전보 : UNW-1030)에 대하여 당국에서는 관련부처와 협의하여 구체적 대응방안을 마련코자 하는바, 본건 검토시 대중동관계에서 우리가 고려해야 할 사항에 관한 귀국의견을 4.20까지 회보하여 주시기 바랍니다. 끝.

1992.12.31. 에 예고문에 의거 일반문서로 재분류됨

검 토 필 (92.6.30.)

0016

| 관리번호 | 92-372 |
|---|---|

| 분류번호 | 보존기간 |
|---|---|
| | |

# 발 신 전 보

번 호 : WUN-0856 920414 1558 WG 종별 :

수 신 : 주 유엔 대사. 총영사

발 신 : 장 관 (연일)

제 목 : UNSCOM 작업단 참여문제

대 : UNW-1030

1. 대호 검토에 참고코자 하니 다음사항 파악 보고바람.

(1) 표제 작업단에의 참여의사 통보국가 및 통보내용(상금 공식통보국이 없는 경우 비공식적으로 UNSCOM측이 파악하고 있는 각국입장)

(2) 통보기한

(3) 동 작업단 요원선발을 위해 유엔측에서 자격심사를 하는지 여부 및 심사할 경우 그 기준

(4) 동 작업단 요원에 대한 보수 및 기타 근무여건(파견에 따르는 제반 경비중 파견국이 부담하는 구체적 범위포함).

2. 대호 서한은 전문용어들이 많고(EOD personnel등 의미불명), 화학무기폐기 작업단의 활동내용에 대해서 구체적 설명이 부족한바, 관련 참고자료들이 있으면 가능한 입수 송부 바람. 끝.

(국제기구국장 김재섭)

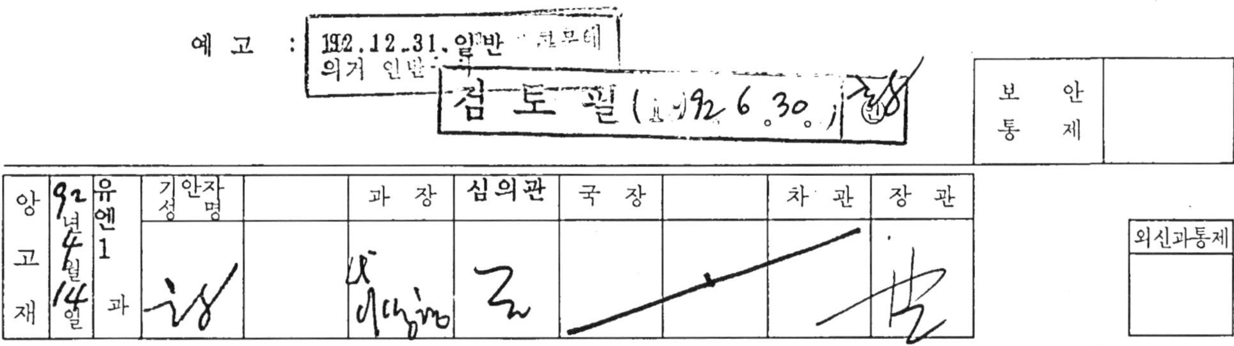

예 고 : 1992.12.31. 일반 의거 인반
검 토 필 (1992.6.30.)

| 보안통제 | |
|---|---|

| 앙고재 | 92년 4월 14일 | 유엔1과 | 기안자 성명 | | 과 장 | 심의관 | 국 장 | | 차 관 | 장 관 |
|---|---|---|---|---|---|---|---|---|---|---|
| | | | | | | | | | | |

| 외신과통제 |
|---|
| |

0017

주 국 련 대 표 부

주국련 20313- 421 1992. 4. 15.

수신 : 장 관

참조 : 국제기구국장

제목 : UNSCOM 작업단

연 : UNW -1107

1. 연호 UNSCOM 의 화학무기폐기작업단 요원 파견과 관련, UNSCOM 에서 이락에 파견하는 각종 팀 요원이 숙지할 보수, 신분보장, 근무여건, 준비사항등을 기록한 자료를 별첨 송부합니다.

2. 동 자료는 금번 파견될 화학무기폐기작업단에도 적용될 기본자료임을 첨언합니다.

첨 부 : UNSCOM 파견 요원 자료. 끝.

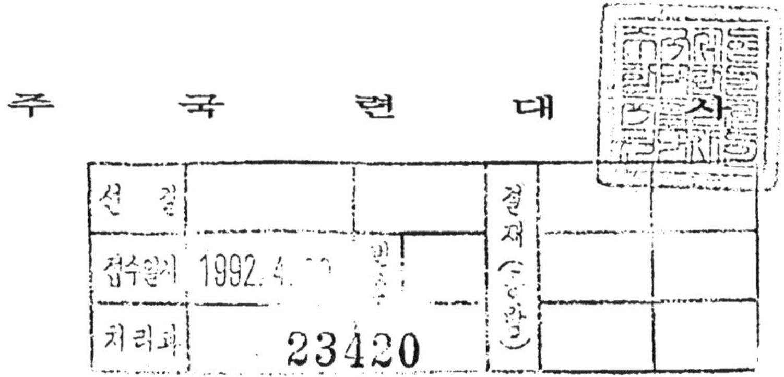
주 국 련 대 사

| 선 결 | | | 결재 공람 | | |
|---|---|---|---|---|---|
| 접수일시 | 1992. 4. | 번호 | | | |
| 처리과 | 23420 | | | | |

0018

**OFFICE OF THE SPECIAL COMMISSION**

5 March 1992

INFORMATION FOR MEMBERS OF INSPECTION TEAMS

**1. UNITED NATIONS STATUS**

While on duty with the U.N. Special Commission (UNSCOM), you, as a member of an UNSCOM inspection team, will enjoy the privileges and immunities accorded to experts performing missions for the United Nations under article VI of the Convention on the Privileges and Immunities of the United Nations of 13 February 1946. To be covered under this Convention, you will be requested to sign a group Special Service Agreement, a type of U.N. contract, which identifies you and your colleagues as experts on mission as well as makes you eligible for coverage under U.N.-provided special insurances, as specified in 5(a) below. Further special arrangements regarding facilities, privileges and immunities for UNSCOM operations have been negotiated with Bahrain and with Iraq. The Chief Inspector is furnished with copies of those arrangements.

**2. TRAVEL DOCUMENTS**

a. Bahrain. As the first leg of their trip, members of UNSCOM inspection teams will be required to assemble in Bahrain, the staging area for inspections into Iraq. Standard time in Bahrain is GMT + 3. Travel to Bahrain, will require, at this time, a national passport and an entry visa for nationals of all countries other than countries members of the Gulf Cooperation Council (Saudi Arabia, Kuwait, Oman, Qatar and the United Arab Emirates) and British nationals. The entry visa will be issued to you at the airport on arrival in Bahrain.

You will be denied entry into Bahrain if your national passport contains an entry/exit stamp from Israel. If this is the case, please obtain a new passport before leaving for Bahrain.

b. Iraq. Standard time in Iraq is GMT + 3. You will fly on a UN aircraft from Bahrain to Iraq and back. Normally, members of inspection teams will enter Iraq on the UN Certificate, a form of "passport" identifying you as a UN expert on mission. These certificates will be given to each inspector in Bahrain. Upon completion of the mission the

0019

certificate will be collected and maintained in Bahrain available for any subsequent deployment. UN certificates which have expired will be extended in Bahrain. Thus, if you already have a certificate, please bring it to Bahrain even if expired.

**NO NEW CERTIFICATES WILL BE ISSUED IN BAHRAIN.** New certificates are issued only at UN Headquarters in New York.

In order to obtain this essential travel document for the first time, it is imperative that you fill out all information required on the UN Certificate application form (a blue original card or a facsimile thereof, as attached), sign the card or the facsimile, attach 8 passport-size photos and return immediately by the most expeditious way (DHL or other express mail if necessary) to:

Ms. Lucy Kotsidis
United Nations Special Commission
Room S-3027
United Nations
New York, New York 10017
U.S.A.

Telephone: (international access code + 1-212-963-9044)

**IF THE INFORMATION IS NOT RECEIVED AT LEAST 7 DAYS PRIOR TO THE TEAM'S ASSEMBLY DATE IN BAHRAIN IT MAY NOT BE POSSIBLE TO OBTAIN THE UN CERTIFICATE IN TIME.**

3. **TRANSPORTATION, HOTEL ACCOMMODATIONS AND OTHER ARRANGEMENTS**

a. Before you leave your place of residence. The United Nations, in accordance with existing United Nations rules and regulations, will provide round-trip transportation on a recognized public carrier, at the most economical rate, via the shortest, most direct route from country of residence to the place of assembly of the teams, which, as indicated above, is Bahrain. UNSCOM's N.Y. Administrative Office will contact you, normally by fax, with information on where to pick up the prepaid ticket. To avoid lengthy reimbursement procedures, every effort should be made to use the prepaid ticket provided.

**You will be advised of a reporting date to the assembly point. Please do not arrive any earlier. Please do not initiate travel, or change travel plans, without UNSCOM approval.**

b. Arrival and stay in Bahrain. UNSCOM has established a Field Office in Bahrain to support inspection activity into Iraq. The Chief of the Field Office is Mr. Alastair

0020

Livingston (office: international access code + 973-320-936; mobile phone: 973-459-273; the Administrative Officer,

Ms. Angelina Hernandez-Griffin, office: international access code + 973-33-6898. In most cases, a representative of the Field Office will meet you at the Manama airport. If no one is at the airport, proceed through immigration and customs, identifying yourself as an UNSCOM inspector, and either take a taxi to the Manama Holiday Inn or call the Holiday Inn (tel. no. 531-122) and ask them to send the hotel mini-bus to pick you up. You may ask the World Travel Service agency at the airport, which represents the U.N. official travel agency at Headquarters, for assistance or to place the call to the hotel.

Hotel accommodations. As indicated above, while in Bahrain you will be staying at the Holiday Inn. Reservations will already have been made for you by UNSCOM on the basis of your approved travel, so there is no need for you to book or confirm hotel accommodations.

Activities while in Bahrain. Several days may be spent in Bahrain for administrative and mission-specific briefings, training and acclimatization prior to entry into Iraq. At this time, you will also be provided with an advance on your daily subsistence allowance for the length of the mission (see 4 below).

c. Iraq. Travel to and from Iraq will be on UN-provided aircraft. All arrangements concerning this travel will have been made by the Bahrain UNSCOM Field Office. To date, transportation within Iraq has been by a combination of UN and Iraqi vehicles. Helicopter transport will be used when distances dictate it. While in Iraq, you will be staying at the Sheraton Hotel, reservations for which will have been made by UNSCOM for the whole team. At this time, there are no easily accessible public international telephone lines from/to Baghdad. Limited personal call will be allowed using the UNSCOM satellite links, but such calls must be paid in cash U.S. dollars and are expensive, approximately $10.00 per minute or fraction thereof. For emergency notification, please follow the instructions given under 7 below.

d. Dispersal. At the end of the mission in Iraq, you will return to Bahrain for a number of days to write the inspection report before returning to your place of residence.

**4. DAILY SUBSISTENCE ALLOWANCE/PER DIEM AND OTHER MONETARY MATTERS**

0021

In addition to roundtrip transportation to and from Baghdad, the United Nations will provide you with a daily subsistence allowance (DSA) for your stay in Bahrain and in Baghdad. At this time, the daily rate for Bahrain is $154.00 and for Baghdad $335.00 for the first sixty days. You will receive a cash advance on arrival in Bahrain. Should the United Nations or other organization provide accommodations during any part of the mission, the DSA will be reduced accordingly.

You are fully responsible for your expenses, including paying hotel bills before check out, meals, telephone calls, etc.

**NOTE WELL**: Hotel bills in Iraq must be paid in cash in U.S. dollars. These bills cannot be paid in any other currency (nor in Iraqi dinars) and no credit cards or travellers cheques are accepted in Iraq. Meals and other expenses may be paid in dinars. The exchange rate is very unfavourable making simple amenities expensive.

Final settlement of all entitlements and claims will take place before your departure from Bahrain for the return trip home.

**5. INSURANCE COVERAGE, HEALTH CERTIFICATION AND MEDICAL SUPPORT**

a. Insurance coverage. You are fully responsible for arranging, at your own expense, such ordinary life, health and other forms of insurance coverage for the period of your service for the United Nation as you consider appropriate. The responsibility of the United Nations is limited solely to the payment of compensation, if appropriate, under the following two schemes:

1. A hazardous duty and malicious acts personal accident insurance coverage begins when the staff member boards the aircraft for the last leg of the flight to the designated duty station, in this case Iraq, and ceases when the staff member deplanes from a flight departing the designated duty station. The sum assured is US$250,000 per person for death or permanent total disablement, or benefits as per proportionate scale for permanent partial disablement.

2. A U.N-financed compensation scheme in the event of death, injury or illness attributable to the performance of official duties on behalf of the United Nations.

The scale of benefits is available through the Chief Administrative Officer, UNSCOM, Room S-3120-D, United Nations Organization, New York, NY 10017, USA.

0022

b. Health considerations. Healthy personnel are essential to the success of the inspection process. Inspection activities will take their toll on everyone, more so in hot weather and on individuals who are not fit. The United Nations requires all personnel to provide a statement from a recognized physician certifying that the individual is in good health, is fit to travel and has had the inoculations required for the countries to which the individual is to travel. For Bahrain and Iraq, the United Nations recommends immunizations for typhoid, tetanus, and also recommends gamma globulin. Additionally, anthrax and plague immunizations are recommended for individuals participating in biological weapons inspections. Although there have been reported cases of cholera, it does not appear to be a significant danger in the areas to which UNSCOM personnel will travel.

To comply with U.N. requirements, please have the attached Health Certificate filled out by your physician and return it to UNSCOM along with your travel certificate application and photographs **(see paragraph 2(b) above)**.

c. Medical support. Emergency medical support is available in Bahrain and in Iraq. An UNSCOM doctor or medical assistant will accompany each inspection team. Evacuation procedures to Kuwait, Bahrain or Western Europe are also in place.

You should bring with you an adequate supply of all personal medications, as re-filling prescriptions may not be possible. Also bring spare spectacles. Sunscreen, chapstick, and salves for rashes are advised. Rashes, stomach aches, and diarrhoea are likely ailments. You will be given a complete medical briefing while in Bahrain.

**6. OTHER USEFUL INFORMATION**

a. Clothing. You are responsible for your own personal clothing. Prudent selection of clothing will contribute significantly to comfortable working conditions and should be adapted to the weather. Temperatures in summer are up to 50 degrees Celsius, in winter, temperatures will drop to zero. In January/March, you will need light-weight daytime clothing with warm sweaters or jackets for the evening. Outerwear providing warmth and rain protection is strongly recommended.

Natural fibre materials such as cotton are cooler and easier to launder; long sleeve shirts will afford protection against sunburn and flying insects. You should bring sufficient clothing for a two-week period in Iraq. Excellent laundry service is available in the hotel in Baghdad, but elsewhere it is unpredictable. Shoes are a most

0023

critical item of clothing. Lightweight, over-the-ankle shoes/boots are advised. Shoes or boots with steel in the sole or toe conduct extremes of cold and heat and can become very uncomfortable. Break in new footwear prior to arriving in Bahrain. Sunglasses are recommended.

You may wear/use military items such as boots and canteens, but you should not wear military uniforms or insignia. The UN will provide you with identifying floppy-brimmed hats and armbands.

Team inspection equipment will be provided at the assembly point. Individuals involved in CBW inspections must bring their own protective gear. They must also bring a respirator with two spare canisters/sets of filters and optical inserts if required.

b. Personal Equipment. Experience gained from inspections to date suggests some personal equipment items may be of benefit to each inspector. These items will have to be provided at individual expense and will not be reimbursed by the U.N. It is strongly recommended that these items be procured before leaving home as there is often no time to do so in Bahrain and the prices there are quite high. Following are suggestions:

Notebook, Dictaphone, or personal notebook computer
Pens/pencils
Portable cassette player
Batteries as appropriate
Secure money pouch
Small compass for orientation
Shoulder bag or backpack

c. Media guidance and government contacts. Press interest in the activities of the Special Commission continues to be high. The authorized spokesman for the team is the Chief Inspector. Results of inspections are considered confidential until authorized for release by the Special Commission. Team members should not make personal reports to their government prior to the completion of the official mission.

d. Photographs. The use of personal cameras in Iraq is normally permitted during leisure activities in civilian areas. However, on the inspection site itself, or going to and from the inspection site, photographs will be taken only by the official team photographers or by individuals specifically designated by the Chief Inspector. These official photographs will be released only with the specific authority of the Special Commission. Further details on the

0024

rules relating to the taking of photographs will be provided during the initial briefing in Bahrain.

**7. EMERGENCY NOTIFICATION.**

UNSCOM must have on record an individual or institution you designate as an emergency point of contact. Please ensure that the information is provided on the attached Inspector Data Sheet and that it is accurate. Family members or your designated point of contact may pass urgent messages to you through UNSCOM headquarters in New York (international access code, if appropriate + 1-212-963-9044/9041) or Field Office Bahrain (international access code + 973-320-936).

**TO REMIND:** **PLEASE FILL OUT AS NECESSARY THE ATTACHED UN CERTIFICATE APPLICATION, INSPECTOR DATA SHEET, HEALTH CERTIFICATE, ATTACH 8 PASSPORT SIZE PICTURES AND RETURN TO THE UNSCOM NEW YORK OFFICE IMMEDIATELY.**

Attachments:

1. Inspector Data Sheet
2. UN Certificate Application
3. Health Certificate

0025

**HEALTH CERTIFICATE**

______________________________ is in good health and is physically fit to travel to Bahrain and Iraq to carry out inspection activities as required by the United Nations. All required inoculations for the travel area have been administered.

______________________________
Physician

______________________________
Date

0026

관리 번호 92-384

원 본

# 외 무 부

종 별 :
번 호 : UNW-1107　　　　일 시 : 92 041 1830
수 신 : 장 관(연일,중동이,기정)
발 신 : 주 유엔 대사
제 목 : UNSCOM 작업단 참여

대:WUN-0856
연:UNW-1030

대호 이락 무기폐기 유엔특별위원회(UNSCOM)의 화학 무계폐기작업단 파견과관련, 4.1. 당관 이수혁 참사관이 동위원회 BARRASS 보좌관을 면담, 파악한 바를 아래 보고함

1. 작업단 파견 결정배경

-연호 UNSCOM 위원장의 화학무기폐기 작업단 참여 요청서한은 각국이 분야별로 제공가능한 구체적인 인원과 장비를 우선 파악하기 위하여 발송한 것으로서각국의 참여의사를 접수한후 각국의 구체적인 분담계획을 작성할 예정이라함

2. 참여의사 통보국가및 통보기한

-현재까지 참여의사를 정식통보한 국가는 없으나 서한발송 대상 27 개국중 7-8 개국 국가가 구체적인 내용을 문의, 관심을 표명한바 있다함

-당초 작업단을 6 월경 파견 계획이었으나 각국의 참여결정이 늦어지면 7 월경 파견 가능성도 있음

-우선 5 월초순까지 참여분야, 요원의 인적사항및 해당분야 경력등을 통보하여 줄것을 요청함

3. 작업단의 활동내용

-동작업단의 주역할은 원칙적으로 이락측이 화학무기를 폐기하는 것을 감독(SUPERVIER)하고 지휘(CONTROL)하기 위한것임

-3-6 개월의 장기근무가 필요한 분야는 화학무기 폐기(DESTRUCTION), 제거(DECONTAMINATION), 폭발물처리전문가(EOD, EXPLOSIVE ORDNANCE DISPOSAL)및 화학분석전문가(ANALYTICAL EXPERTS)이며 단기(수일 또는 수주)근무가 필요한 분야는

국기국 차관 1차보 2차보 중아국 외정실 분석관 청와대 안기부

PAGE 1　　　　92.04.16 09:07
외신 2과 통제관 BX

0027

건물골조기술자(STRUCTURAL ENGINEER), 건물철거기술자등임(이 단기근무자는 이락에 장기상주보다는 화학무기 제조공장등의 내부골조조사와 철거가 필요한 경우 참여를 요청 OCCASIONAL SHORT TOUR CALLS)

-각국이 제공하여 주기를 바라는 장비는 화생방복, 화학무기 탐지기, CCTV, 화학분석기구등임

4. 파견자 자격및 선발

-화학분석전문가, 건축기술자등은 민간인도 좋으나 무기처리분야는 중위 또는 대위급 군인이 업무성격상 적절하다 하며 능통한 영어가 필요하다함

-유엔에서 요원선발 자격심사는 없으며 각국이 추천하는 자를 접수할 것이라함

-각국이 1-3 명정도를 추천하면 이를 종합하여 전체 40-50 명 정도를 모집계획임

5. 보수및 근무여건

-요원의 왕복항공료(한국-이락, 2 등)는 유엔이 부담하며 보수는 일당 $335 이며 숙식부(호텔투숙)는 자비부담임(일당 $335 는 이락에서 1 인 생활에 적절한액수라함) 유엔이 별도의 숙소를 제공할 경우는 일당이 감액됨(근무여건등 관련 참고사항은 금파편 송부함)

-유엔이 항공료와 숙식비를 제공하므로 기타 추가보수는 각국이 결정할 문제라함

6. 기타

-요원 제공국가가 반드시 장비를 제공하여야 되는것은 아니므로 요원제공이불가시 상기 3 항 장비제공을 희망함

-요원의 투숙은 바그다드 시내 호텔에서 집단기거할 계획이나 MUTHANNA 에 숙소 건축도 검토하고 있다함

-작업장소인 MUTHANNA STATE ESTABLISHMENT 는 바그다드에서 북서방향 70KM에 위치하고 있으며 바그다드 시내 호텔에서 기거할 경우 버스 또는 헬기로 출퇴근(버스는 1 시간 반 소요)예정임

(대사 유종하-국장)

예고;92.12.31 일반



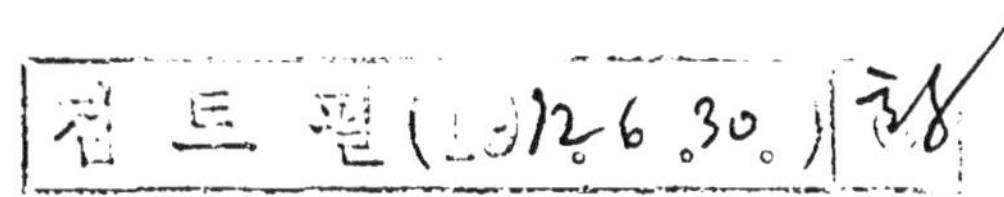

# 외 무 부

110-760 서울 종로구 세종로 77번지 / (02)720-2351 / (02)720-2686

문서번호 중동일 2031- 117 .
시행일자 1992. 4.16.( )

수신 : 국제기구국장
참조

| 선결 | | | 지시 | | |
|---|---|---|---|---|---|
| 접수 | 일자 시간 | | 결재 공람 | | |
| | 번호 | | | | |
| 처리과 | | | | | |
| 담당자 | | | | | |

제목 : UNSCOM 작입단 참여 문제

대 : 연일 2031-124 (92.4.14)

대호 UNSCOM 주관 화학무기 페기 작업단 파견 관련 검토시에 고려해야할 사항에 관한 우리국 의견을 아래와 같이 회보합니다.

- 아 래 -

1. UNSCOM 주관 화학무기 페기 작업단은 유엔 주도하에 구성되는 것인만큼, 우리가 동 작업단에 참여하더라도 한.이라크 양국관계에 직접적 영향을 미칠 가능성은 크지 않을 것으로 사료됨.
2. 그러나, 동화학 무기페기가 유엔의 결의에의해 실시되지만, 이는 현이라크 정부의 의사에 반하는 것이 사실이므로, 지난 3월 유엔의 이라크 핵시설 파괴를 위한 사찰시에 마찰이 있었던점에 비추어 동 작업단과 이라크 정부와의 마찰 가능성을 배제할 수는 없으며, 그럴경우 작업단의 구성원 소속국가에 대한 반감등을 유발시킬 가능성도 있음.
3. 한편, 우리 건설 및 무역업체의 대이라크 미수금이 13억불에 달하고 있으며, 향후 유엔의 대이라크 경제 제재조치가 해제되면 우리나라의 이라크 전후복구 사업 참여등 대이라크 경제관계도 고려되어야 할 것임. 끝.

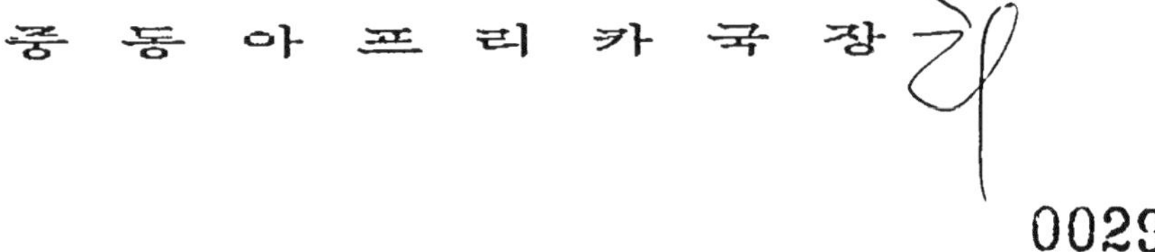


0029

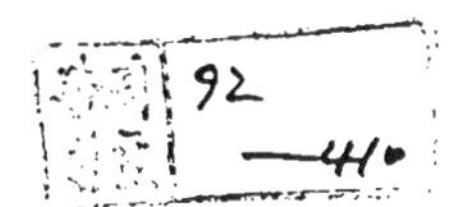

# 외 무 부

110-760 서울 종로구 세종로 77번지 / (02) 720-2334 / (02) 723-3505

문서번호 연일 2031-768
시행일자 1992. 4. 17.
(경유)
수신 국가안전기획부장, 국방부장관(군수국장)

| 취급 | | 장 관 |
|---|---|---|
| 보존 | | |
| 국 장 | 전 결 | |
| 심의관 | | |
| 과 장 | 김ㅇ석 | |
| 기안 | 황준국 | 협조 |

제목 의견문의(UNSCOM 작업단 참여)

연일 2031-352호(92.4.13자)와 관련, 유엔측으로부터 추가로 파악한 사항을 아래 통보하니 검토에 참고하시기 바라며, 본건 검토결과를 가급적 조속히 알려 주시기 바랍니다.

- 아 래 -

1. UNSCOM 화학무기폐기 작업단의 주역할은 이락측이 화학무기를 폐기하는 것을 감독·지휘하는 것임.

2. 동 작업단 요원중 장기근무(3～6개월)가 필요한 분야는 화학무기 폐기 및 제거전문가, 폭발물처리전문가(EOD : Explosive Ordnance Disposal) 및 화학분석전문가이며, 단기근무(수일 또는 수주일)가 필요한 분야는 건물골조기술자, 건물철거기술자등임.

/ 계속 /

노기석
북미과 962-5843

0030

3. 화학분석전문가, 건축기술자등은 민간인도 좋으나, 무기처리분야는 중위 또는 대위급 군인이 적절하며 영어 구사에 어려움이 없어야 함.

4. 동 작업단 요원에게는 유엔에서 항공료 및 일당 $335(숙식비포함)을 제공하며, 유엔이 숙소를 별도 제공할 경우에는 일당이 감액됨.

5. 작업장소인 Muthanna State Establishment는 바그다드에서 북서쪽 70km에 위치하고 있음.

6. 동 작업단에 요원제공이 불가할 때에는 화생방의복, 화학무기탐지기, CCTV, 화학분석기구등 장비만 제공하는 것도 환영함.

예 고 19 1992.12.31. 일반문에 의거 인반문서로 재분됨.

검 토 필 (1992.6.30.)

0031

| 관리 번호 | 92 -425 |
|---|---|

| 분류번호 | 보존기간 |
|---|---|
| | |

# 발 신 전 보

번 호 : WUN-0918 920422 1625 FO 종별 :

수 신 : 주 유엔 대사. 총영사

발 신 : 장 관 (연일)

제 목 : UNSCOM 작업단 참여

대 : UNW-1107

표제관련, 현재까지의 각종 UNSCOM 사찰팀 또는 무기폐기 작업단에의 국별참여현황 및 UNSCOM의 무기폐기활동과 그 구성요원에 대한 최근 이라크측 태도 추이등을 가능한 파악 보고바람. 끝.

(국제기구국장 김재섭)

예 고 : ~~92.12.31. 일반~~ 19 . . . 에 예고문에 의거 인반문서로 재분류

검 토 필 (1992. 6 .30. 서명)

| 보안 통제 | 서명 |
|---|---|

| 앙고재 | 92년 4월 22일 | 유엔1과 | 기안자 성명 | | 과 장 | 심의관 | 국 장 | | 차 관 | 장 관 |
|---|---|---|---|---|---|---|---|---|---|---|
| | | | 서명 | | 김유석 | | | | | 서명 |

| 외신과통제 |
|---|
| |

0032

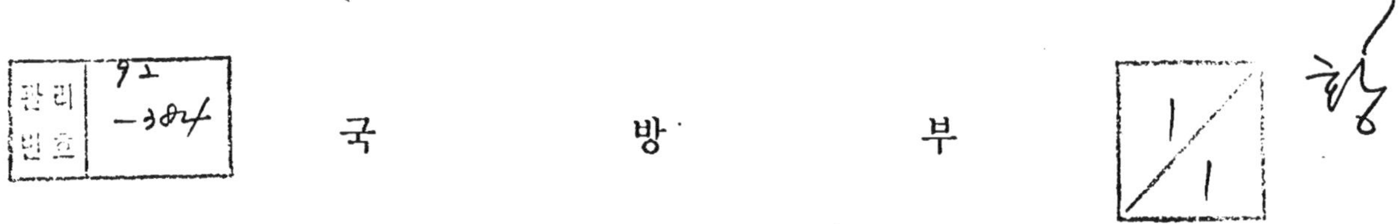


우 140-023 서울 용산구 용산동3가 1번지 / 전화 (02) 793-4772 / 전송 (02) 796-0369

문서번호 군검 24150-040
시행일자 1992. 4. 20
수 신 외무부장관
참 조 국제기구국장

| 선결 | | | 지시 | | |
|---|---|---|---|---|---|
| 접수 | 일자 시간 | | 결재·공람 | | |
| | 번호 | 15152 | | | |
| 처리과 | | | | | |
| 담당자 | | | | | |

제 목 의견 문의 (UNSCOM 작업단 참여) 회신

1. 관련근거 : 연일 2031-352('92. 4. 13) 위 제목

2. 위 근거에 의거, 귀부에서 검토 의뢰한 UNSCOM 작업단 참여 여부를 검토한 결과, 아래와 같이 회신합니다.

가. 동 작업단 구성에 필요한 전문지식을 구비한 현역장교의 선발 파견은 가능함.

나. 동 작업단이 수행할 임무의 성격을 고려할 때 작업단 요원의 계급 구성은 영관장교(소령) 1명과 위관장교(대위) 1명으로 편성하는 것이 적절할 것으로 판단됨.

다. 동 작업단 요원의 파견이 결정되면 관련요원을 선발하여 파견할 수 있도록 추진하겠음. 끝.

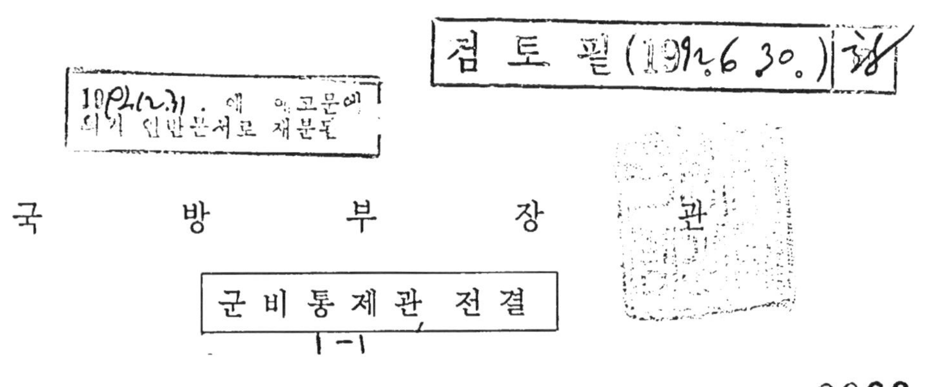


국 방 부 장 관

군비통제관 전결

1-1

0033

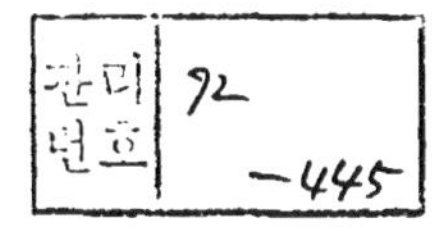

"노는기쁨 순간이고 일한보람 오래간다"

# 국 가 안 전 기 획 부

( ) / 전송

문서번호 국미 400-1177
시행일자 1992. 4. 24. ( )

| 선결 | | | 지시 | | |
|---|---|---|---|---|---|
| 접수 | 일자 시간 | 92.4.27 | | | |
| | 번호 | 15778 | 결재·공람 | | |
| 처리과 | | | | | |
| 담당자 | | | | | |

수신 외무부장관
참조

제목 의견 회신

1. 연일 2031-352, 368로 문의하신 UNSCOM 작업단 참여 관련 의견 회신입니다.

2. 의견

가. 이락 화학무기 폐기작업단에의 아국 요원 파견은

(1) UN 헌장 의무를 수락한 UN 정회원국으로서의 의무이행인 동시에 우리의 평화이미지 및 국제적 위상 제고에 기여하고

(2) 남북한 군축에 대비하여 전문지식 및 경험축적이 가능하며 북한에 대한 심리적 경제효과도 거둘수 있는 이점이 있는 것으로 판단되는바

(3) 동 작업단에 참여하되, 군·민 양 분야에서 경험을 축적한다는 측면에서 해당 전문분야 민간인 및 군인 각 1명정도 파견을 검토하는 것이 바람직할 것으로 사료됩니다.

0034

국미 400-

92. 4.

나. 그러나 동 폐기 작업단에 인원 파견시 파견요원의 신변안전 문제와 향후 이락내 복구사업 참여 및 한·이락 관계 회복에 부담요인이 될 수 있음도 신중히 고려해야 할 것임을 첨언합니다. 끝.

( 92. 12. 31

검 토 필 ( 92. 6 30. )

국 가 안 전 기 획 부

" 노는기쁨 순간이고 일한보람 오래간다"

0035

관리번호 92-442

원 본

# 외 무 부

종 별 :

번 호 : UNW-1198 일 시 : 92 0424 1900

수 신 : 장 관(연일,중동이)

발 신 : 주 유엔 대사

제 목 : UNSCOM 작업단 참여

대:WUN-0918

대호 이락 대량무기파기 위원회(UNSCOM)활동내용및 구성등에 관하여 UNSCOM의 BARRASS 보좌관및 TREVAN 공보관을 통하여 파악한바를 아래보고함

1. 파견실적및 참여국

-91.5-92.4 간 파견한 팀은 핵무기 11 개팀, 화학무기 12 개팀, 생물학무기2 개팀, 미사일 10 개팀등 35 개팀임

-현재까지 UNSCOM 에 요원을 파견한 국가는 알젠틴, 호주, 오스트리아, 바레인, 벨지움, 카나다, 체코, 핀랜드, 프랑스, 독일, 그리스, 헝가리, 인도, 인도네시아, 아일랜드, 이태리, 일본, 화란, 놀웨이, 뉴질랜드, 폴란드, 루마니아,스웨덴, 스위스, 태국, 트리니다트, 영국, 미국, 러시아, 이집트등임

2. 화학무기폐기 활동

-12 개 화학무기팀중 10 개팀은 화학무기생산및 비축실태파악과 폐기방법을강구하기 위하여 파견된 답사팀의 성격이었으며 최근 2 개팀은 화학무기 폐기작업단임. 요원은 팀별로 상이하나 대체적으로 10 여개국 20 여명 전후로 구성됨(10.7-11.8 간 파견된 제 5 차 답사팀은 15 개국 50 명으로 구성, MUTHANNA 에서 정밀답사를 실시함)

-본격적 화학무기폐기작업은 92.2.21-3.24. 간 바그다드 남쪽 400KM 에 있는 KHAMISSIYAH 무기보관소에서 실시되었음. 동작업반은 7 개국 26 명으로 구성되었으며 동작업반 감독하에 122MM 로켓포 463 개를 폐기하였음(GB/GF 합성 신경가스 2.5 톤 분량)

-92.4.5-4.13 간 파견된 2 차 화학무기 폐기반은 8 개국 14 명으로 구성되었는바 동폐기반은 화학무기폐기를 위하여 MUTHANNA 기지에 건설중인 소각로와

국기국 장관 차관 1차보 중아국 분석관 청와대 안기부

PAGE 1

92.04.25 08:22

외신 2과 통제관 CE

0036

신경가스중성화를 위한 가수분해공장(HYDROLYSIS PLANT FOR THE NEUTRALIZATION OF NERVE AGENT)의 건설진척 상황과 안전도를 검사하였음(양공장이 완공되는 7 월부터 본격적인 화학무기 폐기작업을 계획중인바 이를 위하여 UNSCOM 은 한국을포함한 27 개 국가에 요원 추천을 의뢰한 것임)

3. 화학무기종류

-이락이 생산 보유하고 있는 독가스는 MUSTARD 가스와 ORGANOPHOSPHOROUS NERVE AGENTS 로 GB 및 GF 타입이며 GA 타입의 가스 존재도 확인되었다함

-이락측에 의하면 GD 및 VX 계통의 신경가스제조연구도 행해진바 있으나 대량생산은 없었다함

4.UNSCOM 무기폐기활동과 요원에 대한 이락측의 태도

-35 개 UNSCOM 팀이 파견된 동안 3-4 차례에 걸쳐 UNSCOM 팀의 활동에 대한이락정부의 비협조나 반대가 있었고 요원이 바그다드에 도착할시 40 여명의 시위등이 발생하였으나 심각한 상황은 아니었다함

-이락정부는 화학무기폐기반에 대하여는 핵무기 또는 미사일폐기 사찰팀과는 달리 협조적이라 하며 고의적으로 작업단의 활동을 오도하거나 제한하는 행위는 없었다함

-UNSCOM 의 BARRASS 보좌관은 이락정부가 UNSCOM 에 적극 협조함이 제재조치의 조기해제와 직결된다고 인식하고 있는것으로 판단된다고 하고 실제 UNSCOM 의 활동이 전적으로 실무적인 성격이므로 이락이 요원파견국가에 대하여 장차 이를 문제로 삼지는 않을것으로 생각한다는 사견을 피력하였음을 참고로 첨언함

(대사 유종하-국장)

예고:92.12.31 일반고문에 의거 일반문서로 재분류

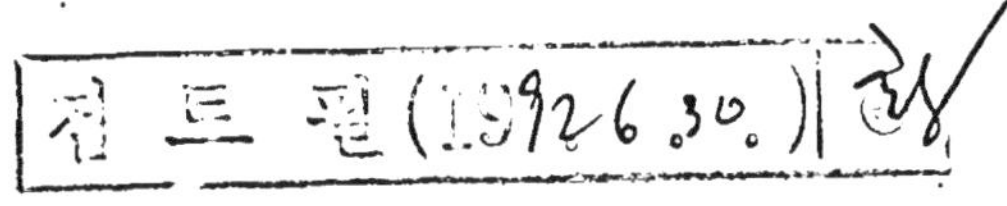

PAGE 2

0037

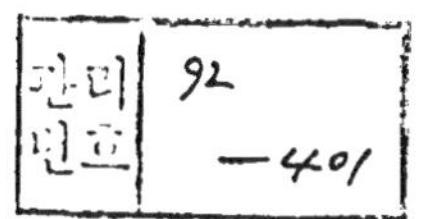
관리번호 92-401

# 외 무 부

110-760 서울 종로구 세종로 77번지 / (02) 720-2334 / (02) 723-3505

문서번호 연일 2031-
시행일자 1992. 4. 27.
(경유)
수신 내부결재
참조

| 취급 | | 차 관 | 장 관 |
|---|---|---|---|
| 보존 | | 전결 | |
| 국 장 | | | |
| 심의관 | (출장중) | 제1차관보 | |
| 과 장 | 김규현 | 중동아국장 | |
| 기안 | 황준국 | | 협조 |

제목 UNSCOM 화학무기 폐기반 참여

유엔특별위원회(UNSCOM)가 요청해온 이라크 화학무기폐기반 참여문제와 관련, 우리의 입장 및 향후 조치계획을 별첨과 같이 건의 드립니다.

첨 부 : 동 조치계획안. 끝.

1992.12.31. 에 예고문에 의거 일반문서로 재분류됨

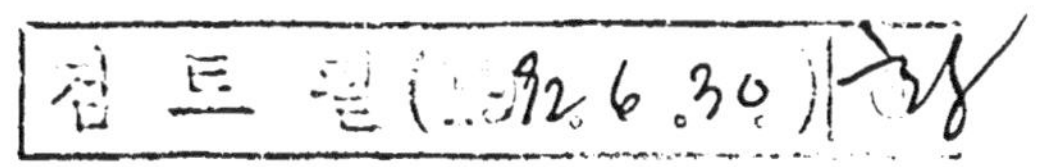
검 토 필 (1992.6.30.)

0038

# UNSCOM 화학무기폐기반 참여에 관한 조치계획(안)

1992.4.27.
유 엔 1 과

## 1. UNSCOM측 요청내용

o 이라크 무기폐기를 위한 유엔특별위원회(UNSCOM)의 Ekeus 위원장은 92.6. 설치예정인 화학무기폐기 작업단에 한국의 참여를 요청해옴. (92.4.3.자 서한)

- 요원 1-2명 파견 또는 장비제공

※ 안보리 상임이사국을 포함한 27개국에 요청
(아시아에서는 호주, 뉴질랜드, 인도, 파키스탄, 일본, 중국, 태국등 포함)

o 동 작업단 개요

- 임 무 : 이라크측의 화학무기 폐기를 감독·지휘
- 규 모 : 30-50명
- 활동기간 : 92.6-12월
- 구 성 : 군인 및 민간인으로서 화학무기의 탐지 및 폐기전문가, 폭발물처리전문가, 화학분석전문가, 건물골조 및 철거 전문가등으로 구성
- 작업장소 : Muthanna State Establishment (바그다드에서 북서쪽 70km)
- 근무조건 : 유엔에서 항공료 및 일당 $335(숙식비 포함) 제공

0039

## 2. 참여에 따른 문제점 검토

(긍정적 측면)

o 유엔의 국제평화 및 안전유지활동에 적극 참여

o 우리 전문가들의 경험축적 및 기술습득
  - 향후 남북한 군축과정에서 활용 가능

(부정적 측면)

o 작업단 구성원 소속국가에 대한 이라크의 반감 유발 가능성
  - 우리 건설 및 무역업체의 대이라크 미수금 13억불
  - 유엔의 대이라크 경제제재 해제후 우리나라의 이라크 전후 복구사업 참여에 영향을 줄 가능성

(평 가)

o 화학무기폐기에 대한 이라크측 태도에 비추어, 우리의 동 작업단 참여가 한·이라크 양국관계에 미치는 영향은 크지 않을 것으로 봄.
  - 우리는 걸프전에 의료단 파견, 전비지원등으로 기참여한 바 있음. → good.
  - 이라크는 핵시설 및 미사일폐기팀과 달리 화학무기작업단에 대해서는 협조적 태도 견지 ?
  ※ 91.5-현재까지 구성된 UNSCOM 작업단은 핵무기, 생화학무기, 미사일 분야등을 포함 모두 35개팀이었으며, 요원파견국은 미, 영, 불, 일등 선진국이외에도 인도, 인니, 이집트등 주요 비동맹국이 포함되어 있음. 비동맹인가?

o 이라크 정정변화 가능성등을 고려할때 유엔제재 참여문제는 이라크 현정권과의 관계에만 국한해서 보기 보다는 중장기적 관점에서 국제평화 증진이라는 원칙에 입각해서 검토해야 할 것임. not correct.

0040

- 다수국가가 우리에 대한 UNSCOM의 요청을 알고 있을 것으로 보며, 파견대상 인력을 갖고 있으면서 참여하지 않을 명분이 약함.

o 우리의 특수한 안보상황에 비추어, 침략자에 대한 국제적 응징 참여에 소극적이라는 인상을 국제사회에 주는 것은 바람직하지 못함.

## 3. 관계부처 의견

(국 방 부)

o 요원파견 방침 결정되면, 화학무기관련 전문지식을 구비한 현역장교 선발 가능
  - 소령 1명 및 대위 1명

## 4. 추진방향(건의)

o 상기 검토내용 및 관계부처 의견에 비추어, 국방부내 전문가 2명 파견을 추진
  - 민간인 보다는 군인이 업무성격이나 사후관리 측면에서 바람직.
  - 1명보다는 2명 파견이 우리의 참여도 제고 및 우리요원의 현지 적응면에서 유리

o 장비 별도제공은 하지않고 파견요원의 활동에 필요한 개인장비 휴대

0041

## 5. 조치계획

- ㅇ 상기 추진방향 청와대 보고(4월말)
- ㅇ 국방부에서 적임자 선발토록 의뢰(5월초)
- ㅇ 선정인원의 인적사항등 유엔측 통보 (5월초)
  - 파견에 따르는 구체사항 유엔측과 협의

- 끝 -

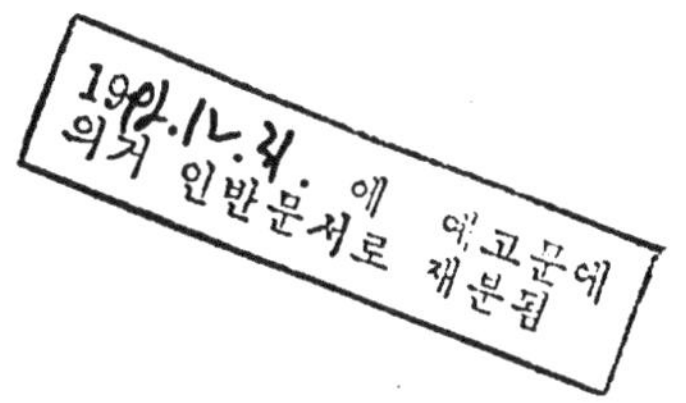


0042

(청와대 특별보고)

# 이라크 化學武器廢棄班 參與

1992. 4. 29.

外 務 部

| 유엔은 이라크 大量破壞武器 廢棄活動의 일환으로 설치되는 化學武器廢棄班에 韓國의 參與를 要請해 온 바, 安企部· 國防部等 關聯部處와의 協議를 거쳐 同 活動에 參與키로 決定하였음을 報告드립니다. |
|---|

1. 유엔側 要請內容(안보리 상임이사국등 27개국에 要請)
   - o 92. 6-12월간 바그다드 인근지역에서 활동예정인 化學武器廢棄班에 韓國의 參與 要請
     - 化學武器 探知 및 廢棄分野의 軍 또는 民間人 專門家 1-2명 派遣 또는 裝備 提供

2. 參與에 따른 問題點 檢討

(肯定的 側面)

- o 유엔의 國際平和 및 安全維持活動에 積極 參與
- o 우리 專門家들의 經驗蓄積 및 技術習得

| 암고제 | 국제연합1과 | 92년4월29일 | 담당 | 과장 | 심의관 | 국장 | 차관보 | 차관 | 장관 |
|---|---|---|---|---|---|---|---|---|---|
| | | | | | | | | | |

0043

(否定的 側面)

o 이라크의 反感誘發, 戰後 復舊事業 참여등에 影響을 줄 가능성

(評　價)

o 우리의 參與가 韓· 이라크 兩國關係에 미치는 影響은 크지 않을 것으로 봄.

- 이라크는 旣설치되었던 化學武器廢棄班에 대하여 協調的 態度 견지(91.5-現在까지 이라크에 派遣된 유엔作業班은 핵무기 11개팀, 화학무기 12개팀등 총 35개)

o 對이라크 유엔制裁 參與問題는 國際平和增進이라는 原則에 입각해서 檢討 必要

- 우리의 특수한 安保狀況에 비추어, 侵略者에 대한 國際的 膺懲에 消極的이라는 인상을 國際社會에 주는 것은 바람직하지 못함.

3. 推進計劃

o 軍 專門家 2명 派遣

- 業務性格이나 事後管理 측면에서 軍人이 적절

o 適任者 選拔(국방부)후 同 派遣에 따르는 구체사항 유엔측과 協議, 施行

- 끝 -

0044

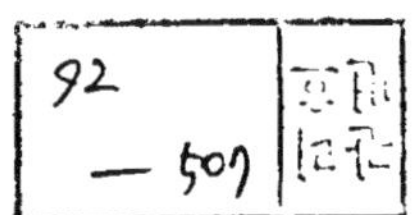

# 외 무 부

110-760 서울 종로구 세종로 77번지 / (02) 720-2334 / (02) 723-3505

문서번호 연일 2031- 415
시행일자 1992. 4. 29.
(경유)
수신 국방부장관
참조 군비통제관

| 취급 | | 장 관 |
|---|---|---|
| 보존 | | |
| 국 장 | 전 결 | |
| 심의관 | | |
| 과 장 | 김△석 | |
| 기안 | 황준국 | 협조 |

제목 UNSCOM 작업단 참여

관련 : 군검 24150-050(92.4.22)

1. 우리부는 유엔의 국제평화 및 안전유지활동에 적극 참여한다는 기본방침에 따라, 유엔특별위원회(UNSCOM)의 이라크 화학무기폐기반에 군 전문가 2명을 파견(개인장비 휴대)하기로 결정하였읍니다.

2. 이에 따라 귀부에서 적격자 2명을 선발하여 주시고, 이들의 전문분야를 명시한 상세 인적사항 및 휴대장비 목록을 지급 회보하여 주시기 바랍니다. 끝.

검열필 통제관

예 고 1992.12.31. 일반문서로 재분류 (일반 고문에 의거 인반문서로 재분류)

검토필(1992.6.30.)

0045

| 관리번호 | 92-416 |
|---|---|

# 국　　　방　　　부

우 140-023 서울 용산구 용산동3가 1번지 / 전화 (02) 793-4772 / 전송 (02) 796-0369

문서번호 군겸 24150-54
시행일자 1992. 5. 8

수　신 외무부장관
참　조 국제기구국장

| 선결 | | | 지시 | | |
|---|---|---|---|---|---|
| 접수 | 일자시간 | 92. 5. 8 | 결재·공람 | | |
| | 번호 | 17771 | | | |
| 처리과 | | | | | |
| 담당자 | | | | | |

제　목 UNSCOM 화학무기 폐기 작업단 파견대상자 (통보)

1. 관련근거 : 외무부 연일 2031-415 ('92.4.29) UNSCOM 화학무기 폐기반 참여

2. 위 근거에 의거, 첨부와 같이 UNSCOM 화학무기 폐기작업단 파견 대상자 2명에 대한 인적사항 및 개인휴대장비 목록을 첨부와 같이 통보합니다.

첨부 : 1. 파견대상자 인적사항 1부.
　　　2. 개인 휴대장비 목록 1부.　끝.

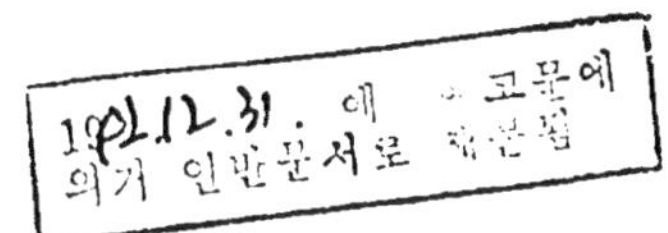


국　　방　　부　　장

군비통제관전결

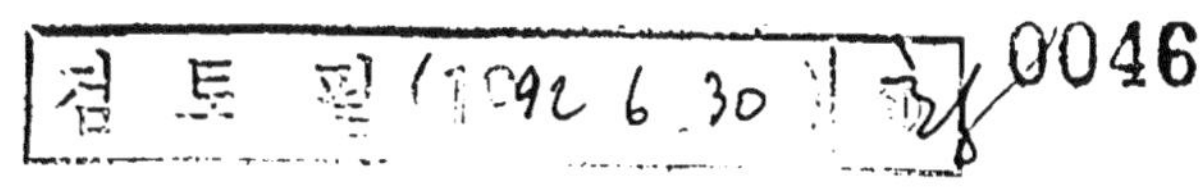


0046

# 공 란

# 공　　란

# 공 란

공　　란

첨부 #2.

# 휴대장비 목록

| 구분 | 장비명 | 단위 | 수량 | 용도 | 비고 |
|---|---|---|---|---|---|
| 개인 방호용 | 방독면 K-1 (Mask) | 개 | 2 | 개인보호 (두부, 호흡기) | 개인당 1 |
| | 침투 보호의 (Chm. Prot. Suit) | 셋 | 4 | 개인보호 (피부 및 피복) | 개인당 2셋 |
| | 해독제 킷 MARK-1 (Antidote Kit) | 킷 | 6 | 신경작용제 응급치료 | 개인당 3킷 |
| | 정화통 (Filter Canister) | 통 | 4 | 방독면 정화통 교환용 | 개인당 2 (예비용) |
| | 피부제독킷 KM258A1 (Skin Decontaminant) | 킷 | 4 | 피부제독 | 개인당 2 |
| 임무 관련 | 화학작용제 탐지킷 KM18A2 (Chm. Agents Detector Kit) | 킷 | 2 | 화학작용제탐지 | 정밀탐지용 |
| | 화학작용제 탐지킷 KM256 | 킷 | 5 | 〃 | 긴급탐지용 |
| | 탐지지 KM9 (Chm. Agents Detector Paper) | 롤 | 5 | 〃 | 신체부위 부착 탐지 |

0051

공　　　　란

공 란

공 란

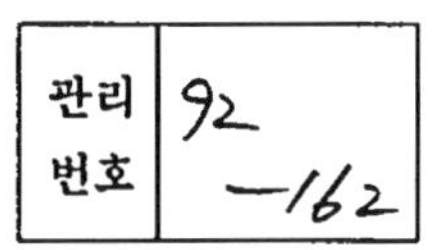

원 본

# 외 무 부

종 별 :

번 호 : UNW-1377 일 시 : 92 0513 1730

수 신 : 장 관(연일)

발 신 : 주 유엔 대사

제 목 : UNSCOM 화학무기 폐기 작업단

대;WUN-1083

1. 대호 UNSCOM 화학무기 폐기작업단 참여와 관련, 금 5.13. UNSCOM 에 대호 2 인의 명단을 통보함

2. 동 UNSCOM WHITTY 보좌관에 의하면 참여요청 대상 27 개국으로부터 매우큰 호응을 받고 있어 금일 현재까지 한국, 미, 영, 일등 13 개국이 참여를 통보해 왔으며 나머지 일부 국가들도 조만간 참여를 결정해 올것으로 예상된다 함

3. 작업단의 구성과 집결일자등은 각국의 통보를 최종 정리한후 결정될 것이나 가능하면 1-2 주내에 구체적 사항을 결정할 계획으로 있다하며 파견일자는 6월말-7 월중으로 예상된다함

4. 복무협정, 집결방법, 제출서류등은 상기 구체적 사항이 결정되는 대로 통보해 주겠다함. 동건 관련사항 통보받는대로 보고 위계임

(대사 유종하-국장)

예고:92.12.31 일반 고문에 의거 일반문서로 재분류됨

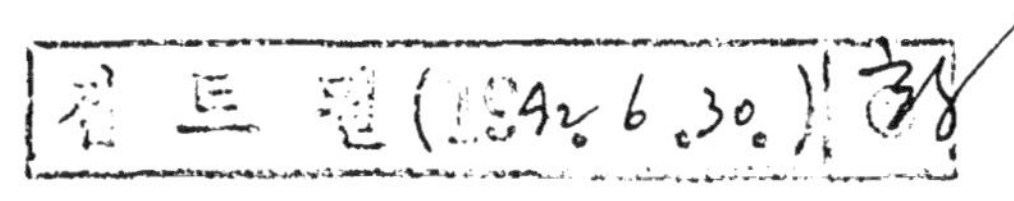

국기국 차관

PAGE 1

92.05.14 06:36

외신 2과 통제관 BZ

0055

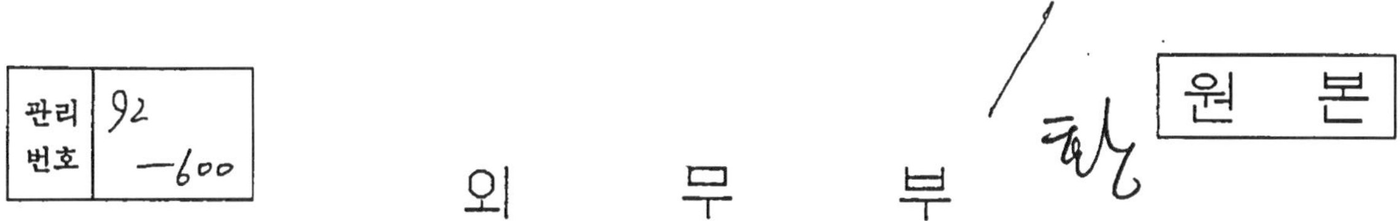


# 외 무 부

종 별 :

번 호 : UNW-1473 일 시 : 92 0521 1600

수 신 : 장 관(연일,중동이,기정)

발 신 : 주 유엔 대사

제 목 : 이락무기 폐기 협조요청

1. 유엔 안보리 이락무기 폐기 특별위원회(UNSCOM) EKEUS 위원장은 5.18 자 본직앞 서한으로 UNSCOM 의 이락무기 조사활동을 위한 아국정부의 협조를 요청하여 왔는바 동 서한 아래와 갈음

가. 정보제공 요청

-이락내 화생무기 및 사정거리 150KM 이상의 미사일의 소재지, 시설물, 자재등과 관련한 정보제공 요청

나. 화생무기.미사일 전문가 추천요청

-UNSCOM 의 필요시 수시 임용할수 있도록 화생무기 및 미사일 전문가 추천요청(전문가 명단을 작성하여 둔후 필요시마다 임여 계획이며 구체적 절차등은 추후 통보예정). 화생무기 분야에서는 군사전문가뿐 아니라 화학처리, DNA 기술,왁친 전문가등도 필요함

다. 모니터 및 확인활동을 위한 각종 장비, 기자재등 제공희망

라. 상기 사항에 관하여 92.6.10 까지 UNSCOM 에 통보 요망

2. 상기 서한 금파편 송부함

(대사 유종하-국장)

예고:92.12.31 일반

검 토 필 (1992. 6. 30.)

국기국 중아국 안기부

PAGE 1

92.05.22 05:32

외신 2과 통제관 FM

0056

| 관리 번호 | 92 -606 |
|---|---|

원 본

# 외 무 부

종 별 :

번 호 : UNW-1501 일 시 : 92 0522 1830

수 신 : 장 관(연일,중동이,기정)

발 신 : 주 유엔 대사

제 목 : 이락 무기폐기

연:UNW-1473, 주국련 2031-113

1. 연호 이락 무기폐기에 관한 연호 안보리 특별위(UNSCOM)의 서한과 관련,당관 이수혁 참사관이 UNSCOM 을 접촉 파악한바에 의하면 지금까지 유엔은 이락이 현재 보유하고 있는 화생무기와 미사일 폐기에 중점을 두고 활동하여 왔으나 금후로는 이와 병행하여 화생무기와 미사일의 생산가능성도 방지하는 활동을 전개할 계획이라함

2. 특히 UNSCOM 은 이락이 민수용으로 쓰이는 화학원료나 화학제품 또는 생산 시설을 무기생산으로 전환할 가능성에 대비하여 이러한 시설을 파악할 필요에서 한국등 이락에 수출한 실적이 있는 국가들에게 관련 정보제공을 요청하였다함

3.MOITORING 요원과 관련, UNSCOM 은 각국으로 부터 연호 서한에서 언급된 관계 분야 전문가 명단을 제출받으면 필요시 해당전문가를 파견할 예정이므로 한국측이 관계분야 전문가를 천거해 주기를 희망하였음,

4. 동 접촉기회에 UNSCOM 측은 MANTHANNA 화학무기 폐기 작업단에 아국인2 명 파견추천에 사의를 표하고 양인을 요원으로 선발, 6 월하순경 파견키로내부 결재중이라 하면서 구체적 사항은 수일내 통보해 주겠다함

(대사 유종하-국장)

예고:92.12.31 일반 문서 의거 일반문서로 재분류됨

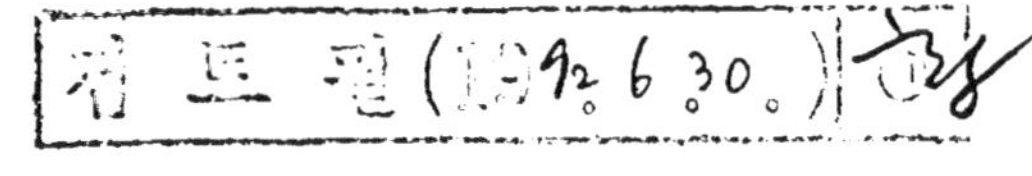

국기국 1차보 중아국 안기부

PAGE 1 92.05.23 07:46

외신 2과 통제관 BZ

0057

분류번호 92/404

# 주 국 련 대 표 부

주국련 2031-113 　　　　　　　　　　　　　　　　　　1992. 5. 22.

수신 장 관

참조 국제기구국장, 중동아프리카국장

제목 이락무기 폐기 감시 협조 요청

연 : UNW - 1473

연호 UNSCOM 위원장의 서한을 별첨 송부합니다.

첨 부 : 서한 1부. 끝.

예고 : 92.12.31 일반.

| 선 람 | | | 결재(공람) | | |
|---|---|---|---|---|---|
| 접수일시 | 1992. 5 26 | 번호 | 1865 | | |
| 처리과 | 361 | | | | |

서한 내용 파악

주 국 련 대 사

0058

UNITED NATIONS  NATIONS UNIES

POSTAL ADDRESS—ADRESSE POSTALE: UNITED NATIONS, N.Y. 10017
CABLE ADDRESS—ADRESSE TELEGRAPHIQUE: UNATIONS NEWYORK

18 May 1992

REFERENCE:

Excellency,

The Special Commission is continuing to plan the operations required to implement the Plan approved by the Security Council in its resolution 715 (1991) for the ongoing monitoring and verification of Iraq's compliance with its obligations not to reacquire any chemical or biological weapons or any ballistic missiles with a range greater than 150 kilometres. These activities will, inter alia, require the compilation of a register of the sites and items in Iraq to be monitored by the Special Commission under the Plan and the conduct of on-site inspections and aerial surveys to verify that no sites or items are used by Iraq for purposes prohibited by resolution 687 (1991). Although obliged by the Plan to do so, Iraq has so far failed to provide to the Special Commission declarations on its relevant dual-purpose capabilities.

The Plan, as approved by the Security Council, covers not only military but also civilian sites, facilities, material, other items or activities that could be involved in contravention of Iraq's obligations under resolution 687 (1991). The Special Commission would like to request the assistance of the Government of the Republic of Korea it in its preparations for carrying out the Plan under resolution 715 (1991) especially the expeditious implementation of monitoring and verification activities under the Plan (a copy of the Plan (S/22871/Rev.1) is attached).

It would be helpful if your Government could furnish the Special Commission with any information available to it, from whatever sources, on the sites, facilities, items and activities in Iraq that fall, or could reasonably expected to fall, under

/...

His Excellency
Mr. Chong-Ha YOO
Ambassador Extraordinary and Plenipotentiary
Permanent Representative of the Republic of
Korea to the United Nations
New York, New York

0059

the terms specified in the Plan. In particular, information on civilian facilities or items having actual or potential capabilities that could be used for purposes prohibited by resolution 687 (1991) would be very welcome. Such information would assist the Special Commission in the analysis of data to be received from Iraq pursuant to the Plan and in planning inspection activities in Iraq, including initial inspections to verify the accuracy of Iraq's declarations and designation of any additional sites by the Special Commission for further inspections.

The Special Commission also invites the Government of the Republic of Korea to designate appropriate experts whose services as inspectors in the implementation of resolution 715 may be available to the Special Commission upon request, and to notify the Commission of their field of expertise and any conditions attached to their services being made available. Based on the designations from the Governments, the Special Commission intends to compose a list of experts available in different fields. The experts required for a specific inspection will be selected from this list. In nominating the designated and selected experts to a specific inspection team, the procedures and arrangements including financial rules established for the current UNSCOM inspection teams will be followed.

The monitoring and verification activities, as envisaged by the Plan under resolution 715, will require specific technical, industrial and scientific expertise. In the chemical and biological areas this includes not only military experts but also process chemists, chemical engineers, plant chemists, experts in sampling and analysis, chemical accountants, fermentation experts, virologists, immunologists, experts in biotechnology and recombinant DNA technology, vaccine production etc...

In the ballistic missile area, the necessary expertise encompasses the different aspects of production and assembly of missiles and their components listed in Annex IV of the Plan, as well as research, development, modification and testing activities related to missiles. Knowledge of Iraq's holdings of missiles and rockets, the procedures for their repair, maintenance, storage, testing and deployment would also be required.

/...

We would welcome any further offers of assistance that your Government may wish to provide to the Special Commission. This may include monitoring technologies, equipment and instruments and sensors, sample analysis support including on-site and out of country, or other technical support for monitoring and verification activities.

It would be appreciated if your Government could give urgent attention to the matter and communicate the response to the Special Commission before 10 June 1992. Any subsequent updates of the information on relevant facilities in Iraq and on offers of expertise, equipment and technical support that may be made available to the Commission by your Government would also be helpful.

Accept, Excellency, the assurances of my highest consideration.

Rolf Ekéus
Executive Chairman
Office of the Special Commission

0061

UNITED NATIONS

S

# Security Council

Distr.
GENERAL

S/22871/Rev.1
2 October 1991

ORIGINAL: ENGLISH

## Plan for future ongoing monitoring and verification of Iraq's compliance with relevant parts of section C of Security Council resolution 687 (1991)

Report of the Secretary-General

### I. GENERAL

#### A. Introduction

1. The present report is submitted in pursuance of Security Council resolution 687 (1991). In paragraph 10 of section C of that resolution, the Security Council requested the Secretary-General, in consultation with the Special Commission, to develop and submit for approval a plan for the ongoing monitoring and verification of Iraq's compliance with its obligations under that paragraph. The Plan is contained in section II of the present report.

2. As outlined in my report to the Security Council of 17 May 1991 (S/22614), the provisions of section C of resolution 687 (1991) lend themselves to a three-stage implementation procedure: gathering and assessment of information; disposal of weapons and facilities and all other items specified in paragraphs 8 and 12 of resolution 687 (1991); and ongoing monitoring and verification of Iraq's compliance. The first two stages are currently being implemented and will continue until their objectives are fully achieved.

3. The Plan submitted in the present report addresses the third stage, i.e. ongoing monitoring and verification of Iraq's compliance with its unconditional obligation not to use, retain, possess, develop, construct or otherwise acquire any weapons or related items prohibited under paragraphs 8 and 9 of resolution 687 (1991). Thus, monitoring and verification will need to cover not only military but also civilian sites, facilities, material and other items that could be used or activities that could be involved in contravention of Iraq's obligations under resolution 687 (1991). The Plan incorporates the additional obligations of Iraq under Security Council resolution 707 (1991) and the corresponding monitoring and verification activities.

91-32425 2644f (E)

/...

0062

4. The Plan should enter into force directly upon its approval by the Security Council, which means that the early stages of its implementation and the later stages of the disposal of existing prohibited weapons, facilities and related items would take place simultaneously. This would, at an early stage, prevent Iraq from developing new capabilities regarding the relevant weapons categories, thus already closing a potential loophole during the first stages of the implementation of section C of resolution 687 (1991). Carefully managed use of available resources would make it possible to carry out the dual tasks in parallel, to great effect. With the gradual completion of the disposal of Iraq's present weapons capabilities, resources can gradually be transferred and streamlined without therefore, at any stage, compromising the efficiency of the verification of Iraq's compliance with its obligations under resolutions 687 (1991) and 707 (1991). In paragraph 14 of its resolution 687 (1991) the Security Council noted that the actions to be taken by Iraq in paragraphs 8, 9, 10, 11, 12 and 13 of that resolution "represent steps towards the goal of establishing in the Middle East a zone free from weapons of mass destruction and all missiles for their delivery and the objective of a global ban on chemical weapons". The implementation of the Plan, developed pursuant to paragraph 10 of resolution 687 (1991), will contribute to an environment conducive to achieving the above-mentioned goal and objective.

## B. Institutional and organizational aspects

5. Bearing in mind that resolutions 687 (1991) and 707 (1991) were adopted by the Security Council acting under Chapter VII of the Charter of the United Nations, it is assumed that the task of carrying out the monitoring and verification provided for under the Plan should be entrusted to an executive body under the authority of the Security Council. This is particularly important should any situation arise of non-compliance by Iraq with its obligations under section C of resolution 687 (1991) and under resolution 707 (1991).

6. The intrinsic interrelationship between paragraphs 8, 9 and 10 of resolution 687 (1991) requires that this body make direct use of the expertise, the information gathered and assessed and the experience gained by the Special Commission established as a subsidiary organ of the Security Council pursuant to paragraph 9 of resolution 687 (1991).

7. In view of these considerations, it would appear most practical and efficient that a compliance unit be organized under the Special Commission in order to carry out the monitoring and verification tasks provided for under the Plan. The present arrangements for staffing would continue on a revised scale, with appropriate support from the Department for Disarmament Affairs. The financing of the Plan would have to be determined by the competent United Nations organs, possibly in the same way as the arrangements agreed upon for the present phase of the Special Commission's work.

0063 /...

8. The operational requirements will be similar to those now in place for the Special Commission. These include a staff at the United Nations Headquarters in New York to assist the Executive Chairman of the Special Commission, compile and analyse information, schedule, plan and organize inspections and aerial overflights, prepare other field operations and provide general administrative support. A staff will be needed in the region to provide logistic, administrative and other support for field operations in Iraq.

### C. Cooperation with the Security Council Committee established by resolution 661 (1990) concerning the situation between Iraq and Kuwait

9. Through resolution 661 (1990) and subsequent related resolutions, including resolution 687 (1991), inter alia, its section F, a comprehensive set of sanctions was established to be implemented by all States against Iraq. The prohibition of the acquisition by Iraq of any weapons and related items specified in paragraphs 8 and 12 of resolution 687 (1991) and of the sale or supply to Iraq by other States of these items is of unlimited duration. However, it cannot be excluded that the Security Council, at a future date, may wish to review the present sanctions regarding items with dual use, i.e. items that could be used for prohibited as well as non-prohibited purposes. In order to ensure that such items are not used for prohibited purposes, the Plan submitted in the present report includes specific provisions for the monitoring and verification, from within Iraq, of any eventual import by Iraq of relevant items with dual use.

10. The efficacy of these provisions would be enhanced if they were complemented by transparency and timely information as regards any future sale or supply by other States to Iraq of relevant items with dual use. Such a comprehensive approach would call for the development of a mechanism that:

(a) Upholds the prohibition on the sale and supply to Iraq by other States of any weapons or related items prohibited under section C of resolution 687 (1991);

(b) Provides for timely information about any sale or supply to Iraq by other States of items that could be used not only for permitted purposes but also for purposes prohibited under resolution 687 (1991).

11. The Plan submitted in the present report contains in its annexes lists of items relevant to the monitoring and verification, from within Iraq, of prohibited items as well as of items with dual use. These should be taken into account in the development of a mechanism related to the sale or supply of items to Iraq by other countries.

12. Such a mechanism should be developed with the cooperation of the Special Commission, the Director General of the International Atomic Energy Agency and the Committee established by resolution 661 (1990) at the earliest possible date, and not later than before the lifting of sanctions covering relevant items.

0064 /...

## II. THE PLAN

### A. Scope

13. In accepting unconditionally Security Council resolution 687 (1991), Iraq has undertaken not to use, retain, possess, develop, construct or otherwise acquire:

(a) Any chemical or biological weapons or any stocks of agents or any related subsystems or components or any research, development, support or manufacturing facilities;

(b) Any ballistic missiles with a range greater than 150 kilometres or any related major parts, including launchers, or any repair or production facilities.

14. In order to ensure Iraq's compliance with these undertakings, the Special Commission, pursuant to resolutions 687 (1991) and 707 (1991), shall, through inspections and through aerial overflights, as well as through the provision of information by Iraq, monitor and verify that activities, sites, facilities, material and other items, both military and civilian, are not used by Iraq in contravention of its obligations under resolutions 687 (1991) and 707 (1991).

15. To this end, the provisions set forth in the Plan and its annexes, which constitute an integral part of the Plan, shall apply.

### B. General provisions

#### 1. Information

16. Iraq shall:

(a) Provide to the Special Commission, on a regular basis, full, complete, correct and timely information on activities, sites, facilities, material and other items, both military and civilian, that might be used for purposes prohibited under paragraph 10 of resolution 687 (1991);

(b) Provide to the Special Commission full, complete, correct and timely information on any additional activities, sites, facilities, material or other items that the Commission may designate for provision of information on a regular basis;

(c) Provide to the Special Commission, fully, completely, and promptly, any additional information or clarification that the Commission may request and respond fully, completely and promptly to any questions or requests from the Special Commission.

Further provisions related to the submission of information are set forth in sections C, D and E and in annexes II, III and IV of the Plan.

/...

0065

## 2. Inspections and aerial overflights

17. The Special Commission shall have the right:

(a) To designate for inspection any site, facility, activity, material or other item in Iraq;

(b) To carry out inspections, at any time and without hindrance, of any site, facility, activity, material or other item in Iraq;

(c) To conduct unannounced inspections and inspections at short notice;

(d) To inspect any number of declared or designated sites or facilities simultaneously or sequentially;

(e) To designate for aerial overflight any area, location, site or facility in Iraq;

(f) To conduct, at any time and without hindrance, both fixed-wing and rotary-wing flights throughout Iraq for all relevant purposes, including inspection, surveillance, aerial overflights (surveys), transportation and logistics without interference of any kind and upon such terms and conditions as may be determined by the Special Commission;

(g) To make full use of its own aircraft with appropriate sensors as necessary and such airfields in Iraq as the Special Commission may determine are most appropriate for its work;

(h) To consider and decide upon requests by Iraq to move or destroy any material, equipment or item relating to its nuclear, chemical or biological weapons or ballistic missile programmes, or material, equipment or any item relating to its other nuclear activities.

18. Iraq shall:

(a) Accept unconditionally the inspection of any site, facility, activity, material or other item declared by Iraq or designated by the Special Commission;

(b) Accept unconditionally aerial overflight of any area, location, site or facility designated by the Special Commission;

(c) Provide immediate and unimpeded access to any site, facility, activity, material or other item to be inspected;

(d) Accept unconditionally and cooperate with the Special Commission in conducting fixed-wing and rotary-wing flights throughout Iraq for all relevant purposes, including inspection, surveillance, aerial overflights (surveys), transportation and logistics upon the terms and conditions determined by the Special Commission;

(e) Accept unconditionally the Special Commission's determinations regarding use of the Commission's aircraft with appropriate sensors as necessary and airfields in Iraq for such aircraft;

(f) Not obstruct aerial overflights or take concealment measures at any area, location, site or facility designated by the Special Commission for inspection or overflight;

(g) Accept unconditionally the inspectors and all other personnel designated by the Special Commission and ensure the complete implementation of the privileges, immunities and facilities of the personnel of the Special Commission and their complete safety and freedom of movement;

(h) Cooperate fully with the Special Commission and facilitate its inspections, overflights and other activities under the Plan;

(i) Accept unconditionally the rights of the Special Commission under the Plan and not take any action to interfere with, impede, or obstruct the exercise by the Special Commission of its functions and rights under Security Council resolutions 687 (1991), 707 (1991) and the Plan;

(j) Designate its Inspection Representative for each inspection to accompany the inspection team in Iraq;

(k) Invite and accept unconditionally the decision of the Special Commission on any requests by Iraq to move or destroy any material, equipment or item relating to its nuclear, chemical or biological weapons or ballistic missile programmes, or material, equipment or any item relating to its other nuclear activities.

19. Further provisions on inspections, aerial overflights, security, privileges and immunities and related provisions are set forth in annex I.

### 3. National implementation measures

20. Iraq shall adopt the necessary measures to implement its obligations under section C of resolution 687 (1991), resolution 707 (1991) and the Plan, in particular:

(a) To prohibit all natural and legal persons under Iraq's jurisdiction or control from undertaking anywhere any activity that is prohibited for Iraq by resolutions 687 (1991), 707 (1991), by other related Security Council resolutions or by the Plan;

(b) To enact penal legislation which, in conformity with international law, shall extend to the activities referred to under subparagraph (a) above undertaken anywhere by any natural or legal persons under Iraq's jurisdiction or control.

/...

0067

21. Iraq shall inform the Special Commission of legislative and administrative measures taken to implement resolutions 687 (1991), 707 (1991), other relevant Security Council resolutions and the Plan, not later than 30 days after the approval by the Security Council of the Plan and thereafter as determined by the Special Commission.

## 4. Non-compliance

22. Should the Special Commission discover any item, including any documentation, that Iraq, under resolution 687 (1991), is obliged to destroy or to yield to the Special Commission for destruction, removal or rendering harmless, the Special Commission shall have the right to take it into custody and shall provide for its disposal, as appropriate. Iraq shall retain no ownership interest in items to be destroyed, removed or rendered harmless pursuant to resolution 687 (1991) and the Plan.

23. Should the Special Commission discover any activity taking place in contravention of resolutions 687 (1991), 707 (1991) or of the Plan, it shall have the right to call upon Iraq to halt the activity and to prevent its recurrence. The Special Commission shall also have the right to take any prohibited item involved, including any documentation, into custody and shall provide for its disposal, as appropriate.

24. Findings by the Special Commission that indicate that Iraq is not in compliance with its obligations under resolutions 687 (1991) and 707 (1991) or the Plan shall be brought to the attention of the Security Council.

## 5. Reports

25. The Special Commission shall, through the Secretary-General, report to the Security Council every six months on the implementation of the Plan and at any other time the Security Council may request.

## 6. Revisions

26. The Plan may only be revised by the Security Council. The Special Commission may, however, after informing the Security Council, update and revise the annexes in the light of information and experience gained in the course of the implementation of resolutions 687 (1991) and 707 (1991) and of the Plan. The Special Commission shall inform Iraq of any such change.

## 7. Entry into force and duration

27. The Plan shall enter into force immediately upon its approval by the Security Council. The duration of the Plan shall be determined by the Security Council.

C. Provisions related to chemical items

28. Chemicals, equipment and facilities set forth herein and in annex II could be used for purposes related to chemical weapons. They shall therefore be subject to monitoring and verification in accordance with the following additional provisions in order to ensure that Iraq does not use, develop, produce or otherwise acquire chemical weapons or related items prohibited under resolution 687 (1991).

29. Chemicals that could be used for the development, production or acquisition of chemical weapons but which also have significant uses for purposes not prohibited by resolution 687 (1991) are set forth in list A in annex II. These chemicals may be used, developed, produced, stored or acquired solely for purposes not prohibited by resolution 687 (1991), subject to the provisions under paragraphs 30 and 31 below, and annex II.

30. Iraq shall, not later than 30 days after the adoption of the Plan by the Security Council, and on a regular basis thereafter, provide to the Special Commission information in accordance with annex II regarding:

(a) The total national quantity of the production, processing or consumption of any chemical specified in list A of annex II and of the import and export of any of these chemicals specifying the supplier or recipient countries involved;

(b) Any site or facility that is involved in production, processing, consumption, storage, import or export of one tonne or more per year of any chemical specified in list A of annex II or that at any time has been involved in activities with any of these chemicals for chemical weapons purposes;

(c) Any site or facility that is involved in production or processing of organophosphorus chemicals or is involved in production of organic chemicals by chlorination;

(d) Any site or facility where production, processing, consumption, storage, import or export of one tonne or more per year of any chemical specified in list A of annex II, or where production or processing of organophosphorus chemicals or where production of organic chemicals by chlorination is planned;

(e) Any import or any other acquisition of equipment or technologies intended for production and processing of any chemical specified in list A of annex II, of any organophosphorus chemical or for production of organic chemicals by chlorination.

31. Should Iraq plan any production, processing, consumption, storage, import or export not notified under paragraph 30 (d) above, it may begin such an activity only after providing to the Special Commission a special notification in accordance with annex II.

0069 /...

32. Chemicals that have little or no use except as chemical warfare agents or for the development, production or acquisition of chemical weapons or which have been used by Iraq as essential precursors for chemical weapons are set forth in list B of annex II. Iraq shall not retain, use, transfer, develop, produce, store, import or otherwise acquire these chemicals. Should Iraq require any chemical specified in list B of annex II, it shall submit a request to the Special Commission specifying precisely the chemical and the quantities required, the site or facility where it is to be used and the purpose of its use. The Special Commission will examine and decide on the request and establish the special arrangements it considers consistent with resolution 687 (1991).

33. Further provisions related to chemical items are set forth in annex II.

## D. Provisions related to biological items

34. Micro-organisms and toxins, equipment and facilities set forth herein and in annex III could be used for purposes related to biological and toxin weapons affecting humans, animals or plants. They shall therefore be subject to monitoring and verification in accordance with the following additional provisions in order to ensure that Iraq does not use, develop, produce or otherwise acquire biological and toxin weapons or related items prohibited under resolution 687 (1991).

35. Iraq shall, not later than 30 days after the adoption of the Plan by the Security Council, and on a regular basis thereafter, provide to the Special Commission information in accordance with annex III regarding:

(a) Any site or facility at which work with toxins or with micro-organisms meeting the criteria for risk groups IV, III or II according to the classification in the 1983 World Health Organization (WHO) Laboratory Biosafety Manual is carried out, or any site or facility at which work with genetic material coding for toxins or genes derived from the aforementioned micro-organisms is carried out;

(b) Any site or facility having a laboratory (unit) meeting the criteria for a "maximum containment laboratory" or "containment laboratory" as specified in the 1983 WHO Laboratory Biosafety Manual, such as those designated as biosafety level 4 (BL4) or P4, biosafety level 3 (BL3) or P3 or equivalent standards and any site or facility being constructed or modified so as to possess such containment capabilities;

(c) Any site or facility at which fermentation or other means for the production of micro-organisms or toxins using vessels larger than 10 litres individually or 40 litres in the aggregate is carried out;

(d) Any site or facility for the bulk storage of toxins or of micro-organisms meeting the criteria for risk groups IV, III or II;

0070 /...

(e) Any site or facility for the production of vaccines;

(f) Any research, development, testing or other support or manufacturing facility for equipment and other items specified in paragraph 1 of annex III;

(g) Any imports, other acquisition or exports of micro-organisms meeting the criteria for risk groups IV, III and II, toxins and vaccines, as well as related equipment and facilities, specifying the supplier or recipient countries involved.

36. Iraq shall, not later than 30 days after the adoption of the Plan by the Security Council, and on a regular basis thereafter, provide to the Special Commission:

(a) A list of all documents of a scientific and technical nature published or prepared by any site or facility engaged in work relating to toxins or micro-organisms meeting the criteria for risk groups IV, III and II, including those of a theoretical nature. Full copies of such documents shall be made available by Iraq to the Special Commission upon request. Documents of a purely diagnostic nature relating to risk group II micro-organisms are excepted;

(b) A description of all work on toxins or micro-organisms meeting the criteria for risk groups IV, III or II as well as of all work being conducted on the dissemination of micro-organisms or toxins into the environment or on processes that would lead to such dissemination, specifying the site or facility involved.

37. Iraq shall provide to the Special Commission in accordance with annex III information on all cases of infectious diseases affecting humans, animals or plants, that deviate, or seem to deviate, from the normal pattern or are caused by any micro-organism meeting the criteria for risk groups IV and III and on all cases of similar occurrences caused by toxins.

38. Iraq shall not:

(a) Import items referred to in paragraph 35 (g) above without giving prior notice to the Special Commission in accordance with annex III. As an exception, the emergency import of vaccines may take place with simultaneous notification to the Special Commission;

(b) Conduct any activities in the field of micro-organisms and toxins except by civilian personnel not in the employ of any military organization. Such activities shall be conducted openly; no classified or secret programmes or activities shall be permitted. The sites or facilities engaged in such activities shall not be under the control of, or owned by, any military organization. Should any military organization need to be involved in such activities for prophylactic or therapeutic purposes, Iraq shall submit a request to the Special Commission specifying precisely the toxins, micro-organisms and the quantities required, the site or facility where they

0071 /...

are to be used and the purpose of their use. The Special Commission will examine and decide on the request and establish the special arrangements it considers consistent with resolution 687 (1991);

(c) Conduct activities on diseases other than those indigenous to or immediately expected to break out in its environment;

(d) Conduct any breeding of vectors of human, animal or plant diseases. Should Iraq need to conduct any such activity, Iraq shall submit a request to the Special Commission specifying precisely its requirements, the vectors to be bred, the site or facility where the activity is to take place and the purpose of the activity. The Special Commission will examine and decide on the request and establish the special arrangements it considers consistent with resolution 687 (1991);

(e) Possess at any one time more than one facility having a laboratory (unit) meeting the criteria for a "maximum containment laboratory" as specified in the 1983 WHO Laboratory Biosafety Manual, such as those designated as biosafety level 4 (BL4) or P4 or equivalent standard. Iraq shall not possess at any one time more than two facilities having a laboratory (unit) meeting the criteria for a "containment laboratory", such as those designated as BL3 or P3 or equivalent standard. Should Iraq require any additional such facilities, Iraq shall submit a request to the Special Commission specifying the precise requirement. The Special Commission will examine and decide on the request and establish the special arrangements it considers consistent with resolution 687 (1991).

39. Further provisions related to biological items are set forth in annex III.

## E. Provisions related to missiles

40. Facilities, equipment, other items and technologies set forth herein and in annex IV could be used for the development, construction, modification or acquisition of ballistic missiles with a range greater than 150 kilometres. They shall therefore be subject to monitoring and verification in accordance with the following additional provisions in order to ensure that Iraq does not use, develop, construct or acquire any ballistic missiles with a range greater than 150 kilometres or related items prohibited under resolution 687 (1991).

41. The prohibition applies to any ballistic missiles or missile delivery systems capable of such a range regardless of payload and to any related major parts, which include missile/rocket stages, re-entry vehicles, solid- or liquid-fuel motors, guidance sets, thrust vector controls, warheads and fusing systems, launchers capable of launching ballistic missiles with a range greater than 150 kilometres and related principal launch equipment, missile transporters and other ground support equipment for such missiles. The prohibition also applies to modification of any missile or any missile delivery system to a ballistic missile with a range greater than 150 kilometres. The prohibition also applies to launch technologies such as tube- or gun-type launchers, which enable such ranges to be achieved.

0072 /...

42. Iraq shall not construct, otherwise acquire or operate sites or facilities for the use, development, production, training or other support of ballistic missiles capable of a range greater than 150 kilometres, including sites or facilities for research, development, modification, manufacture, assembly, testing, storage, repair, training, flight simulating and operational use of such missiles, nor acquire related major parts specified in paragraph 41 and the items listed in paragraph 1 of annex IV for such missiles.

43. Iraq shall, not later than 30 days after the adoption of the Plan by the Security Council, and on a regular basis thereafter, provide to the Special Commission the following:

(a) A list of all its missiles designed for use, or capable of being modified for use, in a surface-to-surface role with a range greater than 50 kilometres, specifying their name and type, type of propulsion, number of stages and/or boosters, guidance systems, payload, warhead and re-entry vehicle types, launcher types, airframe and warhead transporter, ground support equipment and the sites or facilities where these missiles, items or equipment are located;

(b) Information on any project and on any site or facility for such missiles, including sites or facilities for production, assembly, repair and maintenance, storage and operational bases, specifying their locations;

(c) Information on any project and on any site or facility for missile research, development, modification or testing, specifying its locations;

(d) Information on the development, production, export, import or other acquisition, training or other services related to the items, equipment and technologies listed in annex IV, specifying sites or facilities where such items, equipment and technologies are located, the purposes and the projects for which they are being used and the supplier or recipient countries involved.

44. Iraq shall notify the Special Commission in accordance with annex IV of the developmental or test launch of any missile, specifying where and when the launch is to take place.

45. Further provisions related to missiles are set forth in annex IV.

0073

/...

## Annex I

## Detailed provisions related to inspections, aerial overflights, security, privileges and immunities

1. In addition to the basic rights and obligations set forth in paragraphs 17 and 18 of the Plan, the provisions set out in this annex shall apply.

### Scope

2. The Special Commission shall have the right:

(a) To secure any site to be inspected and prevent any material or other item from being taken to or from the site until the inspection is concluded;

(b) To stop and inspect vehicles, ships, aircraft or any other means of transportation within Iraq, any material or other item in movement and to restrict and/or stop movement of material or other items;

(c) To inspect imports or exports of material and other items upon arrival or departure;

(d) To establish special modes of monitoring and verification, including prolonged or continuous presence of inspectors, use of instruments and other arrangements to facilitate monitoring and verification;

(e) To secure full and free access at any time to all sites, facilities, areas, locations, activities, material and other items, including documentation, all persons and all information which, in its judgement, may be necessary for its monitoring and verification activities.

### Notification

3. The Special Commission shall, at a time it considers appropriate, notify Iraq of:

(a) The site, facility, activity, material or other item to be inspected;

(b) The name of the head of the inspection team (the Chief Inspector) and the estimated number of personnel who will take part in the inspection;

(c) The estimated time of departure and arrival of any flight from, to or within Iraq, and other appropriate details, by any aircraft used by the Special Commission.

4. Iraq shall, upon receipt of the name of the Chief Inspector for an inspection, immediately inform the Special Commission of the name of the individual who will be the Iraqi Inspection Representative for the inspection.

## Conduct of inspections or aerial overflights

5. The Special Commission shall have the right:

(a) To request, receive, examine, copy and remove any record, data, information or documentation and to verify inventories;

(b) To examine, retain, move or photograph, including by videotaping, any activity or item;

(c) To conduct interviews with any personnel at a site or facility under inspection, or with any Iraqi official;

(d) To install containment, surveillance and other equipment and devices and to construct facilities for inspection, observation, testing, verification or monitoring activities;

(e) To take samples of any kind and perform on-site analyses of the samples using its own equipment;

(f) To remove and transfer samples outside Iraq for analyses off-site at laboratories of its choice;

(g) To mark, tag or otherwise identify any material or other item;

(h) To use its own instrumentation to collect data during inspections and aerial overflights, including photographic, video, infrared and radar data.

6. Iraq shall:

(a) Provide clarification or explanation of any ambiguity that might arise during an inspection;

(b) Perform, upon request by the Special Commission, analyses of samples in the presence of inspectors, including on-site;

(c) Perform, upon request by the Special Commission, any additional task.

0075 /...

Travel, transport and communications

7. The Special Commission shall have the right:

(a) To unrestricted freedom of entry into and exit from Iraq, without delay or hindrance, for all its personnel, property, supplies, equipment, spare parts, means of transport, material and other items. No visa shall be required of such personnel travelling on United Nations laissez-passer or certificate and possessing an inspection assignment document; Iraq shall ensure prompt issuance of visas of entry and exit for such personnel as may not possess a United Nations laissez-passer or certificate;

(b) To unrestricted freedom of movement within Iraq, without advance notice, delay or hindrance, for all its personnel, property, supplies, equipment, spare parts, means of transport, material and other items;

(c) To fly the United Nations flag on its premises and means of transport;

(d) To use its own means of transport, including fixed- and rotary-wing aircraft, throughout Iraq for all relevant purposes, including inspection, surveillance, aerial overflights (surveys), transportation and logistics;

(e) To use airfields in Iraq for the purposes determined by the Special Commission including landing, take-off, basing, maintenance, refuelling and other support;

(f) To communicate from any place within Iraq, and without censorship or other hindrance, by radio, satellite or other forms of communication, and to connect with the United Nations by its radio and satellite network, as well as by telefax, telephone, telegraph and other means;

(g) To use codes and receive papers, correspondence and other items by courier or sealed bags;

(h) To unrestricted freedom to remove from Iraq, without delay or hindrance, any material or other item, including any documentation, acquired during inspection or other monitoring and verification activities.

8. Iraq shall:

(a) Permit, without delay or hindrance, the Special Commission's personnel, property, supplies, equipment, spare parts, means of transport, material and other items to move within Iraq, without advance notice, as well as to enter or leave Iraq, promptly issuing entry and exit visas if required on national passports and accepting United Nations laissez-passers or United Nations certificates as valid travel documents without requiring visas;

(b) Accept United Nations registration of means of transport on land, sea and in the air and United Nations licensing of the operators thereof;

0076 /...

(c) Provide priority clearance, as well as the basing and all necessary facilities as determined by the Special Commission for any fixed- or rotary-wing aircraft used by the Commission;

(d) Provide, upon the request of the Special Commission, the means of transport, maps or other information needed;

(e) Take every necessary measure to ensure that the inspection team arrives at the site or facility to be inspected by the time notified by the Special Commission;

(f) Provide, upon the request of the Special Commission, appropriate means of communication;

(g) Provide, upon request of the Special Commission, appropriate escort and/or support personnel;

(h) Provide, upon request of the Special Commission, medical, logistical and/or technical support;

(i) Not interfere with or censor any communication to or from the Special Commission or its personnel;

(j) Permit, without delay or hindrance, the Special Commission to remove from Iraq any material or other item, including any documentation, acquired by the Commission during inspection or other monitoring and verification activities.

## Security, privileges and immunities

9. The Special Commission shall have the right to make its own arrangements to ensure the safety and security of its personnel and property and to take custody of any material or other item, including documentation.

10. Iraq shall ensure the safety and security of the personnel and property of the Special Commission and shall provide the arrangements to this end when so requested by the Special Commission.

11. In addition and without prejudice to the foregoing provisions, the Special Commission and any agency of the United Nations system participating in the carrying out of the Plan, its property, funds, assets and personnel shall enjoy the facilities, privileges and immunities provided for in the applicable convention or agreement, namely the Convention on the Privileges and Immunities of the United Nations, the Agreement on the Privileges and Immunities of the International Atomic Energy Agency (IAEA) and the Convention on the Privileges and Immunities of the Specialized Agencies.

12. Iraq shall extend to:

(a) The officers and other members of the Special Commission the privileges and immunities, exemptions and facilities that are enjoyed by diplomatic envoys in accordance with international law;

(b) The officials of the United Nations, of IAEA and any of the specialized agencies of the United Nations, performing functions in connection with the implementation of the Plan, the privileges and immunities applicable to them under articles V and VII of the Convention on the Privileges and Immunities of the United Nations; or articles VI and IX of the Agreement on the Privileges and Immunities of the International Atomic Energy Agency; or articles VI and VIII of the Convention on the Privileges and Immunities of the Specialized Agencies;

(c) The technical experts and other specialists performing functions in connection with the implementation of the Plan the privileges and immunities accorded to experts performing missions for the United Nations, for IAEA or for the specialized agencies of the United Nations under article VI of the Convention on the Privileges and Immunities of the United Nations, article VII of the Agreement on the Privileges and Immunities of the International Atomic Energy Agency, and the relevant annexes to the Convention on the Privileges and Immunities of the Specialized Agencies, respectively.

## Other provisions

13. Iraq shall designate the Iraqi authority responsible for liaison with the Special Commission and shall inform the Special Commission of the name or names of the liaison officers within that authority who shall have the full power and shall take the necessary measures to secure for the Special Commission the effective implementation of the Commission's rights laid down in the Plan.

14. The official points of contact between Iraq and the Special Commission during the course of an inspection shall be the Chief Inspector designated by the Special Commission and the Inspection Representative designated by Iraq.

15. Iraq shall provide, at no cost to the Special Commission, in agreement with the Special Commission, all such premises as may be necessary for the accommodation and fulfilment of the functions of the Special Commission in Iraq. All such premises shall be inviolable and subject to the exclusive control and authority of the Special Commission.

16. All information provided by, and communications from, Iraq to the Special Commission under the Plan shall include the corresponding text in English.

17. For the purposes of the performance of the functions of the Special Commission in implementation of the Plan, the rights, facilities, privileges and immunities conferred in the Plan where necessary supplement and elaborate

upon the rights, facilities, privileges and immunities provided for in the exchange of notes between the Secretary-General of the United Nations and the Minister for Foreign Affairs of Iraq, which entered into force on 14 May 1991, regarding the status, privileges and immunities of the Special Commission as originally established pursuant to paragraph 9 of Security Council resolution 687 (1991).

/...

## Annex II

## Provisions related to chemical items

1. The following list contains chemicals that could be used for the development, production or acquisition of chemical weapons, but which also have significant uses for purposes not prohibited by resolution 687 (1991):

| List A | | Chemical Abstracts Service (CAS) registry No. |
|---|---|---|
| 1. | Chemicals, except for those chemicals specified in list B of this annex, containing a phosphorus atom to which is bonded one methyl, ethyl or propyl (normal or iso) group but not further carbon atoms | |
| 2. | Dialkyl (Me, Et, n-Pr or i-Pr) N,N-dialkyl (Me, Et, n-Pr or i-Pr)-phosphoramidates | |
| 3. | Arsenic trichloride | (7784-34-1) |
| 4. | 2,2-Diphenyl-2-hydroxyacetic acid | (76-93-7) |
| 5. | Quinuclidin-3-ol | (1619-34-7) |
| 6. | N,N-Dialkyl (Me, Et, n-Pr or i-Pr) aminoethyl-2-chloride and corresponding protonated salts | |
| 7. | N,N-Dialkyl (Me, Et, n-Pr or i-Pr) aminoethane-2-ol and corresponding protonated salts | |
| 8. | N,N-Dialkyl (Me, Et, n-Pr or i-Pr) aminoethane-2-thiol and corresponding protonated salts | |
| 9. | Amiton: O,O-Diethyl S-(2-(diethylamino)ethyl) phosphorothiolate and corresponding alkylated and protonated salts | (78-53-5) |
| 10. | PFIB: 1,1,3,3,3-pentafluoro-2-(trifluoromethyl)-1-propene | (382-21-8) |
| 11. | Phosgene | (75-44-5) |

0080 /...

| List A | Chemical Abstracts Service (CAS) registry No. |
|---|---|
| 12. Cyanogen chloride | (506-77-4) |
| 13. Hydrogen cyanide | (74-90-8) |
| 14. Trichloronitromethane (chloropicrin) | (76-06-2) |
| 15. Phosphorus oxychloride | (10025-87-3) |
| 16. Phosphorus trichloride | (7719-12-2) |
| 17. Phosphorus pentachloride | (10026-13-8) |
| 18. Trimethyl phosphite | (121-45-9) |
| 19. Triethyl phosphite | (122-52-1) |
| 20. Dimethyl phosphite | (868-85-9) |
| 21. Diethyl phosphite | (762-04-9) |
| 22. Sulphur monochloride | (10025-67-9) |
| 23. Sulphur dichloride | (10545-99-0) |
| 24. Thionyl chloride | (7719-09-7) |
| 25. Cyclohexanol | (108-93-0) |
| 26. Hydrogen fluoride | (7664-39-3) |
| 27. Ortho-chlorobenzylidenemalononitrile (CS) | (2698-41-1) |
| 28. Potassium fluoride | (7789-23-3) |
| 29. Ammonium bifluoride | (1341-49-7) |
| 30. Sodium bifluoride | (1333-83-1) |
| 31. Sodium fluoride | (7681-49-4) |
| 32. Sodium sulphide | (1313-82-2) |
| 33. Chloroethanol | (107-07-3) |
| 34. Dimethylamine | (124-40-3) |

0081

/...

| List A | Chemical Abstracts Service (CAS) registry No. |
|---|---|
| 35. Dimethylamine hydrochloride | (506-59-2) |
| 36. Potassium cyanide | (151-50-8) |
| 37. Sodium cyanide | (143-33-9) |
| 38. Tri-ethanolamine | (102-71-6) |
| 39. Di-isopropylamine | (108-18-9) |

2. The following list contains chemicals that have little or no use except as chemical warfare agents or for the development, production or acquisition of chemical weapons, or which have been used by Iraq as essential precursors for chemical weapons:

| List B | Chemical Abstracts Service (CAS) registry No. |
|---|---|
| 1. O-Alkyl ($\leq C_{10}$, incl. cycloalkyl) alkyl (Me, Et, n-Pr or i-Pr)-phosphonofluoridates | |
| e.g. Sarin: O-isopropyl methylphosphonofluoridate | (107-44-8) |
| Soman: O-pinacolyl methylphosphonofluoridate | (96-64-0) |
| 2. O-Alkyl ($\leq C_{10}$, incl. cycloalkyl) N,N-dialkyl (Me, Et, n-Pr or i-Pr) phosphoramidocyanidates | |
| e.g. Tabun: O-ethyl N,N-dimethylphosphoramidocyanidate | (77-81-6) |
| 3. O-Alkyl (H or $\leq C_{10}$, incl. cycloalkyl) S-2-dialkyl (Me, Et, n-Pr or i-Pr)-aminoethyl alkyl (Me, Et, n-Pr or i-Pr) phosphonothiolates and corresponding alkylated and protonated salts | |
| e.g. VX: O-ethyl S-2-diisopropylaminoethyl methylphosphonothiolate | (50782-69-9) |

0082 /...

| List B | Chemical Abstracts Service (CAS) registry No. |
|---|---|
| 4. Sulphur mustards: | |
| 2-Chloroethylchloromethylsulphide | (2625-76-5) |
| bis(2-chloroethyl)sulphide: | |
| Mustard gas (H) | (505-60-2) |
| bis(2-chloroethylthio)methane | (63869-13-6) |
| 1,2-bis(2-chloroethylthio)ethane: | |
| Sesquimustard (Q) | (3563-36-8) |
| 1,3-bis(2-chloroethylthio)-n-propane | (63905-10-2) |
| 1,4-bis(2-chloroethylthio)-n-butane | |
| 1,5-bis(2-chloroethylthio)-n-pentane | |
| bis(2-chloroethylthiomethyl)ether | |
| bis(2-chloroethylthioethyl)ether: | |
| O-Mustard (T) | (63918-89-8) |
| 5. Lewisites: | |
| Lewisite 1: 2-chlorovinyldichlorarsine | (541-25-3) |
| Lewisite 2: bis(2-chlorovinyl) chloroarsine | (40334-69-8) |
| Lewisite 3: tris(2-chlorovinyl)arsine | (40334-70-1) |
| 6. Nitrogen mustards: | |
| HN1: bis(2-chloroethyl)ethylamine | (538-07-8) |
| HN2: bis(2-chloroethyl)methylamine | (51-75-2) |
| HN3: tris(2-chloroethyl)amine | (555-77-1) |
| 7. 3-Quinuclidinyl benzilate (BZ) | (6581-06-2) |
| 8. Saxitoxin | (35523-89-8) |
| 9. Ricin | |
| 10. Alkyl (Me, Et, n-Pr or i-Pr) phosphonyldihalides | |
| e.g. methylphosphonyldifluoride | (676-99-3) |
| methylphosphonyldichloride | (676-67-1) |
| 11. Dimethylmethylphosphonate | (756-79-6) |
| 12. O-Alkyl (H or $\leq C_{10}$, incl. cycloalkyl) O-2-dialkyl (Me, Et, n-Pr or i-Pr)-aminoethyl alkyl (Me, Et, n-Pr or i-Pr) phosphonites and corresponding alkylated salts and protonated salts | |
| e.g. QL: O-ethyl O-2-diisopropylaminoethyl methylphosphonite | (57856-11-8) |

0083 /...

| List B | Chemical Abstracts Service (CAS) registry No. |
|---|---|
| 13. O-Alkyl ($\leq C_{10}$, incl. cycloalkyl) alkyl (Me, Et, n-Pr or i-Pr)-phosphonochloridates | |
| e.g. Chloro Sarin: O-isopropyl methylphosphonochloridate | (1445-76-7) |
| Chloro Soman: O-pinacolyl methylphosphonochloridate | (7040-57-5) |
| 14. N,N-Dialkyl (Me, Et, n-Pr or i-Pr) phosphoramidic dihalides | |
| 15. Bis(2-hydroxyethyl)sulphide (thiodiglycol) | (111-48-8) |
| 16. 3,3-Dimethylbutan-2-ol (pinacolyl alcohol) | (464-07-3) |

3. The initial information under paragraph 30 of the Plan to be provided not later than 30 days after the adoption of the Plan by the Security Council shall cover the period from 1 January 1988. Subsequent information shall be provided each 15 January and 15 July and shall cover the six-month period prior to the provision of the information. The advance notifications under paragraph 30 (d) of the Plan shall cover the subsequent six months. The special notifications under paragraph 31 of the Plan shall be provided not later than 30 days in advance.

4. Whenever the information that Iraq is required to provide under section C of the Plan and this annex is equal to nil, Iraq shall provide nil returns.

5. The information on chemicals to be provided under section C of the Plan shall for each chemical include:

(a) The chemical name, common or trade name used by the site or the facility, structural formula and Chemical Abstracts Service registry number (if assigned);

(b) The purposes for which the chemical is produced, processed, consumed, stored, imported or exported;

(c) The total amount produced, processed, consumed, stored, imported or exported.

6. The information on sites or facilities to be provided under section C of the Plan shall for each site or facility include:

(a) The name of the site or facility and of the owner, company or enterprise operating the site or facility;

(b) The location of the site or facility;

0084 /...

(c) A general description of all types of activities at the site or facility;

(d) The sources and amounts of the financing of the site or facility, and of its activities.

7. The location of a site or facility shall be specified by means of the address and a site diagram. Each diagram shall be drawn to scale and shall indicate the boundaries of the site or facility, all road and rail entrances and exits and all structures on the site or facility, indicating their purpose. If the site or facility is located within a larger complex, the diagram shall specify the exact location of the site or facility within the complex. On each diagram, the geographic coordinates of a point within the site or facility shall be specified to the nearest second.

8. In addition to information specified in paragraph 6 of this annex, the following information shall be provided for each site or facility that is or will be involved in production, processing, consumption, storage, import or export of chemicals specified in list A of this annex:

(a) A detailed description of activities related to these chemicals including, as applicable, material-flow and process-flow diagrams, chemical reactions and end-use;

(b) A list of equipment used in activities related to these chemicals;

(c) The production capacity for these chemicals.

9. In addition to information specified in paragraph 6 of this annex, the following information shall be provided for each site or facility that is or will be involved in production or processing of organophosphorus chemicals or in production of organic chemicals by chlorination:

(a) A detailed description of activities related to the relevant chemicals, and the end-uses for which the chemicals are produced or processed;

(b) A detailed description of the processes used in the production or processing of organophosphorus chemicals or in the production of organic chemicals by chlorination, including material-flow and process-flow diagrams, chemical reactions and list of equipment involved.

10. The information on each import to be provided under section C of the Plan shall include:

(a) Specification of each item and the quantity imported and the purpose of its use in Iraq;

(b) Country from which the item is imported and the specific exporter;

(c) Point or port and time of entry of the item into Iraq;

0085 /...

(d) Site or facility where it is to be used;

(e) Name of the specific importing organization in Iraq.

0086 /...

## Annex III

### Provisions related to biological items

1. The following list contains equipment and other items relevant to the acquisition of biological and toxin weapons or biological and toxin weapons capability:

(a) Detection or assay systems specific for risk groups IV, III and II micro-organisms and toxins;

(b) Biohazard containment equipment;

(c) Equipment for the micro-encapsulation of living micro-organisms;

(d) Complex media for the growth of risk groups IV, III and II micro-organisms;

(e) Bio-reactors and fermentation vessels;

(f) Recombinant deoxyribonucleic acid (DNA), equipment and reagents for its isolation, characterization or production and equipment and reagents for the construction of synthetic genes;

(g) Equipment for the release into the environment of biological material;

(h) Equipment for studying the aerobiological characteristics of micro-organisms or toxins;

(i) Equipment for breeding of vectors of human, animal or plant diseases.

2. The initial information under paragraphs 35 and 36 of the Plan to be provided not later than 30 days after the adoption of the Plan by the Security Council shall cover the period from 1 January 1986. Subsequent information shall be provided each 15 January and 15 July and shall cover the six-month period prior to the provision of the information. Notifications under paragraph 38 (a) of the Plan shall be provided not later than 60 days in advance.

3. Whenever the information that Iraq is required to provide under section D and this annex is equal to nil, Iraq shall provide nil returns.

4. The information on each site or facility to be provided under section D of the Plan shall include the following:

(a) The name of the site or facility and of the owner, company, or enterprise operating the facility;

/...

(b) The location of the site or facility (including the address, geographic coordinates to the nearest second, the specific buildings and any structure numbers, location of the facility within any larger complex);

(c) The sources and amounts of financing of the site or facility and of its activities;

(d) The main purpose of the site or facility;

(e) The level of protection, including, as applicable, the number and size of maximum containment or containment laboratories (units);

(f) Scope and description of activities, including, as applicable, a list of types and quantities of micro-organisms, toxins or vaccines and equipment and other items specified in paragraph 1 of this annex;

(g) A list of micro-organisms and toxins, equipment and vaccines imported or uniquely isolated for the use of the site or facility, or exported, indicating the supplier or recipient countries involved.

5. The information on imports to be provided under paragraphs 35 (g) and 38 (a) of the Plan shall cover:

(a) Toxins and micro-organisms meeting the criteria for risk groups IV, III, and II according to the classification in the 1983 WHO Laboratory Biosafety Manual and genetic material coding for toxins or genes derived from the aforementioned micro-organisms;

(b) Equipment and facilities for the production, utilization or storage of micro-organisms meeting the criteria for risk groups IV and III according to the classification in the 1983 WHO Laboratory Biosafety Manual, genetic material coding for toxins or genes derived from the aforementioned micro-organisms, as well as of toxins or vaccines;

(c) Complex media for the growth of micro-organisms meeting the criteria for risk groups IV and III in quantities greater than 100 kilograms;

(d) Equipment for micro-encapsulation of living micro-organisms;

(e) Personnel or material for training or technical support services related to the design, development, use, manufacture or support of items specified in paragraph 35 (a) of the Plan and paragraphs 1 and 5 (a) of this annex;

and shall for each import into Iraq specify:

(a) Types and quantities of micro-organisms, toxins or vaccines;

(b) Quantities of any equipment or other items specified in paragraph 1 of this annex;

0088 /...

(c) Country from which the micro-organisms, toxins, vaccines or items are imported and the specific exporter;

(d) Point or port and time of entry into Iraq;

(e) Site or facility where it is to be used and purpose of its use.

(f) Name of the specific importing organization in Iraq.

6. The information under paragraph 37 of the Plan shall be provided within seven days of the occurrence and the standardized form contained in section III of the annex on confidence-building measures in document BWC/CONF.III/23/II shall be utilized as appropriate.

7. Iraq shall, not later than each 15 April, provide to the Special Commission the copies of the declarations, information and data that Iraq has sent to the United Nations Department for Disarmament Affairs pursuant to the agreements on confidence-building measures, including the exchange of information and data, reached at the Third Review Conference of the Parties to the Convention on the Prohibition of the Development, Production and Stockpiling of Bacteriological (Biological) and Toxin Weapons and on Their Destruction (document BWC/CONF.III/23/II and its annex on confidence-building measures).

/...

## Annex IV

### Provisions related to missiles

1. The following list contains equipment, other items and technologies relevant to the development and manufacture of missiles that could be used in the development and manufacture of ballistic missiles capable of a range greater than 150 kilometres:

(a) Subsystems usable in missile systems that could be used in the development and manufacture of ballistic missiles capable of a range greater than 150 kilometres:

(i) Individual rocket stages;

(ii) Re-entry vehicles, and specially designed equipment therefor;

(iii) Solid- or liquid-fuel rocket engines;

(iv) Guidance sets;

(v) Thrust vector controls;

(vi) Warhead safing, arming, fuzing and firing mechanisms;

(b) Propulsion components and equipment that could be used in the development and manufacture of ballistic missiles capable of a range greater than 150 kilometres:

(i) Rocket-motor cases and production equipment therefor;

(ii) Staging mechanisms and production equipment therefor;

(iii) Liquid-fuel control systems and components therefor, specially designed to operate in vibrating environments of more than 12g/rms between 20/Hz and 2,000/Hz;

(iv) Propellants and constituent chemicals for propellants;

(v) Production technology or production equipment for the production, handling, mixing, curing, casting, pressing, machining and acceptance testing of the liquid- or solid-fuel missile propellants and propellent constituents;

(c) Guidance and control equipment that could be used in the development and manufacture of ballistic missiles capable of a range greater than 150 kilometres:

/...

(i) Gyroscopes, accelerometers and inertial equipment and software therefor;

(ii) Flight control systems usable in missile systems;

(iii) Avionics equipment specially designed or modified for use in unmanned air vehicles or rocket systems and software and components therefor usable in missile systems;

(d) Equipment and technical data for the production of structural composites usable in missiles and components, accessories and software therefor that could be used in the development and manufacture of ballistic missiles capable of a range greater than 150 kilometres;

(e) Pyrolytic deposition and densification equipment and technology that could be used in the development and manufacture of ballistic missiles capable of a range greater than 150 kilometres;

(f) Launch and ground support equipment and facilities usable for missile systems that could be used in the development and manufacture of ballistic missiles capable of a range greater than 150 kilometres;

(g) Analog computers, digital computers or digital differential analysers usable in air vehicles, rocket systems or missile systems that could be used in the development and manufacture of ballistic missiles capable of a range greater than 150 kilometres;

(h) Test facilities and equipment usable for missile systems, to include vibration test equipment using digital control techniques, wind tunnels and test benches for solid- or liquid-fuel rockets that could be used in the development and manufacture of ballistic missiles capable of a range greater than 150 kilometres;

(i) Specially designed software or components for missile design, production or operation that could be used in the development and manufacture of ballistic missiles capable of a range greater than 150 kilometres;

(j) Materials and devices for reduced observables in missile systems that could be used in the development and manufacture of ballistic missiles capable of a range greater than 150 kilometres;

(k) Material and devices for protecting missile systems against nuclear effects that could be used in the development and manufacture of ballistic missiles capable of a range greater than 150 kilometres.

2. The initial information under paragraph 43 of the Plan to be provided not later than 30 days after the adoption of the Plan by the Security Council shall cover the period from 1 January 1988. Subsequent information shall be provided each 15 January and 15 July and shall cover the six-month period

prior to the provision of the information. Notifications under paragraph 44 of the Plan shall be provided not later than 14 days prior to the date of launch.

3. Whenever the information which Iraq is required to provide under section E of the Plan and this annex is equal to nil, Iraq shall provide nil returns.

4. The information on sites or facilities to be provided under section E of the Plan shall for each site or facility include:

(a) The name of the site or facility and of the owner, company or enterprise operating the site or facility;

(b) The location of the site or facility;

(c) The sources and amounts of the financing of the site or facility, and of its activities;

(d) A general description of all types of activities at the site or facility;

(e) List of equipment, other items and technologies specified in paragraph 1 of this annex used or present at the site or facility and their quantities;

(f) A detailed description of activities related to the equipment, other items and technologies specified in paragraph 1 of this annex.

5. The location of a site or facility shall be specified by means of the address and site diagram. Each diagram shall be drawn to scale and shall indicate the boundaries of the site or facility, all road and rail entrances and exits and all structures on the site or facility, indicating their purpose. If the site or facility is located within a larger complex, the diagram shall specify the exact location of the site or facility within the complex. On each diagram, the geographic coordinates of a point within the site or facility shall be specified to the nearest second.

6. The information on each import to be provided under section E of the Plan shall include:

(a) Specification of each item and the quantity imported and the purpose of its use in Iraq;

(b) Country from which the item is imported and the specific exporter;

(c) Point or port and time of entry of the item in Iraq;

0092

/...

(d) Project and site or facility where it is to be used;

(e) Name of the specific importing organization in Iraq.

-----

0093

| 관리 번호 | 92-625 |
|---|---|

| | 분류번호 | 보존기간 |
|---|---|---|
| | | |

# 발 신 전 보

번 호 : WUN-1274 920528 1313 DW 종별 :

수 신 : 주 유엔 대사. 총영사

발 신 : 장 관 (연일)

제 목 : 이라크 무기폐기 협조

대 : UNW-1501

대호, UNSCOM의 요청내용이 매우 광범위함에 비추어 본건 검토에 참고코자하니 아래사항 파악 보고바람.

(1) UNSCOM 의장 서한 발송대상국, 동국가들의 대응동향 및 관련 참고사항

(2) 유엔 안보리 결의내용이외에 UNSCOM 활동의 guideline이 있는지 여부 및 그 내용 (특히 이라크이외 유엔회원국들의 대 UNSCOM 협조와 관련). 끝.

(국제기구국장대리 금정호)

예 고 : 1992.12.31. 일반

검 토 필(1992.6.30.)

| 보안 통제 | |
|---|---|

| 앙 고 재 | 92년 5월 28일 | 유엔1과 | 기안자 성명 | | 과 장 | 심의관 | 국 장 | | 차 관 | 장 관 |
|---|---|---|---|---|---|---|---|---|---|---|
| | | | | | | | | | | |

외신과통제

0094

# 공 란

| 관리 번호 | 92 -631 |
|---|---|

원 본

# 외 무 부

종 별 :

번 호 : UNW-1564 일 시 : 92 0601 1630

수 신 : 장 관(연일)

발 신 : 주 유엔 대사

제 목 : 이락 화학무기 폐기작업단

연:UNW-1501

1. 연호 이락화학무기 폐기작업단 참여와 관련, EKEUS UNSCOM 위원장은 본직앞 서한으로 김강식 소령과 이인식 대위의 동 작업단 참여 결정을 통보하고 아국정부의 최종 동의 여부를 회보하여 줄것을 요청하였음

2. 동작업단에 이대위는 화학무기 폐기반의 ANALYST-SAFETY OFFICER 로, 김소령은 DESTRUCTION MONITORING TEAM 요원으로 임용되며 근무기간은 각각 6 개월임. 구체적 소집일자는 92.7.4 이후 소집 7 일전 통보할 것이므로 7.4. 이후부터는 소집 대기상태에 있어 줄것을 요청함

3. 동서한에서 UNSCOM 측은 상기 내용을 외부에 공표치 말고 비밀로 취급하여 줄것을 요청하였음을 첨언함

4. 동인 파견과 관련한 작업단 구성, 안내서등과 유엔에 제출할 서류등을 6.3. 뉴욕 총영사관 파편 송부하니 필요서류를 기재, 회보바람

(대사 유종하-국장)

예고:92.12.31 일반고문에 의거 일반문서로 재분류

검 토 필 (1992.6.30.)

국기국 장관 차관 1차보 ▇▇ 중아국 분석관 청와대 안기부

PAGE 1

92.06.02 07:39

외신 2과 통제관 BN

0096

## 4. 유엔 이락 化學武器 廢棄班 參與

o 유엔 對이락 武器 廢棄 特別委員會(UNSCOM) 委員長은 우리軍 將校 2명의 이락 化學武器 廢棄班 參與 決定을 우리側에 알려옴.

- 同 廢棄班은 92.7-12월간 총40명 규모로 活動 예정이며, 유엔이 航空料 및 報酬를 提供함.

  * 政府는 4.3 UNSCOM 委員長의 우리側 參與要請 書翰 접수후, 관련부처 協議를 거쳐 상기 2명을 유엔側에 推薦한 바 있음.

0097

관리번호 92-652

# 주 국 련 대 표 부

주국련 2031-119　　　　　　　　　　　　　　　　1992. 6. 1.

수신 : 장 관

참조 : 국제기구국장

제목 : 유엔 이락화학무기 폐기작업단

연 : UNW-1564

1. 연호 아국장교 2명의 유엔 이락화학무기 폐기작업단 참여와 관련, UNSCOM Ekeus 위원장의 본직 앞 서한과 관련자료를 별첨 송부합니다.

2. 상기자료중 유엔에 제출할 서류를 기재, 당관에 송부하여 주시기 바랍니다.

첨 부 : 서한 및 자료. 끝.

예 고 : 92.12.31 일반 예고문에 의거 일반문서로 재분류

점 토 필 (1992. 6.30.)

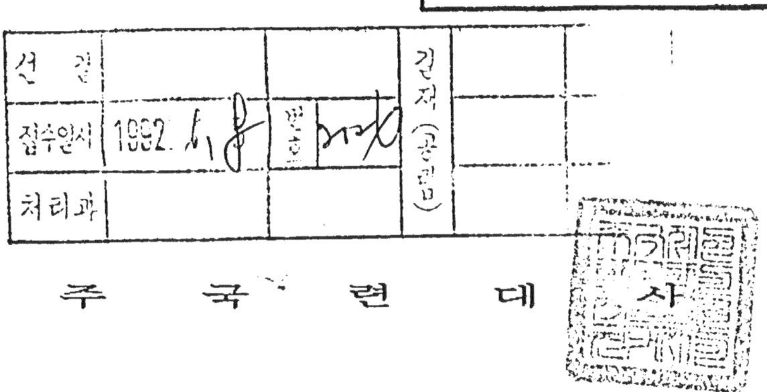

| 선 결 | | | 결재 (공람) | |
|---|---|---|---|---|
| 접수일시 | 1992. 6. 8 | 번호 | | |
| 처리과 | | | | |

주 국 련 대 사

0098

UNITED NATIONS NATIONS UNIES

POSTAL ADDRESS—ADRESSE POSTALE UNITED NATIONS, N.Y. 10017
CABLE ADDRESS—ADRESSE TELEGRAPHIQUE UNATIONS NEWYORK

26 May 1992

REFERENCE:

Excellency,

I last wrote to you on the subject of the destruction of Iraq's chemical warfare capability on 3 April 1992. I would like to take this opportunity to thank your Government for its positive response and to give you more detail in regard to both my scheme of operations and the assistance required to carry out this vital destruction task.

The Chemical Destruction Group will comprise 39 long-term Iraq-based personnel, of which a few will be UN-staff personnel, but the majority will be individuals nominated by member states. The Special Commission will also maintain a register of specialists whose participation will be requested as required.

The Chemical Destruction Group will need to be capable of sustaining both a 24-hour a day presence at Al Muthanna and chemical destruction operations at other locations for 12 to 18 months. To achieve this, I plan to implement a 6-month staffing cycle. However, to ensure continuity, I anticipate half of the initial intake of personnel being replaced after approximately three months.

The Chemical Destruction Group in-country assets will be organized on the basis of a Headquarters and a Destruction Monitoring Sub Group which will operate a two shift system. Each shift will be further sub-divided into three multi-national, multi-function, four person teams.

His Excellency
Mr. Chong-Ha YOO
Ambassador Extraordinary and Plenipotentiary
Permanent Representative of the Republic of Korea
to the United Nations
New York, N.Y.

/...

0099

UNITED NATIONS  NATIONS UNIES



I would therefore be grateful if the Government of the Republic of Korea would make available, for six months, the services of Captain In Sik Lee for employment with the Chemical Destruction Group, as an Analyst/Safety Officer and Major Kang Sik Kim as a Destruction Monitoring Team member. The names of any other specialists you have identified as being available will be entered on the specialist register.

Kindly inform us as soon as possible if this proposal is agreeable to your Government. If so, both Captain In Sik Lee and Major Kang Sik Kim should be placed on seven days notice to move with effect 4 July 1992.

In addition to this request for personnel, I anticipate writing to you again in the near future requesting the assistance of your Government in the provision of equipment.

I enclose with this letter further information relating to the Chemical Destruction Group, a personal data sheet, a health certificate and an application for a UN certificate which must be completed by the personnel you have selected for this mission and returned to UNSCOM at the earliest date. Please treat information relating to this mission as confidential to the Commission and not for public release at this time.

Accept, Excellency, the assurances of my highest consideration.

Rolf Ekéus
Executive Chairman
Office of the Special Commission

0100

**OFFICE OF THE SPECIAL COMMISSION**

**20 MAY 1992**

**CHEMICAL DESTRUCTION GROUP INFORMATION**

GENERAL

1. This background information on UNSCOM's chemical destruction programme and Chemical Destruction Group (CDG) organization is intended to assist supporting states in their planning considerations as well as informing prospective CDG personnel.

2. General information relating to UNSCOM personnel is attached. Additional information will be made available to nominated individuals, through missions, at a later date.

BACKGROUND

3. The Government of Iraq has been directed by the Special Commission to concentrate at Al Muthanna, for subsequent destruction, chemical warfare agents and their precursors. Al Muthanna, which is approximately 75 kilometres NW of Baghdad, is the largest facility of the Muthanna State Establishment (MSE), Iraq's CW organization.

4. The majority of the agent, nerve and mustard, is in bulk containers although significant amounts remain in munitions which are yet to be drained.

5. The principal methods of destruction will be nerve agent caustic hydrolysis and mustard incineration. However, other means including combined explosive/fuel destruction may have to be employed on munitions considered too unstable for either long road moves or drainage.

PERSONAL QUALITIES

6. Personnel nominated for the CDG should have the following personal qualities:

a. Good health.
b. Fitness.
c. Tolerance.

0101

d. Resilience.
e. Stability - no personal problems which will affect performance.
f. A high standard of spoken English and written English in appropriate appointments.
g. Adaptability to new methods.
h. Clean shaven. Facial hair, moustaches excepted, is not permitted on chemical missions.

PROFESSIONAL QUALITIES

7. Personnel nominated for the CDG should have the following professional qualities in addition to any specialised knowledge or expertise:

a. Sound general NBC or equivalent knowledge.
b. Confidence when wearing protective NBC equipment.
c. Adaptability to new methods and equipment.
d. An international driving licence is desirable.

TOUR LENGTH

8. It is anticipated that the chemical destruction programme will operate for 12 to 18 months. The tour length, for those personnel based in Iraq, will be six months with the exception of half the personnel from the first tour who will serve approximately three months to enable the implementation of an overlap and therefore ensure team continuity.

9. Experts from the Specialist Sub Group will be requested as required but usually not for more than 2-3 weeks.

STAFFING

10. UNSCOM would appreciate those states contributing personnel to the CDG undertaking to replace individuals on completion of their tour of duty, or on early departure under any of the following circumstances:

a. Accident.
b. Chemical exposure limit reached.
c. Unsuitability.
d. Compassionate.

0102

HIERARCHY

11. The CDG hierarchy will be based on the appointment held within the CDG.

ORGANIZATION

12. HQ CDG

| | |
|---|---|
| Chief Inspector | - 1 |
| Analyst/Safety Officer | - 2 |
| Doctor | - 2 |
| Medics | - 4 |
| Clerks | - 2 |
| Communicators | - 2 |
| Interpreters | - 1 |
| Driver | - 1 |
| | ===== |
| | **15** |

Specialist Sub Group (SSG) (as required)

Chemical Engineers
Mechanical Engineers
Structural Engineers
Demolition Engineers
EOD Personnel
Maintenance Technicians

Destruction Monitoring Sub Group (DMSG)

Shift HQ Shift HQ

DMT* DMT DMT=12

DMT DMT DMT=12 **TOTAL = 39**

* Destruction Monitoring Team

0103

13. Aircrew will come under HQ CDG when they are supporting CDG operations.

14. HQ CDG personnel, excluding the Chief Inspector, interpreter and driver, will be split between the two shifts.

15. The Shift Headquarters will comprise a Shift Leader, a Deputy Shift Leader and a Shift Administration Officer, all of whom will be members of the four person DMTs.

RESPONSIBILITIES

16. The Chief Inspector, or in his absence his nominated deputy, will be responsible to the Executive Chairman of the Special Commission for all UNSCOM aspects of the chemical destruction programme including direction, operational standards, health and safety.

17. The Destruction Monitoring Sub Group will be responsible to the Chief Inspector for the implementation of such supervision and destruction monitoring activities as are required of the CDG by the Executive Chairman of the Special Commission.

18. Specialists from the Specialist Sub Group will be requested on an as required basis and will be responsible to the Chief Inspector.

JOB DESCRIPTION

19. Those appointments from the organization chart which require further explanation are as follows:

a. Analyst/Safety Officer
The Analyst/Safety Officer will be responsible for the implementation of an analytical quality control regime and ensuring the observation of the UNSCOM "Health and Safety Policy Statement".

b. Shift Leader
In addition to being a member of a DMT, the Shift Leader will be responsible for the day to day activities of the shift.

0104

c. Deputy Shift Leader
In addition to being a member of a DMT, the Deputy Shift Leader will assist the Shift Leader.

d. Shift Administration Officer
In addition to being a member of a DMT, the Shift Administration Officer will be responsible for shift administration.

e. Technical Storeman
Each shift will have a technical storeman who in addition to being a member of a DMT, will be responsible to the Shift Leader for the control and, where appropriate, maintenance of CDG equipment.

## MODUS OPERANDI

20. The CDG will comprise predominantly multi-national, multi-function teams working to UNSCOM standard operating procedures (SOPs) with standardised equipment. UNSCOM SOPs will cover detection, decontamination, demolition, rescue, verification, health and safety and such other activities as is deemed necessary.

## TRAINING

21. Members of the CDG will receive in-country training in the following:

a. Communications.
b. Detection.
c. Decontamination.
d. Equipment use.
e. First aid.
f. Rescue.
g. Verification techniques.

## BRIEFING

22. In addition to information provided to nominated individuals, personnel will receive detailed briefings on all aspects of their employment with the CDG in Bahrain and Baghdad.

0105

WORK REGIME

23. With the exception of some members of the HQ and assigned specialists, personnel will work a 4-day shift as follows:

a. 4 days (96 hours) based at Al Muthanna.
b. 4 days (96 hours) working on chemical tasks at other sites but based in Baghdad.
c. 4 days off, in Baghdad, every 4 weeks.
d. 4 days off, out of country (Bahrain or Cyprus), every 8 weeks.

Note: This regime may need to be modified in the interest of CDG personnel if conditions of climate, work, chemical exposure or general well-being dictate such modifications are necessary.

START DATE

24. It is anticipated that approximately four nominated personnel will be required in Iraq in mid June. The full team will not however be required until the period end of June to mid July.

CALL FORWARD

25. It is anticipated that four nominated personnel will be required in Bahrain on 16 June, and that half the main group will be required in Bahrain on 29 June 1992. However, because factors outside the control of UNSCOM will dictate the date, the remainder of the CDG will be required, they will be placed on seven days notice to move (NTM) with effect 4 July 1992, ie. from 4 July 1992, personnel will be given seven days notice of the requirement to arrive in Bahrain on a nominated date.

ACCOMMODATION

26. UNSCOM will book hotel accommodation for CDG personnel in Bahrain and Baghdad.

27. The CDG compound at Al Muthanna includes office, storage and personnel accommodation.

0106

INDIVIDUAL PROTECTION EQUIPMENT

28. Personnel must bring their own individual protection equipment. They must also bring a respirator with two spare canisters/sets of filters and optical inserts if required.

29. A stock of standardised IPE, including respirators, will be held in Iraq.

GOVERNMENT REPORTS

30. Team members should not make personal reports to their government prior to the completion of the official mission. However, missions of contributing governments will receive regular updates on the progress of CDG operations through UNSCOM New York.

POINT OF CONTACT

31. Queries relating to the CDG should be directed to:

Garth Whitty
CD Team
+ 1-212-963-9026

. . . . .

0107

OFFICE OF THE SPECIAL COMMISSION

5 March 1992

INFORMATION FOR MEMBERS OF INSPECTION TEAMS

**UNITED NATIONS STATUS**

1. While on duty with the U.N. Special Commission (UNSCOM), you, as a member of an UNSCOM inspection team, will enjoy the privileges and immunities accorded to experts performing missions for the United Nations under article VI of the Convention on the Privileges and Immunities of the United Nations of 13 February 1946. To be covered under this Convention, you will be requested to sign a group Special Service Agreement, a type of U.N. contract, which identifies you and your colleagues as experts on mission as well as makes you eligible for coverage under U.N.-provided special insurances, as specified in 5(a) below. Further special arrangements regarding facilities, privileges and immunities for UNSCOM operations have been negotiated with Bahrain and with Iraq. The Chief Inspector is furnished with copies of those arrangements.

**TRAVEL DOCUMENTS**

2 a. Bahrain. As the first leg of their trip, members of UNSCOM inspection teams will be required to assemble in Bahrain, the staging area for inspections into Iraq. Standard time in Bahrain is GMT + 3. Travel to Bahrain, will require, at this time, a national passport and an entry visa for nationals of all countries other than countries members of the Gulf Cooperation Council (Saudi Arabia, Kuwait, Oman, Qatar and the United Arab Emirates) and British nationals. The entry visa will be issued to you at the airport on arrival in Bahrain.

You will be denied entry into Bahrain if your national passport contains an entry/exit stamp from Israel. If this is the case, please obtain a new passport before leaving for Bahrain.

b. Iraq. Standard time in Iraq is GMT + 3. You will fly on a UN aircraft from Bahrain to Iraq and back. Normally, members of inspection teams will enter Iraq on the UN Certificate, a form of "passport" identifying you as a UN expert on mission. These certificates will be given to each inspector in Bahrain. Upon completion of the mission the

0108

certificate will be collected and maintained in Bahrain available for any subsequent deployment. UN certificates which have expired will be extended in Bahrain. Thus, if you already have a certificate, please bring it to Bahrain even if expired.

**NO NEW CERTIFICATES WILL BE ISSUED IN BAHRAIN.** New certificates are issued only at UN Headquarters in New York.

In order to obtain this essential travel document for the first time, it is imperative that you fill out all information required on the UN Certificate application form (a blue original card or a facsimile thereof, as attached), sign the card or the facsimile, attach 8 passport-size photos and return immediately by the most expeditious way (DHL or other express mail if necessary) to:

Ms. Alice Hecht
United Nations Special Commission
Room S-3120D
United Nations
New York, New York 10017
U.S.A.

Telephone: (international access code + 1-212-963-5545)

**IF THE INFORMATION IS NOT RECEIVED AT LEAST 7 DAYS PRIOR TO THE TEAM'S ASSEMBLY DATE IN BAHRAIN IT MAY NOT BE POSSIBLE TO OBTAIN THE UN CERTIFICATE IN TIME.**

**TRANSPORTATION, HOTEL ACCOMMODATIONS AND OTHER ARRANGEMENTS**

3 a. Before you leave your place of residence. The United Nations, in accordance with existing United Nations rules and regulations, will provide round-trip transportation on a recognized public carrier, at the most economical rate, via the shortest, most direct route from country of residence to the place of assembly of the teams, which, as indicated above, is Bahrain. UNSCOM's N.Y. Administrative Office will contact you, normally by fax, with information on where to pick up the prepaid ticket. To avoid lengthy reimbursement procedures, every effort should be made to use the prepaid ticket provided.

**You will be advised of a reporting date to the assembly point. Please do not arrive any earlier. Please do not initiate travel, or change travel plans, without UNSCOM approval.**

b. Arrival and stay in Bahrain. UNSCOM has established a Field Office in Bahrain to support inspection activity into

0109

Iraq. The Chief of the Field Office is Mr. Alastair Livingston (office: international access code + 973-320-936; mobile phone: 973-459-273; the Administrative Officer, Ms. Angelina Hernandez-Griffin, office: international access code + 973-33-6898. In most cases, a representative of the Field Office will meet you at the Manama airport. If no one is at the airport, proceed through immigration and customs, identifying yourself as an UNSCOM inspector, and either take a taxi to the Manama Holiday Inn or call the Holiday Inn (tel. no. 531-122) and ask them to send the hotel mini-bus to pick you up. You may ask the World Travel Service agency at the airport, which represents the U.N. official travel agency at Headquarters, for assistance or to place the call to the hotel.

Hotel accommodations. As indicated above, while in Bahrain you will be staying at the Holiday Inn. Reservations will already have been made for you by UNSCOM on the basis of your approved travel, so there is no need for you to book or confirm hotel accommodations.

Activities while in Bahrain. Several days may be spent in Bahrain for administrative and mission-specific briefings, training and acclimatization prior to entry into Iraq. At this time, you will also be provided with an advance on your daily subsistence allowance for the length of the mission (see 4 below).

c. Iraq. Travel to and from Iraq will be on UN-provided aircraft. All arrangements concerning this travel will have been made by the Bahrain UNSCOM Field Office. To date, transportation within Iraq has been by a combination of UN and Iraqi vehicles. Helicopter transport will be used when distances dictate it. While in Iraq, you will be staying at the Sheraton Hotel, reservations for which will have been made by UNSCOM for the whole team. At this time, there are no easily accessible public international telephone lines from/to Baghdad. Limited personal call will be allowed using the UNSCOM satellite links, but such calls must be paid in cash U.S. dollars and are expensive, approximately $10.00 per minute or fraction thereof. For emergency notification, please follow the instructions given under 7 below.

d. Dispersal. At the end of the mission in Iraq, you will return to Bahrain for a number of days to write the inspection report before returning to your place of residence.

0110

**DAILY SUBSISTENCE ALLOWANCE/PER DIEM AND OTHER MONETARY MATTERS**

4. In addition to roundtrip transportation to and from Baghdad, the United Nations will provide you with a mission subsistence allowance (MSA) for your stay in Bahrain and in Baghdad. At this time, the daily rate for Bahrain is $154.00 and for Baghdad $250.00 although payments are subject to review. You will receive a cash advance on arrival in Bahrain. Should the United Nations or other organization provide accommodations during any part of the mission, the MSA will be reduced accordingly.

5. You are fully responsible for your expenses, including paying hotel bills before check out, meals, telephone calls, etc.

**NOTE WELL**: Hotel bills in Iraq must be paid in cash in U.S. dollars. These bills cannot be paid in any other currency (nor in Iraqi dinars) and no credit cards or travellers cheques are accepted in Iraq. Meals and other expenses may be paid in dinars. The exchange rate is very unfavourable making simple amenities expensive.

6. Final settlement of all entitlements and claims will take place before your departure from Bahrain for the return trip home.

**INSURANCE COVERAGE, HEALTH CERTIFICATION AND MEDICAL SUPPORT**

7 a. Insurance coverage. You are fully responsible for arranging, at your own expense, such ordinary life, health, dental and other forms of insurance coverage for the period of your service for the United Nation as you consider appropriate. The responsibility of the United Nations is limited solely to the payment of compensation, if appropriate, in the event of death, injury or illness attributable to the performance of official duties on behalf of the United Nations.

b. Health considerations. Healthy personnel are essential to the success of the inspection process. Inspection activities will take their toll on everyone, more so in hot weather and on individuals who are not fit. The United Nations requires all personnel to provide a statement from a recognized physician certifying that the individual is in good health, is fit to travel and has had the inoculations required for the countries to which the individual is to travel. For Bahrain and Iraq, the United Nations recommends

0111

immunizations for typhoid, tetanus, and also recommends gamma globulin. Additionally, anthrax and plague immunizations are recommended for individuals participating in biological weapons inspections. Although there have been reported cases of cholera, it does not appear to be a significant danger in the areas to which UNSCOM personnel will travel.

To comply with U.N. requirements, please have the attached Health Certificate filled out by your physician and return it to UNSCOM along with your travel certificate application and photographs (**see paragraph 2 b. above**).

c. Medical support. Emergency medical support is available in Bahrain and in Iraq. An UNSCOM doctor or medical assistant will accompany each inspection team. Evacuation procedures to Kuwait, Bahrain or Western Europe are also in place.

You should bring with you an adequate supply of all personal medications, as re-filling prescriptions may not be possible. Also bring spare spectacles. Sunscreen, chapstick, and salves for rashes are advised. Rashes, stomach aches, and diarrhoea are likely ailments. You will be given a complete medical briefing while in Bahrain.

**OTHER USEFUL INFORMATION**

8 a. Clothing. You are responsible for your own personal clothing. Prudent selection of clothing will contribute significantly to comfortable working conditions and should be adapted to the weather. Temperatures in summer are up to 50 degrees Celsius, in winter, temperatures will drop to zero. In January/March, you will need light-weight daytime clothing with warm sweaters or jackets for the evening. Outerwear providing warmth and rain protection is strongly recommended.

Natural fibre materials such as cotton are cooler and easier to launder; long sleeve shirts will afford protection against sunburn and flying insects. You should bring sufficient clothing for a two-week period in Iraq. Excellent laundry service is available in the hotel in Baghdad, but elsewhere it is unpredictable. Shoes are a most critical item of clothing. Lightweight, over-the-ankle shoes/boots are advised. Shoes or boots with steel in the sole or toe conduct extremes of cold and heat and can become very uncomfortable. Break in new footwear prior to arriving in Bahrain. Sunglasses are recommended.

0112

You may wear/use military items such as boots and canteens, but you should not wear military uniforms or insignia. The UN will provide you with identifying floppy-brimmed hats and armbands.

Team inspection equipment will be provided at the assembly point. Individuals involved in CBW inspections must bring their own protective gear. They must also bring a respirator with two spare canisters/sets of filters and optical inserts if required.

b. Personal Equipment. Experience gained from inspections to date suggests some personal equipment items may be of benefit to each inspector. These items will have to be provided at individual expense and will not be reimbursed by the U.N. It is strongly recommended that these items be procured before leaving home as there is often no time to do so in Bahrain and the prices there are quite high. Following are suggestions:

Notebook, Dictaphone, or personal notebook computer
Pens/pencils
Portable cassette player
Batteries as appropriate
Secure money pouch
Small compass for orientation
Shoulder bag or backpack

c. Media guidance and government contacts. Press interest in the activities of the Special Commission continues to be high. The authorized spokesman for the team is the Chief Inspector. Results of inspections are considered confidential until authorized for release by the Special Commission. Team members should not make personal reports to their government prior to the completion of the official mission.

d. Photographs. The use of personal cameras in Iraq is normally permitted during leisure activities in civilian areas. However, on the inspection site itself, or going to and from the inspection site, photographs will be taken only by the official team photographers or by individuals specifically designated by the Chief Inspector. These official photographs will be released only with the specific authority of the Special Commission. Further details on the rules relating to the taking of photographs will be provided during the initial briefing in Bahrain.

0113

**EMERGENCY NOTIFICATION.**

9. UNSCOM must have on record an individual or institution you designate as an emergency point of contact. Please ensure that the information is provided on the attached Inspector Data Sheet and that it is accurate. Family members or your designated point of contact may pass urgent messages to you through UNSCOM headquarters in New York (international access code, if appropriate + 1-212-963-9044/9041) or Field Office Bahrain (international access code + 973-320-936).

**TO REMIND:** **PLEASE FILL OUT AS NECESSARY THE ATTACHED UN CERTIFICATE APPLICATION, INSPECTOR DATA SHEET, HEALTH CERTIFICATE, ATTACH 8 PASSPORT SIZE PICTURES AND RETURN TO THE UNSCOM NEW YORK OFFICE IMMEDIATELY.**

Attachments:

1. Inspector Data Sheet
2. UN Certificate Application
3. Health Certificate

## DATA SHEET

NAME: ______________________

ADDRESS: ______________________

______________________

______________________

TELEPHONE NUMBERS: OFFICE: ______________________

FAX: ______________ HOME: ______________

NATIONALITY: ______________ DATE OF BIRTH: __________

PLACE OF BIRTH: ______________ SEX: _____ BLOOD TYPE: _____

EMERGENCY NOTIFICATION: NAME: ______________________

ADDRESS: ______________________

______________________

TELEPHONE NUMBER: ______________________

LANGUAGES: ______________________

PASSPORT: TYPE: ______________ NUMBER: ______________

DATE OF ISSUE: ______________ DATE OF EXPIRATION: __________

PLACE OF ISSUE: ______________ CURRENT VISAS: ______________

PRIMARY AREA OF EXPERTISE: CW, BW, NUCLEAR, BALLISTIC MISSILE (circle)

SPECIALTY: ______________________

PREVIOUS INSPECTION EXPERIENCE: ______________________

DATES OF AVAILABILITY: ______________________

UN CERTIFICATE NUMBER (When available): ______________________

**PLEASE FORWARD BY MOST EXPEDITIOUS MEANS THIS DATA SHEET AND EIGHT PASSPORT-SIZE PHOTOS FOR UN CERTIFICATE TO:**

Ms. Alice ·echt
United Nations Special Commission
Room 3120D
United Nations
New York, N.Y. 10017
(Telephone: 212-963-5545)

27 May 1992

0115

PT.84 (3-70) - E.

## APPLICATION FOR UNITED NATIONS CERTIFICATE

INSTRUCTIONS.

1. Please *TYPE* or *PRINT* all information requested.
2. Attach two front view (*shoulder and above*) passport photographs (2 x 2½), printed on thin photographic paper and taken within six months of the date of this application.
3. Print full name on the reverse of each photograph.
4. Submit this form through the appropriate U.N. Office.

(1) NAME: ______ *Last* ______ *First* ______ *Middle*

TITLE: ______ (2)

ADDRESS: *(Local)* ______

NATIONALITY: ______

PASSPORT No.: ______

Tel. No. ______

ISSUED BY *(Country)*: ______

DURATION of CONTRACT: ______

DATE of EXPIRY: ______

PURPOSE of TRAVEL:

Implementation of Security Council Resolution 687 (1991)

TRAVELLING on BEHALF of:

United Nations
*(Name of Organization)*

UN Special Commission (UNSCOM)
*(Division or Section)*

***I certify that the above statements are true to the best of my knowledge.***

(3) ______ *Date* ______ *Signature of Applicant*

Certified that the applicant is entitled to a United Nations Certificate. Please issue valid until
______ *(Not exceeding one year)*

Date: ______ Certifying Officer: ______

Name: ______ Office: ______

***Do not write below this line***

DATE of ISSUE: ______ EXPIRES on: ______ CERT. No.: ______

REVALIDATED: ______ EXPIRES on: ______

PLEASE COMPLETE SECTIONS: 1,2 and 3.

0116

**HEALTH CERTIFICATE**

________________________________ is in good health and is physically fit to travel to Bahrain and Iraq to carry out inspection activities as required by the United Nations. All required inoculations for the travel area have been administered.

________________________________
Physician

________________________________
Date

0117

공 란

| 관리번호 | 92-646 |
|---|---|

원 본

# 외 무 부

종 별 :

번 호 : UNW-1620 일 시 : 92 0604 1920

수 신 : 장 관(연일)

발 신 : 주 유엔 대사

제 목 : 이락무기 폐기

대:WUN-1274

연:UNW-1501

대호 이락무기 폐기에 관한 안보리 특별위(UNSCOM)의 서한과 관련, 추가로 파악한바를 아래보고함

1.UNSCOM 서한 발송대상국

0 UNSCOM 은 안보리 이사국, 주요공업국, 대이락 주요 수출국등 43 개국에 협조서한을 발송하였는바, 상금 구체적으로 회보한 국가는 없으나, 6.10 까지는 회신이 있을것으로 기대함

2. 필요정보내용

OUNSCOM 의 현재까지 활동은 이락내 화생무기및 미사일 폐기에 목적이 있었으나 지금부터는 무기폐기 활동과 병행하여 화생무기 및 미사일 생산 가능성도 방지하는 활동을 전개할 계획으로 이를 위하여 유관 민간시설을 장차 군수시설로전환할 가능성을 파악하자는 것이 금번 정보수집 목적임

0 따라서 한국정부나 한국기업들이 이락 민간 공장의 화생물질 생산, 가공,수요, 저장, 수입 또는 수출에 관한 정보를 가지고 있으면, 이를 UNSCOM 에 제공하여 줄것을 요청하는 것임(예로, 화학원료 생산 공장의 경우 생산화학 원료명,공장명, 위치, 생산능력, 생산공정, 프랜트 건설회사등에 관한 자료)

3. 전문가 파견

0 금번 전문가 파견계획은 무기폐기 작업단의 3-6 개월 파견과를 달리 화생무기생산에 이용될 원료생산이나 미사일 생산에 이용될 가능성이 있는 재료생산 공장이 발견되어 조사가 필요할 경우 5-6 명으로 구성되는 사찰반을 약 2 주(이락현장에 1 주, 보고서 작성을 위해 바레인에 1 주) 파견하는 것임

국기국 차관 1차보 [illegible] 중아국 분석관 청와대 안기부

PAGE 1 92.06.05 09:03

외신 2과 통제관 BN

0119

0 필요 전문가는 화학원료 게조전문가, 화학공장 설계사, 화학성분 분석가,분자생물전문가등 화생무기 및 미사일 생산제조에 필요한 기초원료 생산 관련 전문가임

0 금번의 경우는 직접 무기폐기 작업에 참여하는것이 아니고 민간 생산시설사찰이므로 반드시 군전문가일 필요는 없다함

0 대우는 화학무기 폐기작업단원과 같은 조건임

0 각국이 화학, 생물및 미사일 분야에 각각 1-2 명 추천하면 사찰단 파견시차출할 예정임. 현재로서는 사찰단수와 파견일자등이 결정되지 않았으나 관련 정보가 수집되는대로 이를 확정할 예정이며, 한달에 약 2 개 사찰단 파견이 예상된다함

4. 관련자료

OUNSCOM 의 활동목표, 방향및 파악을 희망하는 화학원료 목록등 관련자료는금 파편 송부함

(대사 유종하-국장)

예고:92.12.31 일반

검 토 필(1992.6.30.)

PAGE 2

0120

주 국 련 대 표 부

주국련 2031- 628 1992. 6. 5.

수신 장 관

참조 국제기구국장, 중동아프리카국장

제목 이락무기 폐기

연 : UNW - 1620

1. 유엔 UNSCOM의 이락무기 폐기활동과 관련, UNSCOM의 활동내용, 방향, 다공약품 목록등이 포함된 "이락의 안보리결의 687 이행의 사찰 및 검증 계획"에 관한 유엔 사무총장의 보고서를 별첨 송부합니다.

2. UNSCOM이 요청한 정보제공과 관련하여, UNSCOM은 이락이 안보리 결의에 의해 관련정보를 제출해야 함에도 불구하고 이를 이행치 않음으로써 일부 유엔 회원국에게 관련 정보제공을 요청하는 것인바, UNSCOM이 필요로 하는 화학, 생물 및 미사일관련 정보는 별첨 보고서 P8-P11 및 관련 부록(AAnnex II, III, IV)에 포함되어 있음을 첨언합니다.

첨 부 : 91.10.2자 유엔 사무총장 보고서(S/22871/Rev.1) 1부. 끝.

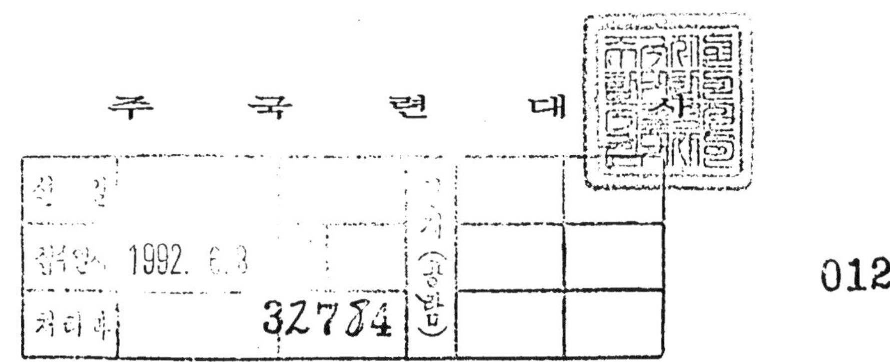

0121

UNITED
NATIONS

S

Security Council



Distr.
GENERAL

S/22871/Rev.1
2 October 1991

ORIGINAL: ENGLISH

# Plan for future ongoing monitoring and verification of Iraq's compliance with relevant parts of section C of Security Council resolution 687 (1991)

## Report of the Secretary-General

## I. GENERAL

### A. Introduction

1. The present report is submitted in pursuance of Security Council resolution 687 (1991). In paragraph 10 of section C of that resolution, the Security Council requested the Secretary-General, in consultation with the Special Commission, to develop and submit for approval a plan for the ongoing monitoring and verification of Iraq's compliance with its obligations under that paragraph. The Plan is contained in section II of the present report.

2. As outlined in my report to the Security Council of 17 May 1991 (S/22614), the provisions of section C of resolution 687 (1991) lend themselves to a three-stage implementation procedure: gathering and assessment of information; disposal of weapons and facilities and all other items specified in paragraphs 8 and 12 of resolution 687 (1991); and ongoing monitoring and verification of Iraq's compliance. The first two stages are currently being implemented and will continue until their objectives are fully achieved.

3. The Plan submitted in the present report addresses the third stage, i.e. ongoing monitoring and verification of Iraq's compliance with its unconditional obligation not to use, retain, possess, develop, construct or otherwise acquire any weapons or related items prohibited under paragraphs 8 and 9 of resolution 687 (1991). Thus, monitoring and verification will need to cover not only military but also civilian sites, facilities, material and other items that could be used or activities that could be involved in contravention of Iraq's obligations under resolution 687 (1991). The Plan incorporates the additional obligations of Iraq under Security Council resolution 707 (1991) and the corresponding monitoring and verification activities.

91-32425 2644f (E) /...

0122

4. The Plan should enter into force directly upon its approval by the Security Council, which means that the early stages of its implementation and the later stages of the disposal of existing prohibited weapons, facilities and related items would take place simultaneously. This would, at an early stage, prevent Iraq from developing new capabilities regarding the relevant weapons categories, thus already closing a potential loophole during the first stages of the implementation of section C of resolution 687 (1991). Carefully managed use of available resources would make it possible to carry out the dual tasks in parallel, to great effect. With the gradual completion of the disposal of Iraq's present weapons capabilities, resources can gradually be transferred and streamlined without therefore, at any stage, compromising the efficiency of the verification of Iraq's compliance with its obligations under resolutions 687 (1991) and 707 (1991). In paragraph 14 of its resolution 687 (1991) the Security Council noted that the actions to be taken by Iraq in paragraphs 8, 9, 10, 11, 12 and 13 of that resolution "represent steps towards the goal of establishing in the Middle East a zone free from weapons of mass destruction and all missiles for their delivery and the objective of a global ban on chemical weapons". The implementation of the Plan, developed pursuant to paragraph 10 of resolution 687 (1991), will contribute to an environment conducive to achieving the above-mentioned goal and objective.

## B. Institutional and organizational aspects

5. Bearing in mind that resolutions 687 (1991) and 707 (1991) were adopted by the Security Council acting under Chapter VII of the Charter of the United Nations, it is assumed that the task of carrying out the monitoring and verification provided for under the Plan should be entrusted to an executive body under the authority of the Security Council. This is particularly important should any situation arise of non-compliance by Iraq with its obligations under section C of resolution 687 (1991) and under resolution 707 (1991).

6. The intrinsic interrelationship between paragraphs 8, 9 and 10 of resolution 687 (1991) requires that this body make direct use of the expertise, the information gathered and assessed and the experience gained by the Special Commission established as a subsidiary organ of the Security Council pursuant to paragraph 9 of resolution 687 (1991).

7. In view of these considerations, it would appear most practical and efficient that a compliance unit be organized under the Special Commission in order to carry out the monitoring and verification tasks provided for under the Plan. The present arrangements for staffing would continue on a revised scale, with appropriate support from the Department for Disarmament Affairs. The financing of the Plan would have to be determined by the competent United Nations organs, possibly in the same way as the arrangements agreed upon for the present phase of the Special Commission's work.

/...

0123

8. The operational requirements will be similar to those now in place for the Special Commission. These include a staff at the United Nations Headquarters in New York to assist the Executive Chairman of the Special Commission, compile and analyse information, schedule, plan and organize inspections and aerial overflights, prepare other field operations and provide general administrative support. A staff will be needed in the region to provide logistic, administrative and other support for field operations in Iraq.

### C. Cooperation with the Security Council Committee established by resolution 661 (1990) concerning the situation between Iraq and Kuwait

9. Through resolution 661 (1990) and subsequent related resolutions, including resolution 687 (1991), inter alia, its section F, a comprehensive set of sanctions was established to be implemented by all States against Iraq. The prohibition of the acquisition by Iraq of any weapons and related items specified in paragraphs 8 and 12 of resolution 687 (1991) and of the sale or supply to Iraq by other States of these items is of unlimited duration. However, it cannot be excluded that the Security Council, at a future date, may wish to review the present sanctions regarding items with dual use, i.e. items that could be used for prohibited as well as non-prohibited purposes. In order to ensure that such items are not used for prohibited purposes, the Plan submitted in the present report includes specific provisions for the monitoring and verification, from within Iraq, of any eventual import by Iraq of relevant items with dual use.

10. The efficacy of these provisions would be enhanced if they were complemented by transparency and timely information as regards any future sale or supply by other States to Iraq of relevant items with dual use. Such a comprehensive approach would call for the development of a mechanism that:

(a) Upholds the prohibition on the sale and supply to Iraq by other States of any weapons or related items prohibited under section C of resolution 687 (1991);

(b) Provides for timely information about any sale or supply to Iraq by other States of items that could be used not only for permitted purposes but also for purposes prohibited under resolution 687 (1991).

11. The Plan submitted in the present report contains in its annexes lists of items relevant to the monitoring and verification, from within Iraq, of prohibited items as well as of items with dual use. These should be taken into account in the development of a mechanism related to the sale or supply of items to Iraq by other countries.

12. Such a mechanism should be developed with the cooperation of the Special Commission, the Director General of the International Atomic Energy Agency and the Committee established by resolution 661 (1990) at the earliest possible date, and not later than before the lifting of sanctions covering relevant items.

0124 /...

## II. THE PLAN

### A. Scope

13. In accepting unconditionally Security Council resolution 687 (1991), Iraq has undertaken not to use, retain, possess, develop, construct or otherwise acquire:

(a) Any chemical or biological weapons or any stocks of agents or any related subsystems or components or any research, development, support or manufacturing facilities;

(b) Any ballistic missiles with a range greater than 150 kilometres or any related major parts, including launchers, or any repair or production facilities.

14. In order to ensure Iraq's compliance with these undertakings, the Special Commission, pursuant to resolutions 687 (1991) and 707 (1991), shall, through inspections and through aerial overflights, as well as through the provision of information by Iraq, monitor and verify that activities, sites, facilities, material and other items, both military and civilian, are not used by Iraq in contravention of its obligations under resolutions 687 (1991) and 707 (1991).

15. To this end, the provisions set forth in the Plan and its annexes, which constitute an integral part of the Plan, shall apply.

### B. General provisions

#### 1. Information

16. Iraq shall:

(a) Provide to the Special Commission, on a regular basis, full, complete, correct and timely information on activities, sites, facilities, material and other items, both military and civilian, that might be used for purposes prohibited under paragraph 10 of resolution 687 (1991);

(b) Provide to the Special Commission full, complete, correct and timely information on any additional activities, sites, facilities, material or other items that the Commission may designate for provision of information on a regular basis;

(c) Provide to the Special Commission, fully, completely, and promptly, any additional information or clarification that the Commission may request and respond fully, completely and promptly to any questions or requests from the Special Commission.

Further provisions related to the submission of information are set forth in sections C, D and E and in annexes II, III and IV of the Plan.

2. Inspections and aerial overflights

17. The Special Commission shall have the right:

(a) To designate for inspection any site, facility, activity, material or other item in Iraq;

(b) To carry out inspections, at any time and without hindrance, of any site, facility, activity, material or other item in Iraq;

(c) To conduct unannounced inspections and inspections at short notice;

(d) To inspect any number of declared or designated sites or facilities simultaneously or sequentially;

(e) To designate for aerial overflight any area, location, site or facility in Iraq;

(f) To conduct, at any time and without hindrance, both fixed-wing and rotary-wing flights throughout Iraq for all relevant purposes, including inspection, surveillance, aerial overflights (surveys), transportation and logistics without interference of any kind and upon such terms and conditions as may be determined by the Special Commission;

(g) To make full use of its own aircraft with appropriate sensors as necessary and such airfields in Iraq as the Special Commission may determine are most appropriate for its work;

(h) To consider and decide upon requests by Iraq to move or destroy any material, equipment or item relating to its nuclear, chemical or biological weapons or ballistic missile programmes, or material, equipment or any item relating to its other nuclear activities.

18. Iraq shall:

(a) Accept unconditionally the inspection of any site, facility, activity, material or other item declared by Iraq or designated by the Special Commission;

(b) Accept unconditionally aerial overflight of any area, location, site or facility designated by the Special Commission;

(c) Provide immediate and unimpeded access to any site, facility, activity, material or other item to be inspected;

(d) Accept unconditionally and cooperate with the Special Commission in conducting fixed-wing and rotary-wing flights throughout Iraq for all relevant purposes, including inspection, surveillance, aerial overflights (surveys), transportation and logistics upon the terms and conditions determined by the Special Commission;

/...

0126

(e) Accept unconditionally the Special Commission's determinations regarding use of the Commission's aircraft with appropriate sensors as necessary and airfields in Iraq for such aircraft;

(f) Not obstruct aerial overflights or take concealment measures at any area, location, site or facility designated by the Special Commission for inspection or overflight;

(g) Accept unconditionally the inspectors and all other personnel designated by the Special Commission and ensure the complete implementation of the privileges, immunities and facilities of the personnel of the Special Commission and their complete safety and freedom of movement;

(h) Cooperate fully with the Special Commission and facilitate its inspections, overflights and other activities under the Plan;

(i) Accept unconditionally the rights of the Special Commission under the Plan and not take any action to interfere with, impede, or obstruct the exercise by the Special Commission of its functions and rights under Security Council resolutions 687 (1991), 707 (1991) and the Plan;

(j) Designate its Inspection Representative for each inspection to accompany the inspection team in Iraq;

(k) Invite and accept unconditionally the decision of the Special Commission on any requests by Iraq to move or destroy any material, equipment or item relating to its nuclear, chemical or biological weapons or ballistic missile programmes, or material, equipment or any item relating to its other nuclear activities.

19. Further provisions on inspections, aerial overflights, security, privileges and immunities and related provisions are set forth in annex I.

### 3. <u>National implementation measures</u>

20. Iraq shall adopt the necessary measures to implement its obligations under section C of resolution 687 (1991), resolution 707 (1991) and the Plan, in particular:

(a) To prohibit all natural and legal persons under Iraq's jurisdiction or control from undertaking anywhere any activity that is prohibited for Iraq by resolutions 687 (1991), 707 (1991), by other related Security Council resolutions or by the Plan;

(b) To enact penal legislation which, in conformity with international law, shall extend to the activities referred to under subparagraph (a) above undertaken anywhere by any natural or legal persons under Iraq's jurisdiction or control.

21. Iraq shall inform the Special Commission of legislative and administrative measures taken to implement resolutions 687 (1991), 707 (1991), other relevant Security Council resolutions and the Plan, not later than 30 days after the approval by the Security Council of the Plan and thereafter as determined by the Special Commission.

## 4. Non-compliance

22. Should the Special Commission discover any item, including any documentation, that Iraq, under resolution 687 (1991), is obliged to destroy or to yield to the Special Commission for destruction, removal or rendering harmless, the Special Commission shall have the right to take it into custody and shall provide for its disposal, as appropriate. Iraq shall retain no ownership interest in items to be destroyed, removed or rendered harmless pursuant to resolution 687 (1991) and the Plan.

23. Should the Special Commission discover any activity taking place in contravention of resolutions 687 (1991), 707 (1991) or of the Plan, it shall have the right to call upon Iraq to halt the activity and to prevent its recurrence. The Special Commission shall also have the right to take any prohibited item involved, including any documentation, into custody and shall provide for its disposal, as appropriate.

24. Findings by the Special Commission that indicate that Iraq is not in compliance with its obligations under resolutions 687 (1991) and 707 (1991) or the Plan shall be brought to the attention of the Security Council.

## 5. Reports

25. The Special Commission shall, through the Secretary-General, report to the Security Council every six months on the implementation of the Plan and at any other time the Security Council may request.

## 6. Revisions

26. The Plan may only be revised by the Security Council. The Special Commission may, however, after informing the Security Council, update and revise the annexes in the light of information and experience gained in the course of the implementation of resolutions 687 (1991) and 707 (1991) and of the Plan. The Special Commission shall inform Iraq of any such change.

## 7. Entry into force and duration

27. The Plan shall enter into force immediately upon its approval by the Security Council. The duration of the Plan shall be determined by the Security Council.

/...

## C. Provisions related to chemical items

28. Chemicals, equipment and facilities set forth herein and in annex II could be used for purposes related to chemical weapons. They shall therefore be subject to monitoring and verification in accordance with the following additional provisions in order to ensure that Iraq does not use, develop, produce or otherwise acquire chemical weapons or related items prohibited under resolution 687 (1991).

29. Chemicals that could be used for the development, production or acquisition of chemical weapons but which also have significant uses for purposes not prohibited by resolution 687 (1991) are set forth in list A in annex II. These chemicals may be used, developed, produced, stored or acquired solely for purposes not prohibited by resolution 687 (1991), subject to the provisions under paragraphs 30 and 31 below, and annex II.

30. Iraq shall, not later than 30 days after the adoption of the Plan by the Security Council, and on a regular basis thereafter, provide to the Special Commission information in accordance with annex II regarding:

(a) The total national quantity of the production, processing or consumption of any chemical specified in list A of annex II and of the import and export of any of these chemicals specifying the supplier or recipient countries involved;

(b) Any site or facility that is involved in production, processing, consumption, storage, import or export of one tonne or more per year of any chemical specified in list A of annex II or that at any time has been involved in activities with any of these chemicals for chemical weapons purposes;

(c) Any site or facility that is involved in production or processing of organophosphorus chemicals or is involved in production of organic chemicals by chlorination;

(d) Any site or facility where production, processing, consumption, storage, import or export of one tonne or more per year of any chemical specified in list A of annex II, or where production or processing of organophosphorus chemicals or where production of organic chemicals by chlorination is planned;

(e) Any import or any other acquisition of equipment or technologies intended for production and processing of any chemical specified in list A of annex II, of any organophosphorus chemical or for production of organic chemicals by chlorination.

31. Should Iraq plan any production, processing, consumption, storage, import or export not notified under paragraph 30 (d) above, it may begin such an activity only after providing to the Special Commission a special notification in accordance with annex II.

/...

32. Chemicals that have little or no use except as chemical warfare agents or for the development, production or acquisition of chemical weapons or which have been used by Iraq as essential precursors for chemical weapons are set forth in list B of annex II. Iraq shall not retain, use, transfer, develop, produce, store, import or otherwise acquire these chemicals. Should Iraq require any chemical specified in list B of annex II, it shall submit a request to the Special Commission specifying precisely the chemical and the quantities required, the site or facility where it is to be used and the purpose of its use. The Special Commission will examine and decide on the request and establish the special arrangements it considers consistent with resolution 687 (1991).

33. Further provisions related to chemical items are set forth in annex II.

D. Provisions related to biological items

34. Micro-organisms and toxins, equipment and facilities set forth herein and in annex III could be used for purposes related to biological and toxin weapons affecting humans, animals or plants. They shall therefore be subject to monitoring and verification in accordance with the following additional provisions in order to ensure that Iraq does not use, develop, produce or otherwise acquire biological and toxin weapons or related items prohibited under resolution 687 (1991).

35. Iraq shall, not later than 30 days after the adoption of the Plan by the Security Council, and on a regular basis thereafter, provide to the Special Commission information in accordance with annex III regarding:

(a) Any site or facility at which work with toxins or with micro-organisms meeting the criteria for risk groups IV, III or II according to the classification in the 1983 World Health Organization (WHO) Laboratory Biosafety Manual is carried out, or any site or facility at which work with genetic material coding for toxins or genes derived from the aforementioned micro-organisms is carried out;

(b) Any site or facility having a laboratory (unit) meeting the criteria for a "maximum containment laboratory" or "containment laboratory" as specified in the 1983 WHO Laboratory Biosafety Manual, such as those designated as biosafety level 4 (BL4) or P4, biosafety level 3 (BL3) or P3 or equivalent standards and any site or facility being constructed or modified so as to possess such containment capabilities;

(c) Any site or facility at which fermentation or other means for the production of micro-organisms or toxins using vessels larger than 10 litres individually or 40 litres in the aggregate is carried out;

(d) Any site or facility for the bulk storage of toxins or of micro-organisms meeting the criteria for risk groups IV, III or II;

/...

0130

(e) Any site or facility for the production of vaccines;

(f) Any research, development, testing or other support or manufacturing facility for equipment and other items specified in paragraph 1 of annex III;

(g) Any imports, other acquisition or exports of micro-organisms meeting the criteria for risk groups IV, III and II, toxins and vaccines, as well as related equipment and facilities, specifying the supplier or recipient countries involved.

36. Iraq shall, not later than 30 days after the adoption of the Plan by the Security Council, and on a regular basis thereafter, provide to the Special Commission:

(a) A list of all documents of a scientific and technical nature published or prepared by any site or facility engaged in work relating to toxins or micro-organisms meeting the criteria for risk groups IV, III and II, including those of a theoretical nature. Full copies of such documents shall be made available by Iraq to the Special Commission upon request. Documents of a purely diagnostic nature relating to risk group II micro-organisms are excepted;

(b) A description of all work on toxins or micro-organisms meeting the criteria for risk groups IV, III or II as well as of all work being conducted on the dissemination of micro-organisms or toxins into the environment or on processes that would lead to such dissemination, specifying the site or facility involved.

37. Iraq shall provide to the Special Commission in accordance with annex III information on all cases of infectious diseases affecting humans, animals or plants, that deviate, or seem to deviate, from the normal pattern or are caused by any micro-organism meeting the criteria for risk groups IV and III and on all cases of similar occurrences caused by toxins.

38. Iraq shall not:

(a) Import items referred to in paragraph 35 (g) above without giving prior notice to the Special Commission in accordance with annex III. As an exception, the emergency import of vaccines may take place with simultaneous notification to the Special Commission;

(b) Conduct any activities in the field of micro-organisms and toxins except by civilian personnel not in the employ of any military organization. Such activities shall be conducted openly; no classified or secret programmes or activities shall be permitted. The sites or facilities engaged in such activities shall not be under the control of, or owned by, any military organization. Should any military organization need to be involved in such activities for prophylactic or therapeutic purposes, Iraq shall submit a request to the Special Commission specifying precisely the toxins, micro-organisms and the quantities required, the site or facility where they

/...

are to be used and the purpose of their use. The Special Commission will examine and decide on the request and establish the special arrangements it considers consistent with resolution 687 (1991);

(c) Conduct activities on diseases other than those indigenous to or immediately expected to break out in its environment;

(d) Conduct any breeding of vectors of human, animal or plant diseases. Should Iraq need to conduct any such activity, Iraq shall submit a request to the Special Commission specifying precisely its requirements, the vectors to be bred, the site or facility where the activity is to take place and the purpose of the activity. The Special Commission will examine and decide on the request and establish the special arrangements it considers consistent with resolution 687 (1991);

(e) Possess at any one time more than one facility having a laboratory (unit) meeting the criteria for a "maximum containment laboratory" as specified in the 1983 WHO Laboratory Biosafety Manual, such as those designated as biosafety level 4 (BL4) or P4 or equivalent standard. Iraq shall not possess at any one time more than two facilities having a laboratory (unit) meeting the criteria for a "containment laboratory", such as those designated as BL3 or P3 or equivalent standard. Should Iraq require any additional such facilities, Iraq shall submit a request to the Special Commission specifying the precise requirement. The Special Commission will examine and decide on the request and establish the special arrangements it considers consistent with resolution 687 (1991).

39. Further provisions related to biological items are set forth in annex III.

## E. Provisions related to missiles

40. Facilities, equipment, other items and technologies set forth herein and in annex IV could be used for the development, construction, modification or acquisition of ballistic missiles with a range greater than 150 kilometres. They shall therefore be subject to monitoring and verification in accordance with the following additional provisions in order to ensure that Iraq does not use, develop, construct or acquire any ballistic missiles with a range greater than 150 kilometres or related items prohibited under resolution 687 (1991).

41. The prohibition applies to any ballistic missiles or missile delivery systems capable of such a range regardless of payload and to any related major parts, which include missile/rocket stages, re-entry vehicles, solid- or liquid-fuel motors, guidance sets, thrust vector controls, warheads and fusing systems, launchers capable of launching ballistic missiles with a range greater than 150 kilometres and related principal launch equipment, missile transporters and other ground support equipment for such missiles. The prohibition also applies to modification of any missile or any missile delivery system to a ballistic missile with a range greater than 150 kilometres. The prohibition also applies to launch technologies such as tube- or gun-type launchers, which enable such ranges to be achieved.

/...

42. Iraq shall not construct, otherwise acquire or operate sites or facilities for the use, development, production, training or other support of ballistic missiles capable of a range greater than 150 kilometres, including sites or facilities for research, development, modification, manufacture, assembly, testing, storage, repair, training, flight simulating and operational use of such missiles, nor acquire related major parts specified in paragraph 41 and the items listed in paragraph 1 of annex IV for such missiles.

43. Iraq shall, not later than 30 days after the adoption of the Plan by the Security Council, and on a regular basis thereafter, provide to the Special Commission the following:

(a) A list of all its missiles designed for use, or capable of being modified for use, in a surface-to-surface role with a range greater than 50 kilometres, specifying their name and type, type of propulsion, number of stages and/or boosters, guidance systems, payload, warhead and re-entry vehicle types, launcher types, airframe and warhead transporter, ground support equipment and the sites or facilities where these missiles, items or equipment are located;

(b) Information on any project and on any site or facility for such missiles, including sites or facilities for production, assembly, repair and maintenance, storage and operational bases, specifying their locations;

(c) Information on any project and on any site or facility for missile research, development, modification or testing, specifying its locations;

(d) Information on the development, production, export, import or other acquisition, training or other services related to the items, equipment and technologies listed in annex IV, specifying sites or facilities where such items, equipment and technologies are located, the purposes and the projects for which they are being used and the supplier or recipient countries involved.

44. Iraq shall notify the Special Commission in accordance with annex IV of the developmental or test launch of any missile, specifying where and when the launch is to take place.

45. Further provisions related to missiles are set forth in annex IV.

/...

## Annex I

## Detailed provisions related to inspections, aerial overflights, security, privileges and immunities

1. In addition to the basic rights and obligations set forth in paragraphs 17 and 18 of the Plan, the provisions set out in this annex shall apply.

### Scope

2. The Special Commission shall have the right:

(a) To secure any site to be inspected and prevent any material or other item from being taken to or from the site until the inspection is concluded;

(b) To stop and inspect vehicles, ships, aircraft or any other means of transportation within Iraq, any material or other item in movement and to restrict and/or stop movement of material or other items;

(c) To inspect imports or exports of material and other items upon arrival or departure;

(d) To establish special modes of monitoring and verification, including prolonged or continuous presence of inspectors, use of instruments and other arrangements to facilitate monitoring and verification;

(e) To secure full and free access at any time to all sites, facilities, areas, locations, activities, material and other items, including documentation, all persons and all information which, in its judgement, may be necessary for its monitoring and verification activities.

### Notification

3. The Special Commission shall, at a time it considers appropriate, notify Iraq of:

(a) The site, facility, activity, material or other item to be inspected;

(b) The name of the head of the inspection team (the Chief Inspector) and the estimated number of personnel who will take part in the inspection;

(c) The estimated time of departure and arrival of any flight from, to or within Iraq, and other appropriate details, by any aircraft used by the Special Commission.

/...

0134

4. Iraq shall, upon receipt of the name of the Chief Inspector for an inspection, immediately inform the Special Commission of the name of the individual who will be the Iraqi Inspection Representative for the inspection.

## Conduct of inspections or aerial overflights

5. The Special Commission shall have the right:

(a) To request, receive, examine, copy and remove any record, data, information or documentation and to verify inventories;

(b) To examine, retain, move or photograph, including by videotaping, any activity or item;

(c) To conduct interviews with any personnel at a site or facility under inspection, or with any Iraqi official;

(d) To install containment, surveillance and other equipment and devices and to construct facilities for inspection, observation, testing, verification or monitoring activities;

(e) To take samples of any kind and perform on-site analyses of the samples using its own equipment;

(f) To remove and transfer samples outside Iraq for analyses off-site at laboratories of its choice;

(g) To mark, tag or otherwise identify any material or other item;

(h) To use its own instrumentation to collect data during inspections and aerial overflights, including photographic, video, infrared and radar data.

6. Iraq shall:

(a) Provide clarification or explanation of any ambiguity that might arise during an inspection;

(b) Perform, upon request by the Special Commission, analyses of samples in the presence of inspectors, including on-site;

(c) Perform, upon request by the Special Commission, any additional task.

/...

Travel, transport and communications

7. The Special Commission shall have the right:

(a) To unrestricted freedom of entry into and exit from Iraq, without delay or hindrance, for all its personnel, property, supplies, equipment, spare parts, means of transport, material and other items. No visa shall be required of such personnel travelling on United Nations laissez-passer or certificate and possessing an inspection assignment document; Iraq shall ensure prompt issuance of visas of entry and exit for such personnel as may not possess a United Nations laissez-passer or certificate;

(b) To unrestricted freedom of movement within Iraq, without advance notice, delay or hindrance, for all its personnel, property, supplies, equipment, spare parts, means of transport, material and other items;

(c) To fly the United Nations flag on its premises and means of transport;

(d) To use its own means of transport, including fixed- and rotary-wing aircraft, throughout Iraq for all relevant purposes, including inspection, surveillance, aerial overflights (surveys), transportation and logistics;

(e) To use airfields in Iraq for the purposes determined by the Special Commission including landing, take-off, basing, maintenance, refuelling and other support;

(f) To communicate from any place within Iraq, and without censorship or other hindrance, by radio, satellite or other forms of communication, and to connect with the United Nations by its radio and satellite network, as well as by telefax, telephone, telegraph and other means;

(g) To use codes and receive papers, correspondence and other items by courier or sealed bags;

(h) To unrestricted freedom to remove from Iraq, without delay or hindrance, any material or other item, including any documentation, acquired during inspection or other monitoring and verification activities.

8. Iraq shall:

(a) Permit, without delay or hindrance, the Special Commission's personnel, property, supplies, equipment, spare parts, means of transport, material and other items to move within Iraq, without advance notice, as well as to enter or leave Iraq, promptly issuing entry and exit visas if required on national passports and accepting United Nations laissez-passers or United Nations certificates as valid travel documents without requiring visas;

(b) Accept United Nations registration of means of transport on land, sea and in the air and United Nations licensing of the operators thereof;

/...

0136

(c) Provide priority clearance, as well as the basing and all necessary facilities as determined by the Special Commission for any fixed- or rotary-wing aircraft used by the Commission;

(d) Provide, upon the request of the Special Commission, the means of transport, maps or other information needed;

(e) Take every necessary measure to ensure that the inspection team arrives at the site or facility to be inspected by the time notified by the Special Commission;

(f) Provide, upon the request of the Special Commission, appropriate means of communication;

(g) Provide, upon request of the Special Commission, appropriate escort and/or support personnel;

(h) Provide, upon request of the Special Commission, medical, logistical and/or technical support;

(i) Not interfere with or censor any communication to or from the Special Commission or its personnel;

(j) Permit, without delay or hindrance, the Special Commission to remove from Iraq any material or other item, including any documentation, acquired by the Commission during inspection or other monitoring and verification activities.

## Security, privileges and immunities

9. The Special Commission shall have the right to make its own arrangements to ensure the safety and security of its personnel and property and to take custody of any material or other item, including documentation.

10. Iraq shall ensure the safety and security of the personnel and property of the Special Commission and shall provide the arrangements to this end when so requested by the Special Commission.

11. In addition and without prejudice to the foregoing provisions, the Special Commission and any agency of the United Nations system participating in the carrying out of the Plan, its property, funds, assets and personnel shall enjoy the facilities, privileges and immunities provided for in the applicable convention or agreement, namely the Convention on the Privileges and Immunities of the United Nations, the Agreement on the Privileges and Immunities of the International Atomic Energy Agency (IAEA) and the Convention on the Privileges and Immunities of the Specialized Agencies.

/...

12. Iraq shall extend to:

(a) The officers and other members of the Special Commission the privileges and immunities, exemptions and facilities that are enjoyed by diplomatic envoys in accordance with international law;

(b) The officials of the United Nations, of IAEA and any of the specialized agencies of the United Nations, performing functions in connection with the implementation of the Plan, the privileges and immunities applicable to them under articles V and VII of the Convention on the Privileges and Immunities of the United Nations; or articles VI and IX of the Agreement on the Privileges and Immunities of the International Atomic Energy Agency; or articles VI and VIII of the Convention on the Privileges and Immunities of the Specialized Agencies;

(c) The technical experts and other specialists performing functions in connection with the implementation of the Plan the privileges and immunities accorded to experts performing missions for the United Nations, for IAEA or for the specialized agencies of the United Nations under article VI of the Convention on the Privileges and Immunities of the United Nations, article VII of the Agreement on the Privileges and Immunities of the International Atomic Energy Agency, and the relevant annexes to the Convention on the Privileges and Immunities of the Specialized Agencies, respectively.

## Other provisions

13. Iraq shall designate the Iraqi authority responsible for liaison with the Special Commission and shall inform the Special Commission of the name or names of the liaison officers within that authority who shall have the full power and shall take the necessary measures to secure for the Special Commission the effective implementation of the Commission's rights laid down in the Plan.

14. The official points of contact between Iraq and the Special Commission during the course of an inspection shall be the Chief Inspector designated by the Special Commission and the Inspection Representative designated by Iraq.

15. Iraq shall provide, at no cost to the Special Commission, in agreement with the Special Commission, all such premises as may be necessary for the accommodation and fulfilment of the functions of the Special Commission in Iraq. All such premises shall be inviolable and subject to the exclusive control and authority of the Special Commission.

16. All information provided by, and communications from, Iraq to the Special Commission under the Plan shall include the corresponding text in English.

17. For the purposes of the performance of the functions of the Special Commission in implementation of the Plan, the rights, facilities, privileges and immunities conferred in the Plan where necessary supplement and elaborate

/...

upon the rights, facilities, privileges and immunities provided for in the exchange of notes between the Secretary-General of the United Nations and the Minister for Foreign Affairs of Iraq, which entered into force on 14 May 1991, regarding the status, privileges and immunities of the Special Commission as originally established pursuant to paragraph 9 of Security Council resolution 687 (1991).

/...

## Annex II

### Provisions related to chemical items

1. The following list contains chemicals that could be used for the development, production or acquisition of chemical weapons, but which also have significant uses for purposes not prohibited by resolution 687 (1991):

| | List A | Chemical Abstracts Service (CAS) registry No. |
|---|---|---|
| 1. | Chemicals, except for those chemicals specified in list B of this annex, containing a phosphorus atom to which is bonded one methyl, ethyl or propyl (normal or iso) group but not further carbon atoms | |
| 2. | Dialkyl (Me, Et, n-Pr or i-Pr) N,N-dialkyl (Me, Et, n-Pr or i-Pr)-phosphoramidates | |
| 3. | Arsenic trichloride | (7784-34-1) |
| 4. | 2,2-Diphenyl-2-hydroxyacetic acid | (76-93-7) |
| 5. | Quinuclidin-3-ol | (1619-34-7) |
| 6. | N,N-Dialkyl (Me, Et, n-Pr or i-Pr) aminoethyl-2-chloride and corresponding protonated salts | |
| 7. | N,N-Dialkyl (Me, Et, n-Pr or i-Pr) aminoethane-2-ol and corresponding protonated salts | |
| 8. | N,N-Dialkyl (Me, Et, n-Pr or i-Pr) aminoethane-2-thiol and corresponding protonated salts | |
| 9. | Amiton: O,O-Diethyl S-(2-(diethylamino)ethyl) phosphorothiolate and corresponding alkylated and protonated salts | (78-53-5) |
| 10. | PFIB: 1,1,3,3,3-pentafluoro-2-(trifluoromethyl)-1-propene | (382-21-8) |
| 11. | Phosgene | (75-44-5) |

/...

0140

| List A | Chemical Abstracts Service (CAS) registry No. |
|---|---|
| 12. Cyanogen chloride | (506-77-4) |
| 13. Hydrogen cyanide | (74-90-8) |
| 14. Trichloronitromethane (chloropicrin) | (76-06-2) |
| 15. Phosphorus oxychloride | (10025-87-3) |
| 16. Phosphorus trichloride | (7719-12-2) |
| 17. Phosphorus pentachloride | (10026-13-8) |
| 18. Trimethyl phosphite | (121-45-9) |
| 19. Triethyl phosphite | (122-52-1) |
| 20. Dimethyl phosphite | (868-85-9) |
| 21. Diethyl phosphite | (762-04-9) |
| 22. Sulphur monochloride | (10025-67-9) |
| 23. Sulphur dichloride | (10545-99-0) |
| 24. Thionyl chloride | (7719-09-7) |
| 25. Cyclohexanol | (108-93-0) |
| 26. Hydrogen fluoride | (7664-39-3) |
| 27. Ortho-chlorobenzylidenemalononitrile (CS) | (2698-41-1) |
| 28. Potassium fluoride | (7789-23-3) |
| 29. Ammonium bifluoride | (1341-49-7) |
| 30. Sodium bifluoride | (1333-83-1) |
| 31. Sodium fluoride | (7681-49-4) |
| 32. Sodium sulphide | (1313-82-2) |
| 33. Chloroethanol | (107-07-3) |
| 34. Dimethylamine | (124-40-3) |

0141 /...

| List A | Chemical Abstracts Service (CAS) registry No. |
|---|---|
| 35. Dimethylamine hydrochloride | (506-59-2) |
| 36. Potassium cyanide | (151-50-8) |
| 37. Sodium cyanide | (143-33-9) |
| 38. Tri-ethanolamine | (102-71-6) |
| 39. Di-isopropylamine | (108-18-9) |

2. The following list contains chemicals that have little or no use except as chemical warfare agents or for the development, production or acquisition of chemical weapons, or which have been used by Iraq as essential precursors for chemical weapons:

| List B | Chemical Abstracts Service (CAS) registry No. |
|---|---|
| 1. O-Alkyl ($\leq C_{10}$, incl. cycloalkyl) alkyl (Me, Et, n-Pr or i-Pr)-phosphonofluoridates | |
| e.g. Sarin: O-isopropyl methylphosphonofluoridate | (107-44-8) |
| Soman: O-pinacolyl methylphosphonofluoridate | (96-64-0) |
| 2. O-Alkyl ($\leq C_{10}$, incl. cycloalkyl) N,N-dialkyl (Me, Et, n-Pr or i-Pr) phosphoramidocyanidates | |
| e.g. Tabun: O-ethyl N,N-dimethylphosphoramidocyanidate | (77-81-6) |
| 3. O-Alkyl (H or $\leq C_{10}$, incl. cycloalkyl) S-2-dialkyl (Me, Et, n-Pr or i-Pr)-aminoethyl alkyl (Me, Et, n-Pr or i-Pr) phosphonothiolates and corresponding alkylated and protonated salts | |
| e.g. VX: O-ethyl S-2-diisopropylaminoethyl methylphosphonothiolate | (50782-69-9) |

/...

0142

| List B | Chemical Abstracts Service (CAS) registry No. |
|---|---|
| 4. Sulphur mustards: | |
| 2-Chloroethylchloromethylsulphide | (2625-76-5) |
| bis(2-chloroethyl)sulphide: | |
| Mustard gas (H) | (505-60-2) |
| bis(2-chloroethylthio)methane | (63869-13-6) |
| 1,2-bis(2-chloroethylthio)ethane: | |
| Sesquimustard (Q) | (3563-36-8) |
| 1,3-bis(2-chloroethylthio)-n-propane | (63905-10-2) |
| 1,4-bis(2-chloroethylthio)-n-butane | |
| 1,5-bis(2-chloroethylthio)-n-pentane | |
| bis(2-chloroethylthiomethyl)ether | |
| bis(2-chloroethylthioethyl)ether: | |
| O-Mustard (T) | (63918-89-8) |
| 5. Lewisites: | |
| Lewisite 1: 2-chlorovinyldichlorarsine | (541-25-3) |
| Lewisite 2: bis(2-chlorovinyl) chloroarsine | (40334-69-8) |
| Lewisite 3: tris(2-chlorovinyl)arsine | (40334-70-1) |
| 6. Nitrogen mustards: | |
| HN1: bis(2-chloroethyl)ethylamine | (538-07-8) |
| HN2: bis(2-chloroethyl)methylamine | (51-75-2) |
| HN3: tris(2-chloroethyl)amine | (555-77-1) |
| 7. 3-Quinuclidinyl benzilate (BZ) | (6581-06-2) |
| 8. Saxitoxin | (35523-89-8) |
| 9. Ricin | |
| 10. Alkyl (Me, Et, n-Pr or i-Pr) phosphonyldihalides | |
| e.g. methylphosphonyldifluoride | (676-99-3) |
| methylphosphonyldichloride | (676-67-1) |
| 11. Dimethylmethylphosphonate | (756-79-6) |
| 12. O-Alkyl (H or $\leq C_{10}$, incl. cycloalkyl) O-2-dialkyl (Me, Et, n-Pr or i-Pr)-aminoethyl alkyl (Me, Et, n-Pr or i-Pr) phosphonites and corresponding alkylated salts and protonated salts | |
| e.g. QL: O-ethyl O-2-diisopropylaminoethyl methylphosphonite | (57856-11-8) |

/...

0143

| List B | Chemical Abstracts Service (CAS) registry No. |
|---|---|
| 13. O-Alkyl ($\leq C_{10}$, incl. cycloalkyl) alkyl (Me, Et, n-Pr or i-Pr)-phosphonochloridates e.g. Chloro Sarin: O-isopropyl methylphosphonochloridate | (1445-76-7) |
| Chloro Soman: O-pinacolyl methylphosphonochloridate | (7040-57-5) |
| 14. N,N-Dialkyl (Me, Et, n-Pr or i-Pr) phosphoramidic dihalides | |
| 15. Bis(2-hydroxyethyl)sulphide (thiodiglycol) | (111-48-8) |
| 16. 3,3-Dimethylbutan-2-ol (pinacolyl alcohol) | (464-07-3) |

3. The initial information under paragraph 30 of the Plan to be provided not later than 30 days after the adoption of the Plan by the Security Council shall cover the period from 1 January 1988. Subsequent information shall be provided each 15 January and 15 July and shall cover the six-month period prior to the provision of the information. The advance notifications under paragraph 30 (d) of the Plan shall cover the subsequent six months. The special notifications under paragraph 31 of the Plan shall be provided not later than 30 days in advance.

4. Whenever the information that Iraq is required to provide under section C of the Plan and this annex is equal to nil, Iraq shall provide nil returns.

5. The information on chemicals to be provided under section C of the Plan shall for each chemical include:

(a) The chemical name, common or trade name used by the site or the facility, structural formula and Chemical Abstracts Service registry number (if assigned);

(b) The purposes for which the chemical is produced, processed, consumed, stored, imported or exported;

(c) The total amount produced, processed, consumed, stored, imported or exported.

6. The information on sites or facilities to be provided under section C of the Plan shall for each site or facility include:

(a) The name of the site or facility and of the owner, company or enterprise operating the site or facility;

(b) The location of the site or facility;

/...

0144

(c) A general description of all types of activities at the site or facility;

(d) The sources and amounts of the financing of the site or facility, and of its activities.

7. The location of a site or facility shall be specified by means of the address and a site diagram. Each diagram shall be drawn to scale and shall indicate the boundaries of the site or facility, all road and rail entrances and exits and all structures on the site or facility, indicating their purpose. If the site or facility is located within a larger complex, the diagram shall specify the exact location of the site or facility within the complex. On each diagram, the geographic coordinates of a point within the site or facility shall be specified to the nearest second.

8. In addition to information specified in paragraph 6 of this annex, the following information shall be provided for each site or facility that is or will be involved in production, processing, consumption, storage, import or export of chemicals specified in list A of this annex:

(a) A detailed description of activities related to these chemicals including, as applicable, material-flow and process-flow diagrams, chemical reactions and end-use;

(b) A list of equipment used in activities related to these chemicals;

(c) The production capacity for these chemicals.

9. In addition to information specified in paragraph 6 of this annex, the following information shall be provided for each site or facility that is or will be involved in production or processing of organophosphorus chemicals or in production of organic chemicals by chlorination:

(a) A detailed description of activities related to the relevant chemicals, and the end-uses for which the chemicals are produced or processed;

(b) A detailed description of the processes used in the production or processing of organophosphorus chemicals or in the production of organic chemicals by chlorination, including material-flow and process-flow diagrams, chemical reactions and list of equipment involved.

10. The information on each import to be provided under section C of the Plan shall include:

(a) Specification of each item and the quantity imported and the purpose of its use in Iraq;

(b) Country from which the item is imported and the specific exporter;

(c) Point or port and time of entry of the item into Iraq;

/...

0145

(d) Site or facility where it is to be used;

(e) Name of the specific importing organization in Iraq.

/...

0146

## Annex III

## Provisions related to biological items

1. The following list contains equipment and other items relevant to the acquisition of biological and toxin weapons or biological and toxin weapons capability:

(a) Detection or assay systems specific for risk groups IV, III and II micro-organisms and toxins;

(b) Biohazard containment equipment;

(c) Equipment for the micro-encapsulation of living micro-organisms;

(d) Complex media for the growth of risk groups IV, III and II micro-organisms;

(e) Bio-reactors and fermentation vessels;

(f) Recombinant deoxyribonucleic acid (DNA), equipment and reagents for its isolation, characterization or production and equipment and reagents for the construction of synthetic genes;

(g) Equipment for the release into the environment of biological material;

(h) Equipment for studying the aerobiological characteristics of micro-organisms or toxins;

(i) Equipment for breeding of vectors of human, animal or plant diseases.

2. The initial information under paragraphs 35 and 36 of the Plan to be provided not later than 30 days after the adoption of the Plan by the Security Council shall cover the period from 1 January 1986. Subsequent information shall be provided each 15 January and 15 July and shall cover the six-month period prior to the provision of the information. Notifications under paragraph 38 (a) of the Plan shall be provided not later than 60 days in advance.

3. Whenever the information that Iraq is required to provide under section D and this annex is equal to nil, Iraq shall provide nil returns.

4. The information on each site or facility to be provided under section D of the Plan shall include the following:

(a) The name of the site or facility and of the owner, company, or enterprise operating the facility;

0147 /...

(b) The location of the site or facility (including the address, geographic coordinates to the nearest second, the specific buildings and any structure numbers, location of the facility within any larger complex);

(c) The sources and amounts of financing of the site or facility and of its activities;

(d) The main purpose of the site or facility;

(e) The level of protection, including, as applicable, the number and size of maximum containment or containment laboratories (units);

(f) Scope and description of activities, including, as applicable, a list of types and quantities of micro-organisms, toxins or vaccines and equipment and other items specified in paragraph 1 of this annex;

(g) A list of micro-organisms and toxins, equipment and vaccines imported or uniquely isolated for the use of the site or facility, or exported, indicating the supplier or recipient countries involved.

5. The information on imports to be provided under paragraphs 35 (g) and 38 (a) of the Plan shall cover:

(a) Toxins and micro-organisms meeting the criteria for risk groups IV, III, and II according to the classification in the 1983 WHO Laboratory Biosafety Manual and genetic material coding for toxins or genes derived from the aforementioned micro-organisms;

(b) Equipment and facilities for the production, utilization or storage of micro-organisms meeting the criteria for risk groups IV and III according to the classification in the 1983 WHO Laboratory Biosafety Manual, genetic material coding for toxins or genes derived from the aforementioned micro-organisms, as well as of toxins or vaccines;

(c) Complex media for the growth of micro-organisms meeting the criteria for risk groups IV and III in quantities greater than 100 kilograms;

(d) Equipment for micro-encapsulation of living micro-organisms;

(e) Personnel or material for training or technical support services related to the design, development, use, manufacture or support of items specified in paragraph 35 (a) of the Plan and paragraphs 1 and 5 (a) of this annex;

and shall for each import into Iraq specify:

(a) Types and quantities of micro-organisms, toxins or vaccines;

(b) Quantities of any equipment or other items specified in paragraph 1 of this annex;

/...

0148

(c) Country from which the micro-organisms, toxins, vaccines or items are imported and the specific exporter;

(d) Point or port and time of entry into Iraq;

(e) Site or facility where it is to be used and purpose of its use.

(f) Name of the specific importing organization in Iraq.

6. The information under paragraph 37 of the Plan shall be provided within seven days of the occurrence and the standardized form contained in section III of the annex on confidence-building measures in document BWC/CONF.III/23/II shall be utilized as appropriate.

7. Iraq shall, not later than each 15 April, provide to the Special Commission the copies of the declarations, information and data that Iraq has sent to the United Nations Department for Disarmament Affairs pursuant to the agreements on confidence-building measures, including the exchange of information and data, reached at the Third Review Conference of the Parties to the Convention on the Prohibition of the Development, Production and Stockpiling of Bacteriological (Biological) and Toxin Weapons and on Their Destruction (document BWC/CONF.III/23/II and its annex on confidence-building measures).

## Annex IV

## Provisions related to missiles

1. The following list contains equipment, other items and technologies relevant to the development and manufacture of missiles that could be used in the development and manufacture of ballistic missiles capable of a range greater than 150 kilometres:

(a) Subsystems usable in missile systems that could be used in the development and manufacture of ballistic missiles capable of a range greater than 150 kilometres:

(i) Individual rocket stages;

(ii) Re-entry vehicles, and specially designed equipment therefor;

(iii) Solid- or liquid-fuel rocket engines;

(iv) Guidance sets;

(v) Thrust vector controls;

(vi) Warhead safing, arming, fuzing and firing mechanisms;

(b) Propulsion components and equipment that could be used in the development and manufacture of ballistic missiles capable of a range greater than 150 kilometres:

(i) Rocket-motor cases and production equipment therefor;

(ii) Staging mechanisms and production equipment therefor;

(iii) Liquid-fuel control systems and components therefor, specially designed to operate in vibrating environments of more than 12g/rms between 20/Hz and 2,000/Hz;

(iv) Propellants and constituent chemicals for propellants;

(v) Production technology or production equipment for the production, handling, mixing, curing, casting, pressing, machining and acceptance testing of the liquid- or solid-fuel missile propellants and propellent constituents;

(c) Guidance and control equipment that could be used in the development and manufacture of ballistic missiles capable of a range greater than 150 kilometres:

/...

0150

(i) Gyroscopes, accelerometers and inertial equipment and software therefor;

(ii) Flight control systems usable in missile systems;

(iii) Avionics equipment specially designed or modified for use in unmanned air vehicles or rocket systems and software and components therefor usable in missile systems;

(d) Equipment and technical data for the production of structural composites usable in missiles and components, accessories and software therefor that could be used in the development and manufacture of ballistic missiles capable of a range greater than 150 kilometres;

(e) Pyrolytic deposition and densification equipment and technology that could be used in the development and manufacture of ballistic missiles capable of a range greater than 150 kilometres;

(f) Launch and ground support equipment and facilities usable for missile systems that could be used in the development and manufacture of ballistic missiles capable of a range greater than 150 kilometres;

(g) Analog computers, digital computers or digital differential analysers usable in air vehicles, rocket systems or missile systems that could be used in the development and manufacture of ballistic missiles capable of a range greater than 150 kilometres;

(h) Test facilities and equipment usable for missile systems, to include vibration test equipment using digital control techniques, wind tunnels and test benches for solid- or liquid-fuel rockets that could be used in the development and manufacture of ballistic missiles capable of a range greater than 150 kilometres;

(i) Specially designed software or components for missile design, production or operation that could be used in the development and manufacture of ballistic missiles capable of a range greater than 150 kilometres;

(j) Materials and devices for reduced observables in missile systems that could be used in the development and manufacture of ballistic missiles capable of a range greater than 150 kilometres;

(k) Material and devices for protecting missile systems against nuclear effects that could be used in the development and manufacture of ballistic missiles capable of a range greater than 150 kilometres.

2. The initial information under paragraph 43 of the Plan to be provided not later than 30 days after the adoption of the Plan by the Security Council shall cover the period from 1 January 1988. Subsequent information shall be provided each 15 January and 15 July and shall cover the six-month period

prior to the provision of the information. Notifications under paragraph 44 of the Plan shall be provided not later than 14 days prior to the date of launch.

3. Whenever the information which Iraq is required to provide under section E of the Plan and this annex is equal to nil, Iraq shall provide nil returns.

4. The information on sites or facilities to be provided under section E of the Plan shall for each site or facility include:

(a) The name of the site or facility and of the owner, company or enterprise operating the site or facility;

(b) The location of the site or facility;

(c) The sources and amounts of the financing of the site or facility, and of its activities;

(d) A general description of all types of activities at the site or facility;

(e) List of equipment, other items and technologies specified in paragraph 1 of this annex used or present at the site or facility and their quantities;

(f) A detailed description of activities related to the equipment, other items and technologies specified in paragraph 1 of this annex.

5. The location of a site or facility shall be specified by means of the address and site diagram. Each diagram shall be drawn to scale and shall indicate the boundaries of the site or facility, all road and rail entrances and exits and all structures on the site or facility, indicating their purpose. If the site or facility is located within a larger complex, the diagram shall specify the exact location of the site or facility within the complex. On each diagram, the geographic coordinates of a point within the site or facility shall be specified to the nearest second.

6. The information on each import to be provided under section E of the Plan shall include:

(a) Specification of each item and the quantity imported and the purpose of its use in Iraq;

(b) Country from which the item is imported and the specific exporter;

(c) Point or port and time of entry of the item in Iraq;

0152 /...

(d) Project and site or facility where it is to be used;

(e) Name of the specific importing organization in Iraq.

-----

0153

# 외 무 부

110-760 서울 종로구 세종로 77번지 / (02) 720-2334 / (02) 723-3505

문서번호 연일 2031-
시행일자 1992.6.8.
(경유)
수신 내 부 결 재
참조

| 취급 | | 차 관 | 장 관 |
|---|---|---|---|
| 보존 | | 전결 출장 | |
| 국 장 | | | |
| 심의관 | | 제1차관보 | |
| 과 장 | 김 | 중동아국장 | |
| 기안 | 황준국 | | 협조 |

제목 이라크 무기폐기관련 유엔 요청

유엔의 이라크무기폐기 특별위원회(UNSCOM)가 요청해 온 이라크무기관련 정보제공 및 무기전문가 추천문제에 대하여 별첨과 같이 대응코자 하오니 재가하여 주시기 바랍니다.

첨 부 : 이라크 무기폐기관련 유엔측 협조요청 대응방안 1부. 끝.

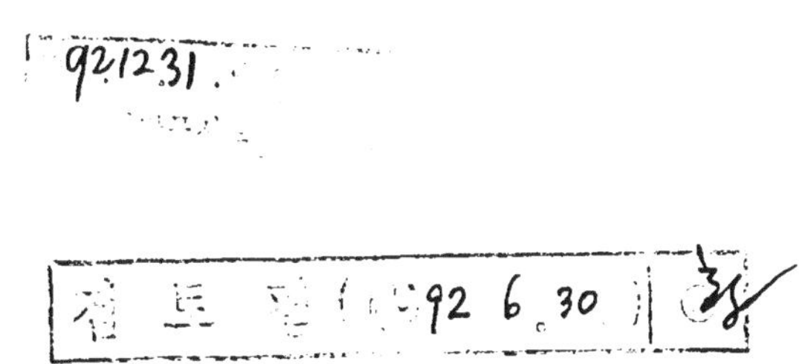
921231.
검 토 필 (1992 6. 30.)

0154

# 이라크 무기폐기 관련 유엔측 협조요청 대응방안

92.6.8.
유엔1과

## 1. UNSCOM측 요청내용

o 이라크 무기폐기를 위한 유엔특별위원회(UNSCOM)의 Ekeus위원장은 UNSCOM의 이라크무기 조사·감시활동을 위하여 하기와 같이 한국정부의 협조를 요청해옴. (92.5.18자 서한)

(1) 정보제공

- 이라크내 화학·생물무기 및 사정거리 150km이상 미사일의 소재지, 관련시설물, 관련물질등에 관한 각종 정보제공 (특히 민수용 시설·물질중에서 군사목적으로의 전용 가능한것 포함)

※ UNSCOM은 무기폐기에 중점을 두어 왔으나 앞으로는 이와 병행하여 이라크의 화생무기 및 미사일의 생산가능성을 봉쇄하는 활동을 전개할 계획

(2) 전문가 추천

- UNSCOM의 필요시 수시 임용할 수 있도록 화생무기 및 미사일 전문가 천거 (전문가 명단작성 예정)

※ 상기서한 발송대상국 : 안보리이사국, 주요공업국, 대이라크 주요수출국등 43개국

0155

## 2. 아측대응시 고려사항

(긍정적 측면)

o 유엔활동에 대한 적극적인 협조자세 과시

o 우리 전문가들의 경험 축적

(부정적 측면)

o 이라크의 반감유발 우려

- 민수용 생산시설까지 대상으로 하는 UNSCOM 활동에 적극 참여하는 것은 유엔회원국으로서의 최소한의 의무이행 수준을 벗어난 것으로 간주할 가능성
- 우리의 대이라크 미수금(13억불), 추후 이라크 복구사업 참여등에 부정적 영향 초래 가능성

o 정보제공을 위한 행정적 부담

- 요청 정보의 내용이 광범위하여 과거 우리의 대이라크 수출실적을 일일히 검토해야 함.
- 관련기업들의 자발적 협조 기대하기 어려움.

(평 가)

o 정보제공에 따른 명분상의 이익에 비해 외교적·행정적 부담이 더 큰 것으로 사료됨.

o 전문가 추천과 관련해서는 UNSCOM 화학무기 폐기반에 파견예정(92.7-12월)인 우리 군장교 2명의 활동상황을 우선 지켜볼 필요가 있음.

- 국방부측에서는 전문가가 상당히 많다고 하나 UNSCOM의 전문가 기준에 적합한지 여부 미상
- 우리 전문가의 참여 결과에 대한 내부평가가 있은후에 전문가 추가 파견 문제를 검토하는 것이 바람직

0156

3. 추진방향 (건의)

o 상기 검토내용에 비추어, UNSCOM측 요청에 적극 대응은 하지 않음.

- UNSCOM측은 6.10.까지 회신 요망하고 있는 바, 추가 요청내지 독촉이 없는한 회신하지 않음
- UNSCOM측 문의시 정부 관련부처에서 검토, 노력하고 있다는 선에서 대응

※ 금번 서한과 유사한 정보제공을 요청하는 92.2.10자 UNSCOM 위원장 명의 서한에 대하여도 회신하지 않았음.

- 끝 -

0157

| 관리 번호 | 92 —659 |
|---|---|

| | 분류번호 | 보존기간 |
|---|---|---|
| | | |

# 발 신 전 보

번 호 : WUN-1388 920609 1649 FQ 종별 :

수 신 : 주 유엔 대사. 총영사

발 신 : 장 관 (연일)

제 목 : 이라크 화학무기 폐기반 참여

대 : UNW-1564, 주국련 2031-119(92.6.1)

1. 우리 요원 2명의 대호 내용에 따른 UNSCOM 화학무기 폐기반 참여에 동의함을 UNSCOM측에 통보바람. 단, 근무기간 6개월을 3개월로 단축할 수 있는지 알아보고 별 문제없이 조정이 가능하다면 변경바람.

2. 아울러 대호 안내자료 내용중 하기사항(3.5자 안내서 P.4) 확인바람.
   - 요원의 1일 보수가 250불로 기재되어, 당초 335불과 차이가 있음.
   - 보험제도 특히 요원의 사망·부상등에 따르는 보상액. 끝.

(국제기구국장 김재섭)

예 고 : 1992.12.31. 일반
19 . . . 에 의거 일반문서로 재분류됨

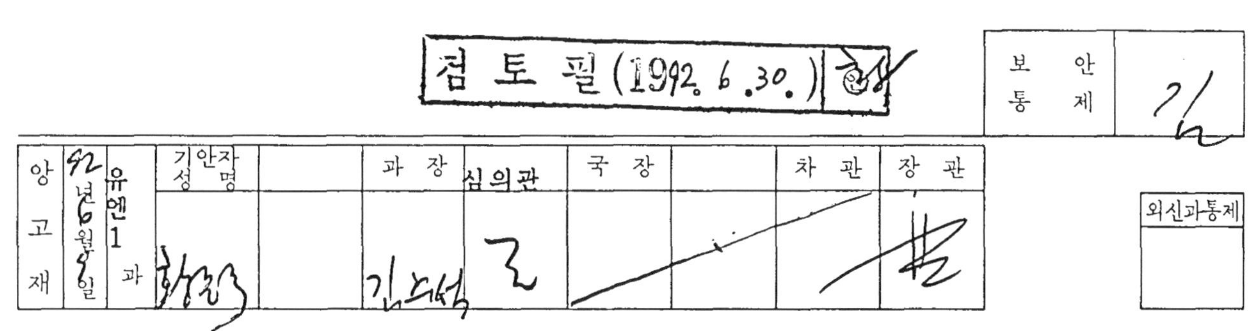

검 토 필(1992. 6. 30.)

| | 보안 통제 | |
|---|---|---|

| 앙 고 재 | 92년 6월 9일 | 유엔1 과 | 기안자 성명 | | 과 장 | 심의관 | 국 장 | | 차 관 | 장 관 |
|---|---|---|---|---|---|---|---|---|---|---|
| | | | 황준국 | | 김도석 | 김 | | | | |

| 외신과통제 |
|---|
| |

0158

| 관리<br>번호 | 92<br>-663 |
|---|---|

원 본

# 외 무 부

종 별 :

번 호 : UNW-1642 일 시 : 92 0609 1700

수 신 : 장 관(연일)

발 신 : 주 유엔 대사

제 목 : 이락 무기 폐기작업단

대:WUN-1388

1. 대호 이락 무기 폐기작업단에 우리요원 2 명 파견기간을 3 개월로 단축하여 줄것을 UNSCOM 에 요청하였는바, UNSCOM 측은 기간조정에 별문제가 없을 것이라는 반응이므로 3 개월로 파견 준비하여도 무방하다고 사료됨

2. 수당은 1 개월 미만의 단기출장의 경우(DAILY SUBSISTENCE ALLOWANCE)는$355, 장기출장의 경우(MISSION SUBSTENCE ALLOWANCE)는 $250 로 조정 되었다함

3. 유엔이 지불하는 보상금은 사망의 경우는 소득등을 감안하고, 부상의 경우는 부상의 정도등에 따라 보상액이 결정되며, 사전 확정된 금액은 없다함. UNSCOM 측에 의하면 보험이 필요한 경우는 요원각자가 개별적으로 해결하여야 한다함

(대사 유종하-국장)

예고: 92.12.31 일반 고문에 의거 일반문서로 재분류

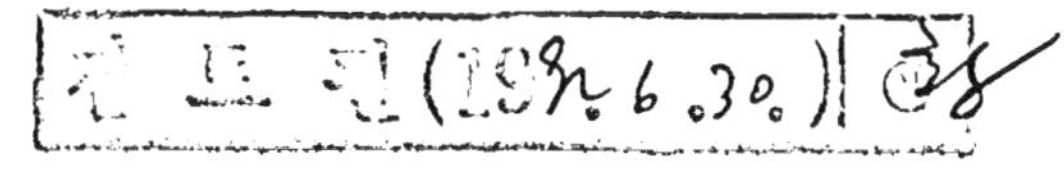

국기국 차관 1차보 분석관 청와대 안기부

PAGE 1

92.06.10 06:49

외신 2과 통제관 BX

0159

관리 번호 92-666

# 외 무 부

원본

종 별 :

번 호 : UNW-1649 일 시 : 92 0609 1830

수 신 : 장 관(연일,중동이)

발 신 : 주 유엔 대사

제 목 : 이락무기 폐기

연:UNW-1620

연호 유엔의 이락무기 폐기활동과 관련, UNSCOM 의 스미도비치 담당관은 연호 2 항에서 언급된 정보외에도 특히 한국 건설회사가 이락에서 지하 시설물 건조나 지상건물을 신축한 공사 실적이 있으면 동 시설물등의 위치, 규모, 공사내용, 추정되는 용도(예로 지하실설물은 플로트늄 생산시설로 사용될수 있으며, 작은 방이 많은 건물을 신축한 경우 이는 화학 실험실등으로 사용할수 있음)등을 UNSCOM 에 제공하여 줄것을 요청하였는바, 동건 검토시 참고바람

(대사 유종하-국장)

예고:92.12.31 일반

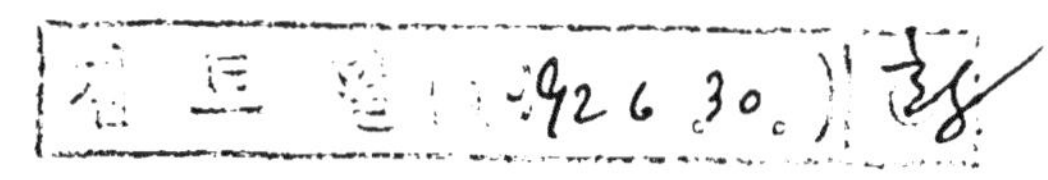

검토필(1992.6.30.)

| 국기국 | 장관 | 차관 | 1차보 | ■■■ | 중아국 | 분석관 | 청와대 | 안기부 |
|---|---|---|---|---|---|---|---|---|

PAGE 1

92.06.10 08:06

외신 2과 통제관 BN

0160

외교문서 비밀해제: 걸프 사태 24
걸프 사태 유엔안전보장이사회 동향 7

초판인쇄 2024년 03월 15일
초판발행 2024년 03월 15일

지은이 한국학술정보(주)
펴낸이 채종준
펴낸곳 한국학술정보(주)
주 소 경기도 파주시 회동길 230(문발동)
전 화 031-908-3181(대표)
팩 스 031-908-3189
홈페이지 http://ebook.kstudy.com
E-mail 출판사업부 publish@kstudy.com
등 록 제일산-115호(2000. 6. 19)

ISBN 979-11-6983-984-6 94340
979-11-6983-960-0 94340 (set)